TABLE OF CONTENTS

PART II: MICROSOFT WORD   **75**

Chapter 4: Getting Started with Word 2010   **77**

Chapter 5: Formatting Documents   **99**

Chapter 6: Creating Outlines   **137**

INTRODUCTION

Welcome to *Microsoft Office 2010 for Windows: Visual QuickStart Guide*. In the pages that follow, you'll find the information and instructions needed to quickly become productive with the key applications in Microsoft Office.

Like other titles in the *Visual QuickStart* series, this book was written primarily as a reference. Unlike a book on a single program, however, this one covers *four* major applications: Word, PowerPoint, Excel, and Outlook. Rather than discuss every command and procedure in excruciating detail (as you'd expect in a one-program book), this book focuses on the commands and procedures you're most likely to actually *use*.

How This Book Is Organized

To make it easy for you to find the information you need at any given moment, the book is divided into major sections called *parts*.

◆ Part I describes the changes you'll find in Office 2010 and provides an introduction to essential Office procedures. Certain tools and features (such as using the new Backstage, working with graphics, and creating charts and tables) work the same regardless of the Office program you're using at the moment. Rather than repeat this material for each application, I present it in Chapters 2 and 3.

◆ Parts II through V are devoted to the individual Office applications—one part for each application.

◆ Part VI provides an introduction to the new Office Web Apps. Using them, you can view, share, and edit Office documents with most current Web browsers.

Which Suites Are Covered?

Microsoft Office 2010 is available in five configurations (or *suites*), each with a different combination of applications (**Table i.1**). With the exception of the Home and Student suite, each suite includes the four core applications discussed in this book: Word, Excel, Outlook, and PowerPoint.

✔ Tip

■ For a solid primer about an earlier version of Microsoft Access, you might want to pick up a copy of *Microsoft Office Access 2003 for Window: Visual QuickStart Guid*e, written by yours truly.

Table i.1

Microsoft Office 2010 Suites					
OFFICE APPLICATIONS	HOME AND STUDENT	STANDARD†	HOME AND BUSINESS	PROFESSIONAL	PROFESSIONAL PLUS†
Word	◆	◆	◆	◆	◆
Excel	◆	◆	◆	◆	◆
PowerPoint	◆	◆	◆	◆	◆
Outlook		◆	◆	◆	◆
OneNote	◆	◆	◆	◆	◆
Publisher		◆		◆	◆
Access				◆	◆
Office Web Apps		◆			◆

†The Standard and Professional Plus suites are available only via volume licensing.

The Office Applications

If you're unfamiliar with any of the programs covered in this book, the following pages provide a quick overview of the tasks for which each one is suited.

Microsoft Office Word 2010

Word is a *word-processing program*. You can use it to write letters, memos, contracts, reports, or the Great American Novel. Because Word is so commonly used in the business world, you'll find that most word-processing documents you receive from others will be Word files.

Like other word-processing programs of the past twenty years, Word uses a *WYSIWYG* (What You See Is What You Get) approach to document formatting, layout, and display. That is, the fonts, paragraph formats, margins, and page breaks you see onscreen will precisely match those in the printout.

If your needs go beyond simple text documents, you can embellish them with tables, clip art, and photos. You can also apply stylish 3-D effects called WordArt to text and insert important titles or bulleted lists as eye-catching SmartArt.

In addition to allowing you to create new documents from scratch, Word provides an array of templates for useful documents and forms. Many can be used as-is or with only minor modification. And if you want to generate personalized mailings, Word has a mail merge feature.

Microsoft Office Excel 2010

Like Word, Excel is the most widely used *spreadsheet* application around. You can use a spreadsheet program to enter, analyze, and summarize large amounts of numerical and text data on a row-and-column grid.

Excel is an excellent tool for performing calculations (via formulas and its built-in functions), as well as for creating colorful, informative graphs. And because so many people use worksheets to record lists, Excel also includes list-management features.

The days of the drab, colorless, single-font worksheet are over. Excel supports mixed fonts, styles, colors, and rotated text, as well as cell background and conditional formatting. To further embellish any worksheet, you can add clip art, pictures, predefined shapes (such as arrows and text balloons), WordArt, and SmartArt.

Microsoft Office PowerPoint 2010

PowerPoint is Office's "best in class" program for creating *presentations*: slide shows with between-slide transition effects, within-slide animations, recorded audio narration, presenter notes, and handouts.

To give your slides a consistent, professional look, you can select one of the included themes or download others from Office.com. You can also create and save templates that include designs and other key elements, such as a company logo or address information.

After you've rehearsed and set the timing for your presentation, it can be played on a computer, professionally output to slides, or used to generate a Web-based presentation.

Microsoft Office Outlook 2010

Outlook's primary function is that of an *email client*. Outlook can send, receive, and manage email for all types of accounts (including certain Web-based ones, such as Hotmail and Windows Live). Outlook 2010 can also be configured to receive Really Simple Syndication (RSS) message feeds.

In addition to providing email capabilities, Outlook can serve as your business and home calendar (allowing you to record and schedule reminders for upcoming appointments, meetings, and other events), handle your to-do list, and manage work and personal contacts.

How to Use This Book

This is a book for beginning to intermediate users of Microsoft Office for Windows. If you're using Office for the first time or already know the basics but want to get more out of your investment in Office, this book is for you. If you learn better from step-by-step instructions and lots of graphic examples than from reference manuals that just describe what the commands do, this book is also for you. Most of all, if you know what you want to do and want to get started in the shortest possible time, this book is *definitely* for you.

I've worked hard to create a book that will let you turn to the directions for any procedure, learn what it does, and then do it yourself. A screen shot illustrates every significant step. The goal is to give you all the information you need and little that you don't, making you productive as quickly as possible. Along the way, you'll find tips that offer helpful information about many of the procedures.

About the Author

Since modern man shoved aside the typewriter in favor of a keyboard, I've been writing computer articles and books. (I was going to say "Since the dawn of time...," but thought it would be a bit much. Thirty-two years of computer-industry writing is a *long* time, though!) My first computer book was published in 1984, and I've written 50+ titles since then. This may not make me the first computer book author or the most prolific, but I must be close on both counts.

My background includes computer periodical/book Editor-In-Chief, as well as Technical Services Director for a software company. I also have a Ph.D. in psychology that I don't use, but the diploma makes a nifty wall hanging.

Part I:
Getting Started

WHAT'S NEW IN OFFICE 2010?

In this chapter, you'll receive a brief overview of the new features and changes introduced in Office 2010—changes in each application, as well as a few major changes that affect all applications and all Office 2010 users.

As mentioned in the introduction, not all new features mentioned in this chapter will be covered in the book (although many of them will). Changes that affect *typical* users will be found in the application chapters.

Office-wide Changes

In addition to the many new features and enhancements that are specific to particular application, Office 2010 includes changes that apply either to the entire suite or to several programs.

File tab/Backstage

In Office 2007, the Office Button was the gateway to the contents of the File menu from previous Office versions. In Office 2010, the Office Button has been eliminated. In its place, each application now has a File tab (**Figure 1.1**). It isn't as flashy like the Office Button, but the fact that it leads one to file-related commands is immediately apparent.

Clicking the File tab switches the screen to the *Microsoft Office Backstage* on which file-related commands for the current document are presented. In Backstage, you can do the following:

◆ Create new documents and open existing documents (**Figure 1.2**)

◆ Save, close, or print the current document

◆ View or change document properties and permissions, check for issues prior to distribution, and manage versions

◆ Share the document via email, fax, or SharePoint server

◆ Generate an Adobe PDF file from the current document

◆ Set application preferences (*Options*)

◆ Exit the application

The Backstage is discussed in Chapter 2.

File tab

Figure 1.1 Click the File tab to display the Microsoft Office Backstage.

Backstage commands

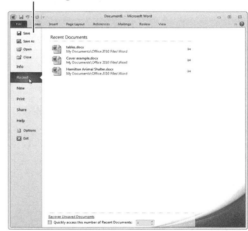

Figure 1.2 Select a file-related command from the list on the left side of the Backstage. For example, click Recent to open a recently used Office document.

Customize the Ribbon

After you're familiar with how an Office 2010 application works, you can bend it to your will by modifying the Ribbon. In the Options section of Backstage, you can add or remove commands from tabs, hide tabs you don't use, rename tabs or groups, and create new tabs. Customizing the Ribbon is explained in Chapter 2.

Paste Options gallery

	B	C	D
	Jan	**Feb**	**Mar**
xpenses	494.60	30.30	72.22
nd fees	375.00	0.00	225.00
ct. 179	0.00	0.00	0.00
ications	0.00	0.00	0.00
. services	109.15	88.74	105.94
	11.51	2.47	6.58
Repairs and maint. (Direct)	0.00	0.00	0.00
Repairs and maint. (Indirect)	3.15	0.00	18.62
Supplies	146.17	72.08	38.93
Taxes and licenses (Direct)	0.00	0.00	0.00
Taxes and licenses (Indirect)	309.48	0.00	0.00
Travel	0.00	0.00	52.00
Utilities (Direct)	51.11	61.26	73.32
Utilities (Indirect)	97.60	304.04	264.70
Utilities (Indirect)			
97.60			
304.04			
264.70			

Paste Preview   *Copied material*

Figure 1.3 In this example, the Utilities (Indirect) data will be transposed and copied to the range A17:A20.

Paste Preview

Although it may sound like a minor change, *Paste Preview* is one of Office 2010's most useful, time-saving enhancements. Although you can continue to paste as you've always done (by switching to the Home tab and clicking the Paste icon in the Clipboard group or by pressing ⌃V), Paste Preview adds a new level of flexibility to paste operations.

If you click the down arrow under the Paste icon, a gallery of Paste Options appears. If you rest the cursor over an option, a ToolTip explains the type of paste that will be performed and shows a preview of the pasted material at the cursor's current position in the document (**Figure 1.3**). You can use Paste Preview to choose exactly the right option *before* committing to the paste.

Image-editing enhancements

Office 2010 now includes a variety of image-editing tools called *Picture Tools*. Available in Word, Excel, PowerPoint, Outlook, and Publisher, the tools are available when you select an image on a document page. Picture Tools (**Figure 1.4**) enable you to alter the brightness, contrast, color, tone, saturation, and sharpening; apply artistic filters; set presentation style, effects, and borders; perform background removal; convert to SmartArt; and crop. Chapter 3 explains how to use the Picture Tools.

Picture Tools tab

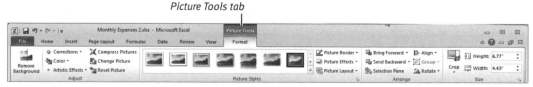

Figure 1.4 When you select a picture in a document, the Picture Tools tab appears (Microsoft Excel shown).

Screen clippings

In addition to dressing up documents with photos, clip art, and images from the Web, you can use the new *screen clipping* feature to insert screen captures into the current Word, Excel, or PowerPoint document. Screen clippings are discussed in Chapter 3.

OpenType typography support

As a successor to TrueType and PostScript Type 1 fonts, Word and Publisher now provide support for OpenType font advanced typography features (**Figure 1.5**).

Cell phones and Office Web Apps

In addition to working with your Word, Excel, PowerPoint, Outlook, and One Note documents in Office 2010, you can view and edit them on Windows Mobile cell phones. For more serious work on Office documents while you're away from your office or home computer, you can access the new *Office Web Apps* using a browser. (Note that Office Mobile 2010 is not part of Office 2010 or the Office Web Apps.)

To use the Office Web Apps, launch a browser, sign in to your Windows Live or Hotmail account, and then navigate to the SkyDrive section of the site. You can work with any document you've uploaded to SkyDrive (**Figure 1.6**), share documents with others, and perform collaborative editing—even when you're away from your main computer. You don't need an installed copy of Office to use the Office Web Apps. For assistance with the Web Apps, see Chapter 22.

OpenType settings

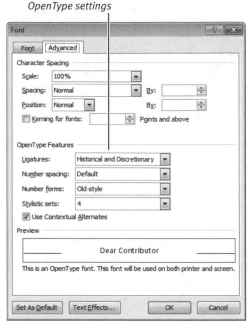

Figure 1.5 In Word, you can set options for selected OpenType text on the Advanced tab of the Font dialog box.

Figure 1.6 A worksheet opened for editing in the Web App version of Excel, as viewed in Internet Explorer 8.

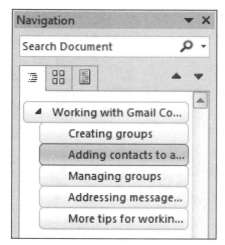

Figure 1.7 Use the Navigation Pane to simplify document navigation. Click a heading, click a page thumbnail, or search for text or a graphic.

Sparklines

	A	B	C	D	E	F
1	Student	Test 1	Test 2	Test 3	Total	Chart
2	Michelle	15	14	16	45	
3	Thomas	18	16	19	53	
4	Adrian	14	9	11	34	
5	Anthony	17	14	18	49	
6	Jonas	20	20	18	58	
7	Heidi	13	15	16	44	
8	Average	16.17	14.67	16.33	47.17	

Figure 1.8 You can create three styles of sparklines: Line, Column (shown here), and Win/Loss.

Application Changes

In this section, you'll learn about application-specific features and changes introduced in Office 2010. While they aren't the only new features and changes, they *are* the most significant ones.

New in Word

◆ The *Navigation Pane* (**Figure 1.7**) is used to navigate the document, rearrange sections, and perform searches

◆ Search for graphics, tables, and equations

◆ Apply *text effects,* such as a colored gradient fill, directly to selected text

◆ The *Selection Pane* simplifies the process of selecting objects within a document

◆ Spell checking now considers the context of a word to determine its proper spelling

New in Excel

◆ Create cell-based charts called *sparklines* (**Figure 1.8**)

◆ Interactive PivotTable filtering via *slicers*

◆ Improved search filtering in tables and PivotTables

◆ More conditional formatting options

◆ More functions with improved accuracy

New in PowerPoint

◆ *Reading View* enables you to review a slide show within the confines of the current document window

◆ Presentations can be divided into sections

◆ *Animation Painter* tool for copying animation properties to other objects

◆ New animations, transitions, and themes

continues on next page

APPLICATION CHANGES

- ◆ Transitions and animations now on separate tabs

- ◆ Improved video editing and formatting

- ◆ Compare presentation versions and combine them into a single presentation

- ◆ Create video from a slide show

- ◆ Slide show broadcasting (requires SharePoint Server)

New in Outlook

General changes

- ◆ Replaces earlier versions' menus with the Ribbon interface (**Figure 1.9**, below)

Email changes

- ◆ *Conversation view* for viewing and handling related messages

- ◆ Execute common actions with a single click by defining *Quick Steps* (**Figure 1.10**)

- ◆ *Mail Tips* prevent Exchange users from making major email mistakes, such as accidentally choosing Reply to All rather than replying to a message's author

- ◆ Receive voice mail messages and faxes in your Inbox (Exchange users only)

- ◆ Additional Exchange features

Calendar changes

- ◆ New *Schedule View* and group scheduling tools

Figure 1.10 To automate common tasks, you can create sets of instructions called Quick Steps.

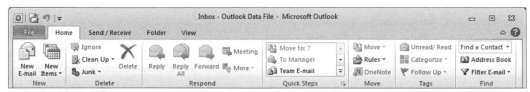

Figure 1.9 Rather than choose commands from menus, you will now use the Ribbon at the top of the Outlook window.

APPLICATION CHANGES

OFFICE BASICS

2

Although the applications in the various Office suites aren't heavily integrated with one another, they do have some similarities. For example, saving files, working with windows, printing, and other basic operations vary little from one Office application to the next. In this chapter, you'll become acquainted with these "Office essentials."

Launching Office Applications

You launch Office applications (such as Word and Excel) in the same manner as you do all other Windows applications.

To launch an Office application:

1. Click the Start button, All Programs, and the Microsoft Office folder (**Figure 2.1**).

   The folder expands, showing all installed Office 2010 applications.

2. Click the Office program you want to run.

   The selected program launches.

✔ Tips

■ You can also launch an Office application by doing any of the following:

   ▲ If you recently ran the application, you can select its name from the list in the Start panel.

   ▲ If you've created them, you can click a Desktop or Quick Launch shortcut icon for the application or any of its documents.

   ▲ Open an Office document by clicking (or double-clicking) its file icon. The document opens in the appropriate Office application.

■ In Windows Vista, you can choose a recently opened Office document from the Start > Recent Items submenu. In Windows 7, each recently used application provides its own recent document list (**Figure 2.2**). Choosing such a document launches the appropriate Office application, if it isn't already running.

■ To quickly open the Start menu, press the Windows logo key on your keyboard.

Start button

Figure 2.1 A common way to launch programs is to choose them from the Start menu (Windows 7 shown).

Figure 2.2 In Windows 7, you can may be able to open a document you've recently worked on by choosing it from the application's Recent pop-out list.

Create button

Figure 2.3 Select a document type or category, and then click Create or Download (depending on whether the template is on your computer or is available online from Office.com).

Using the Backstage

In Office 2007, the core applications had a large, glowing icon in the upper-left corner of the document window called the *Office Button*. Clicking it revealed a page on which you could perform file and document-related tasks, such as opening, saving, and printing, In Office 2010, the Office Button has been replaced by the *File tab*. When you click the tab, the *Microsoft Office Backstage* appears.

In this section, I'll explain the basics of using the Backstage. Application-specific differences will be covered in the application chapters.

To open or close the Backstage:

◆ To open the Backstage, click the File tab.

◆ To close the Backstage, click the File tab again, click a different tab, or press Esc.

Creating a new document

By default, document-based Office programs (Word, Excel, and PowerPoint, for example) automatically create a new, blank document each time you launch the program. To create additional new documents when an Office program is running, perform the steps below.

To create a new document:

◆ *Do either of the following:*

  ▲ Click the File tab, and then click New in the Backstage. Select the type of document you want to create from either of the Templates lists (**Figure 2.3**) and click the Create button.

  ▲ To skip the Backstage and create a standard document, press Ctrl N.

continues on next page

Single- vs. Double-Clicking

Whether it requires a single or double click to open a folder, document, or program on your computer depends on a Folder Options control panel setting:

1. Click the Start button and select Control Panel.

2. Open the Folder Options control panel. (In Windows 7, it's in the Appearance and Personalization group.)

3. In the Click items as follows section of the control panel, select the Single-click or Double-click radio button.

4. Click OK to save the new setting.

✔ Tips

- To create a standard document in Word, Excel, or PowerPoint, select Blank document, Blank worksheet, or Blank presentation, respectively.

- Office has two kinds of templates: those installed on your computer and ones you can download as needed from Microsoft. To use an installed template, select from the Available Templates. For a downloadable template, select a category from the Office.com Templates list.

- To base a new document on one of your own documents, select New from existing in the Available Templates list.

Opening documents

In addition to creating new documents, you can open existing documents—to view, print, or revise them. You can open documents from within Office applications or from the Desktop (simultaneously launching the creating program, if it isn't already running).

To open an existing document from within an Office application:

1. Click the File tab, and click Open (Ctrl O). The Open dialog box appears (**Figure 2.4**).

2. Navigate to the drive and folder that contains the document you want to open.

3. Select the document, and click Open.

   If Folder Options have been set on your PC to open items by single-clicking them (see the sidebar on page 11), the selected document may open without your having to click the Open button.

Figure 2.4 Select an Office document in the Open dialog box and click Open (Windows 7 shown).

Sanitized for Your Protection

When you attempt to open a document that originated from a potentially unsafe source (such as an Internet email attachment), an Office 2010 application will automatically open the file in *Protected View*. Such documents can be read, but not edited. If you trust the document source, click the Enable Editing button in the Protected View yellow banner that appears across the top of the document.

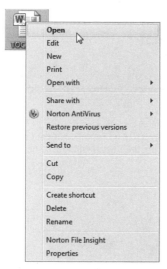

Figure 2.5 You can also open an Office document by right-clicking its file icon and choosing Open.

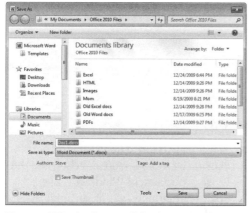

Figure 2.6 Use the Save As dialog box to save a new document. You also use it to save an edited document with a new name, format, or disk location.

Another Way to Save As

From the Backstage, you can quickly specify an alternate Save As format. Click Share, click Change File Type, and select the new format. A Save As dialog box appears with the format already specified.

To open an existing Office document from the Desktop:

1. Locate the document file on the Desktop or in the folder in which it's stored.

2. *Do either of the following:*
   ▲ Click (or double-click) the file icon.
   ▲ Right-click the file icon and choose Open from the context menu that appears (**Figure 2.5**).

   The appropriate Office program launches (if it isn't already running), and the document opens.

✔ Tip

■ In Word, Excel, and PowerPoint, you can also open documents by clicking the File tab, clicking Recent in the Backstage, and choosing a file from the Recent Documents list.

Saving documents

Until you save a document to disk, it exists only in your PC's memory. If you close a document or exit the application without saving, the document and its changes are lost. (Note, however, that if AutoRecover is enabled for the Office program in its Options dialog box, you may be able to recover certain unsaved documents.)

To save a new document:

1. *Do one of the following:*
   ▲ Click the Save icon on the Quick Access Toolbar.
   ▲ Click the File tab, and then click Save or Save As in the Backstage.
   ▲ Press Ctrl S.

   The Save As dialog box opens (**Figure 2.6**).

2. Enter a name in the File name box, navigate to the desired disk and folder, select a file format from the Save as type drop-down list, and click the Save button.

To save an edited document:

◆ *Do either of the following:*

▲ To replace a current Word, Excel, or PowerPoint file with the edited version, click the Save icon in the Quick Access Toolbar, click the File tab and choose Save, or press Ctrl S.

▲ You can save a *copy* of an edited document with a different name, in a different file format, and/or to a new disk location. Click the File tab, and then click Save As. The Save As dialog box appears (see Figure 2.6). Specify a filename, format, and location, and then click the Save button.

Closing documents

It isn't necessary to quit an Office application just to work with another document. When you're done working with a document, you can close it. Closing documents frees up memory for working on other documents.

To close a document:

1. Make the document active that you want to close by doing one of the following:

▲ Click the document's taskbar icon at the bottom of the screen.

▲ Click the View tab. Select the document name from the Switch Windows icon in the Window group (**Figure 2.7**).

2. *Do one of the following:*

▲ Click the File tab, and then click Close in the Backstage (Ctrl W).

▲ Click the close box (X) in the upper-right corner of the document window (**Figure 2.8**). If this is the *only* open document, the application quits.

The document closes. If the document has never been saved or contains unsaved edits, you're given an opportunity to save it.

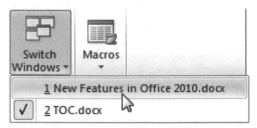

Figure 2.7 You can switch to any open document by selecting its name from the Switch Windows drop-down list.

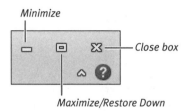

Figure 2.8 You can close a document by clicking its close box.

✔ Tips

■ You can also close a document by right-clicking its taskbar icon and choosing the Close command. In Windows 7, every document grouped within an application's taskbar icon has its own close box (X).

■ Quitting an application automatically closes all open documents. If any of them contain unsaved edits, you're given an opportunity to save each one.

■ Although Excel worksheets share a single interface, each has its own close box (found under the application's close box). Word and PowerPoint documents, on the other hand, open in separate windows.

USING THE BACKSTAGE

Print button   Copies   Preview area

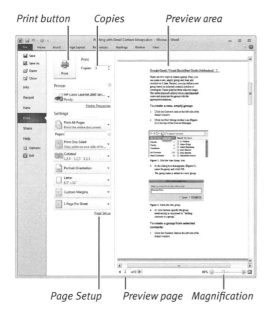

Page Setup   Preview page   Magnification

Figure 2.9 Select a printer, set options, and click the Print button.

✔ Tips

- Not only can you print to a printer that's directly connected to your PC, you may also be able to print to network printers— if you're on a network and have permission to use the network printer.

- If the destination printer isn't listed, you can install it by choosing Add Printer from the Printer drop-down list.

- Use the controls beneath the preview area to change the magnification or the page you're previewing.

- To print specific pages or a range of pages, enter the page numbers and range(s) in the Pages box. Separate pages and ranges with commas, such as 1,3,5-7,9.

- If you save a document after printing, the print settings are also saved.

Printing

The process of printing a document varies little from one Office application to the next. The biggest difference lies in the options you can set. For details on application-specific Print options, see the application's chapters.

Note that you no longer have to request a print preview prior to printing. Office 2010 applications automatically show an onscreen preview of the current print job within the Print section of the Backstage,

To print a document:

1. Open the document you want to print.

2. *Do either of the following:*
   - ▲ Click the File tab. In the Backstage, click Print.
   - ▲ Press Ctrl P.

   The Print section appears (**Figure 2.9**).

3. Select the destination printer from the Printer drop-down list.

4. Specify the number of copies.

5. Indicate the pages to be printed by choosing an option from the first Settings drop-down menu, such as Print All Pages or Print Selection (to print only the currently selected pages).

6. Set other desired options in the Settings section, such as paper size, orientation, and collation.

   As you change settings, they're reflected in the preview area.

7. *Optional:* To change other settings for the print job, such as margins or layout, click the Page Setup text.

8. Ensure that the printer is on and ready to print, and then click the Print button.

   The print job is sent to the selected printer.

USING THE BACKSTAGE

Using the Ribbon

If the most recent version of Office you've used was Office 2003 or earlier (or if this is your *first* version), you're probably wondering what happened to the command menus. To provide easier access to all parts of the Office applications, Microsoft removed the menus from Word, PowerPoint, and Excel 2007. In Office 2010, they finished modifying the core applications by removing Outlook's menus, too. In their place is a new interface known as the *Ribbon*.

The Ribbon (**Figure 2.10**) is the interface for every Word, Excel, PowerPoint, and Outlook document, displayed across the top of the window. Within the Ribbon, similar commands and procedures are listed together on a *tab*, such as Insert or View. Within a tab, procedures are further divided into *groups*, based on similarity of function. To perform a command, you switch to the appropriate tab by clicking its name, locate the group of interest, and then click the command icon or control.

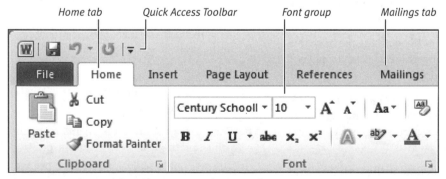

Figure 2.10 A section of the Ribbon interface (Word 2010).

Figure 2.11 When you select a picture in a Word document, the Picture Tools contextual tab appears on the Ribbon. Click the Format tab to set or edit the picture's properties.

Save   *Undo*   *Redo (repeat)*

Figure 2.12 The default Quick Access Toolbar has only a few command icons.

Minimize/Maximize the Ribbon

Figure 2.13 Click this icon to minimize or maximize the Ribbon.

Contextual tabs

When working with certain kinds of items in a document, such as an image or table, a colored *contextual tab* appears above the other Ribbon tabs (**Figure 2.11**). Click a new tab beneath it to view and use commands that are relevant to the selected material. Note that some contextual tabs, such as Table Tools in Word, are divided into *multiple* tabs.

When you're done using a contextual tab's tools, you can dismiss it by selecting a different object in the document or by clicking one of the standard Ribbon tabs.

Quick Access Toolbar

Above the left side of the Ribbon is the *Quick Access Toolbar* (**Figure 2.12**). It has icons for the most basic program procedures, including saving the current document (Word, Excel, PowerPoint), performing a Send/ Receive All (Outlook), undoing commands, and redoing commands. As discussed later in this chapter, you can optionally add commands to the Quick Access Toolbar.

✔ Tips

■ If you like, you can hide the Ribbon so only tab names are displayed. Click the Minimize/Maximize the Ribbon control (**Figure 2.13**) or press Ctrl F1. To access a tab's controls, click its name. When you're done using a tab, the Ribbon automatically minimizes. To restore the Ribbon, click the Minimize/Maximize control again or press Ctrl F1.

■ Instructions for customizing the Ribbon and Quick Access Toolbar are provided later in this chapter.

USING THE RIBBON

Working with Windows

If you occasionally have several documents open, you can arrange and manipulate their windows using Office commands. Window management commands can be found on the View tab in the Window group. Note that the availability, location, and implementation of these commands vary from one Office program to the next.

New Window. The New Window command creates a new instance of the current document. Each new instance is named using the convention *filename:instance number*, such as memo.docx:2. Use the New Window command to view and work in two sections of a document at the same time.

Arrange All. This command simultaneously displays all open documents in an application. In Word, the documents are displayed one above the other. In PowerPoint, they're arranged side-by-side. In Excel, you can specify the arrangement of open documents in the dialog box that appears when you click Arrange All in the Window group of the View tab (**Figure 2.14**).

Cascade. Arranging documents in cascade fashion displays the top edge of each one, enabling you to quickly switch documents by clicking an exposed edge (**Figure 2.15**). In PowerPoint, the Cascade icon can be found in the Window group. In Excel, select this option in the Arrange Windows dialog box (Figure 2.14).

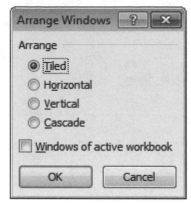

Figure 2.14 In Excel, you have great flexibility in arranging open workbook windows.

Figure 2.15 When you cascade documents, you can see the top edge and title of each one.

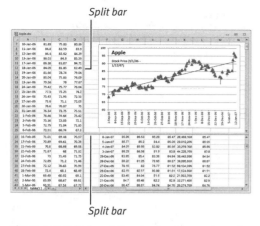

Split bar

Split bar

Figure 2.16 Split the window to simultaneously work in two or four sections of a document.

Click to maximize

Click to restore

Figure 2.17 The Maximize/Restore Down button changes, depending on the window's current state.

Split. Click the Split icon to split the current document into two parts (Word) or four parts (Excel) (**Figure 2.16**), enabling you to work in two or four sections at the same time. In Word, a split bar appears that you position by clicking. In Excel, the split appears above the current cell. You can reposition a split by clicking it and dragging. To remove splits in Excel, click the Split icon. In Word, click the Remove Split icon. You can also remove splits by dragging them off the document's edge.

Save Workspace. This Excel command saves the current arrangement of worksheets within the window so you can restore it later. To restore a saved workspace, open the workspace as you would a worksheet.

Every Office application also supports standard Windows controls and techniques for manipulating windows.

To use standard Windows controls:

◆ *Do any of the following:*

▲ Click the Minimize button (see Figure 2.8) to minimize a window to the taskbar. Click its taskbar icon to restore the window to its original onscreen position and size.

▲ The Maximize/Restore Down button has two states (**Figure 2.17**). When it's a box, you can click it to *maximize* the window, filling the screen. When a window is maximized, the button is a pair of boxes. Click it to restore the window to its original size and position (before you maximized it).

▲ To move a window to a new location, drag it by its title bar.

▲ To manually resize a window, move the cursor over any edge or corner. When the cursor becomes a double arrow, click and drag to change the window's size.

Setting the Magnification

If you're having difficulty reading a Word or Excel document because the type is too tiny or you want a bird's-eye view of a PowerPoint presentation, you can change the document's magnification (or *zoom*).

To set the magnification in Word, Excel, or PowerPoint:

◆ Use the zoom control (**Figure 2.18**) in the bottom-right corner of the document or application window in any of these ways:

▲ Drag the slider to a specific magnification percentage.

▲ Click the – or + button to decrease or increase magnification by 10 percent.

▲ Click the current zoom number to open the Zoom dialog box (**Figure 2.19**).

◆ In the Zoom group on the View tab, you can do either of the following:

▲ Click Zoom to open the Zoom dialog box (Figure 2.19).

▲ Click 100% to zoom the document to its normal magnification.

To set the magnification in Outlook:

◆ In the window for an existing message or a message you're composing, click the Zoom icon in the Zoom group of the Message tab. Set a magnification level in the Zoom dialog box (Figure 2.19), and click OK.

✔ Tip

■ You must set magnification separately for each open document in an application.

Figure 2.18 The zoom control provides three ways for you to set the current magnification.

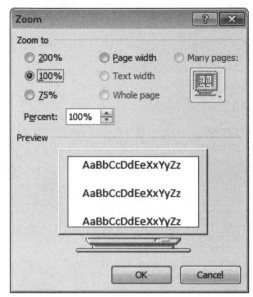

Figure 2.19 Use the Zoom dialog box to set a specific or page-related magnification.

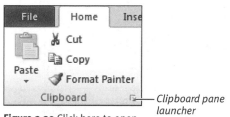
— *Clipboard pane launcher*

Figure 2.20 Click here to open the Office Clipboard.

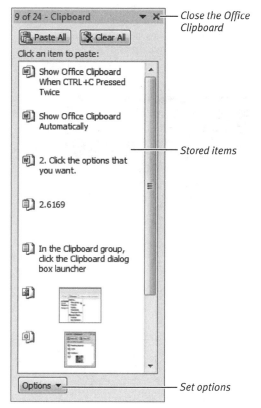
— *Close the Office Clipboard*

— *Stored items*

— *Set options*

Figure 2.21 The Office Clipboard.

Using the Office Clipboard

The Windows *Clipboard* is an area in memory that stores the last item you copied or cut. When you paste an item, it's drawn from the Clipboard. If you copy or cut a new item, it takes the place of the current item stored in the Clipboard. Using the Clipboard, you can insert items into the current document, into a different document, or even into the documents of other applications.

While working in Office, you can continue to use the Windows Clipboard as you've always done. In addition, you can use the *Office Clipboard*, a dedicated clipboard for sharing data among open Office documents. Unlike the Windows Clipboard, the Office Clipboard can store up to 24 items.

To open the Office Clipboard:

◆ **Word, Excel, PowerPoint.** Switch to the Home tab. In the Clipboard group, click the Clipboard pane launcher (**Figure 2.20**).

◆ **Outlook.** In a new message window, select the Message tab. In the Clipboard group, click the Clipboard pane launcher. The Office Clipboard appears (**Figure 2.21**).

To paste Office Clipboard items into a document:

1. Select the spot in the Office document where you want to paste the item(s).

2. *Do one of the following:*
   ▲ To paste an item, click the item in the Office Clipboard scrolling list, or click the item's down arrow and choose Paste from the menu that appears.
   ▲ To simultaneously paste all items stored in the Office Clipboard, click the Paste All button.

USING THE OFFICE CLIPBOARD

To clear items from the Office Clipboard:

◆ *Do either of the following:*

▲ To remove a single item, move the cursor over the item, click the arrow that appears, and choose Delete from the drop-down menu (**Figure 2.22**).

▲ To remove all current items from the Office Clipboard, click the Clear All button (Figure 2.22).

To set Office Clipboard options:

◆ Click the Options button (see Figure 2.21) and choose any of the following options:

▲ **Show Office Clipboard automatically.** Automatically display the Office Clipboard when you copy an item.

▲ **Show Office Clipboard When Ctrl+C Pressed Twice.** Open the Office Clipboard by quickly pressing Ctrl C twice.

▲ **Collect Without Showing Office Clipboard.** Items are added to the Office Clipboard without displaying it.

▲ **Show Office Clipboard on Taskbar.** Add a taskbar icon for the Office Clipboard when it is active.

▲ **Show Status Near Taskbar When Copying.** A status message appears when a new item is copied to the Office Clipboard (**Figure 2.23**).

To close the Office Clipboard:

◆ *Do the following:*

▲ **Word, Excel, PowerPoint.** Click the Office Clipboard's close box (X) or click the Clipboard pane launcher (see Figure 2.20).

▲ **Outlook.** Click the Office Clipboard's close box (see Figure 2.21).

Figure 2.22 To remove a single item, choose Delete from the drop-down menu.

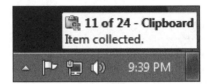

Figure 2.23 A message like this can be displayed to denote a newly copied item.

✔ Tips

■ If you add more than 24 items to the Office Clipboard, the oldest item is automatically deleted to make room for the new item.

■ To paste from the Windows Clipboard rather than from the Office Clipboard, use the normal Paste command (click the Paste toolbar icon or press Ctrl V).

■ The last item copied or cut also becomes the current item in the Windows Clipboard.

■ Items remain in the Office Clipboard until you exit all Office programs.

The Mechanics of Copy, Cut, Paste, and Drag-and-Drop

Most Windows and Macintosh programs allow you to copy and cut text and objects to the Clipboard, and then paste the most recently copied or cut material to another location in the same document, a different document, or a document in another program. These procedures allow you to easily duplicate or move material. The last copied or cut item remains on the Clipboard and is available for pasting until a new copy or cut is performed.

Some programs also support the direct procedure of *drag-and-drop*, enabling you to accomplish a cut/paste or copy/paste by simply dragging the material to a new location. Unlike copying or cutting, drag-and-drop doesn't use the Clipboard.

Surprisingly, many novice and seasoned computer users don't understand or take advantage of these marvelous time-saving techniques. Let's review how they work in Office 2010. Note that these same commands and procedures are often available in other Windows applications, too.

If you want to perform a *copy-and-paste*:

1. Select the text or object(s) that you want to copy.

2. Click the Copy icon in the Clipboard group (see Figure 2.20) or press Ctrl C. The copied material is stored in the Windows Clipboard. If the Office Clipboard is active, the material is also stored there.

3. To select a destination for pasted text, position the text insertion mark at the spot in the document where you want to paste. To paste object(s), click the approximate location on the page where you want to paste the material.

4. Click the Paste icon in the Clipboard group (see Figure 2.20) or press Ctrl V. The material appears at the destination location.

If you want to perform a *cut-and-paste*:

1. Select the text or object(s) you want to cut. Unlike copying, cutting is a destructive procedure and removes the selected material from its original location.

2. Click the Cut icon in the Clipboard group (see Figure 2.20) or press Ctrl X. The cut material is stored in the Windows Clipboard. If the Office Clipboard is active, the material is also stored there.

3. Select a destination for the cut material (as described for copying). Click the Paste icon in the Clipboard group (see Figure 2.20) or press Ctrl V to execute the paste.

You can also use *drag-and-drop* to perform a move or copy:

1. Select the material to be moved or copied. When a drag-and-drop is performed within a document, the material is moved. When performed between documents or applications, the material is copied.

2. Drag the selected material to the desired destination. Release the mouse button to complete the move or copy.

USING THE OFFICE CLIPBOARD

Customizing Office

You can modify any Office program to make it easier to use and better suit your working style by setting preferences, customizing the Quick Access Toolbar and the Ribbon, and assigning keyboard shortcuts to commands.

Setting preferences

Preference settings (called *options* in Office) determine how common procedures work in a given Office application. Essentially, by modifying these settings, you're instructing the application to "perform this action when I do this, rather than doing that." In Excel, for example, you can specify the direction that cell selection moves when you press (Enter) and whether to hide or show the formula bar. Although the default behaviors for commands and procedures are designed to meet the needs of most users, you can customize the way any Office application operates by changing its preference settings.

To view or change preferences:

1. In a running Office application, click the File tab to go to the Backstage.

2. Click Options.
   The *application name* Options dialog box appears (**Figure 2.24**).

3. Select an options category from the list on the left side of the dialog box.

4. View and change options settings, as desired.

5. *Optional:* To view or change settings in other categories, repeat Steps 3–4.

6. To enable all changes that you've made to the settings, click OK. Otherwise, to ignore changes (or if you've made no changes), click Cancel.
   The Options dialog box closes.

Option categories

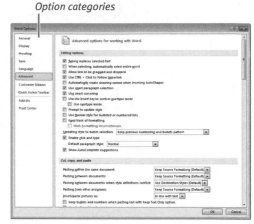

Figure 2.24 Select an option category, view or change settings, and click OK.

✔ Tips

- Some option categories don't fit on a single screen. Use the scroll bar on the right side of the dialog box to view the additional options.

- Most preference settings apply to the application. A few, however, affect only the current document, such as the When calculating this workbook settings in the Advanced section of Excel Options.

Click to open the list

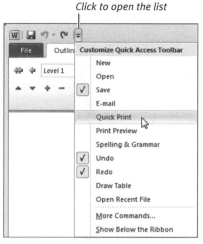

Figure 2.25 Many common commands can be chosen from this drop-down list.

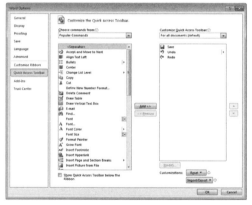

Figure 2.26 Select a command from the left-hand list and click Add to add it to the Quick Access Toolbar.

Customizing the Quick Access Toolbar

The Quick Access Toolbar in each Office application (see Figure 2.12) initially contains only a few command icons. However, you are free to expand it by adding commands for other procedures. The advantage of doing this is that commands on the Quick Access Toolbar are always available to you, regardless of which Ribbon tab you're using.

To add commands to the Quick Access Toolbar:

◆ *Do either of the following:*

▲ Click the Customize Quick Access Toolbar icon at the right side of the toolbar and choose new commands from the list that appears (**Figure 2.25**). Checked commands will appear in the toolbar.

▲ Click the File tab to go to the Backstage, and click Options. In the *application name* Options dialog box, select the Quick Access Toolbar category. To add a command to the toolbar (**Figure 2.26**), select it from the list on the left and click Add. When you're done making changes, click OK.

✔ Tips

■ Another way to reach the Quick Access Toolbar section of the Options dialog box is to choose More Commands from the drop-down list (Figure 2.25).

■ To remove a command from the toolbar, choose it from the list (Figure 2.25) to remove its check mark. If the command isn't listed, open the Options dialog box, select the command in the right-hand list (Figure 2.26), and click Remove.

CUSTOMIZING OFFICE

Customizing the Ribbon

In Office 2010, you aren't stuck with the standard Ribbon configuration for each program. If you like (although most won't bother), you can customize the Ribbon by adding, removing, reordering, and renaming groups, tabs, and commands.

Keep the following in mind as you customize an Office application's Ribbon:

◆ Although you can remove any group from a tab or move it to a new position within the tab (or even to a different tab), you cannot remove or move *command icons* within the default tabs.

◆ Items that cannot be modified are shown in gray text.

◆ You can add commands icons to *any* tab or group, whether it's a default or custom tab or group.

To customize the Ribbon:

1. In the application you want to customize, open the Backstage by clicking the File tab.

2. Click Options.
   The *application name* Options dialog box opens.

3. Select Customize Ribbon in the category list (**Figure 2.27**).

4. *Do any of the following:*
   ▲ **Show or hide a tab.** Add or remove the tab's check mark in the right-hand pane. For example, you can display the Developer tab in Excel, allowing you to record macros. Similarly, you can hide tabs you don't use.
   ▲ **Move a tab or group.** Select the tab or group in the right-hand pane, and then click the Move Up or Move Down button.

Customize Ribbon category   *Move Up/Move Down*

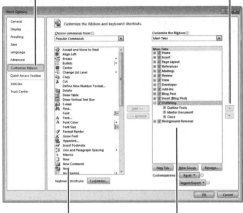

Command list   Current tabs, groups, and commands

Figure 2.27 You make changes to the Ribbon in this section of an application's Options dialog box.

CUSTOMIZING OFFICE

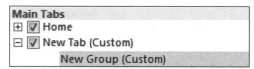

Figure 2.28 When adding a tab, it appears beneath the currently selected tab (in this case, Home). Like other items, however, you can change its position.

Figure 2.29 You can rename a tab (top), as well as a group or command (bottom). When renaming a group or command, you can also select an icon to represent it.

▲ **Create a new tab.** In the right-hand pane, select the tab beneath which the new tab will be added. Click New Tab. A tab named New Tab (Custom) is inserted into the list, as well as a placeholder for the tab's first group (**Figure 2.28**). Rename the tab and group (**Figure 2.29**) by selecting each one and clicking Rename.

▲ **Create a new group.** In the right-hand pane, select the group beneath which the new group will be added. Click New Group. A group named New Group (Custom) is inserted into the list. Rename the group by selecting it and clicking Rename.

▲ **Add a command to a custom group.** Select a command set from the drop-down list above the left-hand pane. Select the group in the right-hand pane to which you want to add the command and click Add.

▲ **Remove a command.** Select the command in the right-hand pane and click Remove. (You can only remove commands previously added to a custom group; defaults are grayed out.)

▲ **Rename a tab, group, or command.** Select the tab, group, or command in the right-hand pane and click Rename (Figure 2.29). Note that you can only rename items that aren't grayed out.

5. Click OK to accept the changes.

The document window appears, reflecting the Ribbon changes.

✔ Tips

■ To go directly to the Customize Ribbon section of the Backstage, right-click any Ribbon tab and choose Customize the Ribbon from the drop-down menu.

■ You can also change an item's position by dragging it up or down.

■ To restore the default Ribbon, click Reset and choose Reset all customizations from the drop-down menu.

■ To remove only the changes you've made to a specific tab, select the tab or any of its components in the right-hand pane, click Reset, and choose Reset only selected Ribbon tab from the drop-down menu.

Modifying Word keyboard shortcuts

To make it simpler to execute your favorite Word 2010 commands, you can assign keyboard shortcuts to them, as well as change existing shortcuts.

To view, change, or assign keyboard shortcuts:

1. In Word 2010, click the File tab to go to the Backstage.

2. Click Options.

   The Word Options dialog box appears.

3. Select Customize Ribbon from the category list on the left side of the dialog box.

4. Click the Customize button beneath the left pane (**Figure 2.30**).

   The Customize Keyboard dialog box appears (**Figure 2.31**).

5. Select a category from the Categories list and select a command to modify from the Commands list.

   The current keyboard shortcuts (if any) assigned to the command are displayed.

6. Press the keyboard shortcut that you want to assign to the command. Click Assign.

   Keyboard shortcuts normally consist of a letter or number key, plus one or more of these modifier keys: Shift, Ctrl, or Alt. Function keys, such as F7, can also be used as keyboard shortcuts—alone or in combination with other modifiers.

7. If desired, repeat Steps 5 and 6 for additional commands.

8. To accept all changes, click Close.

Figure 2.30 Click this button to view or modify Word's keyboard shortcuts.

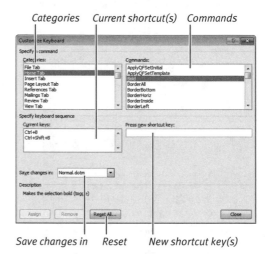

Figure 2.31 View, change, or assign keyboard shortcuts in the Customize Keyboard dialog box.

✔ Tips

■ Be extremely careful when assigning or changing shortcuts. If the key combination you specify is currently assigned to another command, it is reassigned *without warning* to the selected command.

■ Shortcuts are either assigned to the default Word template (Normal.dotm) for all new documents or to the current document, depending on your Save changes in selection.

■ To remove a currently assigned shortcut, select it in the Current keys list for the command and click Remove.

■ To restore all default Word shortcuts, click Reset All.

CUSTOMIZING OFFICE

Document Management Tools

Regardless of the core application you're running, you can use the following tools to safeguard your Office documents or prepare them to be shared:

- **AutoRecover options.** In Options, you can instruct an Office program to automatically save documents every so many minutes, protecting you from accidental data loss.

- **Document Inspector.** When sharing a document publicly or with a select set of users, the Document Inspector can be used to strip the document of embedded personal information, hidden text, invisible content, and the like.

- **Compatibility Checker.** Use this tool to quickly determine if there are compatibility issues with the current document that could affect users of earlier versions of this Office application.

- **Protect Document.** You can assign a password to any document to help prevent unauthorized access to its contents.

- **Document Properties.** Every saved document has properties that you and others can view, such as author, size, pages, word count, and when it was last changed. There are also optional properties you can set, such as a title, tags, and comments.

Identify Yourself

To automatically use your name as the author of your Office documents, you must *personalize* your copy of Office. This information is also used to identify the edits and comments of the various contributors.

1. In Word, open a document and click the File tab to go to the Backstage. Click Options.

2. In the General section of the Word Options dialog box, enter your user name and initials. Click OK.

AutoRecover options

As you work on a Word, Excel, or PowerPoint document, Office can automatically save a draft copy whenever changes are noted during a specified interval. Enabling this *AutoRecover* option protects your work in the event of a crash. When you issue a normal Save command, autosaved draft files created in prior intervals are automatically deleted. By default, AutoRecover options are enabled.

To enable document autosaving:

1. Click the File tab to open the Backstage.

2. Click Options.

   Backstage is exited and the Options dialog box for the application opens.

3. Select the Save category.

   AutoRecover options can be found in the Save documents section (**Figure 2.32**).

4. To enable AutoRecover, click the Save AutoRecover information every X minutes check box and specify an autosave frequency (in minutes).

   As you work on a document, Office will automatically save a copy in the designated location at the specified interval.

5. *Optional:* Check Keep the last Auto Recovered file if I close without saving.

   If you mistakenly close a document file without saving your changes, a draft version will automatically be saved.

6. To close the Options dialog box, click OK to accept the new settings or click Cancel to ignore changes you've made (if any).

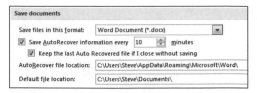

Figure 2.32 Set AutoRecover options in the Save category of each application's Options dialog box.

✔ Tips

■ AutoRecover must be enabled separately for each Office application.

■ Do *not* use AutoRecover as a substitute for regular manual Saves. If the interval is set to 10 minutes, you still risk losing that many minutes of document edits—depending on when you made your last edit and when the last autosave occurred.

■ Frequent disk accesses drain laptop batteries. Laptop users may want to increase the AutoRecover interval.

DOCUMENT MANAGEMENT TOOLS

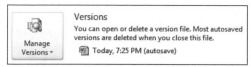

Figure 2.33 One draft of the current document is listed, as well as the date and time of its autosave.

Figure 2.34 When you open an autosaved version, Compare and Restore buttons help simplify the restoration process.

Reviewing pane   Original

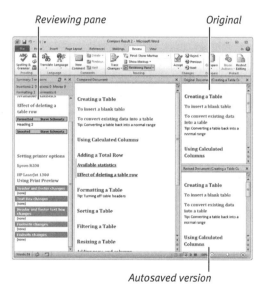

Autosaved version

Figure 2.35 A comparison document shows the differences between original and autosaved versions.

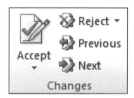

Figure 2.36 For each change, click Accept or Reject. Click Previous and Next to navigate among the changes.

To view or restore a previous version of the current document:

1. Click the File tab to go to the Backstage.

The Info section is automatically selected. Autosaved versions of the document are shown in the Versions area (**Figure 2.33**).

2. Click the name of the autosaved file that you want to view.

The file opens. A yellow bar at the top of the document presents two buttons: Compare and Restore (**Figure 2.34**).

3. Compare the autosaved version to the most recently saved version by clicking the Compare button.

A dialog box informs you if there are no differences between the autosaved version and the last saved version. Otherwise, a new document appears (**Figure 2.35**) that shows the differences.

4. *Do one of the following:*

▲ To selectively accept or reject each change, click buttons in the Changes group (**Figure 2.36**).

▲ Close the comparison document and click the Restore button (Figure 2.34) to overwrite the most recently saved version with this autosaved version.

▲ Close the comparison document and the autosaved version. Continue working with the most recently saved version of the document.

DOCUMENT MANAGEMENT TOOLS

To delete an autosaved version:

1. Click the File tab to open the Backstage. The Info section is automatically selected.

2. In the Versions area, the autosaved versions of the current document are listed (see Figure 2.33).

3. *Do either of the following:*
   - ▲ Right-click a specific version and choose Delete this version from the context menu (**Figure 2.37**).
   - ▲ Click the Manage Versions icon and choose Delete All Draft Versions from the drop-down menu.

4. To exit the Backstage, click the File tab or press Esc.

✔ Tips

- ■ Documents that were closed without saving are also listed in the Recent section of the Backstage.

- ■ You can also view autosaved versions of the current document by clicking the Manage Versions icon and choosing Recover Draft Versions.

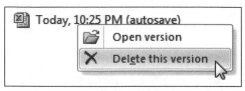

Figure 2.37 You can selectively delete autosaved versions of the current document.

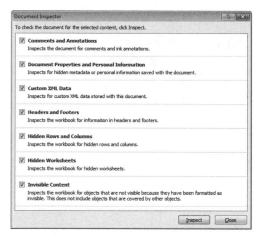

Figure 2.38 Remove check marks from the items you want to ignore (if any), and then click Inspect.

Issue

Figure 2.39 Found material is marked with an exclamation point (!). Click the Remove All button to eliminate it from the document.

✔ Tips

■ Basic issues are automatically listed to the right of the Check for Issues icon in the Info section of the Backstage.

■ Think carefully before saving the changes to the original document. You can't Undo a Save.

Document Inspector

Before sharing an Office document with someone or openly posting it on the Web, you should be aware that it can contain data you may not wish to share. Examples include comments and revision marks, as well as *invisible data*, such as personal information and text formatted as hidden. You can run the Document Inspector to find and remove this material.

To run the Document Inspector:

1. Open the Office document. Click the File tab to go to the Backstage.

   The Info section is automatically selected.

2. Click the Check for Issues icon and choose Inspect Document.

   The Document Inspector dialog box appears (**Figure 2.38**).

3. Remove check marks from elements you don't want to examine. Click Inspect.

   The document is examined and the results are presented (**Figure 2.39**).

4. To eliminate a found element from the document, click its Remove All button.

5. Dismiss the Document Inspector by clicking Close.

6. If material has been removed, *do one of the following:*

   ▲ To incorporate Document Inspector changes into the original document, click the File tab and click Save, click the Save icon in the Quick Access Toolbar, or press Ctrl S.

   ▲ Save the Document Inspector changes in a *new* file. Click the File tab, click Save As, and save the revised document using a new name. Send this copy to the recipient rather than the original document.

DOCUMENT MANAGEMENT TOOLS

Compatibility Checker

With each new Office version, new features are introduced and older ones modified. As a result, although a current document can still be opened by a previous version of Office, the new and modified features may not be supported. Before sharing a document with someone who runs Office 2003, for example, you can run the Compatibility Checker to alert you to potential problems.

1. Open the Office document. Click the File tab to go to the Backstage.

   The Info section is automatically selected.

2. Choose Check Compatibility from the Check for Issues icon's drop-down menu.

   The Compatibility Checker launches and lists incompatibilities (**Figure 2.40**).

3. *Optional:* To restrict the check to particular versions of Office, select them from the Select versions to show drop-down list.

4. Examine each incompatibility and decide whether you want to correct it.

   To go directly to a listed incompatibility, click its Find text.

5. *Optional:* If the document will regularly be shared with users of earlier Office versions, click the Check compatibility when saving... check box to automatically alert you to new issues.

6. Close the dialog box by clicking OK.

7. After correcting any significant issues, you can share the document by clicking the File tab, clicking Save As, and specifying the older file format in the Save As dialog box.

View this incompatibility in the document

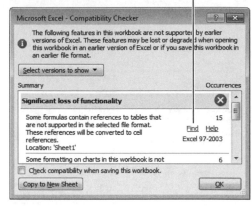

Figure 2.40 Review the noted compatibility issues.

✔ Tips

- Help lists incompatibilities between Office 2010 and earlier versions. It also provides suggestions on how to correct (or avoid) them.

- You can convert a file that's in an older Office format to an Office 2010 document by clicking the Convert icon in the Info section. (This icon is only displayed when working on an older document, denoted by [Compatibility Mode] in the title bar.)

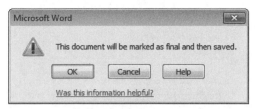

Figure 2.41 To mark this document as final, click OK.

Figure 2.42 This banner appears atop any document marked as final.

Protecting documents

Whether a document will be distributed to others in your office or school, will be sent around the world (via the Web), or will never leave your PC, Word offers several ways for you to protect it. The two simplest options are as follows:

◆ Mark the document as final, changing it to read-only to prevent additional changes.

◆ Encrypt the document, requiring a password to open and work with it.

To mark a document as final:

1. Open the Office document. Click the File tab to go to the Backstage.

   The Info section is automatically selected.

2. Click the Protect Document (Word), Presentation (PowerPoint), or Workbook (Excel) icon and choose Mark as Final from the drop-down menu.

   A dialog box appears (**Figure 2.41**).

3. Click OK.

   The document is marked as final and saved. An explanatory dialog box appears.

4. Click OK to dismiss the dialog box.

   The document is now read-only. When it's opened, any user (including you) will be discouraged from editing the document.

✔ Tip

■ Mark as Final is not a *secure* means of protecting a document because:

   ▲ When opened in earlier Office versions, the document can be freely edited.

   ▲ To override Mark as Final, a user need only click the Edit Anyway button (**Figure 2.42**).

   ▲ To change it back to a normal Office 2010 document, anyone can reissue the Mark as Final command.

DOCUMENT MANAGEMENT TOOLS

To encrypt a document:

1. With the document open in Office, click the Protect Document (Word), Presentation (PowerPoint), or Workbook (Excel) icon and choose Encrypt with Password from the drop-down menu.

   The Encrypt Document dialog box appears (**Figure 2.43**).

2. Enter the password you will use to open the file. Click OK.

3. Reenter the password in the Confirm Password dialog box. Click OK.

4. When you're done working with the document, save the changes. Saving enables the encryption and password protection.

   When you or another user attempt to open the document, a Password dialog box will appear (**Figure 2.44**). Unless the correct password is entered, the document will refuse to open.

✔ Tips

- To remove encryption and password protection from a document, choose Encrypt with Password again and *delete* the password that's shown. (You must first open the document by supplying the password before you can remove the password.)

- If you forget a document's password, you will not be able to open it. It's a good idea to either keep a record of the password in a secure place or retain an unencrypted copy of the document.

- Digital signatures and restricted permissions are other protection features supported by Office, but they require you to enroll in optional services.

Figure 2.43 Enter the password you will use to open this document.

Figure 2.44 A password dialog box appears whenever someone tries open to the document.

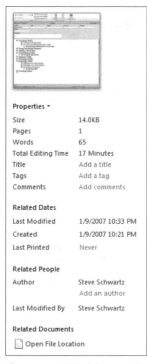

Properties ▾

Size	14.0KB
Pages	1
Words	65
Total Editing Time	17 Minutes
Title	Add a title
Tags	Add a tag
Comments	Add comments

Related Dates

Last Modified	1/9/2007 10:33 PM
Created	1/9/2007 10:21 PM
Last Printed	Never

Related People

Author	Steve Schwartz
	Add an author
Last Modified By	Steve Schwartz

Related Documents

☐ Open File Location

Figure 2.45 A Word document's current properties.

Close box

Figure 2.46 Common document properties can be entered or edited in the Document Panel.

Document properties

As in previous versions of Office, there are a variety of *properties* you can set for a document to help identify, categorize, indicate its current status, and so on. Properties can be assigned to assist your own tracking needs or to provide additional information when you'll be sharing the document with others, such as a workgroup.

To set or view document properties:

1. Open the Office document. Click the File tab to go to the Backstage.

   The Info section is automatically selected. Property information is displayed on the right side of the Backstage (**Figure 2.45**).

2. *Do any of the following:*

   ▲ You can edit basic properties by typing directly into Properties pane fields. Most properties that you can edit are shown in light gray, such as Tags, Comments, and Author.

   ▲ To display additional properties in the pane (such as Status, Subject, and Company), click Properties and choose Show All Properties from the drop-down menu. Like the basic properties, many of these can also be edited in the pane.

   ▲ You can use the Document Panel (**Figure 2.46**) to view, add, or edit several key properties. Choose Show Document Panel from the Properties drop-down menu. When you're done, click the Document Panel's close box.

   ▲ To view, add, or edit all possible properties, open the Properties dialog box by choosing Advanced Properties from the Properties drop-down menu or from the Document Properties drop-down menu at the top of the Document Panel (Figure 2.46).

DOCUMENT MANAGEMENT TOOLS

Getting Help

Office applications can draw help information from files stored on your computer, as well as from Office.com (using an active Internet connection). Simple help is provided by means of *ToolTips* (tiny pop-up windows).

To view a ToolTip:

◆ Rest the cursor over a command or control. A ToolTip (including its keyboard shortcut, if any) appears (**Figure 2.47**).

To get help with an Office application:

◆ Click the Microsoft Office Help icon (**Figure 2.48**) or press F1.
A Help window appears (**Figure 2.49**).

To work in an Office Help window:

1. *Do any of the following:*
   ▲ To view the main Help page, click the Home (house) icon at the top of the Help window.
   ▲ To display/hide Help's content list, click the Table of Contents (book) icon.
   ▲ To read information on a topic, click its blue *link text*. (When you move the cursor over link text, an underline appears beneath the text.)
   ▲ To search Help for a particular topic, type search text in the box and click the Search icon.
   ▲ To go backward or forward among pages you've viewed, click the Back or Forward icon.
   ▲ To change the size of the Help text, click the Change Font Size icon.
   ▲ To print the current help topic, click the Print (printer) icon.

2. When you're done using Help, click the Help window's close box (X).

Figure 2.47 The explanation offered by a ToolTip is generally sufficient to understand what a command icon does.

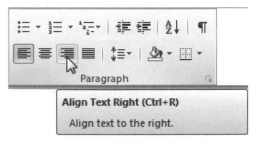

Figure 2.48 Click this icon in the upper-right corner of an application or document window.

Figure 2.49 An Office 2010 Help window.

Figure 2.50 Click the text in the corner of the Help window to indicate which help information to use.

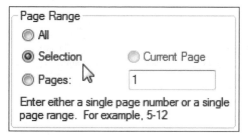

Figure 2.51 You can also print selected text from a Help topic.

✔ Tips

■ To switch between offline and online help information, click the drop-down menu in the lower-right corner of the Help window (**Figure 2.50**) and choose an option.

■ You can click the triangle to the right of the Search icon to specify the *scope* of the search.

■ You can copy Help text and paste it into other documents, such as those of Word or OneNote. Select the text (including images, if you like) and press Ctrl C. The selected material is copied to the system Clipboard. If the Office Clipboard is active, it's also stored there.

■ To print a partial Help topic, select the desired text and click the Print icon. In the Print dialog box, set Page Range to Selection (**Figure 2.51**), and click OK.

GETTING HELP

Quitting an Office Program

As when working with other Windows programs, when you're done using an Office application, you *exit* it.

To quit an Office application:

1. *Do one of the following:*
   - ▲ Click the application's close box (X).
   - ▲ Click the File tab, and then click Exit (**Figure 2.52**).
   - ▲ Press Alt F4.

2. If an open document contains unsaved changes, a dialog box appears (**Figure 2.53**). Otherwise, the program quits immediately.

Figure 2.52 Click Exit in the Backstage to quit the current Office application.

Figure 2.53 When you exit a program, you'll get an opportunity to save any edited documents.

Tables, Charts, and Art

3

Although many documents consist solely of page after page of text or numbers, you can make your Office documents more informative and attractive by adding tables, charts, and artwork, such as photos, clip art, WordArt, and SmartArt.

In this chapter, you'll learn how to insert these items into your documents; embellish artwork by adding color, 3-D effects, and rotation; and specify how surrounding text will wrap around them. You'll also learn about Office 2010's new image-editing tools.

Inserting Tables

The old way to add a table to a document mimicked using a typewriter. Using tabs, text and data were carefully aligned in columns. Word, PowerPoint, and Outlook avoid this rigmarole by letting you place a spreadsheet-style row-and-column table wherever you like.

As shown in **Figure 3.1**, you can insert or create a table in any of the following ways:

◆ Specifying the number of rows and columns by dragging or entering numbers in a dialog box

◆ Manually drawing the table grid

◆ Converting existing text to a table

◆ Importing part of an Excel worksheet

◆ Selecting a Quick Table template and replacing its data with your own

Table-creation options differ somewhat among the three applications.

To insert a table:

1. Set the text insertion mark at the spot in the document where you want to insert the table.

2. On the Insert tab, click the Table icon to reveal the drop-down menu (**Figure 3.1**).

3. *Do one of the following:*

    ▲ **Insert table by highlighting.** In the top section of the drop-down menu, highlight squares to specify the table's dimensions, such as 4 x 5. To place the table, click the lower-right square of the highlighted selection.

    ▲ **Insert table via dialog box.** Choose Insert Table. In the Insert Table dialog box (**Figure 3.2**), specify the number of columns and rows, select an AutoFit behavior, and click OK.

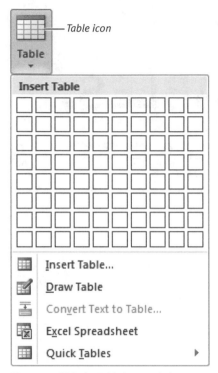

Figure 3.1 Click the Table icon and choose a table insertion method.

Figure 3.2 For additional precision when creating a table, use the Insert Table dialog box.

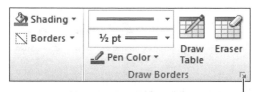

Borders and Shading dialog box launcher

Figure 3.3 These tools are available when drawing a table on a document page.

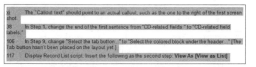

Figure 3.4 Select the text to convert to a table. (For Office to determine how to arrange the text, it should normally be delimited with Returns, tabs, or commas.)

Figure 3.5 Set conversion options and click OK to create the table.

Figure 3.6 If you need the full capabilities of Excel to manipulate your data, you can embed a worksheet in your document rather than use a normal table.

▲ **Create table by drawing.** Choose Draw Table and use the pencil tool to draw the table's line segments. Other Table Tools (**Figure 3.3**) allow you to remove lines (Eraser); change the line style, width, or color; add or remove cell borders; and apply cell shading.

▲ **Convert existing text to a table.** In Word or Outlook, select the text to convert (**Figure 3.4**) and choose Convert Text to Table. In the Convert Text to Table dialog box (**Figure 3.5**), verify the number of columns and rows, set an AutoFit behavior, ensure that the correct text separator is specified, and click OK.

▲ **Insert a worksheet.** Choose Excel Spreadsheet to embed a worksheet in the current document (**Figure 3.6**). Use Excel procedures to enter data, create formulas, and format cells.

▲ **Insert a Quick Table.** In Word or Outlook, choose a table from the Quick Tables submenu to insert a fully formatted table into the document. Replace the sample titles and data with your own information.

✔ Tips

■ When using the Insert Table dialog box, the default behavior is to create fixed-width columns. If you select AutoFit to contents, each column will automatically expand as needed to fully display the longest text string in the column.

■ If you switch to a cell-formatting tool (Shading or Borders) while drawing a table, you drop out of drawing mode. To resume drawing, click the Draw Table icon.

■ Table Tools can be used to modify *any* table. Click the Draw Table icon in the Draw Borders group (Figure 3.3). Click the icon again when you're done editing the table.

Entering Data Into a Table

Unless you converted existing text to a table or inserted a Quick Table, you're now staring at an empty grid. Table cells can contain virtually anything that might be found in an Office document, such as text, numeric data, images, and charts.

To enter data into a table:

1. Click in the first cell in which you want to enter data. (In most newly created tables, the top-left cell is automatically selected.)

2. *Do one of the following:*

   ▲ Type or paste text into the cell.

     If the cell is fixed width, text will wrap within the cell as needed. If an AutoFit option has been applied, the column will expand to fit the longest character string within it.

   ▲ On the Insert tab, select an item from the Illustrations or Images group to insert into the cell (**Figure 3.7**), such as a picture, clip art image, or shape.

     In Word and Outlook, objects are inserted into cells. That is, if you insert an object, the row height and column width adjust to accommodate the object. In PowerPoint, on the other hand, objects float on the slide. They aren't inserted *into* cells.

   ▲ Paste a copied object or use drag-and-drop to move it into the cell.

3. To enter additional data into the table, *do either of the following:*

   ▲ Press Tab to move to the next cell or Shift Tab to move to the previous cell (**Figure 3.8**). Note that if you tab out of the bottom-right cell, a new row will automatically be created.

   ▲ Click in the next cell into which you want to enter data.

Figure 3.7 In addition to pasting, you can insert images and objects by choosing commands from the Illustrations group on the Insert tab.

Figure 3.8 Tabbing from cell to cell (as indicated by the arrows) works as it does in a spreadsheet, such as Excel.

✔ Tip

■ Whenever you're working in a table, the Table Tools contextual tab automatically appears at the top of the Ribbon, along with its Design and Layout tabs.

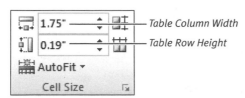

Figure 3.9 To precisely set row or column sizes, enter numbers in these boxes.

Figure 3.10 Choose an option from the AutoFit drop-down menu to set a table to fixed column widths or to AutoFit to match cell contents.

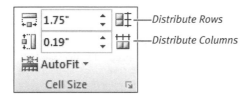

Figure 3.11 To split the total space allotted to several selected rows or columns, click one of these icons.

■ If a row or column contains an object, neither the row height nor the column width can be made smaller than the object. To reduce the row height or column width, you must first reduce the object's size.

Modifying the Table Grid

Unless you plan *very* carefully when creating a table, you'll usually find that the grid needs some modification in order to fit the data. For example, you may need to change the size of the entire table, modify row heights or column widths, change line colors or widths, or color individual cells or the entire table.

To change the size of table elements:

◆ *Do any of the following:*

▲ To change the table size, move the cursor over the table's lower-right corner, and click and drag. To resize proportionately, hold down [Shift] as you drag.

▲ To manually change a column width, move the cursor over the column's right edge until it turns into a double arrow. Drag to the left or right to resize the column.

▲ To manually change a row height, move the cursor over the row's bottom edge until it turns into a double arrow. Drag up or down to resize the row.

▲ To precisely set column widths or row heights, select the columns or rows, and click the Layout tab. Enter a number (in inches) into the Table Column Width or Table Row Height box in the Cell Size group (**Figure 3.9**).

▲ To change a table from AutoFit to fixed-width columns (or vice versa), click the Layout tab and choose an option from the AutoFit icon's drop-down menu in the Cell Size group (**Figure 3.10**).

✔ Tips

■ You can evenly distribute the total width of several selected columns or the total height of several selected rows. Click the Distribute Columns or Distribute Rows icon in the Cell Size group (**Figure 3.11**).

MODIFYING THE TABLE GRID

To remove or add rows or columns:

◆ *Do any of the following:*

▲ To delete rows or columns, click the Layout tab, select the rows or columns, and choose an option from the Delete icon's drop-down menu in the Rows & Columns group (**Figure 3.12**).

▲ To insert rows or columns, select the cell above or below which you want to insert rows or to the right or left of which you want to insert columns. Click an Insert icon in the Rows & Columns group (**Figure 3.13**). To insert more rows or columns, click the icon once for each additional row or column.

To merge or split cells:

1. Make the table active and then click the Layout tab.

2. *Do one of the following:*

▲ To merge cells into a single cell (to create a title row, for example), select the cells and click the Merge Cells icon in the Merge group (**Figure 3.14**).

▲ To reverse a merge or split a single cell into multiple cells, select the cell, click the Split Cells icon, and set options in the Split Cells dialog box (**Figure 3.15**).

▲ To divide a table into two tables, select a cell and click the Split Table icon. The rows above the selected cell become the first table; the selected row and the rows beneath it become the second table.

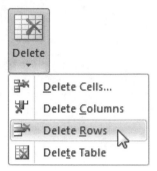

Figure 3.12 Delete selected rows, columns, or an entire table by making a choice from the Delete drop-down menu.

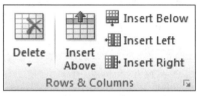

Figure 3.13 Select an Insert command.

Figure 3.14 Click an icon in the Merge group to merge selected cells, split one cell into several, or divide a table into two tables.

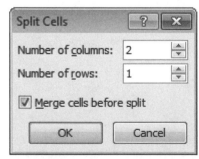

Figure 3.15 You can split a cell into two or more cells.

Borders and Shading dialog box launcher

Figure 3.16 Set line properties by choosing options in the Draw Borders group.

✔ Tips

■ For help selecting table elements, you can choose commands from the Select icon in the Table group on the Layout tab.

■ You don't have to select *entire* rows or columns. Just select enough cells so the application knows what to do. For instance, when modifying one row or column, you can select a single cell in the row or column. To modify two columns, you can drag-select two adjacent cells.

■ You can change individual line properties using the Draw Table tool (Figure 3.16).

■ To selectively remove cell borders, click them with the Eraser tool (Figure 3.16).

■ If you want to simultaneously apply multiple border and/or shading properties to selected cells, click the Borders and Shading dialog box launcher (Figure 3.16) or choose Borders and Shading from the Borders drop-down menu in the Table Styles group.

To change border properties:

1. To modify one or more lines (*borders*) of one or more table cells, begin by selecting the cell(s).

2. In the Draw Borders group on the Design tab, choose a line style, width, and pen color to apply (**Figure 3.16**).

3. Open the Borders drop-down menu in the Table Styles group and choose the border or borders to affect.

   The chosen line style, width, and color are applied to the specified borders.

4. If desired, repeat Step 3 to apply the current line properties to other borders of the selected cells.

To apply cell shading:

1. Select the cells to which you want to apply a background color.

2. Open the Shading menu in the Table Styles group. The Shading menu provides a live preview of any color over which the cursor is hovered. Click to select and apply a color.

To apply a table style to a table:

1. Make the table active by clicking in a cell.

2. On the Design tab, select a Table Style. If the desired style isn't shown, click the down arrow to the right of the visible styles to reveal the entire list. A live preview is shown for any style over which the cursor is hovered. Click a style to apply it to the table.

3. *Optional:* Check options in the Table Style Options group to modify the table style, such as formatting a bottom row differently because it will contain totals.

Formatting Table Data

Like other text in an Office document, table cells can have character and paragraph formatting applied to them.

To apply formatting to cell data:

1. Select the words, sentences, or cells to which the formatting will be applied.

2. To apply paragraph formatting to the selection, *do any of the following:*

   ▲ In the Alignment group (**Figure 3.17**) of the Layout tab, click an icon to set the paragraph alignment.

   ▲ In the Paragraph group (**Figure 3.18**) of the Home tab (PowerPoint and Word) or the Basic Text group of the Message tab (Outlook), you can click icons to set alignment; decrease or increase the indent; or apply a bullet, number, or multilevel list format.

   ▲ Move the cursor up or right-click the selected text to reveal the Mini toolbar (**Figure 3.19**). By clicking its icons, you can center-align paragraphs, as well as decrease or increase the indent.

3. To apply character formatting to the selection, *do any of the following:*

   ▲ In the Font group (**Figure 3.20**) of the Home tab (PowerPoint and Word) or the Basic Text group of the Message tab (Outlook), you can change the font, size, style, color, and highlighting of the selected text.

   ▲ In the Styles group of the Home tab (Word only), you can apply a defined style to the selected text.

   ▲ Move the cursor up or right-click the selected text to reveal the Mini toolbar (Figure 3.19). Apply formatting by clicking icons on the Mini toolbar.

Figure 3.17 Set paragraph alignment by clicking an icon.

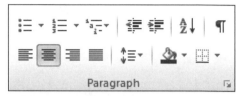

Figure 3.18 In addition to setting the alignment, you can apply bullet and number formats by clicking icons in the Paragraph group.

Figure 3.19 The Mini toolbar.

Clear Formatting

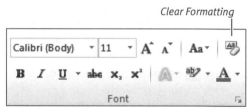

Figure 3.20 Use controls in the Font group to apply character formatting to selected text.

✔ Tips

■ If a cell contains several paragraphs, each can have a different paragraph format.

■ You can also use keyboard shortcuts to apply character and paragraph formatting.

Figure 3.21 Create the formula in this dialog box.

Formula cell

Figure 3.22 To recalculate a formula, right-click the formula cell and choose Update Field from the context menu.

Calculations in Tables

You can include simple row- or column-based formulas in tables to compute statistics, such as sums and averages. You can also sort a table numerically or alphabetically.

To enter a formula into a cell:

1. Click in the cell that will contain the formula.

   Generally, the cell will be in the bottom row or the rightmost column.

2. On the Layout tab, click the Formula icon in the Data group.

   The Formula dialog box appears (**Figure 3.21**).

3. Type an Excel-style formula in this form:

   =function(LEFT/RIGHT/ABOVE/BELOW)

   The word in parentheses determines the cells that are included in the calculation. For example, to total the cells above the current cell, you'd use =SUM(ABOVE).

4. *Optional:* Select a format for the result from the Number format drop-down list.

5. Click OK.

   The calculation is performed and the result is displayed.

✔ Tips

- When performing complex calculations, it's better to insert an Excel worksheet than to create formulas in a standard table.

- To copy a supported function into the Formula box, select the function name from the Paste function drop-down list.

- If the data on which a formula is based changes, the result doesn't automatically update. To force a recalculation, right-click the formula cell and choose Update Field (**Figure 3.22**).

To sort a table:

1. Select the table you want to sort.

2. In the Data group on the Layout tab, click the Sort icon.

The Sort dialog box appears (**Figure 3.23**, below).

3. Select a sort field from the Sort by drop-down list, a data Type (Text, Number, or Date), and a sort order (Ascending or Descending).

4. *Optional:* To sort by more columns, repeat Step 3 for additional Then by sections.

5. For My list has, click a radio button to indicate whether the table has a *header row* (column labels).

6. Click OK to perform the sort (**Figure 3.24**).

✔ Tip

■ Sorting a table works the same as sorting a range in Excel. Information in each table row is treated as a *record*. When you pick a column by which to sort, data in the other columns of each record remains associated.

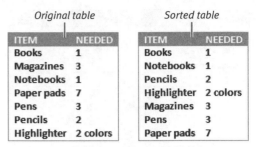

Figure 3.24 To sort this table numerically by the second column, the options set were Sort by: Needed column, Type: Number, Ascending, and Header row.

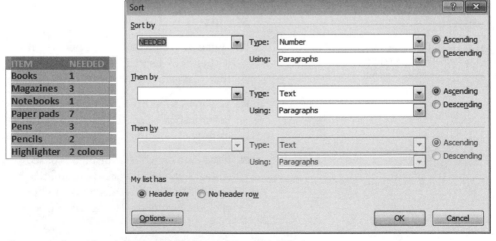

Figure 3.23 Set options in the Sort dialog box and then click OK.

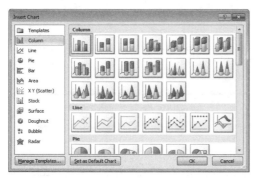

Figure 3.25 Select a chart type from the left column, select a style icon, and click OK.

	A	B	C	D	E	F	G
1	Student	Test 1	Test 2	Test 3			
2	Michelle	15	14	16			
3	Thomas	18	16	19			
4	Adrian	14	9	11			
5	Anthony	17	14	18			
6	Jonas	20	20	18			
7	Heidi	13	15	16			
8		To resize chart data range, drag lower right corner of range.					

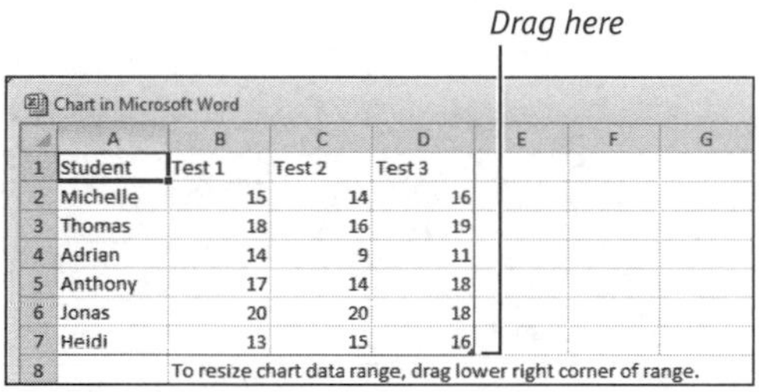

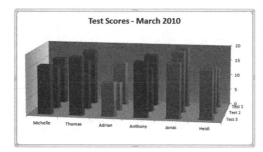

Figure 3.26 In the Excel worksheet that appears, replace the sample data with your own data.

Figure 3.27 You can change any element in the initial chart, such as adding a title, selecting new fonts, and picking a flashier background.

Creating Charts

Excel's charting tools also enable you to create charts in Word, PowerPoint, and Outlook. The chart is embedded in the document and its data is stored in an Excel worksheet.

To create a chart:

1. On the Insert tab, click the Chart icon in the Illustrations group.

   The Insert Chart dialog box appears (**Figure 3.25**).

2. Select the type of chart you want to create and click OK.

   An Excel worksheet appears, containing sample data.

3. Replace the sample data with your data and labels by typing/pasting (**Figure 3.26**).

   The chart is constructed as you enter data.

4. If your data's range doesn't match the sample's range, drag the bounding box's lower-right corner (Figure 3.26) so the range matches that of your data.

   In some cases, Excel will automatically adjust the bounding box for you.

5. *Optional:* Embellish and modify the chart (**Figure 3.27**) by choosing options from the Design, Layout, and Format tabs.

   For more information on creating and modifying charts, see Chapter 12.

✔ Tip

- You can copy an Excel chart and paste it into Word, PowerPoint, or Outlook. The option you choose from the Paste icon's menu will dictate whether the chart will be linked to its data or treated as an embedded picture.

About Adding Graphics and Objects

By clicking icons on the Insert tab (**Figure 3.28**), you can add many common types of images and objects to Office documents. There are also features that help you create your own graphics, such as WordArt, SmartArt, and common shapes.

An image can be placed *inline* with text or as a floating *object* that text wraps around. Images can be loaded from disk, copied from open documents in other programs, or dragged directly into your document from an open document in certain other programs.

Office 2010 provides its own tools for modifying and embellishing graphics. For instance, you can do the following:

◆ Crop an image, removing unwanted parts

◆ Change an image's brightness or contrast

◆ Recolor a picture by adding a color cast

◆ Add a border in any combination of color, line width, and line style

◆ Apply special effects, such as bevel, glow, 3-D rotation, and shadow (**Figure 3.29**) or artistic effects, such as marker, texturizer, or photocopy

◆ Set text-wrap instructions for the image

Office 2010's image-editing tools are discussed at the end of this chapter.

✔ Tip

■ In Internet Explorer, many images are also clickable links. If you attempt to place such an image in your document via drag-and-drop, the link may appear rather than the image. You *can*, however, use copy-and-paste with such images.

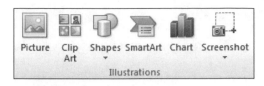

Figure 3.28 You can click icons in the Illustrations, Images, or Text groups to add images and objects to a document.

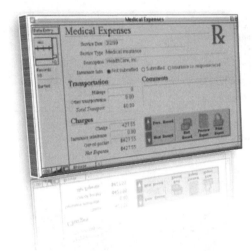

Figure 3.29 Using Picture Tools commands, you can convert an image to impressive artwork.

Figure 3.30 Select a picture and click Insert.

Figure 3.31 The image appears in the document.

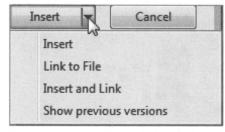

Figure 3.32 Click the arrow beside the Insert button to specify file linking or embedding.

Adding Pictures

You can insert almost any photo or drawing from your hard disk into a PowerPoint, Excel, Word, or Outlook document.

To insert a picture:

1. On the Insert tab, click the Picture icon in the Illustrations group (Word, Excel, and Outlook) or Images group (PowerPoint).

   The Insert Picture dialog box appears (**Figure 3.30**).

2. Navigate to the drive and folder that contains the picture. Select the picture, and click the Insert button.

   The picture appears in the document (**Figure 3.31**).

✔ Tips

- You can click and drag a handle on any corner or edge of a placed picture to change its size. Drag a corner handle to resize the image proportionately.

- The Insert button also has a drop-down menu (**Figure 3.32**). Your menu choice determines whether a *copy* of the image is embedded in the document (Insert) or the image is *linked* to the file (Link to File) on your hard disk. Use Insert when a document will be shared with others. Use Link to keep a document's file size small.

- You can also insert a picture via copy-and-paste. Open the picture or the document in which it's embedded, select the picture, and choose Edit > Copy ($\boxed{\text{Ctrl}}\boxed{\text{C}}$). Switch to the Office document, set the text insertion mark, and click Paste in the Clipboard group on the Home tab or press $\boxed{\text{Ctrl}}\boxed{\text{V}}$.

- You can add a descriptive *figure caption* to a photo or picture by right-clicking the image and choosing Insert Caption from the context menu.

Adding Clip Art

Clip art images are simple drawings and photos that you can use to embellish flyers, memos, brochures, party invitations, and the like. Office 2010 includes a healthy selection of clip art, supplemented by downloadable online images.

To insert clip art:

1. On the Insert tab, click the Clip Art icon in the Illustrations or Images group.

   The Clip Art pane appears (**Figure 3.33**).

2. *Do one of the following:*

   ▲ To search your hard disk and the online collection of clip art images (requires an active Internet connection), ensure that Include Office.com content is checked.

   ▲ To restrict the search to material on your hard disk, remove the check mark.

3. Click the down arrow beside the Results should be box and specify the acceptable type(s) of media.

4. Type a search string in the Search for box and click Go.

   Icons for matching media appear in the results area of the Clip Art pane.

5. To insert a found image into the document, *do one of the following:*

   ▲ Double-click the image icon.

   ▲ Drag the image onto the document.

   ▲ Select the icon, click the down arrow that appears beside the icon, and choose Insert from the drop-down menu (**Figure 3.34**).

✔ Tip

■ To learn more about an item (such as its size or file type), choose Preview/Properties (Figure 3.34).

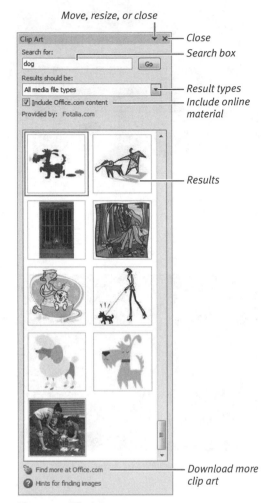

Figure 3.33 Clip Art pane.

Move, resize, or close
Close
Search box
Result types
Include online material
Results
Download more clip art

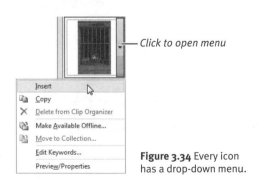

Click to open menu

Figure 3.34 Every icon has a drop-down menu.

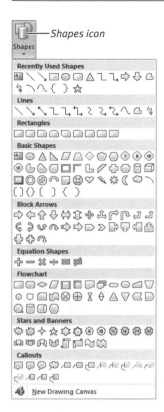

—*Shapes icon*

Figure 3.35 Select a shape from the gallery.

Adding Shapes

Office includes a variety of predefined shapes (such as cubes, arrows, cartoon balloons, and flowchart elements) that you can insert into documents. A shape can optionally be assigned a color, shadow, and 3-D effects. You can insert text into many shapes.

To insert a shape:

1. On the Insert tab, click the Shapes icon in the Illustrations group and select a shape (**Figure 3.35**).

2. Using the drawing cursor (+), click and drag in the document to create the shape.

   To draw a uniform shape (a circle or square rather than an ellipse or rectangle, for example), press Shift as you draw.

3. Release the mouse button to complete the shape.

4. *Optional:* Apply color (**Figure 3.36**) to the selected shape by doing the following:

   ▲ **Apply a style.** On the Format tab, choose a style from the Shape Styles gallery.

   ▲ **Apply a solid, gradient, picture, or pattern fill.** On the Format tab, click the Shape Fill icon in the Shape Styles group. Choose an option from the drop-down menu.

   ▲ **Specify an outline.** Choose settings from the Shape Outline and/or Shape Effects drop-down menus.

   ▲ **Apply a complex style.** Click the Format Shape dialog box launcher icon in the lower-right corner of the Shape Styles group. The dialog box appears, enabling you to apply a variety of color, line, size, rotation, and special effects to the shape.

5. *Optional:* Change the shape's size or rotation by dragging its handles.

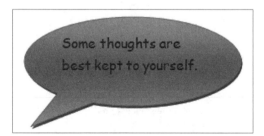

Figure 3.36 You can create a cartoon balloon, apply a color or gradient fill, and then enter and format text.

✔ Tip

■ Text can be added to most shapes. Some require only that you click in them and type. Right-click other shapes, and choose Add Text or Edit Text from the context menu. You can apply character and paragraph formatting to the added text.

ADDING SHAPES

Using a Drawing Canvas

If a drawing will require multiple shapes, you may find it easier to work in a special area called a *drawing canvas* (**Figure 3.37**).

To create and use a drawing canvas (Word and Outlook only):

1. Each drawing canvas is created as an inline graphic. Position the text insertion mark where you want the drawing canvas to appear.

2. On the Insert tab, click the Shapes icon in the Illustrations group and choose New Drawing Canvas from the menu.

   A drawing canvas appears.

3. When working on the canvas, use tools on the Insert and Format tabs to insert and modify shapes. Use the commands in the Arrange group (**Figure 3.38**) to group objects, align objects with one another, and specify layering.

✔ Tips

- You can create as many drawing canvases as you need.

- To resize a drawing canvas, you can drag a corner or edge.

- Drawing canvases are objects. Using Format tab commands, you can set a text wrap for it, fill it with color or a gradient, add a shadow, or apply 3-D effects.

- When you're done drawing, you can resize the canvas to fit tightly around the drawn shapes. Right-click any edge and choose Fit from the context menu (**Figure 3.39**).

- To delete a drawing canvas, right-click it and choose Cut from the context menu (Figure 3.39).

Figure 3.37 A new drawing canvas.

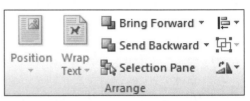

Figure 3.38 Commands in the Arrange group are useful for arranging and grouping drawing elements.

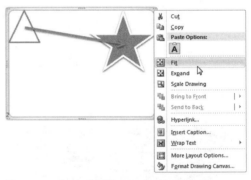

Figure 3.39 Apply the Fit command to resize a drawing canvas to the smallest possible size that encloses all of its elements.

That Little Yellow Dot

When you select an inserted shape, you may see a tiny yellow dot around the outside of or within the shape. You can click and drag the dot to modify a property of the shape. For example, when you drag the dot in the cartoon balloon shown in Figure 3.36, you can change the direction and length of the balloon's handle.

Categories   Preview

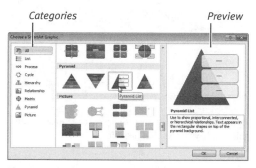

Figure 3.40 Select a SmartArt graphic from this dialog box. Click OK to insert it into the document.

Pop-out panel

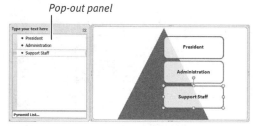

Figure 3.41 It may be easier to type text in the pop-out panel than to enter it directly into the elements.

✔ Tips

- To format several objects the same way, select the objects (drag a selection rectangle around them or Ctrl-click each one) and apply the formatting.

- To delete an unneeded element, select it and press Del. To create more elements, select an element at the same level in the pop-out panel and press Enter. (Note, however, that not all SmartArt objects support additional elements.)

- In PowerPoint, you can convert a text object (such as a set of bullet points) to SmartArt by clicking the Convert to SmartArt Graphic icon in the Paragraph group on the Home tab.

Adding SmartArt

A *SmartArt* object is a ready-made combination of shapes and text. You can use SmartArt to create bullet lists and organizational charts, show processes, and illustrate relationships. SmartArt is available in all core applications.

To insert SmartArt:

1. On the Insert tab, click the SmartArt icon in the Illustrations group.

   The Choose a SmartArt Graphic dialog box appears (**Figure 3.40**).

2. Select a graphic category from the list on the left side of the dialog box.

   SmartArt graphics for the category are shown in the center of the dialog box.

3. Select a SmartArt graphic.

   A preview and explanation for the graphic are displayed.

4. To insert the selected SmartArt graphic into the document, click OK.

5. To replace text and picture placeholders with your own material, *do the following:*

   ▲ **Text.** Click a text placeholder and type. Or click the arrows on the left edge of the SmartArt graphic's border and enter text in the pop-out panel that appears (**Figure 3.41**).

   ▲ **Picture.** Click a picture placeholder. The Insert Picture dialog box appears. Select an image from disk and click Open.

6. You can format a selected element by choosing options from the Format tab. To change the SmartArt graphic's design or color scheme, add elements, or reorder or reorganize the elements, choose options from the Design tab.

Inserting Screenshots

Office 2010 includes a new feature you can use to capture an image of any open window or a selected portion of the screen and insert it as a picture into your document. If you don't have a Windows screenshot utility, you can use this feature to embellish a Word document with a picture of the worksheet on which you're working or capture part of a Web page for inclusion in an Outlook email message, for example.

To insert a screenshot into an Office document:

1. To specify where you'd like to place the screenshot, *do the following:*

   ▲ In Word or Outlook, click to set the text insertion mark.

   ▲ In PowerPoint, click a picture placeholder. In slides that have no picture placeholder, it's sufficient to switch to that slide.

   ▲ In Excel, no action is necessary. A screenshot is added as a floating object.

2. On the Insert tab, click the Screenshot icon in the Illustrations or Images group.

   A drop-down menu and gallery of available windows appears (**Figure 3.42**).

3. *Do one of the following:*

   ▲ To insert an image of an open window, select it in the Available Windows list.

   ▲ To capture a potion of the visible screen, choose Screen Clipping. Using the crosshair cursor that appears, drag to select an area of the screen.

   The window or clipping is inserted into the document (**Figure 3.43**). Resize and format the image as you like.

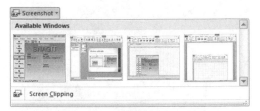

Figure 3.42 The Available Windows list shows thumbnails of all windows that are eligible to be used as screenshots.

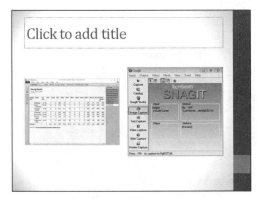

Figure 3.43 This PowerPoint slide contains two screenshots: a OneNote page and a utility window.

✔ Tip

■ You must prepare for a screenshot. First, because minimized windows aren't listed in the Available Windows list (Figure 3.42), you must open any window that you want to capture. Second, if you want to create a screen clipping, you must ensure that the area you need to capture isn't obscured by other windows.

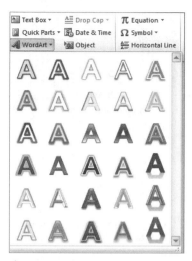

Figure 3.44 Select a style from the WordArt gallery.

Figure 3.45 Replace this text placeholder with your own text.

Figure 3.46 An example of WordArt.

Creating WordArt

WordArt is a decorative text object that you create by applying a special effect to text and optionally stylizing it using object-formatting commands. Although WordArt is too flashy for many business and school documents, it's great for flyers, party invitations, brochures, and PowerPoint slide text.

To create WordArt:

1. *Optional:* Select text in the document that you want to convert to WordArt.

   WordArt can be created from existing text or typed in the WordArt placeholder.

2. On the Insert tab, click the WordArt icon in the Text group and select a WordArt style (**Figure 3.44**).

   A placeholder appears (**Figure 3.45**) or the selected text is converted to WordArt.

3. If the WordArt text box contains a place-holder (Your text here), replace it with your text by typing or pasting.

4. Using commands on the Format tab, other Ribbon tabs (such as Home and Message), and the Mini toolbar, set the font, size, style, and alignment for the WordArt. Additional formatting options can be found in the WordArt Styles group of the Format tab.

5. Resize the WordArt bounding box (Figure 3.45) as desired.

6. If necessary, reposition the WordArt by dragging it to a new location (**Figure 3.46**).

✔ Tips

- In Excel, WordArt is always created as placeholder text. It cannot be created by first selecting existing cell text.

- You can specify a text-wrap setting for WordArt as described later in this chapter.

Adding a Text Box

A *text box* is a rectangular container object for text. Text boxes are commonly used to set off important snippets of text (such as the quote shown in **Figure 3.47**) from the main text. Magazines often use text boxes (without the surrounding border or background) to print blurbs that summarize and draw attention to the article in which they're embedded.

> See a penny, pick it up, and all the day you'll have one cent.
> —*Steve Schwartz, 1963*

Figure 3.47 This is an example of a text box formatted with a gradient fill.

To create a text box:

1. On the Insert tab, click the Text Box icon in the Text group and choose Draw Text Box from the drop-down menu.

   A drawing cursor (+) appears.

2. Click and drag to draw the box.

   When you release the mouse button to complete the box, a text insertion mark appears inside the box.

3. Type or paste text into the box.

4. Format the text using commands on the Mini toolbar or the Home tab. If necessary, you can resize the box to fit the text by dragging a side or corner handle.

5. *Optional:* Format the box using tools on the Format tab.

6. *Optional:* The default text-wrap setting for a text box is In Front of Text. You can choose a different setting from the Wrap Text drop-down menu in the Arrange group of the Format tab.

7. Drag the box into the desired position. Move the cursor over any edge until it becomes a plus with arrowheads and then drag.

✔ Tips

- Word's Text Box drop-down menu also contains a gallery of predefined boxes.

- To delete a text box, select it and press Del.

Figure 3.48 Click Create Link to establish a link between text boxes.

Linking Text Boxes

You can also use text boxes to create complex documents (such as newsletters) that are normally tackled with a desktop publishing program. To facilitate this use, text boxes in Word or Outlook can be *linked* to allow text to automatically flow from one text box into the next:

1. Create the initial text box, and type or paste your text into it.

2. Create a second text box, but leave it empty. (You can create a link only to an empty text box.)

3. Select the first text box or set the text insertion mark inside it.

4. On the Format tab, click the Create Link icon (**Figure 3.48**, above) in the Text group. Click the empty text box to establish the link.

If you later want to break the link between text boxes, select the first text box and click the Break Link icon in the Text group.

ADDING A TEXT BOX

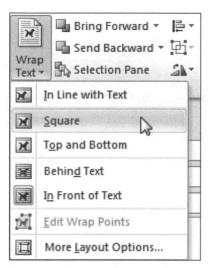

Figure 3.49 Choose a wrapping option from the Wrap Text drop-down menu.

Figure 3.50 If an object must appear in a particular location on the page, you can apply settings from the Position tab of the Layout dialog box.

Setting Text Wrap

Whether you're placing photos, charts, clip art, WordArt, SmartArt, text boxes, or another object type on document pages, each object must have a *text wrap* setting. This setting determines how surrounding text interacts with the object: whether it wraps around the object or enables the object to be placed beneath or on top of the text.

To set text wrap for an object:

1. Select the object.

2. On the Format tab, choose an option from the Wrap Text drop-down menu in the Arrange group (**Figure 3.49**).

3. Drag the object into position.

   The surrounding text wraps around the object as specified.

✔ Tips

■ You also use the Wrap Text drop-down menu (Figure 3.49) to switch an object from inline to floating or vice versa:

   ▲ To convert a floating object to an inline object, choose In Line with Text.

   ▲ To convert an inline object to a floating object, choose any command other than In Line with Text.

■ You can add a watermark or stamp to a page, such as Confidential or Not for Distribution. Create a text box with large type (72 pt., for example), set the text color to a light gray, and then choose Behind Text as the Wrap Text setting.

■ Two additional wrap styles (Through and Tight), as well as specific position settings, can be set in the Layout dialog box (**Figure 3.50**). To open the dialog box, choose More Layout Options from the Wrap Text menu (Figure 3.49).

SETTING TEXT WRAP

Resizing, Moving, and Rotating Objects

Using the handles that surround any selected object, you can manually resize, move, or rotate the object.

To change an object's size:

1. Select the object.

   Handles appear around the object (**Figure 3.51**).

2. *Do either of the following:*

   ▲ To change only an object's height or width, drag an edge handle. Resizing an object in this manner does *not* maintain its original proportions.

   ▲ To proportionately change both the object's height and width, hold down (Shift) while dragging a corner handle.

To move an object:

1. Select the object.

2. Move the cursor over the object until the cursor changes to a plus symbol with arrowheads:

   ▲ In drawn objects, photos, and clip art, click anywhere inside the object and drag.

   ▲ In a text box, drag any edge of the box.

   ▲ In a table, move the cursor over the upper-left corner and drag the plus symbol that appears (**Figure 3.52**).

3. Release the mouse button when the object is in the desired position.

To rotate an object:

1. Select the object.

   Handles appear around the object.

2. To rotate the object, click the green rotate handle, and drag to the left or right.

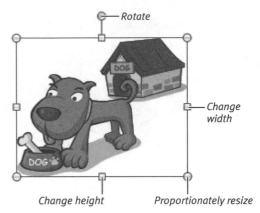

Rotate — Change width — Change height — Proportionately resize

Figure 3.51 Every selected object is surrounded by handles.

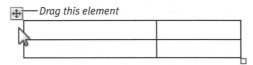

Drag this element

Figure 3.52 To change a table's position, drag here.

About Layers

An Office document can have multiple layers. A page that contains only text or a single object has one layer. However, when you create or place *additional* objects on the page, each object can either be on the same layer as the other material or on its own layer—on top of or beneath other objects and text.

To change a selected object's layer, choose a command from the Bring to Front or Send to Back drop-down menu in the Arrange group on the Format tab. Ensure that In Line with Text is *not* the Wrap Text setting (see previous page).

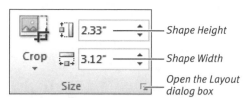

Figure 3.53 The Size group.

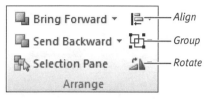

Figure 3.54 Choose a rotation option from the Rotate icon. Each command has a live preview.

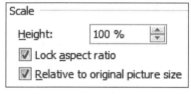

Figure 3.55 The behavior of the Size boxes in Figure 3.53 is determined by the Lock aspect ratio setting.

Using the Selection Pane

Use the Selection Pane when you have trouble selecting a placed object (so you can move it or alter its formatting, for example). Open the pane by switching to the Format tab and clicking the Select or Selection Pane icon in the Editing group. All objects on the current page are listed in the pane; visible objects are marked with an eye symbol.

To select an object, click its name. If the object is obscured by another object, click the covering object's eye symbol to temporarily hide it and enable you to work directly with the obscured object.

✔ Tips

■ Some objects, such as tables, cannot be rotated.

■ To proportionately resize artwork, such as a photo or clip art, it isn't necessary to hold down [Shift] as you drag a corner handle.

■ You can also change the size or rotation of objects by specifying exact amounts:

▲ **Size.** Type a number or click an arrow in the Shape Height or Shape Width box in the Size group of the Format tab (**Figure 3.53**).

▲ **Rotation.** Click the Rotate icon in the Arrange group on the Format tab (**Figure 3.54**), and choose an option from the drop-down menu. To set a specific rotation angle, choose More Rotation Options.

■ Dimensions entered in the Size group boxes resize only the selected dimension or proportionately resize the object, depending on a setting in the Layout dialog box. Click the icon at the bottom of the Size group (Figure 3.53). In the Layout dialog box, switch to the Size tab, add or remove the check mark from Lock aspect ratio (**Figure 3.55**), and click OK.

■ If you've carefully placed several objects and want to move them, it's easier if you *group* them first. Select the objects and choose Group from the Group icon menu. To later separate the objects (enabling you to work with them individually again), choose Ungroup from the Group menu.

■ To align two or more selected objects with one another, choose a command from the Align icon's menu in the Arrange group.

■ The Arrange group in Word has a Position icon menu that you can use to position an object relative to the surrounding text.

RESIZING, MOVING, AND ROTATING OBJECTS

Image-editing Tools

With Office 2010, you may find that it's no longer necessary to have a separate image-editing program to clean up, crop, or otherwise modify photos you want to include in documents. Whenever you select an inserted photo, the Picture Tools tab appears, providing a variety of image-editing tools and enhancement options.

As you'll learn in this section, you can do the following with any photo placed in an Office document:

◆ Adjust the brightness, contrast, and sharpness

◆ Alter the color saturation or tone

◆ Apply artistic effects

◆ Apple style settings, such as a frame or border

◆ Turn a photo into a SmartArt object

◆ Crop an image to remove distracting elements or reform it to match a shape, such as a heart

◆ Remove the background, leaving only the photo's main subject

◆ Compress pictures to reduce the document's size

◆ Replace one picture with another, retaining the same size and applied formatting as the original

◆ Revert to the original photo, discarding all formatting changes

✔ Tips

■ When working with Format tab galleries, you may need to scroll the document to prevent the gallery from obscuring the photo you're editing.

■ When experimenting with effects in a drop-down gallery, you can restore the image to its previous state by selecting the first effect (labelled "None"). In the Format Picture dialog box, click Reset.

■ Edits affect only the way an image looks on the document page. The original photo stored on disk remains unchanged. To make *permanent* edits and corrections to a photo, *do either of the following:*

▲ Make your edits with a dedicated image-editing program, such as Adobe Photoshop.

▲ Right-click the image in your Office document, choose Save as Picture from the context menu that appears, and save the edited photo. You can overwrite the original file or save it with a new name, location, and/or file format.

IMAGE-EDITING TOOLS

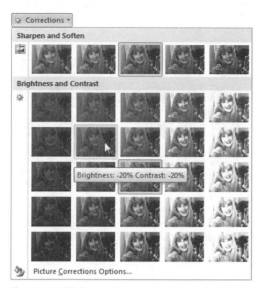

Figure 3.56 Click to apply a new brightness/contrast or sharpness setting.

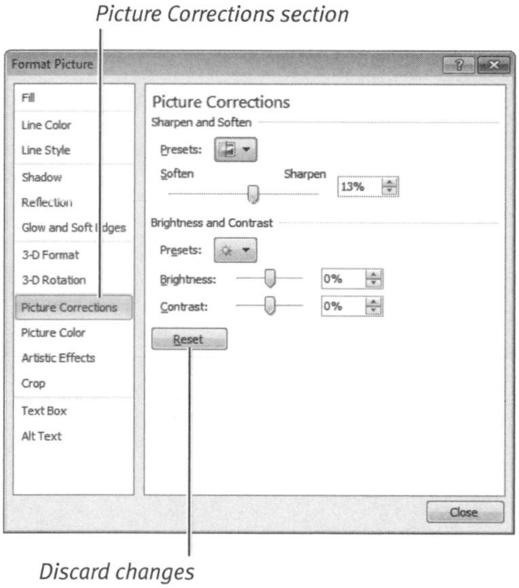

Picture Corrections section

Discard changes

Figure 3.57 One advantage of using the Format Picture dialog box is that you can adjust brightness and contrast independently.

Adjusting brightness, contrast, and sharpness

Because of lighting conditions or inappropriate use of a flash, it's not unusual for a photo to be too dark or bright, muddy looking (when shot with a Web cam, for instance), or soft (common with scanned photos). Depending on the degree of the problem, you may be able to salvage the photo by adjusting the brightness, contrast, and/or sharpness.

To adjust the brightness, contrast, or sharpness:

1. Select the inserted photo in the Office document.

   The Picture Tools contextual tab appears. Click the Format tab if it isn't automatically selected.

2. Click the Corrections icon in the Adjust group.

   The drop-down gallery (**Figure 3.56**) shows brightness/contrast combinations and sharpness settings that you can apply.

3. *Do either of the following:*

   ▲ As you hover the cursor over a thumbnail, a live preview of the setting is shown on the photo. Click the thumbnail to apply that setting.

   ▲ For more precise corrections, choose Picture Corrections Options. The Format Picture dialog box appears. Using the controls in the Picture Corrections section (**Figure 3.57**), adjust the brightness, contrast, and softness. Click Close when you're done making changes.

✔ Tip

■ When experimenting in the Picture Corrections section of the Format Picture dialog box, you can discard your changes by clicking the Reset button (Figure 3.57).

IMAGE-EDITING TOOLS

Setting color saturation and tone

Office also has tools that enable you to adjust the overall color saturation (*density*) and the color tone (*temperature*). Using these tools, you can brighten up a washed-out or faded shot, change a photo's mood, or create a duotone, for example.

To change the color saturation or tone:

1. Select the inserted photo in the Office document.

   The Picture Tools contextual tab appears. Click the Format tab if it isn't automatically selected.

2. Click the Color icon in the Adjust group. A drop-down gallery appears (**Figure 3.58**).

3. *Do any of the following:*

   ▲ As you hover the cursor over a thumbnail, a live preview of the setting is shown on the photo. Click the thumbnail to apply that setting.

   ▲ To create a duotone from the photo, click an icon in the Recolor section of the gallery. To use a different recoloring shade, choose More Variations.

   ▲ For more precise corrections, choose Color Picture Options. The Format Picture dialog box appears. Using the controls in the Picture Color section (**Figure 3.59**), adjust the saturation and tone. Click Close when you're done making changes.

✔ Tips

■ To change a color photo into a black-and-white image, select Grayscale in the Recolor area (Figure 3.58). Select Sepia or a orange/tan color to create a traditional duotone image.

■ The Black and White: 50% Recolor option provides an effect similar to Kodalith film—black and white only; no gray shades.

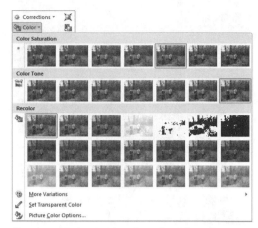

Figure 3.58 Select settings from the Color gallery to change a photo's color saturation or tone.

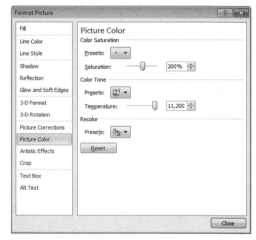

Figure 3.59 Use options in the Format Picture dialog box to simultaneously change multiple color settings for the current picture.

■ For some images, it can be useful to set a *transparency color*. Areas that match the selected color will allow objects, photos, and text beneath the photo to show through. Choose Set Transparency Color from the Color drop-down menu (Figure 3.58). Use the eyedropper tool to select the color in the photo that will be treated as transparent.

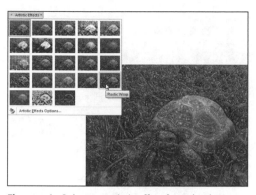

Figure 3.60 Select an artistic effect from the drop-down gallery.

Figure 3.61 Use the Artistic Effects section of the Format Pictures dialog box to apply custom settings to an artistic effect, such as altering the grid size of the Light Screen effect.

Applying artistic effects

Occasionally, you may want to transform a photo into something artistic or funky. Office 2010 has more than two dozen artistic effects that you can apply to photos, such as Marker, Light Screen, and Glow Edges.

1. Select the inserted photo in the Office document.

   The Picture Tools contextual tab appears. Click the Format tab if it isn't automatically selected.

2. Click the Artistic Effects icon in the Adjust group.

   A drop-down gallery appears (**Figure 3.60**).

3. As you hover the cursor over a thumbnail, a live preview of the effect is shown on the photo. Click the thumbnail to apply that setting.

✔ Tips

- Choosing Artistic Effects Options from the Artistic Effects menu enables you to fine-tune the settings of many effects (**Figure 3.61**).

- Another way to open the Format Picture dialog box is to select the photo and click the launcher icon in the bottom-right corner of the Picture Styles group on the Format tab. You can also right-click the photo and choose Format Picture from the context menu that appears.

IMAGE-EDITING TOOLS

Adding a border or frame

When you insert a photo into a document, it's added unaltered. Other than its own natural colors, a photo has no frame or border. While this is fine—typical, in fact—for photos inserted into email messages, photos in Word documents often look better with a border.

To add a border or frame to a photo:

1. Select the inserted photo in the Office document.

   The Picture Tools contextual tab appears. Click the Format tab if it isn't automatically selected.

2. In the Picture Styles group, *do one of the following:*

   ▲ To apply a solid or dashed border to the photo, click the Picture Border icon and choose options from the drop-down menu (**Figure 3.62**). Revisit the menu for each additional line option you want to apply.

   ▲ Choose a decorative frame (**Figure 3.63**) from the Picture Styles gallery.

   ▲ Choose a more esoteric frame (such as a 3-D or reflection frame) from the Picture Effects submenus.

✔ Tips

■ Advanced line style settings can be specified in the Line Color and Line Style sections of the Format Picture dialog box (see Figure 3.61).

■ You can remove a previously added line border by choosing No Outline from the Picture Border drop-down menu.

■ To convert a selected image to a SmartArt object, select an option from the Picture Layout drop-down gallery.

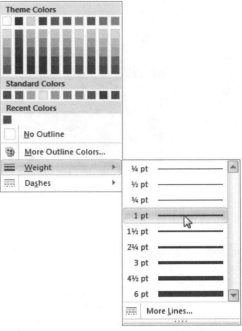

Figure 3.62 To apply a border, choose line options from the Picture Borders drop-down menu.

Figure 3.63 You can make certain photos stand out by adding a stylish frame.

Figure 3.64 Cropping handles appear at all corners and sides.

Discard   Keep   Discard

Figure 3.65 Drag one or more handles to show the area of the photo that you want to keep.

Cropping photos

As framed in the camera, shots often contain extraneous material that you may wish to eliminate by judiciously *cropping* the photo. Picture Tools enables you to crop manually, match a desired aspect ratio, or conform to a selected shape.

To crop a photo manually:

1. Select the inserted photo in the Office document.

   The Picture Tools contextual tab appears. Click the Format tab if it isn't automatically selected.

2. Click the Crop icon in the Size group.

   Cropping handles appear around the picture (**Figure 3.64**). The photo's current height and width are shown in boxes in the Size group.

3. When the cursor is over a crop handle, its shape changes to match that of the handle. Drag handles to remove the unwanted portions of the picture.

   The area to be cropped out is shown in gray (**Figure 3.65**).

4. To complete the process, click anywhere else on the document page or press Esc.

✔ Tips

- To crop proportionately from one corner, Shift-drag the corner handle. To crop equally from two edges, Ctrl-drag an edge handle. To crop equally from all edges, Ctrl-drag any corner handle.

- While cropping, you can also drag the image around while retaining the current crop dimensions. Click in the gray area and drag.

- You can use the Compress Pictures tool to reduce the photo's size by discarding the cropped-out portions.

IMAGE-EDITING TOOLS

To crop to match a shape:

1. Select the inserted photo in the Office document.

   The Picture Tools contextual tab appears. Click the Format tab if it isn't automatically selected.

2. Choose Crop to Shape and select a shape from the Crop icon's drop-down menu (**Figure 3.66**).

   The photo is cropped to match the shape.

To crop to an aspect ratio:

1. Select the inserted photo in the Office document.

   The Picture Tools contextual tab appears. Click the Format tab if it isn't automatically selected.

2. Click the Crop icon in the Size group and choose a ratio from the Aspect Ratio submenu (**Figure 3.67**).

   Crop dimensions that match the aspect ratio are overlaid on the photo.

3. If necessary, adjust the area that will be cropped by clicking in the gray area of the photo and dragging.

4. To complete the process, click anywhere else on the document page or press Esc.

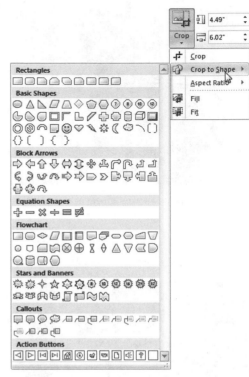

Figure 3.66 Choose a shape from the gallery.

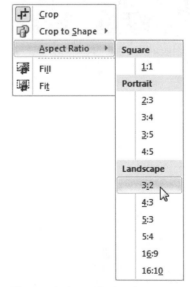

Figure 3.67 Aspect Ratio submenu.

IMAGE-EDITING TOOLS

Background Removal tools

Figure 3.68 The subject is displayed normally, while the material to be eliminated is shown in purple.

Figure 3.69 With a clearly defined subject and a background like this, results can be exceptional.

✔ Tip

- When adding and removing areas to keep, increasing the magnification can help.

Removing the background

You can use the Remove Background command to isolate part of a photo, removing all material around it. The command's effect is similar to *masking* in Photoshop.

To remove the background:

1. Select the inserted photo in the Office document.

    The Picture Tools contextual tab appears. Click the Format tab if it isn't automatically selected.

2. Click the Remove Background icon in the Adjust group.

    The Background Removal tools appear and Office guesses the photo's subject (**Figure 3.68**).

3. *Optional:* Adjust the selection marquee by dragging its handles to include less or more material.

4. If necessary, adjust the selected material by doing any of the following:

    ▲ To expand the selection, click the Mark Areas to Keep icon and draw lines to denote the new areas.

    ▲ If extraneous material is selected, click the Mark Areas to Remove icon and draw lines to mark areas to be eliminated from the selection.

    ▲ If a drawn line doesn't have the desired effect, click the Delete Mark icon and then click the mark(s) you want to remove.

5. *Do one of the following:*

    ▲ To complete the background removal (**Figure 3.69**), click Keep Changes, press (Esc), or press (Enter).

    ▲ To abort the process, click Delete All Changes.

IMAGE-EDITING TOOLS

Compressing pictures

Given the high megapixel cameras now being sold, photos can take up considerable space in documents, presentations, and email messages. Using the Compress Picture command, you can reduce the resolution of individual photos or all photos in an Office document, reducing the document's size.

To compress one or more pictures:

1. Select the placed photo that you want to compress. (If you want to compress all photos in the document, it doesn't matter which photo you select.)

   The Picture Tools contextual tab appears. Click the Format tab if it isn't automatically selected.

2. Click the Compress Pictures icon in the Adjust group (**Figure 3.70**).

   The Compress Pictures dialog box appears (**Figure 3.71**).

3. *Set the following options:*

   ▲ **Apply only to this picture.** To compress only the selected photo, check this option. To compress all photos in the document, remove the check mark.

   ▲ **Delete cropped areas of pictures.** If the selected photo(s) have been cropped, set this option to delete the cropped areas. (Cropping does not delete the cropped-out areas. It merely hides them.)

   ▲ **Target output.** This resolution setting determines the amount of compression to be applied to the photo(s).

4. Click OK to perform the compression.

   If the results are satisfactory, save the document. If not, click the Undo icon in the Quick Access Toolbar or press [Ctrl][Z].

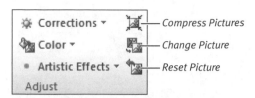

Figure 3.70 Other commands in the Adjust group.

Figure 3.71 The Compress Pictures dialog box.

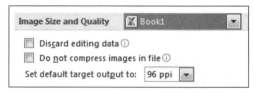

Figure 3.72 Specify compression settings for the chosen document.

✔ Tip

■ By default, Office compresses all photos placed in a document. To view or change the default setting, click the File tab. In the Backstage, click Options and select the Advanced category in the *application* Options dialog box. Make any desired changes in the Image Size and Quality section (**Figure 3.72**).

IMAGE-EDITING TOOLS

Figure 3.73 Navigate to the appropriate drive and folder, and select a replacement photo.

Replacing one photo with another

Use this command to replace a selected photo with a different one from disk while retaining the current size and formatting applied to the selected photo.

To replace a photo:

1. Select the inserted photo in the Office document.

   The Picture Tools contextual tab appears. Click the Format tab if it isn't automatically selected.

2. Click the Change Picture icon in the Adjust group (see Figure 3.70).

   The Insert Picture dialog box appears (**Figure 3.73**).

3. Select a replacement photo and click Insert.

   The new photo replaces the original in the document.

Resetting edits

If you've been experimenting with formatting options for an inserted photo, you can restore the original image using the Reset Picture command.

To reset all edits for an image:

1. Select the inserted photo in the Office document.

   The Picture Tools contextual tab appears. Click the Format tab if it isn't automatically selected.

2. Click the Reset Picture icon in the Adjust group (see Figure 3.70).

   All edits are removed from the photo.

IMAGE-EDITING TOOLS

Part II:
Microsoft Word

GETTING STARTED WITH WORD 2010

Microsoft Office Word is a word-processing application—perhaps the most widely used word-processing application in existence. You can use Word to write letters, memos, reports, and essays. Because it is so pervasive and allows you to save in a variety of file formats, there's an excellent chance you can create a version of a given Word document that can be opened by almost any recipient.

In this introductory chapter, you'll learn about the Word interface, working in different views, and entering and editing text. For information on launching and quitting Word, as well as performing basic document-related tasks, such as creating, opening, saving, and closing documents, see Chapter 2.

✔ Tip

■ Every Word document—whether new or opened from disk—opens in its own window. Clicking a document's close box (X) closes only that document. To close *all* documents and quit Word, you must individually close every open document or click the File tab and click Exit in the Backstage.

The Word Interface

Figure 4.1 (below) shows the interface elements you'll use when creating and editing Word documents. Many, such as the Ribbon, File tab, and Quick Access Toolbar, can also be found in Excel, PowerPoint, and Outlook.

File tab. Click this tab to perform file-related activities in Office Backstage (**Figure 4.2**), such as creating, opening, saving, and printing. Click Options to set Word preferences. To open a document on which you've recently worked, click its name in the Recent list. The Exit command can also be found here.

Quick Access Toolbar. Icons for common commands (such as Save, Undo, and Redo) can be found on this customizable toolbar.

Figure 4.2 When printing the current document in the Backstage, Page Setup options and a print preview are automatically displayed.

Figure 4.1 Elements of the Word 2010 interface.

Figure 4.3 Click text links in Word Help to view help topics. Click the close box (X) or exit Word to dismiss Word Help.

Help. Click this icon or press F1 to open the Word Help window (**Figure 4.3**).

Ribbon. The Ribbon is Office's replacement for the program menus found in Word 2003 and prior versions. Similar commands and procedures are listed together on a tab, such as Insert or View. Within each tab, procedures are further divided into groups, based on similarity of function. To perform a command, you switch to the appropriate tab by clicking its name and then click the command's icon or control.

Rulers. Click the View Ruler icon to hide or show the horizontal and vertical rulers. Use the controls on the horizontal ruler to set or change tab stops and indents for the currently selected paragraph(s). The vertical ruler is visible only on the document page that contains the text insertion mark.

Styles pane. To make it easier to apply a Word character or paragraph style to selected text, you can display the Styles pane by clicking the launcher icon at the bottom of the Styles group on the Home tab. Click a style name to apply it to currently selected text.

Office Clipboard. The Office Clipboard is shared among Office applications and allows you to copy and paste multiple items within a document, between documents, and even between applications. To show the Office Clipboard pane, click the launcher icon at the bottom of the Clipboard group on the Home tab. Click the pane's close box (X) to dismiss the pane.

Document. Most of Word's window is reserved for the current word-processing document. You can close the Office Clipboard and other panes to increase the display area for the document.

Scroll bar and scroll box. You can click in the scroll bar or drag the scroll box to navigate through a document's pages.

Page indicator. This indicator displays the current page number, as well as the total number of pages in the document. Click the indicator to open the Find and Replace dialog box to the Go To tab (**Figure 4.4**).

Words indicator. This indicator shows the word count for the document. If text is selected, it shows the number of words in the selection. Click the indicator to open the Word Count dialog box (**Figure 4.5**).

Proofing indicator. This indicator shows if there are proofing errors that need to be addressed, such as misspellings, repeated words, or extra spaces between words. Click the indicator to move from one suspected error to the next.

View controls. Click an icon to switch views (**Figure 4.6**). You can also switch views by clicking the View tab and then clicking an icon in the Document Views group. The purpose of each view is explained in the next section.

Zoom controls. Change the current magnification by dragging the slider, clicking the + (increase) or – (decrease) button, or clicking the zoom percentage icon.

Close. Click the close box (X) to close an open document or to quit Word. (When the current document is the only one that's open, clicking the close box quits Word.) You can also close the active document by clicking Close in the Backstage (see Figure 4.2).

✔ Tip

■ Any Word pane, such as Styles or the Navigation Pane, can be displayed as a docked pane or a floating palette. To make a docked pane float, drag it by its title bar to a new location. To dock a floating pane, slowly drag it off either side of the document window until it snaps into place.

Figure 4.4 On the Go To tab, you can go to a specific page by entering a page number and clicking Go To.

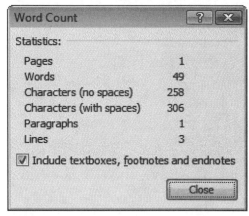

Figure 4.5 For detailed word count information, open the Word Count dialog box.

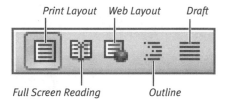

Figure 4.6 You can quickly change views by clicking an icon at the bottom of the document window.

Figure 4.7 The Document Views group contains the same five view icons as the ones in the status bar.

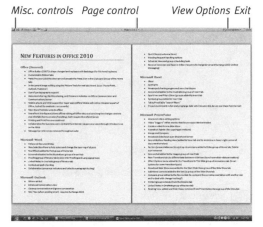

Figure 4.8 Full Screen Reading view is especially useful for proofing documents, as well as reading ones you download or receive as email attachments.

Figure 4.9 View Options menu.

Working in Different Views

Depending on what you currently want to do with a document, you can work in any of Word's *views*: Print Layout, Full Screen Reading, Web Layout, Outline, and Draft. Each view serves a particular purpose, as described below. To switch views, you can click an icon in the status bar (see Figures 4.1 and 4.6) or click an icon in the Document Views group on the View tab (**Figure 4.7**).

Print Layout view

Standard documents, such as letters, memos, and reports, are often written and edited in Print Layout view. One advantage of working in this view is its adherence to *WYSIWYG* (what you see is what you get). The margins, headers, and footers correspond to the printed output. Pages are shown as equivalent pieces of paper with physical breaks between pages.

Full Screen Reading view

If want to read or review a document, Full Screen Reading view (**Figure 4.8**) can help simplify the task.

To control Full Screen Reading view:

1. *Do any of the following:*
   - ▲ To show single pages or pairs of facing pages, choose Show One Page or Show Two Pages from the View Options menu (**Figure 4.9**).
   - ▲ To preview the pages as they'll print, choose Show Printed Page from the View Options menu.
   - ▲ To change the text magnification, choose Increase Text Size or Decrease Text Size from the View Options menu.
   - ▲ To enable or disable editing, choose Allow Typing from the View Options menu.

continues on next page

WORKING IN DIFFERENT VIEWS

▲ To change pages, click an arrow button at the bottom of any page; click the left or right arrow icon in the Page controls; or press an arrow key, (Page Down), or (Page Up).

▲ To go directly to a page, click the Page control and choose a command from its menu, such as Go to First Page, Go to Last Page, or Go To (**Figure 4.10**).

▲ If you're reviewing a document, you can choose Track Changes commands from the bottom of the View Options menu (see Figure 4.9).

▲ Choose other commands from the icons in the upper-left corner of the screen (**Figure 4.11**).

2. To exit Full Screen Reading view, click the close box (X) in the upper-right corner of the screen or press (Esc).

Web Layout view

Use Web Layout view to create, view, and edit pages as they'll appear online when opened in a browser. By choosing Save As in the Backstage, you can save pages in several Web-compatible formats.

Outline view

Use Outline view to create, view, and edit outlines. (The initial table of contents for this book was created in Outline view.) For information about working in Outline view, see Chapter 6.

Draft view

Work in Draft view when speed is of primary importance. In Print Layout view, physical pages and breaks are drawn. Draft view displays a document as a continuous text scroll; page breaks are denoted by dashed lines. Because repagination occurs almost instantly as you compose, this is an ideal view if you have an older, slower computer.

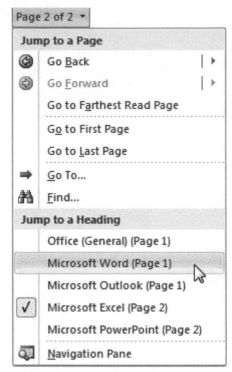

Figure 4.10 Navigation commands can be chosen from the Page control drop-down menu.

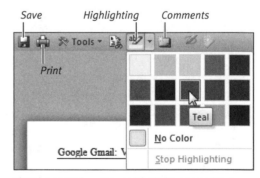

Figure 4.11 Click an icon to highlight selected text, add a comment, save changes, or print.

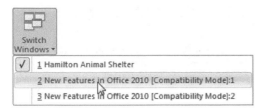

Figure 4.13 You can make any open document active by choosing its name from the Switch Windows menu.

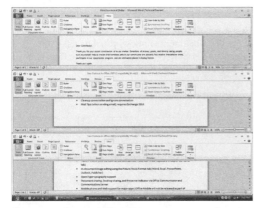

Figure 4.14 Arrange All enables you to see and work with multiple open documents.

Managing Windows

When you create a new Word document or open an existing document, each one opens in a separate window. Because it's common to work with several documents at once, Word provides window-management commands in the Window group of the View tab (**Figure 4.12**, below).

To manage open document windows:

◆ *Do any of the following:*

▲ To create another instance of the current document, click the New Window icon. Edits made in any instance of a window affect the document.

Each new instance has the same name as the original, followed by a colon and a number. For example, a new instance of memo.docx would be named memo.docx:2.

▲ To bring a document to the front and make it the *active document*, choose its name from the Switch Windows menu (**Figure 4.13**).

Because every open Word document is represented by a taskbar button, you can also switch documents by clicking the appropriate taskbar button.

▲ To view all open documents at the same time, click Arrange All. The documents are displayed in a stack (**Figure 4.14**) or side by side. To work in one of the windows, click in the document to make it active.

continues on next page

Figure 4.12 The Window group (View tab).

MANAGING WINDOWS

▲ To work with a pair of open documents, click View Side by Side. If more than two documents are open, the Compare Side by Side dialog box appears (**Figure 4.15**). Select the second document and click OK.

▲ When working in View Side by Side mode, you can make the two documents scroll together by clicking the Synchronous Scrolling icon. This feature is useful for comparing two versions of the same document.

▲ To close the active Word document, click its close box (X), press (Alt)(F4) or (Ctrl)(W), or click the File tab and then click Close in the Backstage.

▲ To close a Word document (regardless of whether it's the active document), you can right-click its taskbar button or right-click any blank spot in its title bar and choose Close from the context menu that appears (**Figure 4.16**).

✔ Tip

■ If you're running Windows 7, taskbar buttons are different from earlier versions of the operating system (OS). If you have multiple Word documents open, they are grouped together within a single Word taskbar button. To close one of the open documents, rest the cursor over the Word taskbar button, move up to highlight the document you want to close, and click its close box (X) (**Figure 4.17**). As in earlier versions of the OS, you can still right-click the document name and choose Close from the pop-up menu that appears.

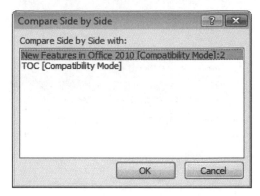

Figure 4.15 After clicking the View Side by Side icon in the first document window, you'll be asked to select the comparison document (if more than two documents are open).

Figure 4.16 You can close any document or application in the taskbar by right-clicking its button and choosing Close from the pop-up menu.

Figure 4.17 In Windows 7, documents of the same type are grouped within an application taskbar button.

MANAGING WINDOWS

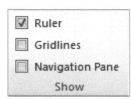

Figure 4.18 Click check boxes in the Show group to enable or disable display options.

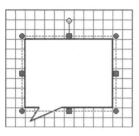

Figure 4.19 Gridlines can make it easier to place objects.

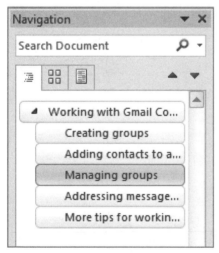

Figure 4.20 Use the Navigation Pane to quickly move to a desired spot in a document.

Setting Display Options

In addition to using the zoom controls to change the magnification (see "Setting the Magnification" in Chapter 2), you can show or hide the following elements in the document window by clicking check boxes in the Show group on the View tab (**Figure 4.18**):

◆ **Ruler.** Use the ruler to position objects, set paragraph indents, and set tab stops.

◆ **Gridlines.** When enabled, each page is overlaid with a visible grid (**Figure 4.19**). Placed objects automatically snap to the nearest grid intersection.

◆ **Navigation Pane.** In Word 2010, the Navigation Pane (**Figure 4.20**) replaces the Document Map. Use the Navigation Pane to move directly to a specific document page, heading, or search result. For instructions, see "Using the Navigation Pane," later in this chapter.

To show/hide rulers:

◆ *Do either of the following:*
  ▲ On the View tab in the Show group, click the Ruler check box.
  ▲ Click the View Ruler icon at the top of the vertical scroll bar (see Figure 4.1).

To show/hide gridlines:

◆ On the View tab in the Show group, click the Gridlines check box.

To show/hide the Navigation Pane:

◆ On the View tab in the Show group, click the Navigation Pane check box. To switch among viewing document headings, page thumbnails, and search results, click a tab at the top of the Navigation Pane. To close the pane, click its close box (X) or remove its check mark from the Show group (Figure 4.18).

Entering Text

If you've previously used a word-processing program, you're already familiar with the basics of entering text. On the other hand, if you're *new* to word processing, you'll need to know the following information.

To enter text:

1. Create a new document or open an existing document.

2. *Do one of the following:*

   ▲ **New document.** The text insertion mark is automatically positioned at the top of the first document page (**Figure 4.21**).

   ▲ **Existing document.** The text insertion mark is set at the beginning of the document. Scroll to the page where you want to begin entering new text, such as the end of the last page. Click to set the text insertion mark.

3. Type your text.

   Entered text appears at the text insertion mark. In a new document, the text is formatted with the default font and the paragraphs are left-aligned.

4. As you type, text automatically wraps as needed to fit within the current paragraph's margins. When you want to begin a new paragraph, press (Enter).

✔ Tips

■ For information on changing character or paragraph formatting (such as applying a different font or centering title text), see Chapter 5.

■ You can add text copied from other documents to a Word document by clicking the Paste icon in the Clipboard group of the Home tab (**Figure 4.22**) or by pressing (Ctrl)(V).

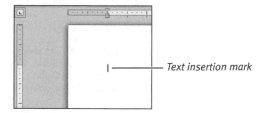

Figure 4.21 In a new or opened document, the text insertion mark is set at the beginning of the document.

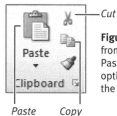

Figure 4.22 To paste copied text from the Clipboard, click the Paste icon. To reveal other Paste options, click the arrow beneath the Paste icon.

Using Click-and-Type

If you're more comfortable working with a typewriter than with a word-processing program, you can use Word's *click-and-type* feature to approximate a typewriter.

Instead of typing from the text insertion mark at the top of a new document or the bottom of an opened document, you can double-click any blank spot below either of these points. Word sets the text insertion mark at the double-clicked spot and automatically adds sufficient paragraph returns to fill in the gap above.

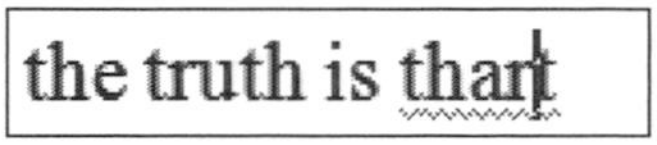

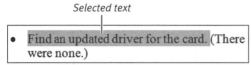

Figure 4.23 Set the text insertion mark to the right or left of the text you want to delete.

Selected text

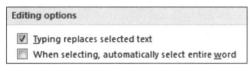

Figure 4.24 Selected text is highlighted like this.

Editing options

☑ Typing replaces selected text
☐ When selecting, automatically select entire word

Figure 4.25 To simplify text selection, remove the check mark from the second check box in the Editing options section.

Selecting Partial Words

If you find that you're frequently (and automatically) selecting entire words when trying to select partial words, the reason is that a Word Options setting is getting in your way.

To change this setting, click the File tab. In the Backstage, click Options. In the Word Options dialog box, select the Advanced category and remove the check mark from When selecting, automatically select entire word (**Figure 4.25**, above). Click OK to save the new setting.

Basic Text Editing

You can use any of the following techniques to correct errors in a document and make other desired changes, such as adding text. The techniques vary, depending on whether you are changing selected or unselected text.

To delete unselected text:

1. Position the text insertion mark immediately to the right or left of the text you want to correct or remove (**Figure 4.23**).

2. *Do one of the following:*
   ▲ To delete the *previous* character (the one to the left), press ⟨Backspace⟩.
   ▲ To delete the *next* character (the one to the right), press ⟨Del⟩ or ⟨Delete⟩.
   To delete additional characters, continue pressing ⟨Backspace⟩, ⟨Del⟩, or ⟨Delete⟩.

3. If necessary, replace the deleted text by typing new characters.

To delete or replace selected text:

1. To select text (**Figure 4.24**) to be deleted or replaced, *do one of the following:*
   ▲ Set the text insertion mark at one end of the text to be selected, and then drag to or ⟨Shift⟩-click the opposite end.
   ▲ Set the text insertion mark at one end of the text to be selected, and then— while holding down ⟨Shift⟩—press arrow keys to move to the end of the text.
   ▲ Double-click to select a word or triple-click to select a paragraph.

2. *Do one of the following:*
   ▲ To *delete* the selected text, press ⟨Del⟩, ⟨Backspace⟩, or ⟨Delete⟩.
   ▲ To *replace* the selected text, type the replacement text. When you begin typing, the selected text is deleted.

BASIC TEXT EDITING

To insert new text:

1. Position the text insertion mark where you want to add the new text.

   You can insert new text anywhere in a document.

2. *Do either of the following:*

   ▲ Type the new text.

   ▲ Paste the new text by clicking the Paste icon in the Clipboard group of the Home tab or by pressing Ctrl V.

✔ Tips

■ You can also delete text by *cutting* it. Unlike a normal deletion, cut text is stored in the Clipboard (and the Office Clipboard), where it's available for pasting. To cut selected text, click the Cut icon in the Clipboard group of the Home tab (see Figure 4.22) or press Ctrl X.

■ You can use *drag-and-drop* to move selected text from one location to another—either within a document or between Word documents. This is equivalent to performing a cut-and-paste.

■ If you want a drag-and-drop to leave the original text intact (working as a copy-and-paste rather than as a cut-and-paste), drag the selected text using the *right* mouse button. From the context menu that appears at the destination (**Figure 4.26**), choose Copy Here.

■ To undo the most recent edit, immediately click the Undo icon in the Quick Access Toolbar (**Figure 4.27**) or press Ctrl Z. (Note that you can undo multiple actions by clicking the Undo icon's down arrow.)

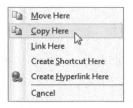

Figure 4.26 When right-dragging text, you can elect to perform a copy rather than a move.

Figure 4.27 You can often reverse your most recent action.

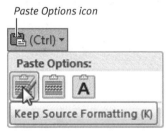

Figure 4.28 Choose a formatting method from the Paste Options drop-down menu.

Controlling Paste Formatting

When you paste text into a Word document, its formatting is determined by settings in the Advanced section of the Word Options dialog box. Depending on the text's source and whether the styles conflict, either the original formatting is retained or the text is reformatted to match the surrounding text at the destination. However, you can override the default Paste formatting.

When pasting, the Paste Options icon appears at the end of or beneath the pasted text (**Figure 4.28**, above). Click the icon to choose a formatting option.

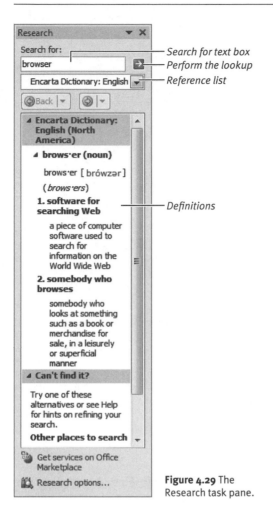

Figure 4.29 The Research task pane.

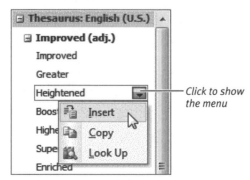

Figure 4.30 To use a synonym in the current document, click its down arrow and choose an option.

Using the Proofing Tools

Word includes a dictionary, thesaurus, and spelling/grammar checker that you can use to help with writing and editing. Spelling and grammar can be checked *on the fly* (as you type) or run as a traditional full-document or selected-text check.

To look up a word's definition:

◆ *Do either of the following:*

▲ If the word is in the current document, select it, right-click it, and choose Look Up > Encarta Dictionary from the context menu that appears.

▲ Switch to the Review tab, and click the Research icon in the Proofing group. In the Research pane (**Figure 4.29**), type or paste the word into the Search for box, select Encarta Dictionary from the drop-down list, and click the green arrow button.

The word's definition is displayed in the task pane.

To find a synonym for a word:

◆ *Do either of the following:*

▲ If the word is in the current document, select it, right-click it, and open the Synonyms submenu in the context menu that appears. To replace the word, choose a synonym from the list.

▲ Switch to the Review tab, and click the Thesaurus icon in the Proofing group. In the Research pane (Figure 4.29), type or paste the word into the Search for box and then click the green arrow button. (If the word is preselected in the document, it will automatically appear in the Search for box.)

To use a listed synonym in your document, click the down arrow beside the word, and choose Insert or Copy (**Figure 4.30**).

To check spelling/grammar as you type:

1. When the Check spelling as you type preference is enabled (see the Tip at the end of this section), each suspected spelling or grammatical error is marked with a wavy, colored underline.

2. **Spelling.** To correct or dismiss a marked spelling error, right-click the underlined text and choose one of these options from the context menu (**Figure 4.31**):

   ▲ To accept a suggested correction (if any are listed), choose a replacement spelling from the words listed at the top of the context menu.

   ▲ Choose Ignore to skip this instance of the word, leaving it unchanged.

   ▲ Choose Ignore All to ignore all instances of the flagged spelling in the document.

   ▲ If the spelling is correct, choose Add to Dictionary to ensure that the word is never flagged again—in this or any other document.

3. **Grammar.** To correct or dismiss a marked grammar error, right-click the underlined text. Choose one of the following options from the context menu (**Figure 4.32**):

   ▲ Choose the suggested fix to let Word make the correction.

   ▲ Choose Ignore if you believe the grammar is correct or if you want to manually make the correction.

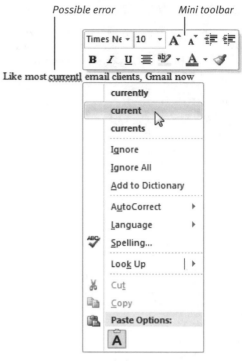

Figure 4.31 Right-click a marked spelling error and choose an option from the context menu.

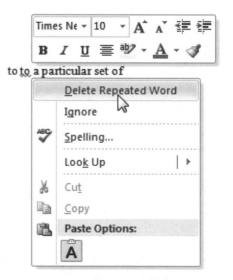

Figure 4.32 Grammatical errors can be handled by accepting a proposed correction or by choosing Ignore.

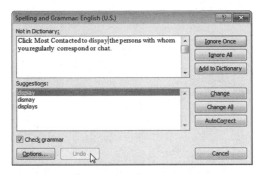

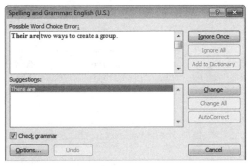

Figure 4.33 Suspected spelling errors (top) are marked in red and grammatical errors (bottom) are shown in green. Both are displayed in context in the top section of the dialog box.

Correcting Letter Case Errors

Has this happened to you? You accidentally press Caps Lock instead of Shift and now your newly typed text reads SUSAN JONES. Or while entering mailing addresses, your assistant decides not to bother with capitalization. You can fix many such errors by choosing a correction from the Change Case icon's menu in the Font group on the Home tab.

To check spelling/grammar for selected text or the entire document:

1. *Optional:* To restrict the check to a specific portion of the document, select the text to be checked.

2. *Do one of the following:*
   - ▲ On the Review tab, click the Spelling & Grammar icon in the Proofing group.
   - ▲ Press F7 .

   If suspected errors are identified, the Spelling and Grammar dialog box appears (**Figure 4.33**).

3. **Spelling.** To handle a suspected spelling error, *do one of the following:*
   - ▲ To accept a suggested correction (if any are listed), select it in the list and click Change.
   - ▲ To accept a suggested correction and apply it throughout the document, select it in the list and click Change All.
   - ▲ Edit the misspelled word in the Not in Dictionary box and click Change.
   - ▲ To accept the flagged word as spelled correctly, click Ignore Once to ignore this instance of the word or click Ignore All to ignore all instances of this word found in the document.
   - ▲ To accept the flagged word as spelled correctly and add it to the Office user dictionary (so it isn't flagged in later checks), click Add to Dictionary.
   - ▲ If the flagged word is one that you routinely misspell this way, select the correct spelling in the Suggestions list and click AutoCorrect. The misspelling is added to the AutoCorrect list and will automatically be corrected as you type in future writing sessions.

continues on next page

4. Grammar. To handle a suspected grammatical error, *do one of the following:*

▲ Click the button labeled with the correction, such as Delete or Change, if one is presented.

▲ If you believe the grammar is correct or you intend to rewrite the text, click Ignore Once to ignore the flagged error.

▲ Rewrite the text in the top half of the dialog box and click Change.

✔ Tips

■ To set spelling/grammar checking preferences, click the File tab and then click Options. In the Word Options dialog box, select the Proofing category (**Figure 4.34**), make any desired changes, and click OK.

■ You can go directly to the Proofing section of the Word Options dialog box by clicking the Options button in the Spelling and Grammar dialog box.

■ Word 2010 can consider the context of words when performing spelling/grammar checks (**Figure 4.35**), allowing it to flag words that are spelled properly but are incorrect (distinguishing among *to*, *too*, and *two*, for example).

■ If you choose Ignore or Ignore All for a suspected spelling or grammar error, the error will not reappear in subsequent spelling/grammar checks. To reconsider such errors, click the Recheck Document button in the Proofing section of the Word Options dialog box (Figure 4.34).

■ The AutoCorrect feature automatically corrects common typos and misspellings as you type. To view or edit the current AutoCorrect word list (**Figure 4.36**), click the AutoCorrect Options button in the Proofing section of the Word Options dialog box (Figure 4.34).

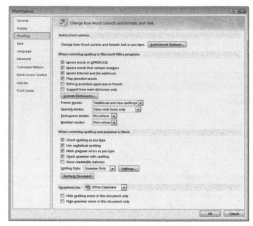

Figure 4.34 Set preferences for the proofing tools in the Proofing section of the Word Options dialog box.

Are their to many words in this sentence?

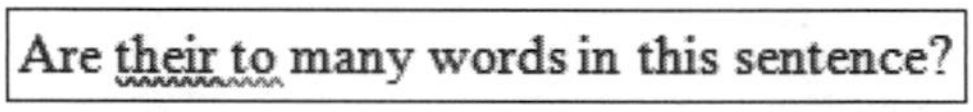

Figure 4.35 Although *their* and *to* are proper words, Word can flag them as incorrect if you've enabled Use contextual spelling in the Proofing section of the Word Options dialog box.

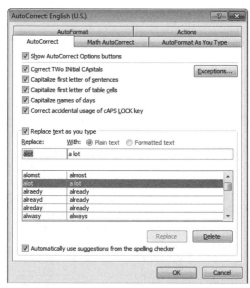

Figure 4.36 Add words that you commonly misspell to the AutoCorrect list.

Find tab   Search string

Show additional options

Figure 4.37 To perform a simple search, enter a search string in the Find what box and click Find Next.

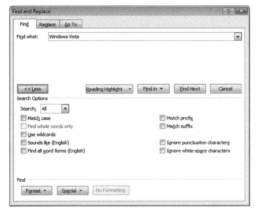

Figure 4.38 You can expand the dialog box to set additional Find options.

Finding and Replacing Text

Using the Find and Replace dialog box, you can search for any text string and optionally replace it with another. In addition to performing standard text searches, you can search for and replace special items, such as paragraph characters (¶), graphics, or text formatted in a specific font. Note that simple text searches are best performed in the Navigation Pane, described at the end of this chapter.

To perform a Find:

1. On the Home tab, click the Replace icon in the Editing group (Ctrl H).

   The Find and Replace dialog box appears, open to the Replace tab.

2. Click the Find tab.

3. Enter a search string in the Find what box (**Figure 4.37**).

4. *Optional:* To set additional options and criteria, click the More >> button. The dialog box expands (**Figure 4.38**):

   ▲ To perform a more precise search, set options in the Search Options area. For instance, you can ensure that found text exactly matches the letter case of the search string (Match case) or specify the search direction (Search drop-down menu).

   ▲ To search for a special character such as a tab, insert it into the Find what box by choosing the character from the Special button's menu.

   ▲ To find only text with certain formatting (such as a particular font), choose an option from the Format button menu.

   continues on next page

FINDING AND REPLACING TEXT

5. To begin the search, *do one of the following:*

  ▲ Click Find Next.

  ▲ Choose an option from the Find in button's menu to restrict the search to a particular document component.

  Word highlights the first match, if any. Otherwise, a dialog box informs you that the search text wasn't found (**Figure 4.39**).

6. *Do either of the following:*

  ▲ To search for the next match, click Find Next. Repeat as necessary.

  ▲ When you're finished, click Cancel or click the close box (X).

To perform a Find/Replace:

1. On the Home tab, click the Replace icon in the Editing group ([Ctrl][H]).

  The Find and Replace dialog box appears, open to the Replace tab.

2. Enter a search string in the Find what box and a replacement string in the Replace with box (**Figure 4.40**).

3. *Optional:* To set additional options and criteria, click the More >> button. The dialog box expands (**Figure 4.41**).

4. *Do either of the following:*

  ▲ To simultaneously replace every matching instance, click Replace All.

  ▲ To selectively replace text after examining each possible match, click Find Next. Word highlights the first match, if one is found. Click Replace if you want to make the replacement, or click Find Next to skip this instance and go to the next match. Continue as necessary.

5. When you're finished, click Cancel or click the close box (X).

Figure 4.39 If the search string isn't found, this dialog box appears. A similar dialog box is presented after all matches have been found and viewed.

Show additional options

Figure 4.40 Enter Find what and Replace with strings.

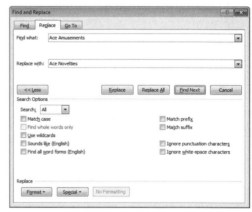

Figure 4.41 You can expand the dialog box to enter more specific criteria.

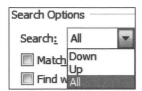

Figure 4.42 You can control the search direction and scope.

✔ Tips

■ Regardless of the command you use to open the Find and Replace dialog box, you can switch between Finds and Replaces by clicking the appropriate tab.

■ To restrict a Find or Replace to only *part* of a document, select the text before you execute the Find or Replace.

■ The initial direction and scope of a search are determined by the text insertion mark and your choice in the Search drop-down menu (**Figure 4.42**) in the bottom half of the Find and Replace dialog box. A search starts from the text insertion mark and proceeds in the direction specified in the Search drop-down menu as follows:

▲ If Down or Up is chosen, the search proceeds to the bottom or top of the document or selection. When the bottom or top is reached, a dialog box asks if you'd like to search the rest of the document.

▲ If All is chosen from the Search menu, the search starts from the text insertion mark, continues downward until the end is reached, and then wraps around to the beginning in order to complete the search.

■ When you replace text without checking Match case (see Figure 4.41), capitalization of the replacement text (Replace with) will match that of the replaced text (Find what).

■ It's sometimes important to check Find whole words only (see Figure 4.41) when performing a Replace. For example, when attempting to replace every instance of John with Mike, checking Find whole words only will prevent Johnson from being changed to Mikeson.

FINDING AND REPLACING TEXT

Entering Symbols and Special Characters

Some characters—especially symbols, such as copyright (©)—can be extremely difficult to type. Using the Symbol drop-down gallery or the Symbol dialog box, you can easily insert a symbol or other character from any font that's installed on your computer.

To insert a symbol or other character:

1. Set the text insertion mark at the spot in your text where you want to insert the symbol or other character.

2. In the Symbols group on the Insert tab, click the Symbol icon.

3. *Do either of the following:*

   ▲ Choose the character from the Symbol drop-down gallery (**Figure 4.43**). The character is inserted into the text.

   ▲ Choose More Symbols to open the Symbol dialog box (**Figure 4.44**). To insert a character, double-click it or select it and click Insert. Click the Close button or the close box (X) to dismiss the dialog box.

✔ Tips

- When inserting a character, Word uses the font at the text insertion mark. To use a different font (Webdings, for example, contains unusual characters not found in other fonts), choose it from the Font drop-down menu in the Symbol dialog box.

- To use a special character throughout a document, insert it once, select the character, copy it ((Ctrl)(C)), and then paste the character ((Ctrl)(V)) wherever it's needed.

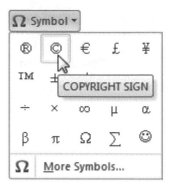

Figure 4.43 Common symbols can be selected from this gallery.

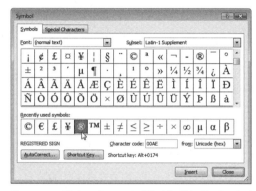

Figure 4.44 To insert a symbol that isn't in the Symbol gallery or one from a different font, use the Symbol dialog box.

Headings

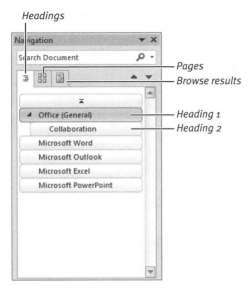

Pages
Browse results

Heading 1
Heading 2

Figure 4.45 You can jump directly to important headings.

Figure 4.46 You can also display pages as graphic thumbnails.

Using the Navigation Pane

As mentioned, the Office 2010 Navigation Pane replaces the Document Map from earlier versions of Word. In addition to quickly jumping to important document sections by clicking a thumbnail or text heading, you can do the following:

◆ Execute Finds to locate text in the document that marks the spot to which you want to go

◆ Rearrange document sections by dragging their headings in the Navigation Pane

◆ Search for other material, such as tables, graphics, equations, footnotes/endnotes, and reviewer comments

To open/close the Navigation Pane:

◆ To open the Navigation Pane, switch to the View tab and click the Navigation Pane check box in the Show group (see Figure 4.18), click the Find icon in the Editing group on the Home tab, or press Ctrl F.

◆ To close the pane, click its close box (X) or remove the check mark from the Navigation Pane check box in the Show group.

To go to a particular page or heading:

◆ To go to a heading, click the Headings tab in the Navigation Pane. In the list that appears (**Figure 4.45**), click the desired heading.

Only paragraphs to which you've applied a *Heading* style (such as Heading 1, Heading 2, and so on) are listed in the pane. To learn about Word styles, see Chapter 5.

◆ To go to a page, click the Pages tab in the Navigation Pane. Click the thumbnail of the desired page (**Figure 4.46**).

USING THE NAVIGATION PANE

To perform a text search:

1. *Optional:* To set specific search options (such as Match case or Find whole words only), click the down arrow to the right of the search box and choose Options from the drop-down menu.

   The Find Options dialog box appears (**Figure 4.47**). Set options and click OK.

2. Type search text in the box at the top of the Navigation Pane. Word searches as you type. Matches are highlighted in the document. The contents of the Navigation Pane depend on the tab that's selected:

   ▲ **Headings.** Any heading that contains a match is highlighted in yellow.

   ▲ **Pages.** Any page that contains a match is displayed; all others are hidden.

   ▲ **Browse results.** Matches are shown in context in the Navigation Pane (**Figure 4.48**).

3. To go to a match, *do any of the following:*

   ▲ In the Navigation Pane, click a heading, thumbnail, or text result.

   ▲ Click the up (Previous) or down (Next) icons in the Navigation Pane.

   ▲ Press [Enter] to go to the next match.

✔ Tips

■ Choose the Find, Replace, or Go To command from the upper section of the drop-down menu to open the normal Find and Replace dialog box (see Figure 4.40).

■ To find non-text items in the current document, choose a command from the lower half of the drop-down menu: Graphics, Tables, Equations, Footnotes/Endnotes, or Comments. To navigate among the found items, click the Previous and Next icons (Figure 4.48).

■ To end a search, click the close box (X) to the right of the search box or press [Esc].

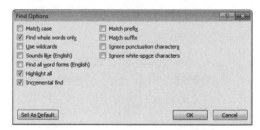

Figure 4.47 You can set the same search options that appear in the Find and Replace dialog box (see Figure 4.41).

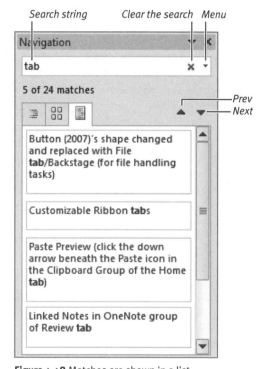

Figure 4.48 Matches are shown in a list.

USING THE NAVIGATION PANE

FORMATTING DOCUMENTS

Writing text is only part of what you'll do with Word. (If your main interest is in generating a lot of text with as few interruptions as possible, you can probably do it faster using a simple text editor, such as Notepad.) In order to create documents that are attractive and pleasant to read, you must add *formatting*.

Word supports three kinds of formatting:

- *Document formatting* affects the entire document and is primarily related to page settings, such as paper size, margins, orientation, sections, and columns. Other document formatting commands enable you to insert page, section, and column breaks; insert blank and cover pages; and add headers and footers.

- *Paragraph formatting* applies to entire paragraphs and is used to set alignment, indents, and line spacing. You can also create numbered or bulleted lists.

- *Character formatting* can be applied to selected words, sentences, or paragraphs and includes attributes such as font, size, color, and style.

To simplify the process of consistently applying paragraph and character formatting to material in a document, you can define *styles*.

Specifying Page Settings

To set basic document formatting, you choose options from the icon menus in the Page Setup group on the Page Layout tab (**Figure 5.1**). These settings normally affect the entire document.

To set paper size and orientation:

◆ **Paper size.** Click the Size icon and choose a standard paper size from the drop-down menu.

   If you want to use a special paper size, choose More Paper Sizes. On the Paper tab of the Page Setup dialog box, select Custom size from the Paper size drop-down list, specify the paper's width and height, and click OK.

◆ **Orientation.** Pages can be laid out and printed in normal fashion (*portrait*) or sideways (*landscape*). Choose Portrait or Landscape from the Orientation menu.

◆ **Columns.** Certain types of documents look better and are easier to read when arranged in multiple columns. To format a new document or reformat an existing one in this manner, choose the number of columns or a two-column layout (Left or Right) from the Columns drop-down menu (**Figure 5.2**).

◆ **Margins.** Set margins for the document by choosing an option from the Margins drop-down menu (**Figure 5.3**). To set margins that differ from the ones listed, choose Custom Margins and enter the desired settings on the Margins tab of the Page Setup dialog box.

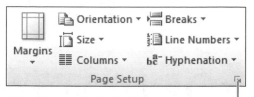

Page Setup dialog box Launcher

Figure 5.1 Specify page settings by choosing options from the Page Setup group on the Page Layout tab.

Figure 5.2 Choose a number or type of column.

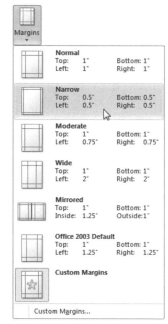

Figure 5.3 Choose margins from the Margins drop-down menu.

— View Ruler

Figure 5.4 On the ruler, drag a column's right margin to change its width.

Tabs

Apply to menu

Figure 5.5 You can also specify page settings on the tabs of the Page Setup dialog box.

✔ Tips

■ To change a column's width, drag the right margin of the column in the horizontal ruler (**Figure 5.4**).

If the ruler isn't visible, switch to the View tab and click the Ruler check box in the Show group. Or you can click the View Ruler icon (found beneath the right side of the Ribbon).

■ To restore a multi-column document to a single column, choose One from the Columns menu (see Figure 5.2).

■ Although it's uncommon, you can change page settings in mid-document (switching from portrait to landscape mode or setting new margins, for instance). Click the Page Setup dialog box launcher (see Figure 5.1). On the appropriate tab of the Page Setup dialog box (**Figure 5.5**), set new options, choose This point forward from the Apply to drop-down menu, and click OK.

■ You can also use the Page Setup dialog box to apply new settings to the *entire* document. Choose Whole document from the Apply to drop-down menu.

■ Although you may be tempted, it's usually inappropriate to set left or right margins of zero (0). First, many printers can't print from edge to edge. For instance, laser printers often have a *no-print zone* of 0.2–0.25" on each margin. Second, documents with tiny margins are often difficult to read because the lines are so long.

■ You can specify page settings at any time: before you begin writing, after you've finished, or at any point in between.

SPECIFYING PAGE SETTINGS

Modifying the Background

You can choose options from the Page Background group (**Figure 5.6**) on the Page Layout tab to add color, a watermark/rubber stamp, or a border to every document page.

In general, you should apply background settings sparingly and only to special documents. Color and borders, for example, are best reserved for party invitations, ads, and flyers. On the other hand, a watermark can be extremely useful when applied to certain business documents, marking them as drafts or confidential, for example.

To add a background color to each page:

◆ Click the Page Color icon, and *do one of the following:*

▲ Select a color from the Theme Colors or Standard Colors palette (**Figure 5.7**).

▲ To choose among all possible colors, choose More Colors. Select a color in the Colors dialog box and click OK.

▲ To apply a color gradient, texture, pattern, or picture to the background, choose Fill Effects. Select options from the tabs of the Fill Effects dialog box (**Figure 5.8**) and click OK.

▲ To remove a previously applied color, choose No Color.

✔ Tip

■ Document text may be easier to read on certain color, gradient, texture, pattern, and picture backgrounds than on others. For instance, if you choose a dark color, you may need to change the text color to one that contrasts better with the new background.

Figure 5.6 Change the page background by choosing options from this group.

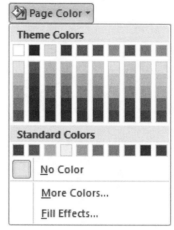

Figure 5.7 The selected color will be applied to every document page.

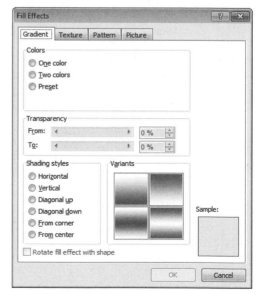

Figure 5.8 The Fill Effects dialog box.

MODIFYING THE BACKGROUND

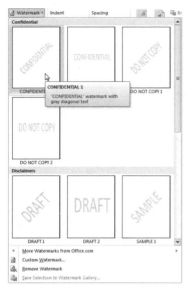

Figure 5.9 Common text watermarks can be chosen from the gallery.

Figure 5.10 To create a custom watermark or customize one of the gallery choices, set options in the Printed Watermark dialog box.

To apply a preset watermark:

◆ Click the Watermark icon and choose one of the preset watermarks from the gallery (**Figure 5.9**).

The watermark is applied to all pages.

To apply a custom watermark:

1. Click the Watermark icon and choose Custom Watermark from the gallery (Figure 5.9).

   The Printed Watermark dialog box appears (**Figure 5.10**).

2. *Do one of the following:*

   ▲ To use a text string as the watermark, select Text watermark; choose or type a text string; and choose settings for the language, font, size, color, and layout. For a fainter watermark, ensure that Semitransparent is checked.

   ▲ To use an image as the watermark, select Picture watermark. Click the Select Picture button to select an image file from your hard disk. You can choose a magnification for the image from the Scale drop-down menu or leave it set to Auto for the optimal size that will fit on the document page without cropping. Click the Washout check box for a fainter image.

   ▲ To remove an existing watermark from the document, select No watermark.

3. Click Apply to add the watermark to the document pages. If you don't like its appearance, you can change the settings and click Apply again.

4. When you're satisfied with the watermark, click OK to close the dialog box.

MODIFYING THE BACKGROUND

✔ Tips

- You can also remove a watermark by choosing Remove Watermark from the Watermark gallery menu (see Figure 5.9).

- You can apply a text watermark *or* a picture watermark—not both. If you switch types, the current watermark is replaced.

- Check the watermark's appearance with and without Semitransparent or Washout.

To add borders around each page:

1. Click the Page Borders icon.

   The Borders and Shading dialog box appears (**Figure 5.11**). Select the Page Border tab.

2. Click an icon in the Setting list to specify the type of border you want to create.

3. Set line properties by choosing options from the Style, Color, Width, and Art drop-down menus.

   Your choices are reflected in the Preview area of the dialog box.

4. From the Apply to drop-down menu, indicate the document pages to which the border will be applied.

5. Click OK.

✔ Tips

- To remove an existing page border or to begin designing one from scratch, select None in the Setting list.

- To remove individual lines from the border or to add a line, click that side of the box or the matching icon in the Preview area.

- Rather than create a line border, you can use artwork (such as pencils, scrollwork, or trees) as the border by choosing an image from the Art drop-down menu (**Figure 5.12**).

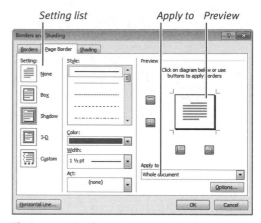

Figure 5.11 Select border settings on the Page Border tab of the Borders and Shading dialog box.

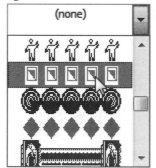

Figure 5.12 Use artwork to add a festive or eye-catching border to a flyer or party invitation.

To create a group from selected contacts:

1. Click the Contacts link on the left side of the Gmail window.

2. Display the contact records from which you want to select group members by doing one of the following (see Figure 1):

Figure 5.13 In Draft view, automatic page breaks are shown as dotted lines.

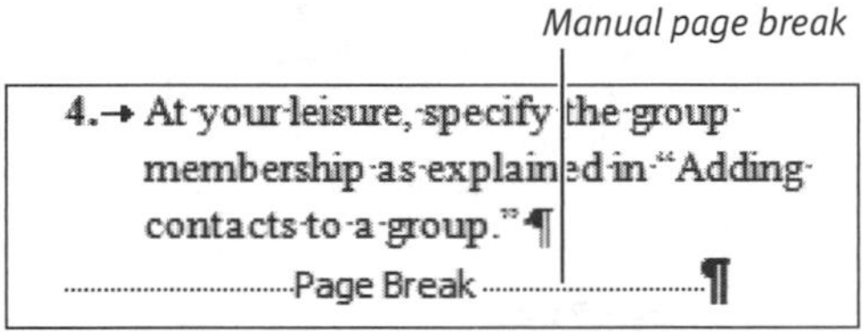

Manual page break

4.→ At your leisure, specify the group membership as explained in "Adding contacts to a group." ¶
                    Page Break   ¶

Figure 5.14 When invisible characters are made visible, manual page breaks are clearly marked.

Avoiding Widows and Orphans

In word processing, a single line at the end of a page is referred to as a *widow*; a single line at the beginning of a page (normally, the final line of a paragraph that began on the previous page) is called an *orphan*. Layout rules suggest that both look amateurish and should be avoided.

If you carefully define and use *paragraph styles* (see "Working with Styles" in this chapter), you can automatically avoid widows and orphans. For example, when specifying the style for a header, you can enable a combination of Widow/Orphan control, Keep with next, and Keep lines together. For body text paragraphs, Widow/Orphan control will suffice.

Inserting Breaks

Word adds an *automatic page break* wherever it's needed, based on the margins and the style setting of the paragraph that will be broken or moved to the next page. As you add or delete text, the automatic breaks are adjusted as needed; that is, Word *repaginates* as you type. In Print Layout and Full Screen Reading views, breaks are shown as new physical pages. In Draft view, they're indicated by dotted lines (**Figure 5.13**).

Occasionally, breaks appear in spots where you'd prefer they not occur. For example, a key quote may be split between two pages. You can prevent this by inserting a *manual break* wherever it's needed. In addition to inserting manual page breaks, you can insert column and section breaks.

To insert a manual page break:

1. Set the text insertion mark at the start of the line on which you want to start the new page.

2. *Do one of the following:*
    ▲ On the Insert tab, click the Page Break icon in the Pages group.
    ▲ On the Page Layout tab, click the Breaks icon in the Page Setup group and choose Page.
    ▲ Press Ctrl Enter.
    A page break is created at the text insertion mark.

✔ Tips

■ The safest time to insert page breaks is after you've finished writing and editing.

■ To remove a manual page break, select it and press Backspace, Delete, or Del. It's easiest to do when the breaks are visible (**Figure 5.14**). To display normally invisible characters, click the Show/Hide ¶ icon in the Home tab's Paragraph group.

To insert other types of manual breaks:

1. Set the text insertion mark at the start of the line where you want to insert the break.

2. On the Page Layout tab, click the Breaks icon in the Page Setup group. From the drop-down menu (**Figure 5.15**), *do one of the following*:

   ▲ Choose Column to break the current column in a multi-column layout. The text following the text insertion mark will begin in the next column.

   ▲ Choose a command from the Section Breaks part of the menu to create or indicate the start of a new section.

   The column or section break is inserted.

✔ Tip

■ Unless you're writing a lengthy or complex report, you're unlikely to divide a document into sections. (I suspect that most Word users don't even know this feature exists.) Use sections when you want to use chapter-relative page numbering or dramatically change formatting in the middle of a document (switching between a single- and multi-column layout, for example).

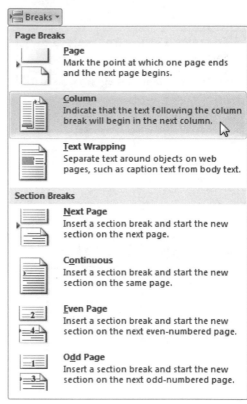

Figure 5.15 You can insert manual breaks for new pages, columns, or sections by choosing a command from the Breaks drop-down menu.

INSERTING BREAKS

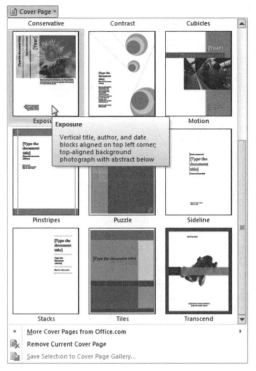

Figure 5.16 Choose a cover page from the gallery.

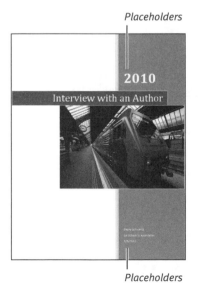

Placeholders

Placeholders

Figure 5.17 To complete the cover page, replace the placeholder text.

Adding a Cover Page or Blank Page

You can add a preformatted *cover page* (or title page) to some documents. A cover page is especially useful for reports. The cover page is automatically placed at the beginning of the document and contains placeholders for important text elements such as the title, author, and date. Only one cover page is allowed per document. If you add another, it replaces the current one.

When writing a report or book that will be bound on the left edge, it's traditional to start each new section or chapter on a right-hand page. As such, if there's no material for the facing page (on the left), the page must be blank. You can insert blank pages anywhere you wish.

To add a cover page:

1. On the Insert tab, click the Cover Page icon in the Pages group and choose a cover page from the gallery (**Figure 5.16**). The cover page is added as the first page.

2. Replace the placeholder text with your own text (**Figure 5.17**).

✔ Tips

- To view additional cover pages, move the cursor over the More Cover Pages from Office.com submenu and wait for the page thumbnails to download.

- When you replace one cover page with another, filled placeholders remain filled.

- To remove a cover page, choose Remove Current Cover Page from the Cover Page drop-down menu.

To insert a blank page:

1. Set the text insertion mark where you want to add a blank page.

2. On the Insert tab, click the Blank Page icon in the Pages group (**Figure 5.18**).

   A blank page is added at the text insertion mark by inserting two page breaks (**Figure 5.19**). As necessary, text is reflowed around—but not into—the blank page.

✔ Tips

- You can leave an inserted blank page blank or type text on it.

- To remove a blank page, delete the two manual page breaks and the blank paragraphs that were inserted. It's easiest to select and delete these items if you've enabled Show/Hide ¶ in the Paragraph group on the Home tab.

Figure 5.18 Click Blank Page to add a blank page at the text insertion mark.

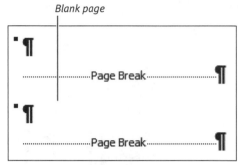

Figure 5.19 To create a blank page, Word inserts a new paragraph surrounded by a pair of manual page breaks.

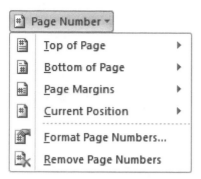

Figure 5.20 To insert only a page number into a header, footer, or margin, choose an option from the Page Number drop-down menu.

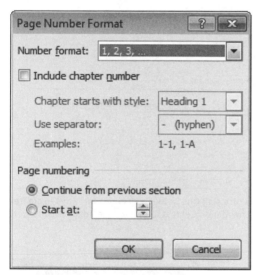

Figure 5.21 To start numbering with a number other than 1, select a different number format, or apply chapter-relative numbering, set options in the Page Number Format dialog box.

Figure 5.22 Click this icon when you're ready to resume editing the document.

Adding Headers or Footers

Headers and footers are reserved areas at the top and bottom of each page, respectively, in which you can display important text, such as a page number, date, filename, or text string (*Confidential*, for instance). Header and footer styles can be chosen from a gallery or created from scratch.

To add a header or footer that contains only a page number:

1. On the Insert tab, click the Page Number icon in the Header and Footer group (**Figure 5.20**). Choose a number style from the appropriate position gallery: Top of Page (header), Bottom of Page (footer), or Page Margins (left or right margin).

2. *Optional:* To specify a numbering format (such as chapter-relative numbering) or a starting number, choose Format Page Numbers from the Page Number menu. Make any desired changes in the Page Number Format dialog box (**Figure 5.21**) and click OK.

3. To return to the body of the document, click Close Header and Footer in the Close group of the Design tab (**Figure 5.22**) or double-click anywhere in the body.

✔ Tips

- To remove all inserted page numbers, click the Page Number icon and choose Remove Page Numbers (Figure 5.20).

- Although the intent of the Page Number command is to add page numbering as the *sole* element in a header, footer, or margin, you can add other elements by following the instructions in "To add a preformatted header or footer" and "To create a custom header or footer."

To add a preformatted header or footer:

1. On the Insert tab, click the Header or the Footer icon in the Header & Footer group. Choose a style from the drop-down gallery (**Figure 5.23**).

   If you intend to show different header or footer text for odd and even pages, be sure to choose the correct one for the currently displayed page. If the same information will be shown on odd and even pages, it doesn't matter whether you choose an odd or an even page style. The chosen style will be displayed on *every* page.

2. Make any necessary edits to the header or footer elements. For example, you can:

   ▲ Delete unwanted elements.

   ▲ Replace placeholder text by typing.

   ▲ Select an option, such as a date, from a placeholder's drop-down menu (**Figure 5.24**).

   ▲ Replace one element with another by deleting the original element, clicking the Quick Parts icon in the Insert group, and choosing Field. Common fields can also be chosen from the Quick Parts > Document Property submenu.

   ▲ Insert and position a new element. Add a text alignment tab for the new element by choosing Insert Alignment Tab from the Position group on the Design tab.

3. If you want the header or footer to be different on odd and even pages, click the Different Odd & Even Pages check box in the Options group of the Design tab. Then repeat Steps 1–2 for the opposite page—that is, odd or even.

4. To return to the body of the document, click Close Header and Footer in the Close group of the Design tab or double-click anywhere in the body.

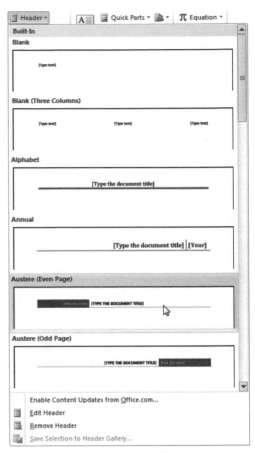

Figure 5.23 One of the most expedient ways to create a header or footer is to pick a style from the gallery.

Figure 5.24 Some header/footer fields have a menu from which you can choose a setting or option.

To create a custom header or footer:

1. *Do either of the following:*

   ▲ In the Header & Footer group on the Insert tab, click the Header or Footer icon and choose Edit Header or Edit Footer from the drop-down menu.

   ▲ In Print Layout view, double-click in the header or footer area.

   The text insertion mark appears in the header or footer (**Figure 5.25**).

   continues on next page

Footer area　Header area　　Header & Footer Tools contextual tab　Close Header/Footer

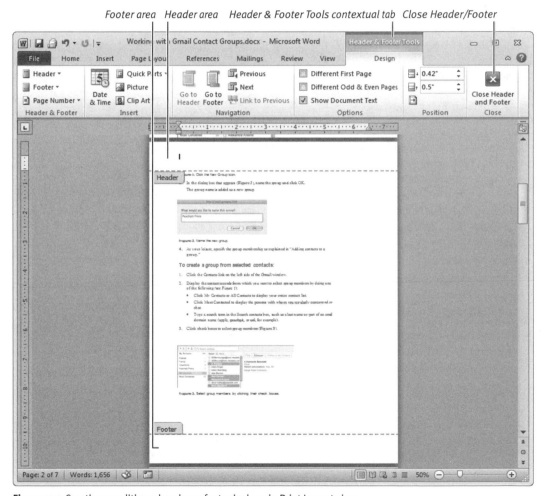

Figure 5.25 Creating or editing a header or footer is done in Print Layout view.

2. To insert header or footer elements, *do any of the following:*

▲ Type a text string, such as the author's name, filename, or document title.

▲ To insert the current date, time, or both, click the Date & Time icon in the Insert group of the Design tab. Select a format from the Date and Time dialog box (**Figure 5.26**). To show the current date and time each time you open the document, click Update automatically. Otherwise, the date/time entered at this moment will be treated as static text. Click OK.

▲ To insert a page number, click the Quick Parts icon in the Insert group and choose Field. In the Field dialog box (**Figure 5.27**), select Page from the field list, select a number format from the Format list, and click OK.

3. To insert another element, click the Insert Alignment Tab icon in the Position group. In the Alignment Tab dialog box (**Figure 5.28**), select a position in the header or footer for the new element (Left, Center, or Right) and click OK. Repeat for a third element, if desired.

By default, an element on the left side of the page is left-aligned with the left margin, a center element is center-aligned between the two margins, and a right element is right-aligned with the right margin.

4. When you're done entering and editing elements in the header or footer area, *do either of the following:*

▲ Edit the other area by clicking in it.

▲ Click Close Header and Footer in the Close group (see Figure 5.22 or 5.25).

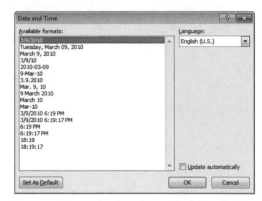

Figure 5.26 Insert the date, time, or both by selecting a format from the Date and Time dialog box.

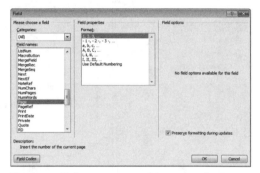

Figure 5.27 To insert page numbers, select the Page field name and specify a display format.

Figure 5.28 Set an alignment for the new element and click OK.

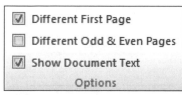

Figure 5.29 The Options group.

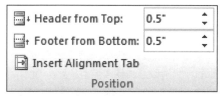

Figure 5.30 You can change the distance of the header or footer from the top or bottom of the page, respectively.

- You can reposition the header or footer by entering new settings in the Header from Top or Footer from Bottom boxes in the Position group (**Figure 5.30**).

- To *edit* a header or footer (whether it's gallery-based or one that you created from scratch), follow these same steps. Any element can be deleted or replaced.

✔ Tips

- If you find the body text distracting, you can temporarily hide it by removing the check mark from Show Document Text in the Options group (**Figure 5.29**). When you finish working with the header and footer, the body text will reappear.

- If you base a document on a template, you should note that the template may contain a gallery from which you can choose other header and footer styles.

- You can also add graphics to a header or footer, such as a logo or horizontal rule. To insert a graphic element, click the Picture or Clip Art icon in the Insert group.

- Text in a header or footer can be formatted as you like. Select a header or footer element or the entire header or footer. Choose formatting commands from the Mini toolbar or from the Font group on the Home tab.

- A Page field can be preceded by text, such as the word Page. Position the text insertion mark before the page number in the header or footer, and then type Page and a space.

- Page 1 of certain documents (such as a report with a title or cover page) often has no header/footer or it may need to contain special text. Click the Different First Page check box in the Options group (Figure 5.29). You can then leave the page 1 header and footer blank or create a *different* page 1 header and/or footer.

- To create different headers and footers on even/left and odd/right pages (as is often done for books and other publications with facing-page spreads), click the Different Odd & Even Pages check box (Figure 5.29).

ADDING HEADERS OR FOOTERS

Paragraph Formatting

In Word, a *paragraph* (**Figure 5.31**) is any amount of text (a word, line, sentence, or multiple sentences) that ends with a paragraph mark (¶). You finish a paragraph and begin a new one by pressing Enter. This action inserts a paragraph mark.

Generally, the new paragraph will have the same formatting as the previous one. The exception is when the *style* assigned to the current paragraph is designed to be followed by a paragraph of a different style. For instance, a heading style is typically followed by a body text style.

Paragraph formatting, such as alignment or indents, can be applied to a selected paragraph by choosing options from the Paragraph group on the Home tab (**Figure 5.32**), the Mini toolbar, or the Paragraph dialog box. You can also apply formatting by choosing a *paragraph style* (discussed later in this chapter).

Paragraph formatting has nothing to do with font, size, style, or color. It is concerned solely with alignment, spacing between lines, indents from one or both margins, and so on.

✔ Tips

- Normally, paragraph marks are invisible, but you can show them by clicking the Show/Hide ¶ icon (Ctrl *) in the Paragraph group on the Home tab. Other normally hidden characters, such as tabs, spaces, and line breaks, also become visible.

- You can force certain characters (such as paragraph marks) to *always* display. Click the File tab to go to the Backstage and then click Options. In the Word Options dialog box, select the Display category, click the check boxes of the items you always want to show (**Figure 5.33**), and click OK.

> **Interviewer:** Can you explain to our readers how you get the ideas on what to write about and how you go about preparing and then writing the book?¶
> ¶
> **Steve:** When I first started writing books, I specifically chose topics that held great interest for me—assuming that others shared those same interests. I quickly discovered that this is an excellent way to starve. Now, I try to focus more on fulfilling what I perceive to be major user needs; i.e., I'm "market driven." With the current move by many software companies to omit manuals from their products, for example, there is a real need for easy-to-follow books that explain in depth how a program works, what its features do, why you would use one feature rather than another to accomplish a particular task, and so on. In most cases, help files are no substitute for decent documentation. And if there's no documentation at all, this is often a great reason to write a book.¶

Figure 5.31 Here are three paragraphs, each ending with a paragraph mark. The middle one is a blank paragraph.

Paragraph dialog box launcher

Figure 5.32 The Paragraph group contains icons for common paragraph-formatting commands.

Always show these formatting marks on the screen	
☐ Tab characters	→
☐ Spaces	···
☐ Paragraph marks	¶
☐ Hidden text	abc
☐ Optional hyphens	¬
☐ Object anchors	⚓
☐ Show all formatting marks	

Figure 5.33 Check the items that will always be shown, regardless of the status of Show/Hide ¶.

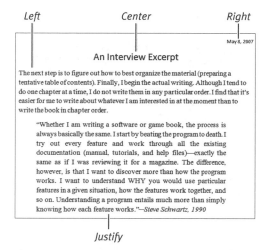

Figure 5.34 No matter how short or long, every paragraph has an alignment.

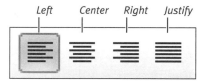

Figure 5.35 Click an alignment icon in the Paragraph group.

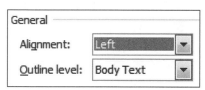

Figure 5.36 In the Paragraph dialog box, choose an option from the Alignment drop-down menu.

Setting Alignment

A paragraph's *alignment* determines its position in relation to the margins. Every paragraph must have one of the following alignments (**Figure 5.34**):

◆ **Left.** The left edge of the paragraph is flush with the left margin and the right edge is ragged. Body text of most documents is left-aligned.

◆ **Right.** The right edge of the paragraph is flush with the right margin and the left edge is ragged.

◆ **Center.** Each line of the paragraph is automatically centered between the two margins. Center alignment is sometimes applied to titles and other headings.

◆ **Justify.** Both edges of the paragraph are flush with a margin. As necessary, Word adjusts the spacing between words to enable each line to be flush with the margins. Magazine copy and block quotations are often justified.

To set paragraph alignment:

1. Select one or more paragraphs.

   To select a single paragraph, it's sufficient to set the text insertion mark in it. To select multiple paragraphs, drag a selection through at least part of each one.

2. *Do one of the following:*

   ▲ On the Home tab, click an alignment icon in the Paragraph group (**Figure 5.35**).

   ▲ Press an alignment keyboard short-cut: Left Ctrl L, Center Ctrl E, Right Ctrl R, or Justify Ctrl J.

   ▲ In the Paragraph dialog box, click the Indents and Spacing tab, choose an alignment (**Figure 5.36**), and click OK.

   ▲ Click the Center alignment icon on the Mini toolbar.

Setting Indents

Every paragraph has three indents that you can set to specify the distance between the text and the left/right margins:

- **Left.** Distance from the left margin.

- **Right.** Distance from the right margin.

- **First line.** Distance from the left margin that applies only to the paragraph's first line of text.

Indents are automatically set for bulleted and numbered lists (*hanging indents*). You can set equal left and right indents of 0.5" or 1" to format a block quote. Indents can be set on the horizontal ruler or in the Paragraph dialog box. Any or all indents can be set to 0.

To set indents:

- Select one or more paragraphs, and then *do any of the following:*
  - ▲ **Paragraph group (Home tab).** To increase or decrease the left indent in increments of 0.5", click the Increase Indent or Decrease Indent icon in the Paragraph group (**Figure 5.37**) or on the Mini toolbar.
  - ▲ **Paragraph group (Page Layout tab).** Enter numbers (in inches) in the Left and/or Right box (**Figure 5.38**).
  - ▲ **Paragraph dialog box.** You can also set exact indents on the Indents and Spacing tab (**Figure 5.39**). To create a first line indent (similar to starting each paragraph by pressing (Tab)), choose First line from the Special drop-down menu and set the indent. To create a hanging indent for a bulleted or numbered list, choose Hanging from the Special drop-down menu.
  - ▲ **Horizontal ruler.** You can manually set indents by dragging markers on the horizontal ruler (**Figure 5.40**).

Decrease Indent

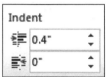

Increase Indent

Figure 5.37 Click an icon to decrease or increase the left indent by half an inch.

Figure 5.38 You can set precise left and right indents.

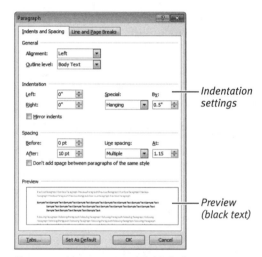

Figure 5.39 You can create any kind of indent in the Paragraph dialog box.

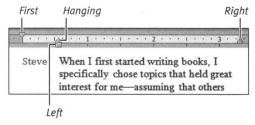

Figure 5.40 To create this outdent, I dragged the first line indent marker to the left.

✔ Tips

■ You can use the Paragraph dialog box to create an *outdent* (extending to the left of the left margin) by entering a negative number for the left indent (see Figure 5.40).

■ When setting indents on the ruler, you'll note the following behaviors:

▲ The first line and right indent markers move independently of other markers.

▲ The left and hanging indent markers move as a pair.

▲ When you drag the left indent marker, it and the hanging indent marker maintain their current distance from the first line indent marker.

▲ Drag the hanging indent marker to change its distance (and that of the left indent marker) from the first line indent marker.

Working with Tabs

The ability to set indents and create tables in Word has virtually eliminated the need to use tabs in most documents. However, if you *do* need them to create a column of numbers aligned on the decimal point, for example, here's what you should know:

◆ By default, you can press Tab at the start of or within a paragraph to space to the next 0.5" increment on the ruler.

◆ To set a left tab for selected paragraphs, click the desired spot on the horizontal ruler.

◆ To create other types of tab stops (right, center, decimal, or bar), modify existing tab stops, or specify a *leader character* (such as a string of periods), double-click a tab marker on the ruler. Make the necessary changes in the Tabs dialog box.

◆ Change a tab stop position by dragging its marker or by entering a new position in the Tabs dialog box.

◆ You can remove a tab stop by dragging its marker from the ruler onto the document page.

SETTING INDENTS

Creating Lists

Bulleted and numbered lists are special kinds of hanging indent paragraphs. The hanging portion is either a bullet character (such as a filled or empty circle, diamond, or check mark) or a sequential number. You can create such lists *automatically* (depending on settings in Word Options) or *manually* (by applying a bullet or number format to a set of paragraphs).

You can also create lists with multiple levels of indents. These *multilevel lists* can contain sublists beneath any list item.

To enable automatic bulleted and numbered lists:

1. Open the Word Options dialog box by clicking the File tab, followed by the Options button.

2. Select the Proofing category.

3. Click the AutoCorrect Options button near the top of the dialog box.

4. In the AutoCorrect dialog box, select the AutoFormat As You Type tab.

5. In the Apply as you type section of the dialog box (**Figure 5.41**), enable Automatic bulleted lists and Automatic numbered lists.

6. Click OK to close the AutoCorrect dialog box.

7. Click OK to close the Word Options dialog box.

✔ Tip

- This is a one-time procedure. You'll have to revisit it only if you want to stop automatically creating one or both list types.

Figure 5.41 Enable the automatic creation of bulleted and numbered lists by clicking these check boxes.

Before, During, or After?

It's important to understand that paragraph and character formatting can be applied at *any* time: before you begin typing a paragraph or text block, as you type it, or after you've written and edited it.

And there's no single best approach— it depends on your writing style. For example, if you're making a numbered list, you can start a new paragraph, apply the number format, and then type the first item. For each additional paragraph you create, the numbering increments. On the other hand, it can be just as easy to write the entire list, select it, and *then* apply the numbered paragraph format.

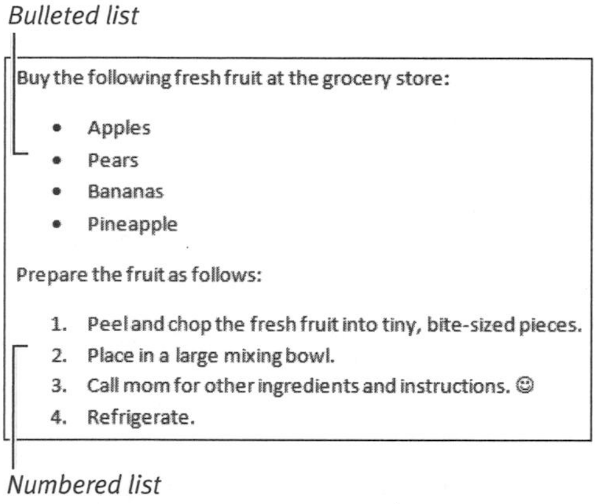

Bulleted list
Buy the following fresh fruit at the grocery store:
Apples
Pears
Bananas
Pineapple
Prepare the fruit as follows:
1. Peel and chop the fresh fruit into tiny, bite-sized pieces.
2. Place in a large mixing bowl.
3. Call mom for other ingredients and instructions. ☺
4. Refrigerate.
Numbered list

Figure 5.42 Examples of an automatic bulleted list and a numbered list.

Bullets
Numbering
Multilevel List

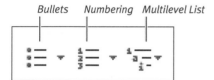

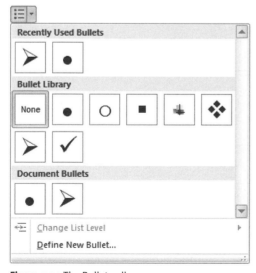

Figure 5.43 You can create a list by clicking an icon or by choosing a style from a drop-down gallery.

Recently Used Bullets
Bullet Library
None
Document Bullets
Change List Level
Define New Bullet...

Figure 5.44 The Bullet gallery.

To automatically create a list:

1. At the beginning of a new paragraph, *do one of the following:*
   - **Bulleted list.** To create the first item, type an asterisk (*) and a space. The asterisk is converted to a bullet.
   - **Numbered list.** To create the first item, type 1. and a space. This item becomes the first in a numbered list.
2. Finish the item paragraph and press Enter. Additional consecutive paragraphs you create by pressing Enter will continue the bullets or numbering.
3. To complete the final list item (**Figure 5.42**), press Enter twice.

To manually create a list:

1. *Do either of the following:*
   - To create a bulleted or numbered list using the most recently applied bullet or number style, click the Bullets or Numbering icon in the Paragraph group of the Home tab (**Figure 5.43**) or on the Mini toolbar.
   - Select a specific bullet or numbering style from the Bullets or Numbering icon's gallery (**Figure 5.44**).
2. Finish the item paragraph and press Enter. Additional consecutive paragraphs that you create by pressing Enter will continue the bullets or numbering.
3. To complete the final list item, press Enter twice.

✔ Tips

- You can also end a bullet or numbered list by clicking the Bullets or Numbering icon in the Paragraph group (see Figure 5.43).

- There are other characters you can type (followed by a period and a space) to automatically start a numbered list with a different numbering format, such as a., A., i., and I.

- To type additional text directly beneath a bulleted or numbered point without interrupting the bullets or numbering (**Figure 5.45**), end the previous line by pressing Shift Enter to create a *line break*. Type the additional text on the new line. When you press Enter to end the line or paragraph, the bullets or numbering will resume.

- You can change the bullet or numbering style for an existing list. Select all bulleted or numbered points, and then select a style from the Bullet or Numbering gallery (see Figure 5.44). A live preview appears as you rest the cursor on a style.

- To change a list from bullets to numbers or vice versa, click the other icon in the Paragraph group of the Home tab (see Figure 5.43) or on the Mini toolbar.

- You can sort a bulleted list alphabetically, numerically, or in date order. Select the items, click the Sort icon in the Paragraph group on the Home tab, and set options in the Sort Text dialog box (**Figure 5.46**).

- You can change the formatting of all bullets and numbers in a list. Click one to select them all. Apply character formatting (such as a new font, boldface, or a color) by choosing options from the Font group on the Home tab or from the Mini toolbar.

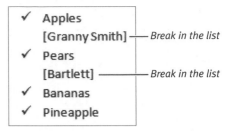

Figure 5.45 You can interrupt a list without ending it.

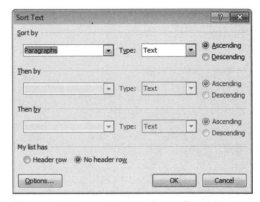

Figure 5.46 These settings can be used to sort a bulleted list alphabetically.

CREATING LISTS

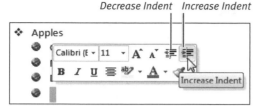

Decrease Indent *Increase Indent*

Figure 5.47 To set or change an item's level, click the Decrease Indent or Increase Indent icon.

Figure 5.48 A multilevel bulleted list.

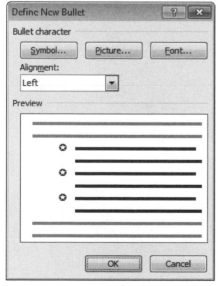

Figure 5.49 You can create new bullets by choosing a symbol character or an image.

To create a multilevel list:

1. Begin an automatic or manual list by following the previous task instructions.

2. To enter an item at a new level, click the Increase Indent icon in the Paragraph group of the Home tab (see Figure 5.37) or on the Mini toolbar (**Figure 5.47**).

   Additional items created at the same indent level by pressing [Enter] will have the same bullet or number style.

3. To convert an item to a higher level, click the Decrease Indent icon in the Paragraph group of the Home tab (see Figure 5.37) or on the Mini toolbar (Figure 5.47).

4. To specify the bullet or number format to be applied to each level, click the Multilevel List icon in the Paragraph group of the Home tab and select a style from the gallery.

   Your list is reformatted to match the gallery selection (**Figure 5.48**).

✔ Tips

- To select all items at a particular level in a bulleted or numbered list, click the bullet or number for any item at that level.

- You can substitute other bullets for the ones in the gallery. Click the down arrow beside the Bullets icon in the Paragraph group of the Home tab and choose Define New Bullet (see Figure 5.44). Or right-click any selected bullet and choose Bullets > Define New Bullet from the context menu. In the Define New Bullet dialog box (**Figure 5.49**), click Symbol or Picture to select a character from an installed font (such as Symbol, Wingdings, or Webdings) or to use an image file, respectively.

- You can also change levels by pressing [Tab] (increase) or [Shift][Tab] (decrease).

CREATING LISTS

Changing Paragraph and Line Spacing

Paragraph attributes also include the space between lines, as well as the space before and after a paragraph. Although line spacing and between-paragraph spacing are defined as part of every paragraph style, there are times when you'll want to change these settings. For instance, if a document is a few lines too long, you can make it fit in fewer pages by reducing the line spacing. Similarly, if an instructor insists on *double-spaced text* (a typewriter term), you can approximate it on a computer by increasing the line spacing of all paragraphs.

To change line spacing for paragraphs:

1. Select the paragraph(s) that will be affected by the new setting.

2. Click the Line and Paragraph Spacing icon in the Paragraph group of the Home tab, and choose one of the following from the drop-down menu (**Figure 5.50**):

   ▲ Choose a number, representing the space between each pair of lines. (Double spacing is 2.0, for example.)

   ▲ Choose Line Spacing Options. The Paragraph dialog box opens. On the Indents and Spacing tab, set the Line spacing (**Figure 5.51**), and click OK.

   The selected paragraphs are reformatted.

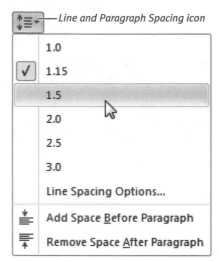

Line and Paragraph Spacing icon

Figure 5.50 The Line and Paragraph Spacing drop-down menu.

Figure 5.51 You can select a line spacing option from this drop-down list.

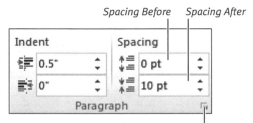

Spacing Before   *Spacing After*

Paragraph dialog box launcher

Figure 5.52 Enter numbers in these boxes to set the before and after spacing.

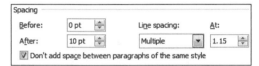

Figure 5.53 Set the before and after spacing (in points), and then click OK.

■ In general, it's best to avoid applying new spacing settings directly to paragraphs. Unless you're consistent, you may end up with a very ugly document. Instead, modify the document's paragraph *styles*. Doing so will ensure consistency because all paragraphs to which you've assigned a particular style will automatically update to reflect the new settings. Styles are discussed later in this chapter.

To change the before or after spacing for selected paragraphs:

1. Select the paragraph or paragraphs that will be affected by the new settings.

2. *Do one of the following:*

   ▲ In the Paragraph group on the Page Layout tab (**Figure 5.52**), enter numbers (in points) in the Spacing Before and/or Spacing After boxes.

   ▲ At the bottom of the Paragraph group on the Home or Page Layout tab, click the Paragraph dialog box launcher (Figure 5.52). On the Indents and Spacing tab of the Paragraph dialog box, enter numbers (in points) in the Before and/or After boxes (**Figure 5.53**). Click OK to close the dialog box.

   ▲ In the Paragraph group of the Home tab, click the Line and Paragraph Spacing icon. Choose Add (Remove) Space Before Paragraph or Add (Remove) Space After Paragraph (see Figure 5.50) to add a 12-point space or remove the current space.

   The new before/after spacing is applied to the selected paragraphs.

✔ Tips

■ To set line spacing in *points* (72 per inch), choose Exactly from the Line spacing drop-down menu (Figure 5.53).

■ New line spacing and before/after settings affect only the currently selected paragraphs. To apply these settings to an entire document, set the text insertion mark and press Ctrl A. Or click the Select icon in the Editing group of the Home tab and choose Select All.

■ If a paragraph or paragraph style is set for no (0) space before and after, it may be difficult to distinguish from surrounding paragraphs.

Character Formatting

Character formatting is formatting that you selectively apply to words, phrases, lines, sentences, or paragraphs. To make a phrase stand out in its sentence, you might format it as italic, boldface, blue, or underlined. If the sentence containing the phrase was formatted with the Arial font, you might apply a variation of the font, such as Arial Narrow or Arial Black.

If you're applying a character format as you type (rather than by selecting existing text), you can think of the formatting as an on/off sequence. You turn the formatting feature on, type the new text, and then turn the feature off when you want to return to the original formatting.

If you want to easily reapply complex character formatting to other text in the document, you can use the Format Painter.

To apply formatting as you type:

1. To switch to a different character formatting, *do one of the following:*

   ▲ Choose character-formatting options from the Font group on the Home tab (**Figure 5.54**).

   ▲ Choose character-formatting options from the Mini toolbar (**Figure 5.55**).

   ▲ Click the Font dialog box launcher (Figure 5.54) or press [Ctrl][D]. Choose new settings in the Font dialog box (**Figure 5.56**) and click OK.

2. Type the text that you want to format with the chosen attribute(s).

3. Disable the attributes chosen in Step 1 by clicking their icons again. If you changed fonts, you can revert to the original font by choosing its name from any Font menu or scrolling list.

Clear Formatting

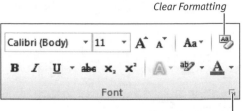

Font dialog box launcher

Figure 5.54 Common character-formatting attributes can be chosen from the Font group on the Home tab.

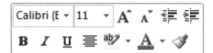

Figure 5.55 The Mini toolbar provides only basic character-formatting options.

Figure 5.56 Every supported character-formatting attribute can be selected in the Font dialog box.

To apply formatting to existing text:

1. Select the text to which you want to apply a different character formatting.

2. *Do any of the following:*

   ▲ Choose character-formatting options from the Font group on the Home tab (see Figure 5.54).

   Rest the cursor over any icon to see a ToolTip description of its function.

   ▲ Choose character-formatting options from the Mini toolbar (see Figure 5.55).

   ▲ Click the Font Dialog Box Launcher (see Figure 5.54). Choose settings in the Font dialog box (see Figure 5.56) and click OK.

To remove character formatting:

1. Select the text from which you want to remove character formatting.

2. *Do any of the following:*

   ▲ To remove *all* character formatting (leaving only plain text), click the Clear Formatting icon in the Font group of the Home tab (see Figure 5.54).

   ▲ To selectively remove formatting (when you've applied multiple attributes to the selected text), click icons of the formats you want to remove in the Font group or Mini toolbar.

   ▲ Click the Font Dialog Box Launcher (see Figure 5.54). Choose new settings in the Font dialog box (see Figure 5.56) and click OK.

Changing the Default Font

Whenever you create a new, blank Word document and begin typing, the font used is the *default font.* You can easily change the default font, if you like.

1. Open the Font dialog box.

   The font, style, size, and other attributes of the currently selected text are shown.

2. To specify attributes other than those of the selected text, select a font and other attributes from the drop-down lists and check boxes.

3. Click the Set as Default button. In the dialog box that appears, select All documents based on the Normal.dotm template. Click OK.

4. Click OK to close the Font dialog box.

To use the Format Painter to duplicate formatting:

1. Select the text whose formatting you want to duplicate or position the text insertion mark within that text.

2. Click the Format Painter icon in the Clipboard group of the Home tab (**Figure 5.57**) or press [Ctrl][Shift][C]. The Format Painter cursor appears.

3. Drag to select the target text (**Figure 5.58**). The copied character formatting is applied to the target text.

✔ Tips

■ You also can open the Font dialog box by pressing [Ctrl][D].

■ Many character-formatting commands have keyboard shortcuts. You can apply or remove their formatting by pressing the keys listed in **Table 5.1**.

■ You can use the Format Painter to duplicate character *and* paragraph formatting. Select the entire paragraph before clicking the Format Painter icon.

■ You can apply copied character attributes to *multiple* selections by double-clicking the Format Painter icon. One by one, drag-select each destination text string. When you're finished, click the Format Painter icon again.

■ You can easily apply new attributes to multiple text strings that currently share the same formatting. Select any one of the text strings and switch to the Home tab. Click the Select drop-down menu in the Editing group and choose Select Text with Similar Formatting. As you choose new character formatting, it'll be applied to *all* the text selections.

Format Painter icon

Figure 5.57 The Format Painter tool.

Format Painter cursor

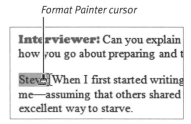

Figure 5.58 Using the Format Painter, it's easy to duplicate text formatting.

Table 5.1

Character-Formatting Keyboard Shortcuts	
KEYPRESS	DEFINITION
[Ctrl][B]	Boldface
[Ctrl][I]	Italic
[Ctrl][U]	Underline (single)
[Ctrl][Shift][D]	Underline (double)
[Ctrl][Shift][W]	Underline words but not spaces
[Ctrl][Shift][K]	Small capital letters (caps)
[Ctrl][=]	Subscript
[Ctrl][+]	Superscript
[Ctrl][<]	Decrease font size
[Ctrl][>]	Increase font size
[Shift][F3]	Change letter case
[Ctrl][Spacebar]	Remove manual character formatting

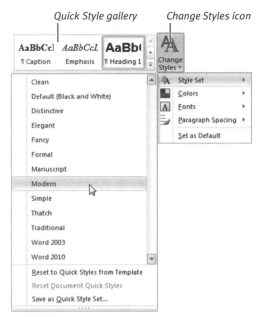

Quick Style gallery   *Change Styles icon*

Figure 5.59 Choose a new Quick Style set from the Style Set submenu.

Working with Styles

A *style* is a set of formatting instructions you can apply to selected paragraphs or text. By applying styles rather than manually formatting a document, you can ensure that the formatting is consistent throughout—resulting in a document with a professional appearance.

The *Quick Style gallery* (found in the Styles group on the Home tab) contains a subset of all defined styles for the current document. Designed to help you easily apply the most common paragraph and character styles to selected text, Quick Styles encourage users who have previously ignored styles to start using them.

If you create a document from scratch, there are several Quick Style sets available to you, each designed to convey a certain style and tone. If you create a document from a template, a Quick Style set may be included with the template. You can customize the active Quick Style set by adding new styles and removing unwanted ones.

To switch Quick Style sets:

1. Click the Change Styles icon in the Styles group of the Home tab.

2. From the Style Set submenu, choose a new style set (**Figure 5.59**). As you drag the cursor over each set name, a live preview of the resulting style changes is applied to all visible text.

   The current Quick Style set is replaced by the chosen set.

WordArt and Text Effects

In Chapter 3, you learned how to create *WordArt*, a decorative text object. In Word, you can use the Text Effects command to apply the same decorative effects without changing the selected text into an object.

1. Select the text (such as a heading) that you want to format.

2. On the Home tab, click the Text Effects icon in the Font group and choose an effect from the gallery. Each effect provides a live preview.

You can modify other characteristics of the text (such as its font, size, or color) without losing the applied text effect.

To apply a style:

1. Select a text string or paragraph to which you want to apply a style.

2. Open the Quick Style gallery. Move the cursor over a style icon (**Figure 5.60**).

   A preview of the style is displayed on the text.

3. If this is the correct style, click its icon to apply it to the text.

To add a new stye to the current set:

1. You can create new Quick Styles from formatted text or paragraphs in the current document. Begin by applying the desired character formatting to some text or by applying paragraph formatting to a paragraph.

2. Select the formatted word, text string, or paragraph.

3. Choose Save Selection as a New Quick Style from the Quick Style gallery menu (Figure 5.60).

   The Create New Style from Formatting dialog box appears (**Figure 5.61**).

4. Name the new style and click Modify.

   A new dialog box appears (**Figure 5.62**).

5. Make any additional formatting changes that are required. Ensure that the setting for Style type matches the kind of style you want to create: Character, Paragraph, or Linked (paragraph and character). Click the Format button to view other options. Click OK to return to the previous dialog box.

6. Click OK.

   An icon for the style appears in the Quick Style gallery. The style definition is added to the document's style list.

Figure 5.60 The gallery for a Quick Style set.

Figure 5.61 Name the new style.

Figure 5.62 Make any necessary changes and click OK.

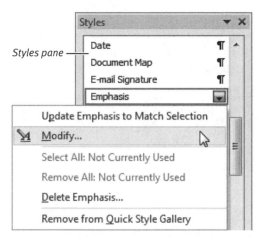

Styles pane

Figure 5.63 The Styles pane lists *all* defined styles for the document. To open the pane, click the Styles dialog box launcher at the bottom of the Styles group.

To modify a style by example:

1. Make the desired changes to a text string or paragraph that is formatted with the style you want to modify.

2. Select the modified text or paragraph, right-click the selection, and choose Styles > Update *style name* to Match Selection.

   This command can also be chosen from the context menu that appears when you right-click the style's icon in the Quick Style gallery.

To modify a style using a dialog box:

1. *Do either of the following:*

   ▲ Right-click the style icon in the Quick Style gallery and choose Modify.

   ▲ In the Styles pane (**Figure 5.63**), click the down-arrow beside the style name and choose Modify.

   A Modify Style dialog box appears, identical to the one shown in Figure 5.62.

2. Make any desired changes. (Additional options can be chosen by clicking the Format button.) Click OK.

   The modified style definition is stored. Text or paragraphs formatted with the style automatically update to conform to the new definition.

WORKING WITH STYLES

✔ Tips

■ To add a previously defined (but unlisted) style to the current Quick Style set, click the style's down-arrow in the Styles pane. Choose Add to Quick Style Gallery.

■ To remove a style from the current set, right-click its icon in the gallery and choose Remove from Quick Style Gallery. (Note that this only removes the style from the gallery. It does *not* delete the style from the document's style definitions.)

■ To *delete* a style (permanently removing it from a document's style list), click the down-arrow beside the style name in the Styles pane and choose Delete *style name* (see Figure 5.63). Text or paragraphs that are presently formatted with the style revert to the default formatting.

■ To remove all formatting applied by choosing a particular style, click the down-arrow beside the style's name in the Styles pane and choose Clear Formatting.

■ To apply a different style to all text/paragraphs previously assigned a given style, click the down-arrow beside the style in the Styles pane and choose Select All x Instance(s). Reformat the selected material by clicking a new style or by choosing formatting options from the Home tab.

■ Another way to open or close the Styles pane is to press [Alt][Ctrl][Shift][S].

■ As an alternative to the Styles pane, you can open a floating window from which you can choose styles to format selected text (**Figure 5.64**). Choose Apply Styles from the bottom of the Quick Style gallery.

Close

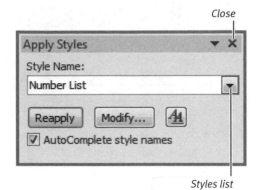

Styles list

Figure 5.64 Like the Styles pane, the Apply Styles window contains the complete list of defined styles for the current document. Select a style from the list or type its name.

Merge Formatting

By adding specially formatted placeholder text called *merge fields* to a document and combining it with data from a second document created in Word, Excel, Outlook, or another application, you can *merge* the two documents—creating a separate, customized version of the Word document for each data record. For example, by inserting name and address placeholders in the main document, you could create a mail merge. A personalized letter containing their address and using their first name in the greeting line could be generated for each person.

The easiest way to learn how to perform a merge is to use the Mail Merge Wizard to walk you through the process. As an example, you'll generate a series of personalized letters. To follow along, create an Excel worksheet similar to the one in **Figure 5.65**. Each row is a data record. Be sure to create at least three or four records.

donation list.xlsx

	A	B	C	D	E	F	G
1	First	Last	Address	City	State	Zip	Donation
2	Amy	Fredericks	3226 State Street	Menlo Park	CA	94025	$ 25
3	Dave	Johnson	2480 Christina Lane	Walnut Creek	CA	94596	$ 5
4	Mike	Smith	35 James Rd.	Cocoa	FL	32926	$ 125
5	Steve	Anderson	677 Lillian Ave	Sudbury	MA	01776	$ 5
6	James	Barr	4125 Leeway Trail	Ormond Beach	FL	32174	$ 2
7	Douglas	Simons	299 NW 72nd Circle	Vancouver	WA	98665	$ 10
8	Josiah	Jefferson	13267 Skyline Dr.	Golden Valley	MN	55422	$ 20
9	Andrea	Harrison	3645 Michael St.	Carson City	NV	89703	$ 25
10	Sheri	Slainee	79879 E. Prince Dr., #42	Scottsdale	AZ	85255	$ 5
11	James	Kern	332 Sea Island Dr	Dana Point	CA	92629	$ 50
12	Josh	Kimes	2171 Skipper Lane	Lake Havasu City	AZ	86403	$ 100
13	Jill	Nelson	20 Archway Drive	Slingerlands	NY	12159	$ 50
14	Robert	Eliason	5310 Henderson Street	Duluth	MN	55804-1111	$ 10
15	Russ	Sanders	4000 Wildrose	Flagstaff	AZ	86001	$ 10

Sheet1 / Sheet2 / Sheet3 /

Figure 5.65 Data in this worksheet will be merged with a Word form letter.

To perform a merge using the Mail Merge Wizard:

1. In Word, create a document similar to the one shown in **Figure 5.66** (below).

   Leave space for the mail merge fields.

2. Open the Mail Merge task pane by selecting the Mailings tab, clicking the Start Mail Merge icon in the Start Mail Merge group, and choosing Step by Step Mail Merge Wizard.

   The Mail Merge task pane appears on the right side of the window (**Figure 5.67**).

Figure 5.67 The Mail Merge Wizard: Step 1.

Salutation   *Donor address*   *Donation amount*

Hamilton Animal Shelter
1867 Jones Drive
Hamilton, MA 01886

Thank you for your recent contribution of to our shelter. Donations of money, goods, and time by caring people such as yourself help us ensure that homeless pets in our community are properly fed, receive inexpensive shots, participate in our spay/neuter program, and are ultimately placed in loving homes.

Thank you again.

Sincerely,

Steven Schwartz
President

Figure 5.66 The merge letter can be based on an existing document like this one or created from a template.

MERGE FORMATTING

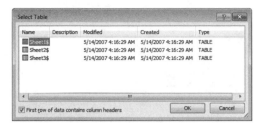

Figure 5.68 Select the first sheet in the workbook. Because the first row of the sheet contains the merge field names, ensure that the check box is checked.

Include/exclude check boxes

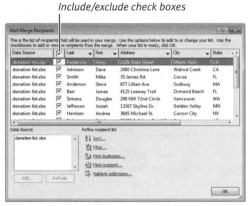

Figure 5.69 Review the data, ensure that it looks correct, and specify the records to include.

3. Click the Letters radio button and then click Next: Starting document (at the bottom of the task pane).

Step 2 of 6 appears in the task pane.

4. *Select one of the following:*

▲ **Use the current document.** If the merge document is open and onscreen, select this option.

▲ **Start from template.** If you haven't created the document, select this option. Click the Select template text that appears and then pick a template, such as the Origin Letter.

▲ **Start from existing document.** If you've already created the document but it isn't open, select this option, select the document from the list that appears, and click the Open button.

5. At the bottom of the task pane, click Next: Select recipients.

Step 3 of 6 appears in the task pane.

6. Select Use an existing list and then click Browse.

The Select Data Source dialog box appears.

7. Navigate to the drive and folder in which you saved the Excel data file, select the file, and click Open.

The Select Table dialog box appears (**Figure 5.68**).

8. Select the first sheet (Sheet1$), ensure that First row of data contains column headers is checked, and click OK.

The Mail Merge Recipients dialog box appears (**Figure 5.69**).

9. *Optional:* You can omit a recipient by removing the check mark before his or her last name. Click OK when you're ready to continue.

continues on next page

MERGE FORMATTING

10. At the bottom of the task pane, click Next: Write your letter.

Step 4 of 6 (**Figure 5.70**) appears.

11. To select the spot for the recipient's address in the form letter, set the text insertion mark at the beginning of the line beneath the return address. Click the Address block... text in the task pane.

The Insert Address Block dialog box appears (**Figure 5.71**).

12. Select a format for displaying each person's name. Click the arrows above the preview area to ensure that the names and addresses are displayed correctly. Click OK.

The Address Block merge field is inserted into the letter (**Figure 5.72**).

13. Set the text insertion mark where the greeting line ("Dear ...") will appear: two lines below the Address Block field. Click the Greeting line... text in the task pane.

The Insert Greeting Line dialog box appears (**Figure 5.73**).

14. Select options from the drop-down lists to format the greeting line. Click the arrows above the preview area to see how the greeting line looks when filled with your data. Click OK to continue.

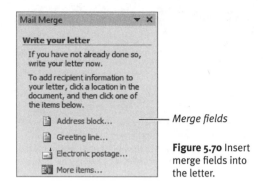

— *Merge fields*

Figure 5.70 Insert merge fields into the letter.

Name format   *Preview area*

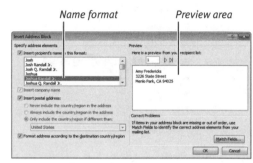

Figure 5.71 Select a format for the recipient's name to specify how it will be displayed in the address block.

Merge field

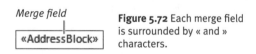

Figure 5.72 Each merge field is surrounded by « and » characters.

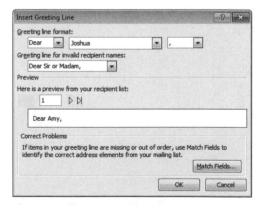

Figure 5.73 The Insert Greeting Line dialog box.

Figure 5.74 Select a merge field to add at the text insertion mark.

Donation merge field

> contribution of $«Donation» to our shelter.

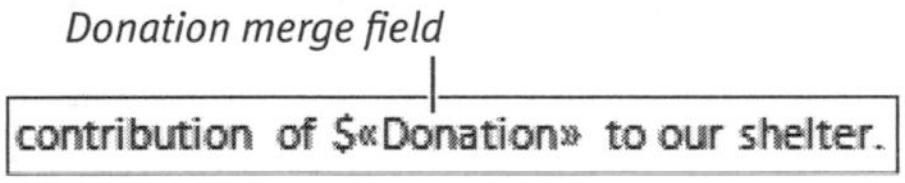

Figure 5.75 Add a $ immediately before the Donation merge field.

15. Now you'll add a placeholder for the donation amount. In the first line of the letter, set the text insertion mark after "...contribution of..." Then click More items... in the task pane.

The Insert Merge field dialog box appears (**Figure 5.74**).

16. Select the Donation field and click Insert.

The Donation merge field is inserted into the letter.

17. Close the dialog box by clicking Close.

18. The Donation merge field must be preceded by and followed by a space. If either space is missing, insert it now.

19. Type a dollar sign ($) immediately to the left of the merge field (**Figure 5.75**).

When the merge procedure extracts the Excel data, the dollar sign will be ignored. But you can add it to the letter.

20. At the bottom of the task pane, click Next: Preview your letters.

Step 5 of 6 appears, displaying a merge letter (**Figure 5.76**).

continues on next page

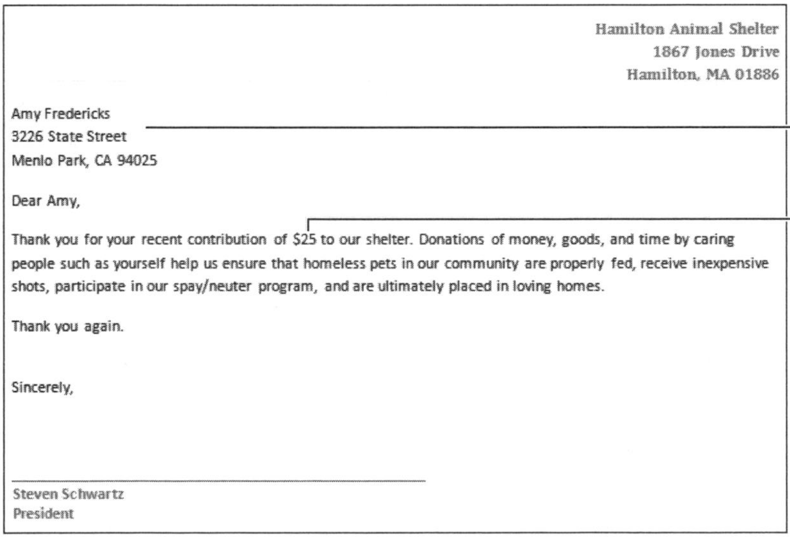

Hamilton Animal Shelter
1867 Jones Drive
Hamilton, MA 01886

Amy Fredericks —————————————————— *Address block*
3226 State Street
Menlo Park, CA 94025

Dear Amy,

Thank you for your recent contribution of $25 to our shelter. —— *Donation amount* Donations of money, goods, and time by caring people such as yourself help us ensure that homeless pets in our community are properly fed, receive inexpensive shots, participate in our spay/neuter program, and are ultimately placed in loving homes.

Thank you again.

Sincerely,

Steven Schwartz
President

Figure 5.76 The form letter now displays data from the Excel file.

21. Click buttons to examine the recipient letters (**Figure 5.77**). If you see a person whom you don't want to include in the merge, click Exclude this recipient.

    Navigation buttons are also available in the Preview Results group in the Ribbon.

22. At the bottom of the task pane, click Next: Complete the merge.

23. In Step 6 of 6, *do one of the following:*

    ▲ Click Print... to merge directly to a connected printer. A separate letter will be printed for each recipient.

    ▲ Click Edit individual letters... to generate a new Word document as the merge output.

    A Merge to Printer or Merge to New Document dialog box appears (**Figure 5.78**).

24. Specify the records to use in the merge and click OK.

✔ Tips

■ You can format merge fields. Be sure to select the entire field, including the surrounding bracket characters.

■ In the final task pane, the option to Edit individual letters serves several important functions. First, it allows you to edit— or delete—individual letters. Second, because this option generates an ordinary Word document, you can save it on disk as documentation of the mailing. Finally, after you proof the letters and make any necessary edits, printing this document is the same as choosing the Print option. A letter is produced for each recipient.

■ In the final step, you can further control the output by clicking icons on the Mailings tab. In particular, if you click Auto Check for Errors in the Preview Results group, additional options appear (**Figure 5.79**).

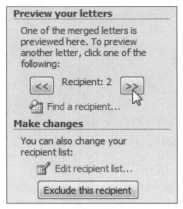

Figure 5.77 Examine the letters and, if desired, exclude certain recipients.

Figure 5.78 Specify which records to include in the printout or the Word output document.

Figure 5.79 You can specify how Word will handle errors discovered during the merge.

6

CREATING OUTLINES

If you remember high school or college, you probably remember *outlines* (lists of key points organized into headings and subheadings), too. To demonstrate that you had a thorough plan, teachers may have required you to create an outline before starting a paper or report.

Even after you've left school, you may find that writing an outline is an excellent way to get organized. Whether you're about to write an important report, preparing to give a presentation or lecture, or planning a complicated home renovation, you can create an outline to ensure that you've hit the important points or steps in the proper order. Although dedicated outlining applications may be easier to use or have more features, many users will find Word's Outline view sufficient for handling basic outlining tasks.

✔ Tip

Outline view isn't only for outlines. Because it has some unique tools, such as the ability to collapse sections and easily reorganize paragraphs, it's sometimes helpful to use Outline view to polish a normal document.

About Outline View

As far as Word is concerned, a document is a document. Nothing distinguishes an outline from any other Word document. Outline is merely a *view* you can work in—just like Print Layout view. The only real difference is that Outline view provides special tools for working with outlines.

Figure 6.1 Click the Outline icon to switch to Outline view.

To enter or exit Outline view:

1. Click the View tab on the Ribbon.

2. Click the Outline icon in the Document Views group (**Figure 6.1**).

The current document is displayed in Outline view (**Figure 6.2**, below). The Outlining tab appears and is automatically selected.

3. To exit from Outline view, click the Close Outline View icon on the Outlining tab (Figure 6.2).

Outline

Figure 6.3 Or click the Outline icon at the bottom of the document window.

✔ Tips

■ You can also switch to Outline view by clicking the Outline icon at the bottom of the document window (**Figure 6.3**, above).

■ While working in Outline view, you can freely switch tabs to apply formatting, insert objects, and the like.

Figure 6.2 A document in Outline view.

Figure 6.4 The level of each point is indicated by its indentation and (typically) its formatting. Each paragraph is considered a separate point.

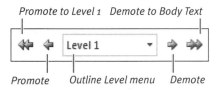

Figure 6.5 To set or change a point's level, you can use these tools.

Figure 6.6 A comment is preceded by a solid bullet symbol, rather than a plus (+) or minus (–).

Point Symbols

A point that has one or more subordinate points is preceded by a plus (+) symbol. A point that has no subordinate points is preceded by a minus (–) symbol.

Starting an Outline

A Word outline consists of outline points and, optionally, comments. Each point is assigned a *level* (**Figure 6.4**); the higher the level, the more important the point. For example, the outline for this book consists of parts, chapters, main headings, and secondary headings, assigned Levels 1, 2, 3, and 4, respectively.

To create an outline:

1. In a new document, click the View tab. Click the Outline icon in the Document Views group (see Figure 6.1).

   A minus (–) symbol appears, ready for you to enter the first point.

2. Type the first point and press Enter.

   The cursor moves to a new line.

3. *Do one of the following:*

   ▲ To treat the new point as Level 1, enter the text for the point and press Enter.

   ▲ Use the tools in the Outline Tools group (**Figure 6.5**) to demote this to a Level 2 point by choosing Level 2 from the Outline Level menu, clicking the Demote icon, or pressing Alt Shift →.

   ▲ To treat the new text as a *comment* (**Figure 6.6**) rather than a point, choose Body Text from the Outline Level menu or click the Demote to Body Text icon.

4. Continue entering outline points. By default, when you press Enter to create a new point, the level of the point matches that of the one immediately above it.

✔ Tip

■ You can *promote* a selected point by choosing a higher level from the Outline Level menu, clicking Promote to Level 1, or clicking Promote (or pressing Alt Shift ←) to raise the level by one.

STARTING AN OUTLINE

Reorganizing an Outline

Creating an outline generally involves a certain amount of reorganizing: changing point levels, adding and deleting points, and moving points and sections to new spots. The first step in reorganizing is to select the point or points that you want to manipulate.

To select outline points:

◆ *Do one of the following:*

  ▲ **Single point or comment.** Click to the left of the point or comment.

  ▲ **Point and its subordinate points.** Double-click to the left of the main point (**Figure 6.7**).

  ▲ **Contiguous series of points.** Click to the left of the first point and drag down.

  ▲ **Noncontiguous series of points.** Ctrl-click to the left of each point.

✔ Tip

■ Selecting a collapsed point also selects its subordinate points.

To insert a new point:

1. Click at the end of the point immediately before where you want to insert the new point and then press Enter.
   A line for the new point appears (**Figure 6.8**), set to the same level as the point above it.

2. *Optional:* You can change the new point's level by using a tool in the Outline Tools group (see Figure 6.5).

To delete one or more points:

◆ Select the point or points, and press Del, Delete, or Backspace.

✔ Tip

■ Deleting a collapsed point also deletes its subordinate points.

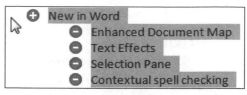

Figure 6.7 Double-click to the left of a point to select the point and its subordinate points, if any.

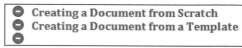

Figure 6.8 To make room for a new point, I clicked to the right of Template and pressed Enter.

Level Formatting

If you don't care for the fonts, color, or other aspects of the default level formatting applied to your outline, you're free to change it.

◆ *To change the formatting of selected words or entire points,* use normal formatting techniques. You can set options on the Home tab, use the Mini toolbar, or select text and then right-click it.

◆ *To change the formatting for a level throughout the outline,* format a single point for that level, right-click it, and then choose Styles > Update Heading *number* to Match Selection. (The style names for Levels 1–6 are Heading 1–6; comments use the Normal style.)

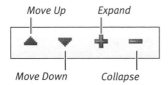

Figure 6.9 Click a Move icon to move the selected point(s) one line at a time.

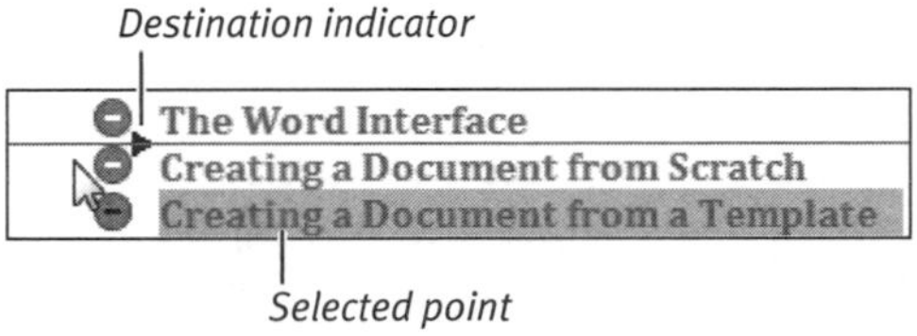

Destination indicator

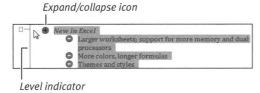

Selected point

Figure 6.10 You can drag selected points up or down in the outline.

Expand/collapse icon

Level indicator

Figure 6.11 You can promote or demote selected points by dragging to the left or right.

To move points up or down:

◆ *Do one of the following:*

▲ Click the Move Up or Move Down icon in the Outline Tools group (**Figure 6.9**). Each click moves the selected point(s) up or down one line in the outline.

▲ Cut the selected point(s) by pressing Ctrl X, click to set the text insertion mark where you want to insert the point(s), and then paste by pressing Ctrl V.

▲ Click the symbol that precedes the point or group of points you want to move, and then drag up or down to the destination (**Figure 6.10**). When you release the mouse button, the dragged point(s) are moved to the new location.

To promote or demote points:

◆ To change the level of points, *do one of the following:*

▲ Use the tools in the Outline Tools group (see Figure 6.5) to demote (Alt Shift →) or promote (Alt Shift ←) the selected point(s).

▲ Drag the symbol that precedes a point (and its subordinates, if any) to the left or right (**Figure 6.11**). Release the mouse button to set the new level.

✔ Tip

■ When moving, promoting, or demoting points, mistakes are commonplace. To correct a move that goes awry, click the Undo icon in the Quick Access Toolbar or press Ctrl Z. To undo *multiple* actions, click the down arrow beside the Undo icon and choose the last action you want to correct. The selected action and all the actions above it in the drop-down list will be undone.

REORGANIZING AN OUTLINE

Changing Display Settings

Word provides viewing features and tools (**Figure 6.12**) to make it easier to work with outlines. You can collapse sections to focus on the rest of the outline; hide lower-level, less significant levels so only important details are visible; or remove level formatting to make it simpler to read the outline.

To change display settings:

◆ *Do any of the following:*

▲ **Collapse sections.** To collapse a section, double-click the + symbol that precedes the section's main point. Or with the section's main point selected, click the Collapse icon in the Outline Tools group (see Figure 6.9) or press [Alt][Shift][−]. The section and all its subordinate sections and points collapse (**Figure 6.13**).

▲ **Expand sections.** To expand a collapsed section, double-click the + symbol that precedes the section's main point. Or with the section's main point selected, click the Expand icon in the Outline Tools group (see Figure 6.9) or press [Alt][Shift][+]. The section and its subordinate sections expand.

▲ **Show Level.** To focus on higher-level points, you can choose a level number from the Show Level drop-down menu (**Figure 6.14**). Only points at that level or higher are then displayed; lower-level points are collapsed. To view the full outline again, choose All Levels from the drop-down menu.

▲ **Hide formatting.** Remove the check mark from Show Text Formatting to display the entire outline in a single default font, size, and style.

▲ **Show First Line Only.** Click this check box to hide additional lines of text beyond the first for each outline point.

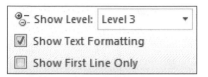

Figure 6.12 View options are set in this section of the Outline Tools group.

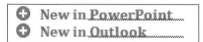

Figure 6.13 Collapsed sections are denoted by a squiggly underline. To expand collapsed points, double-click the symbol beside their section heading.

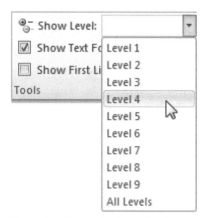

Figure 6.14 Choose the lowest level to display from this drop-down menu.

✔ Tip

■ To print an outline, click the File tab. In the Backstage, click Print and then click the Print button. Note that collapsed points will not print. If Show Text Formatting isn't checked (Figure 6.12), the printout will be in a single default font.

SHARING WORD DOCUMENTS

7

Some Word documents are destined never to leave your hard disk. You might mail a printout of selected documents as letters, but the actual *files* are meant for your use only.

Other Word documents, however, are meant to make the rounds. You may intend to email them to a friend, share them on the company network, put them out for review by members of a workgroup, or post them on the Web. In this chapter, you'll learn about tools for sharing such documents.

✔ Tips

■ See Chapter 2 for information on protecting documents by marking them as final or password-protecting them.

■ See Chapter 22 for information on sharing Word, PowerPoint, and Excel documents via the new Office Web Apps.

Choosing a File Format

The most straightforward way to share Word documents is to provide the file—on disk, by email, or via a download link on your Web site. However, the decision concerning which *file format* to use (**Figure 7.1**) depends on the recipient's software and whether the document needs to be editable. The most commonly used Save As formats include:

◆ **Word Document (.docx)**. These native Word 2007/2010 files can be read and edited only by owners of Word 2007 or Word 2010, or by people who have installed the converter software for Office 2000, XP, or 2003.

◆ **Word 97–2003 Document (.doc)**. This binary file format is the one used by Word 97–2003 documents. Recipients with Word 97 or higher (including Word 2007 and 2010) can read and edit .doc files.

◆ **Rich Text Format (.rtf) and Plain Text (.txt)**. Rich Text Format is a good choice for files that must retain their formatting and be readable by other word-processing applications. Plain Text files can be read and edited by *all* word-processing programs and text editors, but character and paragraph formatting are removed.

◆ **PDF (.pdf)**. This is the most common format for the Web distribution of read-only documents that remain true to their original formatting. These Adobe Acrobat files can be opened with Adobe Reader, Apple's Preview, and similar utilities.

✔ Tip

■ Users of Office XP, 2000, or 2003 can download the free Microsoft Office Compatibility Pack from microsoft.com to enable their version of Office to read native Word, Excel, and PowerPoint 2007–2010 documents.

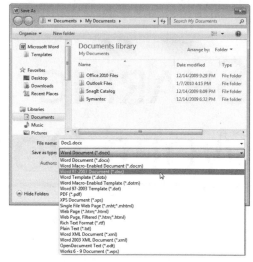

Figure 7.1 To save a copy of a Word document in a different format, click the File tab, click Save As, select a format from the Save as type drop-down list, name the file, and click Save.

Emailing a Document as the Message Body

In addition to emailing documents as attachments, you can send them as the *body* of a message. To do so, you must add a command to the Quick Access Toolbar:

1. Click the File tab, followed by Options.

2. Select the Quick Access Toolbar category in the Word Options dialog box.

3. Select All Commands from the Choose commands from drop-down list.

4. Select Sent to Mail Recipient, click the Add button, and then click OK.

To email any active Word document as the message body, click the new Send to Mail Recipient icon, enter recipients, and click the Send a Copy toolbar icon.

Send Using E-Mail   Send options

Figure 7.2 To email a document from within Word, click the File tab, select Share, and choose an option from the Send Using E-mail commands.

Attached document

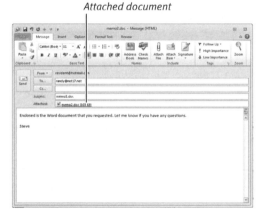

Figure 7.3 You can easily enclose the current document in an email message without leaving Word.

✔ Tip

■ Like many file types, XPS files can be opened only by certain programs such as Internet Explorer 7/8 and XPS Viewer.

Emailing Word Documents

As explained in Chapter 19, *any* kind of document (including Word files) can be sent as an attachment to an email message. In addition to attaching the file within Outlook or another email client, you can attach Word documents to messages from within Word.

To send a Word document as a message attachment:

1. In Word, open the document you want to send via email. Ensure that any recent changes have been saved.

2. *Optional:* To send the document as Word 97–2003, Rich Text Format, or Plain Text format, click the File tab, choose Save As, and save a copy of the document in the desired format.

   The document in the new format becomes the active document.

3. Click the File tab, select Share, and then select Send Using E-mail. Click one of the following command icons (**Figure 7.2**):

   ▲ **Send as Attachment.** A message window opens with the current document attached as a Word file (**Figure 7.3**). Enter recipients, type the message text, and click Send.

   ▲ **Send as PDF, Send as XPS.** A message window opens with the current document attached as an Adobe Acrobat (PDF) or XML Paper Specification (XPS) file. Enter recipients, type the message text, and click Send.

   ▲ **Send as Internet Fax.** The document is transmitted as a fax using an Internet Fax service. If you don't have a fax service provider, you can enroll with one after choosing this option.

   The document is transmitted.

Change Tracking

When multiple people will be working on, reviewing, or commenting on a document, you can use Word's *change tracking* features to simplify and coordinate the process. When change tracking is enabled, you can see every modification made to a document: deletions, insertions, and formatting changes. If multiple people are editing the document, each person's changes are differentiated from everyone else's. During the writing and editing or at the end of the process, the document's author can finalize the document, accepting or rejecting each suggested change.

To enable/disable change tracking:

◆ *Do either of the following:*

▲ Click the Review tab, click the Track Changes icon in the Tracking group, and choose Track Changes.

▲ Press Ctrl Shift E.

When enabled, the Track Changes icon turns orange (**Figure 7.4**).

To set tracking options:

1. Click the Review tab, click the Track Changes icon in the Tracking group, and choose Change Tracking Options.

   The Track Changes Options dialog box appears (**Figure 7.5**).

2. Make any desired changes and click OK.

To set the view for change tracking:

1. On the Review tab, choose an option from the Display for Review drop-down menu (**Figure 7.6**).

   Original refers to the original document, prior to any edits. *Final* displays the document as if all changes have been accepted.

2. Click the Show Markup icon and choose Balloons, followed by a method for displaying revisions.

Track Changes enabled   Display for Review menu

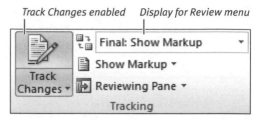

Figure 7.4 Change tracking and its options are set in the Tracking group on the Review tab.

Figure 7.5 You can set the color and formatting of various edits in the Track Changes Options dialog box.

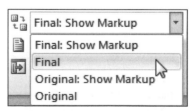

Figure 7.6 Choose a display option for the document from this menu.

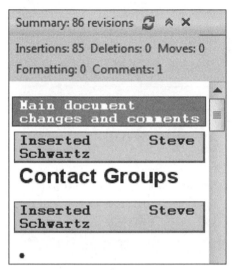

Figure 7.7 The Reviewing Pane presents all edits in a scrolling list. Double-click any entry to scroll the document directly to that edit.

Figure 7.8 Process revisions by clicking these Changes icons.

- To accept or reject *all* edits, choose Accept All Changes in Document or Reject All Changes in Document from the Accept or Reject icon's menu.

- If you mistakenly accept or reject an edit, you can reverse your action by immediately clicking the Undo icon in the Quick Access Toolbar or by pressing [Ctrl][Z].

- Excel has change tracking, too. When it's enabled (in the Changes group on the Review tab), users can hover the cursor over any changed cell to see the change details. PowerPoint, on the other hand, only allows you to add comments.

To process document revisions:

1. *Optional:* Open the Reviewing Pane (**Figure 7.7**) by clicking the Reviewing Pane icon and choosing a display option: Vertical or Horizontal.

2. Click in the document at the point where you want to start and, using the icons in the Changes group (**Figure 7.8**), *do the following for each revision:*

   ▲ To accept the current revision, click the Accept icon or choose an option from the icon's drop-down menu. (Accepting a revision incorporates the edit into the text.)

   ▲ To reject the current revision, click the Reject icon or choose an option from the icon's drop-down menu. (Rejecting a revision removes the edit.)

   ▲ Temporarily ignore a revision by clicking the Next or Previous icon.

✔ Tips

- You don't have to share a document to use change tracking. You can use it to track and manage your own edits, too.

- Another way to view the content of edits and comments is to move the cursor over them in the body of the document. A pop-up box will appear.

- You can close the Reviewing Pane by clicking its icon or the pane's close box.

- Any reviewer can insert comments into the text. Comments can be used for any purpose, such as explaining the reason for an edit or pointing out material that needs to be rewritten. To insert a comment, set the insertion mark or select the text to which the comment refers, click the New Comment icon in the Comments group, and type the comment. Comments are identified by the reviewer's initials, followed by a number, such as [SS3].

CHANGE TRACKING

Comparing Documents

Whether you're working alone on an important document or with others, it can be helpful to compare two versions to see what's been changed. (This assumes, of course, that you've saved multiple versions of the document or, at least, an original and a current version.)

To compare two versions of a document:

1. On the Review tab, click the Compare icon in the Compare group and choose Compare from the drop-down menu.

   The Compare Documents dialog box appears (**Figure 7.9**).

2. Select the original and revised documents from the drop-down lists.

   If a document isn't listed, click its Browse icon to locate the document on disk.

3. If the bottom half of the dialog box is hidden, click the More button to reveal the document-comparison options.

4. Review and set options, and then click OK.

   The comparison document is created and displayed (**Figure 7.10**).

✔ Tips

- You can compare *any* two versions of the same document—not just the first and last or the previous and current versions.

- Each pane in the comparison document has its own close box.

- If a document has undergone multiple revisions, you'll find it more manageable to compare the last two versions than to compare the original and final.

- Compare Documents can also be used to compare the last saved version with an autosaved version. See Chapter 2 for more details on using Compare Documents.

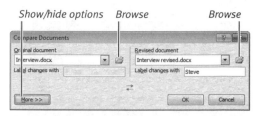

Show/hide options Browse Browse

Figure 7.9 Select the original and revised documents, set options, and click OK.

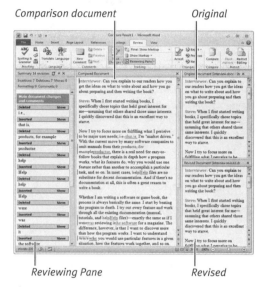

Comparison document Original

Reviewing Pane Revised

Figure 7.10 You can customize the display by choosing commands from icon menus, such as Show Markup, Reviewing Pane, and Show Source Documents.

Other Office Sharing Tools

If you need to share your Office 2010 documents with users of earlier versions, the Document Inspector and Compatibility Checker are two very helpful utilities. Both can be found in the Info section of the Backstage, as described in Chapter 2.

In addition, the Share section of the Backstage contains a Change File Type command that you may find easier to use than choosing Save As file formats.

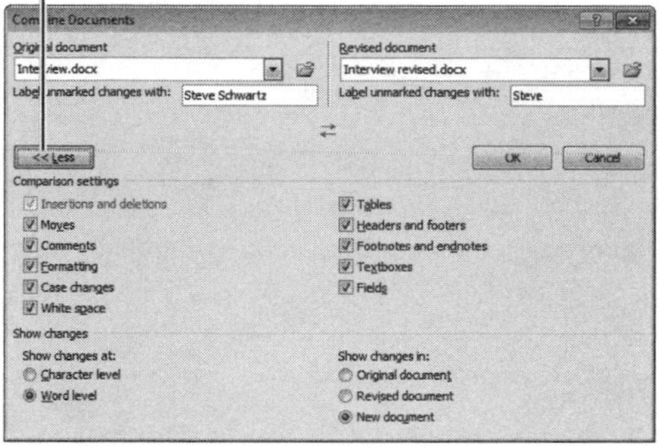

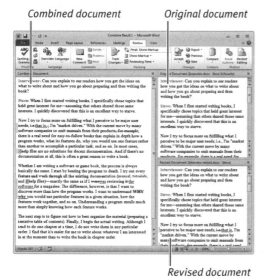

Show/hide options

Figure 7.11 Select the two documents, set options, and click OK.

Combined document   *Original document*

Revised document

Figure 7.12 The combined document appears in a new window. You can open the Reviewing Pane to process the revisions.

✔ Tip

- Creating a combined document does *not* save it to disk. If you'd like a permanent copy of the combined document, remember to save!

Combining Documents

If multiple reviewers are independently reviewing the same document, you can use the Combine command to merge their edits and comments (two documents at a time) into a single master document. Then the author or group leader can process the revisions, as explained previously in "Change Tracking."

To merge two documents:

1. On the Review tab, click the Compare icon in the Compare group and choose Combine from the drop-down menu.

   The Combine Documents dialog box appears (**Figure 7.11**).

2. Select the two documents from the drop-down lists.

   If a document isn't listed, click its Browse icon to locate the document.

3. If the bottom half of the dialog box is hidden, click the More button to reveal the procedure options.

4. At the bottom of the dialog box, select Show changes in: New document. Review the other options and then click OK.

   The combined document is created and displayed (**Figure 7.12**).

5. Save the combined document by clicking the File tab to go to the Backstage and then clicking Save As.

6. If more documents need to be merged with the new, combined document, repeat Steps 1–5, but specify the combined document saved in Step 5 as one of the documents.

7. *Optional:* To process the revisions, open the Reviewing Pane (see Figures 7.7 and 7.10) by clicking the Reviewing Pane icon and choosing a display option: Vertical or Horizontal.

Publishing Blog Entries

Another way to share written information is to publish it to a Web log (*blog*). Blog journals can be viewed in any browser. To create your own blog, you must register with a blog service provider, such as Windows Live Spaces (`http://spaces.msn.com`) or Blogger (`www.blogger.com`). Many providers host blogs without charge.

To configure Word for blog work:

1. If you haven't registered with a blog service, do so before proceeding.

2. The first time you issue a blog-related command in Word, the Register a Blog Account dialog box appears. Click Register Now.

3. In the New Blog Account dialog box (**Figure 7.13**), select your blog service from the drop-down list, and click Next.

4. In the New *service* Account dialog box (**Figure 7.14**), enter the user name and password for your blog account. Click the Remember Password check box.

5. Click the Picture Options button.
   The Picture Options dialog box appears (**Figure 7.15**).

6. Select your blog service from the Picture provider drop-down list and click OK.
   If your blog service isn't listed or your blog posts won't contain images, select None - Don't upload pictures.

7. Click OK to close the New *service* Account dialog box.

✔ Tip

■ If the Picture Options dialog box doesn't list your service, you may still be able to upload pictures to your blog. For instructions, see the blog service's Help pages.

Figure 7.13 Select your blog service. Click Next.

Figure 7.14 To enable Word to transmit blog posts to your account, enter your user name and password.

Figure 7.15 Select the blog's picture-hosting service from the drop-down list.

Entry title   Entry text

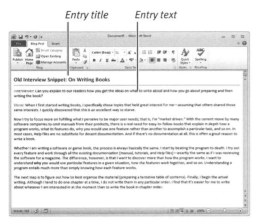

Figure 7.16 Enter a title for the entry and write the text.

Figure 7.17 Here's how the blog entry looks when viewed in a browser.

Figure 7.18 Tools for publishing posts, editing previous posts, and managing blog accounts can be found in the Blog group.

To create and publish a blog entry:

1. Click the File tab to go to the Backstage, and select New.

2. Select the Blog post icon in the Available Templates list, and then click Create.

    A blog post template appears. The Ribbon tabs and icons provide the tools to write, format, and post your blog entry.

3. Create the new blog entry by typing the entry text and replacing the title place-holder with a title (**Figure 7.16**).

4. When you're satisfied with the entry, click the Publish icon and choose Publish from the drop-down menu that appears.

    The new entry is posted to your blog (**Figure 7.17**).

5. To view your blog, click the Home Page icon in the Blog group.

✔ Tips

- You can also publish an existing Word document as a blog entry rather than starting from the template. Click the File tab, select Share, select Publish as Blog Post, and click the Publish as Blog Post button. Replace the title placeholder with a title and make any desired edits to the content. When you're satisfied with the entry, click the Publish icon and choose Publish from the drop-down menu.

- To edit a previously published blog entry, click Open Existing in the Blog group (**Figure 7.18**). In the Open Existing Post dialog box, select the entry you want to edit and click OK. Make the changes, and then publish it as you did before.

- To delete a blog post, use the tools provided by the blog service.

- To add, change, or delete blog accounts, click the Manage Accounts icon.

Part III:
Microsoft Excel

GETTING STARTED WITH EXCEL 2010

8

Excel is Office 2010's spreadsheet program. You use Excel to create, analyze, and manage documents called *workbooks* that contain text and numeric data. Workbooks can consist of simple lists (address books, club rosters, and collections) or complex calculations (bookkeeping systems, sales and expense tracking, engineering computations, and manufacturing measurements).

To get you started, this chapter presents the following essential Excel 2010 topics:

◆ Working with the Excel interface

◆ Understanding workbooks and worksheets

◆ Selecting cells and ranges

◆ Entering and editing data

◆ Reorganizing worksheets

◆ Filling cells

◆ Importing data

◆ Finding and replacing data

◆ Sorting data

◆ Naming cells and ranges

◆ Password-protecting workbooks

The Excel Interface

Before we jump into how to use Excel, take a moment to examine **Figure 8.1** (below). It shows many of the Excel interface components you'll be using. You'll note that some elements, such as the Ribbon, Quick Access Toolbar, and Backstage, can also be found in Word, PowerPoint, and Outlook.

Backstage. Click the File tab to go to the Backstage (**Figure 8.2**) to perform file-related activities, such as creating, opening, saving, and printing documents. Click Options to set Excel preferences. To open a document on which you've worked, click its filename in the Recent list. The Exit command can also be found in the Backstage.

File tab   Recent Documents list

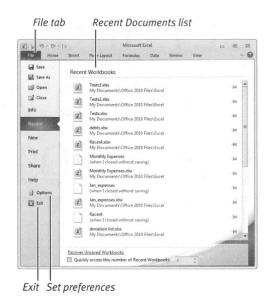

Exit   Set preferences

Figure 8.2 The Backstage.

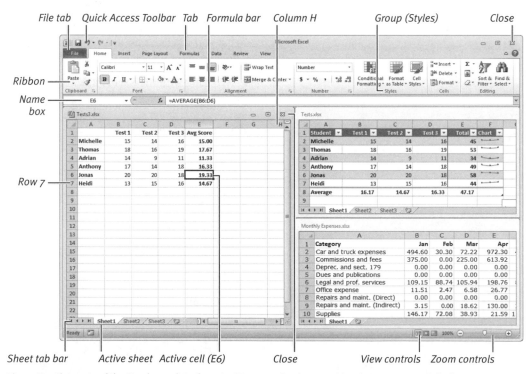

Figure 8.1 Elements of the Excel 2010 interface. In this example, three workbooks are open and tiled.

THE EXCEL INTERFACE

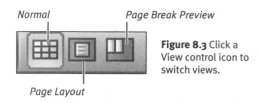

Normal *Page Break Preview*

Figure 8.3 Click a View control icon to switch views.

Page Layout

Quick Access Toolbar. Common commands are found here, such as Save, Undo, and Redo.

Ribbon. The Ribbon is what Office now uses rather than menus. Similar commands and procedures are listed together on a *tab*, such as Insert or View. Within a tab, procedures are further divided into *groups*, based on similarity of function. To perform a command, you switch to the appropriate tab by clicking its name and clicking the command's icon.

Sheet tab bar. A workbook can contain multiple worksheets (or *sheets*). This area of the document window displays the names of all worksheets in the current workbook. To switch worksheets, click the sheet's name.

Active sheet. This is the sheet that you're currently viewing and/or editing.

Columns and rows. A worksheet is a grid of columns and rows. Columns are designated by letter and rows are numbered. A *column* consists of all cells directly beneath a column letter. A *row* is the string of cells to the right of a row number.

View controls. Click an icon to switch views (**Figure 8.3**). You can also change views by selecting the View tab and clicking an icon in the Workbook Views group. Use Normal or Page Layout view to work with or view your data. Full Screen view is useful when you want to view a worksheet at the largest possible size (without the Ribbon). Before you print, you can switch to Page Break Preview to examine and manually adjust the page breaks.

Zoom controls. You can change the current magnification by dragging the slider, clicking + (increase) or – (decrease), or clicking the zoom percentage number.

Close. Workbooks and Excel each contain a close box that you can click to close an open workbook or to quit Excel, respectively.

Active cell. This is the currently selected cell (indicated by a heavy black border), named by combining the intersection of column and row. For example, E6 is in column E, row 6. The active cell name is shown in the name box, and the cell's column letter and row number are highlighted.

Name box. The name box performs a variety of functions, including displaying the name of the active cell and creating *names* (a descriptive name for a cell or range, such as SalesTax or Budget). Names are also referred to as *range names* and *named ranges*.

Formula bar. Data and formulas can be entered in the formula bar or directly into the active cell. The formula bar displays any formula or data contained in the active cell.

THE EXCEL INTERFACE

Workbooks and Worksheets

An Excel document consists of a single workbook containing one or more worksheets. A *worksheet* (or sheet) has numbered rows and lettered columns that form a grid. The intersection of a row and column is called a *cell* (**Figure 8.4**). You can enter text data, numeric data, or formulas into the cells. Unlike in other programs you may have used, data doesn't have to be entered from the top down, left to right. You can use any cells that you want, leaving blank rows and columns as best suits the data.

A setting in the General section of Excel Options (**Figure 8.5**) determines the initial number of worksheets in a new workbook. Depending on the data you're entering and analyzing, you can ignore all worksheets but the first or use the others for a completely different type of data or related data. Because Excel lets you perform calculations across worksheets within a workbook, you can also use one sheet to consolidate the data in other sheets. For example, in a bookkeeping workbook, you might collect each month's data in a separate sheet and use another sheet to calculate annual figures, based on the data in the monthly sheets.

Worksheets are managed using the *Sheet tab bar*, found in the bottom-left corner of every workbook window (**Figure 8.6**). To make a different worksheet active, you click its name. You can add, delete, and change the order of the sheets. You can also rename a sheet to make it easier to identify.

To rename a worksheet:

◆ Right-click the tab of the worksheet you want to rename and choose Rename from the context menu (**Figure 8.7**). Type a new name and press ⌷Enter⌷.

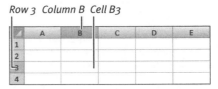

Row 3 Column B Cell B3

Figure 8.4 A worksheet is a grid composed of rows and columns.

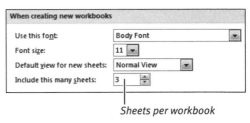

Sheets per workbook

Figure 8.5 To set Excel preferences (such as the number of sheets per workbook), click the File tab to go to the Backstage and then click Options.

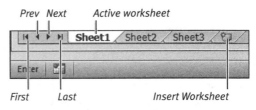

Prev Next Active worksheet

First Last Insert Worksheet

Figure 8.6 You use the Sheet tab bar to make a worksheet active and to manage your worksheets. Each worksheet is represented by a named tab. Click the arrow icons to view additional sheets.

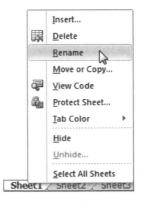

Figure 8.7 Right-click a worksheet's tab to reveal this context menu.

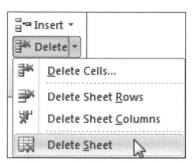

Figure 8.8 You can delete or insert sheets by choosing a command from the Delete or Insert icon.

Worksheet icon

Figure 8.9 To insert a new worksheet, ensure that Worksheet is selected and click OK.

Creating New Workbooks

Although you can continue to add sheets to a workbook, you'll want to create a *new* workbook whenever you begin a project:

◆ To immediately create a new standard workbook, press Ctrl N.

◆ To create a specific type of workbook, click the File tab and click New. In the Available Templates gallery, select Blank workbook, a template, or New from existing. Click the Create button.

To delete a worksheet:

◆ *Do either of the following:*
  ▲ Right-click the tab of the worksheet you want to delete and choose Delete from the context menu (see Figure 8.7).
  ▲ Switch to the Home tab, click the worksheet's tab in the Sheet tab bar (to make the worksheet active), and choose Delete Sheet from the Delete drop-down menu in the Cells group (**Figure 8.8**).

If the worksheet contains data, a warning dialog box appears. Otherwise, the worksheet is immediately deleted.

To insert a new worksheet:

◆ *Do one of the following:*
  ▲ Click the Insert Worksheet icon in the Sheet tab bar (see Figure 8.6) or press Shift F11 .
  ▲ Right-click a worksheet name in the Sheet tab bar and choose Insert from the context menu. On the General tab of the Insert dialog box (**Figure 8.9**), select Worksheet and click OK.
  ▲ Switch to the Home tab, and choose Insert Sheet from the Insert drop-down menu in the Cells group.

The new worksheet is appended to the end of the sheet list or inserted to the right of the currently selected sheet.

To change the order of worksheets:

◆ Drag the worksheet's name to a new position in the Sheet tab bar (see Figure 8.6). As you drag, a tiny triangle shows the sheet's position. Release the mouse button to complete the move.

WORKBOOKS AND WORKSHEETS

Cell and Range Selection

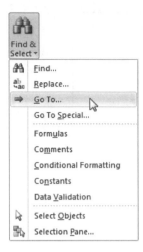

Whether you're preparing to enter, edit, or format data, the first step is to select a cell or cell range. Following are some cell-selection techniques.

To select cells:

◆ **Single cell.** *Do one of the following:*

▲ Scroll to bring the cell into view and then click the cell.

▲ Press a navigation key (such as ⬅,
➡, ⬆, ⬇, Tab, Shift Tab, Enter, or
Shift Enter) to move into the cell. See the Tips on the following page for other useful key combinations.

▲ On the Home tab, choose Go To (Ctrl G) from the Find & Select icon's menu in the Editing group (**Figure 8.10**). In the Go To dialog box (**Figure 8.11**), select or type the cell address or name (if a name has been assigned to the cell). Click OK.

▲ Type the cell address, range, or name in the name box (**Figure 8.12**) and press Enter.

▲ To find a cell based on its contents, choose Find from the Find & Select icon's drop-down menu (Figure 8.10). In the Find dialog box, enter the text, number, date, or time contained in the cell and click Find Next. When the desired cell is selected, click Close. See "Finding/Replacing Data," later in this chapter, for additional options.

Figure 8.10 To go to a cell address or range, choose Go To from the Find & Select menu.

Figure 8.11 To specify a destination, enter an address, range, or name in the Reference text box or select a recently visited address, range, or name.

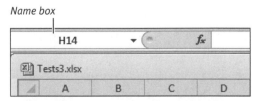

Figure 8.12 Type an address, range, or name in the name box.

CELL AND RANGE SELECTION

Anchor (B2)

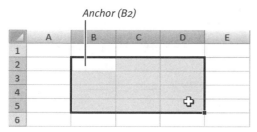

Figure 8.13 To select a range, click a cell in one corner of the range and drag to the opposite corner.

Click to select entire worksheet

Selected column (A)

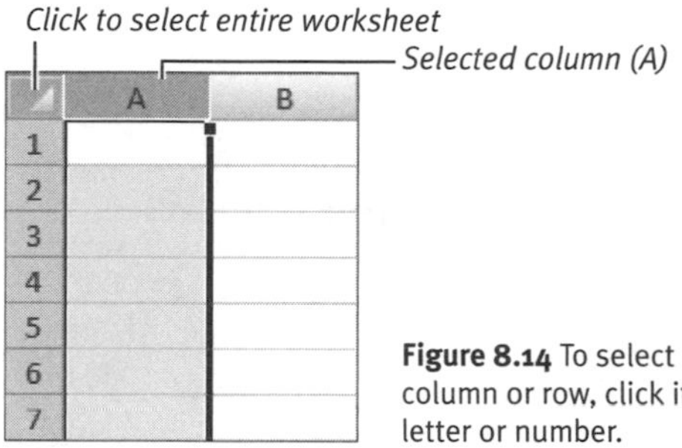

Figure 8.14 To select a column or row, click its letter or number.

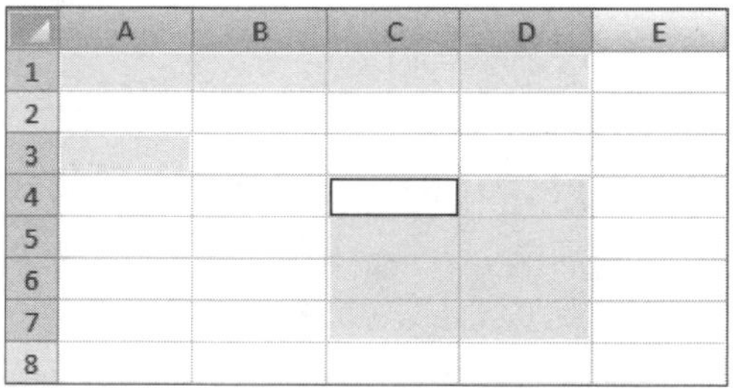

Figure 8.15 You can also select any combination of cells, ranges, rows, and columns (marked with light blue highlighting).

- ■ Press Ctrl End to select the last cell in the active area of the worksheet, Home to move to the first cell in the current row, or Ctrl Home to move to cell A1.

- ■ Press Ctrl and an arrow key to move to the next filled cell in the specified direction. If there are no other filled cells, the first or last cell in the row or column will be selected.

- ◆ **Contiguous cell range.** *Do one of the following:*
  - ▲ Click a cell in any corner of the range (called the *anchor*) and drag to the opposite corner to select the additional cells (**Figure 8.13**).
  - ▲ To select an entire column or row, click its letter or number (**Figure 8.14**).
  - ▲ To select the entire worksheet, click the intersection of the column and row headings (Figure 8.14).
  - ▲ On the Home tab, choose Go To (Ctrl G) from the Find & Select icon's menu in the Editing group (see Figure 8.10). In the Go To dialog box (see Figure 8.11), enter the cell range in the form

    start cell:end cell

    such as a1:d4. If you've named the range (see "Naming Cells and Ranges," later in this chapter), you can enter its name rather than the range. Click OK.
  - ▲ Enter the cell range or its name in the name box (see Figure 8.12) and press Enter.

- ◆ **Noncontiguous cells and ranges.** While pressing Ctrl, click or click-and-drag to select the cells, ranges, columns, and/or rows (**Figure 8.15**).

✔ Tips

- ■ If you need to regularly return to a cell or range, naming it will enable you to easily do so using the Go To command or the name box (see "Naming Cells and Ranges," later in this chapter).

- ■ You can speed the entry of new data by preselecting the destination range. After each entry, press Tab or Enter to move through the range in left-to-right or top-to-bottom fashion, respectively.

CELL AND RANGE SELECTION

Entering Data

A cell can contain one or more lines of text, a number, a date, a time, or a formula that results in one of these data types. To enter data into a cell, follow the instructions below. (Formulas are discussed in Chapter 10.)

To enter data into a cell:

1. Select the cell into which you want to enter data, making it the active cell.

   You can select a cell by clicking in it. For other cell-selection methods, see the previous section.

2. *Do one of the following:*

   ▲ **Text.** Type or paste the text.

   ▲ **Number.** Type or paste the number.

   ▲ **Date.** Type a date in a recognizable format, such as 9-12-06, 09/12/2006, or 12-Sep-06. Date components must be separated by a slash (/) or hyphen (–) character.

   ▲ **Time.** Type a time in a recognizable format, such as 4:, 4:07, 4:07:53, 4:07 p, 4 pm, or 16:07. Time components must be separated by a colon (:).

   When a 12-hour time is entered, such as 10:43, it is assumed to be AM. To indicate PM, you must enter the time in military (24-hour) format or follow the time with p or pm, such as 6:15 p or 6:15 pm. Morning times can optionally be followed by an *a* or *am*, such as 7:15 a or 7:15 am.

3. To complete the entry, click another cell or press a navigation key, such as Enter or Tab. See **Table 8.1** for options.

Table 8.1

Keystrokes to Complete a Cell Entry	
KEYSTROKE	**DIRECTION**
Tab, →	Right
Shift Tab, ←	Left
Enter, ↓	Down
Shift Enter, ↑	Up

Using Entry AutoComplete

When you enter text or a combination of text and numbers into a cell, Excel checks the current column for matching entries. If one is found, Excel proposes it. To accept this AutoComplete entry, press Enter. To ignore it, continue typing.

Changing the Behavior of Enter

Normally, pressing Enter when you finish entering data into a cell causes the cursor to move down, selecting the cell directly beneath the current cell. However, if you like, you can change the behavior of the Enter key:

1. Click the File tab. Click Options.

2. In the Excel Options dialog box, select the Advanced category.

3. Select a cursor-movement direction from the Direction drop-down list. (This is the first item in the Editing options section).

4. Click OK.

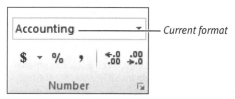

Figure 8.16 You can force line breaks within a cell.

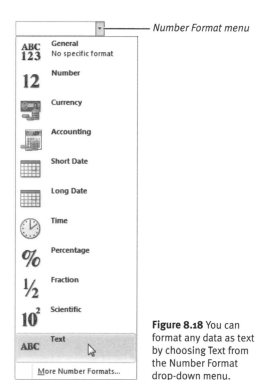

Figure 8.17 You can see the formatting for the active cell in the Number group on the Home tab.

Figure 8.18 You can format any data as text by choosing Text from the Number Format drop-down menu.

✔ Tips

■ If a cell shows a string of # characters (#####), it means that the number in the cell is too large to display. To display the complete number, widen the column (see Chapter 9).

■ To enter multiple lines of text, numbers, dates, or times into a cell (**Figure 8.16**), press Alt Enter to insert a line break between each pair of lines.

■ To enter today's date into a cell, press Ctrl ;. To enter the current time, press Ctrl Shift ;.

■ If you want the data to display differently, select the cell and apply formatting (see Chapter 9). The current formatting for the active cell is shown in the Number Format box in the Number group on the Home tab (**Figure 8.17**).

■ If you enter a number that begins with one or more zeros, Excel discards the zeros. This presents a problem with some ZIP codes, for example. To force Excel to retain leading zeros, choose Text from the Number Format menu (**Figure 8.18**) in the Number group before entering the data.

■ Excel distinguishes between data *display* (determined by formatting) and what is *stored*. When performing calculations, Excel uses the stored data, regardless of what's shown in the cells. For example, when calculating a sales tax of 7.75% on a $12.50 purchase, the result is 0.9675. When formatted as Currency, the number displays as $0.97, the result rounded to two decimal places. If you create a formula in another cell that adds the sale amount ($12.48) to the sales tax, the result is 13.46875—*not* $13.47.

Editing Data

As you create and work with a worksheet, you can correct errors, update data with new values, and revise formulas.

To edit the contents of a cell:

1. Select the cell whose contents you want to change.

2. You can edit in the formula bar or in the cell itself. To set the text insertion mark and begin editing, click in the formula bar or double-click in the cell.

   If the cell contains a formula, the formula appears (**Figure 8.19**). Otherwise, the data is shown.

3. Make the desired changes.

4. To finish the edits, *do one of the following:*

   ▲ Press a navigation key, such as Enter, to move to another cell (see Table 8.1).

   ▲ Click another cell.

   ▲ Click the check mark (✔) icon in the formula bar (**Figure 8.19**).

✔ Tips

■ You can use the same editing techniques you use when modifying other kinds of Windows documents. For example, press Backspace to delete the character to the left, press Del or Delete to delete the character to the right, or press any of these keys to delete selected text. To replace a string, select it and type the replacement or delete the string and then type.

■ The cursor keys are active while editing. Press ← or → to move one character in the desired direction; press Ctrl ← or Ctrl → to move one string at a time.

■ To rearrange data within a cell, you can cut (Ctrl X) selected data, set the text insertion mark where you want to move the data, and then paste (Ctrl V).

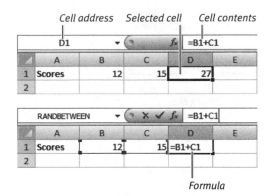

Figure 8.19 When you select a cell (top), its contents are shown in the formula bar. When you set the text insertion mark for editing (bottom), the result is replaced in the cell by the actual formula.

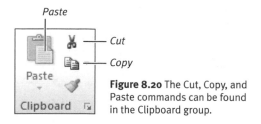

Figure 8.20 The Cut, Copy, and Paste commands can be found in the Clipboard group.

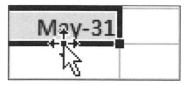

Figure 8.21 When the cursor changes to this symbol, you can drag the selected cell(s) to a new location.

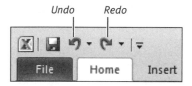

Figure 8.22 To undo your last action, click the Undo icon. To undo multiple actions, choose an action from the Undo icon's drop-down menu.

Reorganizing a Worksheet

In addition to editing cell contents, you can rearrange the data. You can move cells to other locations, add or delete cells (automatically shifting the affected surrounding cells), and insert or delete rows and columns.

To move cells to another location:

1. Select the cell or range you want to move.

2. *Do one of the following:*

   ▲ Cut the cell/range by pressing Ctrl X or by clicking the Cut icon in the Clipboard group on the Home tab (**Figure 8.20**). Select the destination cell or the cell in the upper-left corner of the destination range. Press Enter, press Ctrl V, or click the Paste icon in the Clipboard group.

   ▲ Move the cursor over the border of the selected cell or range (**Figure 8.21**). Drag the selected cell to the destination cell or the selected range to the cell that will serve as the upper-left corner of the destination range. Release the mouse button to complete the move.

Neither procedure *deletes* the original cells. Their data is simply moved to the new location.

✔ Tips

■ Whether performed by cut-and-paste or drag-and-drop, cell/range moves are *destructive*. If you select a destination that already contains data, the old data will be replaced by the moved data. If this happens unintentionally, immediately click the Undo icon in the Quick Access Toolbar (**Figure 8.22**) or press Ctrl Z.

■ To move data between worksheets, use cut-and-paste.

To copy cells to another location:

1. Select the cell or range you want to copy.

2. *Do one of the following:*

   ▲ Copy the cell/range by pressing Ctrl C or by clicking the Copy icon in the Clipboard group on the Home tab (see Figure 8.20). Select the destination cell or the cell in the upper-left corner of the destination range. Press Enter, press Ctrl V, or click the Paste icon in the Clipboard group on the Home tab.

   ▲ While pressing Ctrl, move the cursor over the border of the selected cell or range. A tiny plus symbol is added to the cursor (**Figure 8.23**). Drag the cell/range to the destination cell or to the cell in the upper-left corner of the destination range.

✔ Tip

■ Rather than just clicking Paste, you can click the arrow beneath Paste to reveal a gallery of Paste options (**Figure 8.24**). If you rest the cursor on an option, a ToolTip explains the option and a preview appears on the worksheet.

To insert cells:

1. Select the cell or range where you want to insert new, blank cells.

2. *Do one of the following:*

   ▲ On the Home tab, click the Insert icon in the Cells group and choose Insert Cells (**Figure 8.25**).

   ▲ Right-click the cell or range and choose Insert from the context menu.

3. In the Insert dialog box (**Figure 8.26**), select Shift cells right or Shift cells down, and then click OK.

   Cells affected by the insertion are shifted to make room for the inserted cell(s).

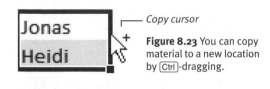

— Copy cursor

Figure 8.23 You can copy material to a new location by Ctrl-dragging.

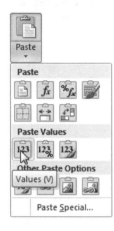

Figure 8.24 You can choose advanced Paste options from this gallery.

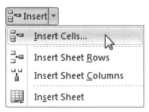

Figure 8.25 Choose Insert Cells from the Insert menu.

Figure 8.26 When inserting new cells, you must specify how surrounding cells will be affected.

Reorganizing a Worksheet

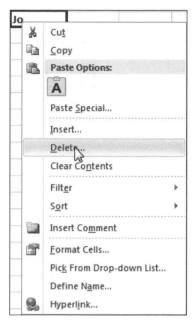

Figure 8.27 Right-click a selected cell or range, and then choose Delete.

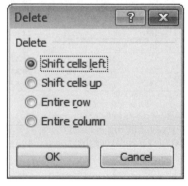

Figure 8.28 Specify how neighboring cells should shift in response to the cell or range deletion.

To delete cells:

1. Select the cell or range you want to delete.

2. *Do one of the following:*
   ▲ On the Home tab, click the Delete icon in the Cells group and choose Delete Cells from the drop-down menu.
   ▲ Right-click the cell or range and choose Delete from the context menu that appears (**Figure 8.27**).

3. In the Delete dialog box (**Figure 8.28**), select Shift cells left or Shift cells up, and then click OK.

   Surrounding cells affected by the deletion are shifted to close the space left by the deleted cell(s).

To insert a row:

1. Select the row where you want to insert a new row.

2. *Do one of the following:*
   ▲ On the Home tab, click the Insert icon in the Cells group (see Figure 8.25).
   ▲ Right-click any cell in the selected row and choose Insert from the context menu (Figure 8.27).

   The new row appears. The selected row and all those beneath it shift down one.

✔ Tips

■ You can also select a single cell in the row where you want to insert a new row. However, you must then choose Insert Sheet Rows from the Insert icon's menu (see Figure 8.25) or select Entire row in the Insert dialog box (see Figure 8.26).

■ To insert *multiple* rows, select as many rows as you want new rows and click the Insert icon. You can also right-click any cell in the selected rows and choose Insert from the context menu (Figure 8.27).

REORGANIZING A WORKSHEET

To insert a column:

1. Select the column where you want to insert a new column (**Figure 8.29**, top).

2. *Do either of the following:*
   - ▲ On the Home tab, click the Insert icon in the Cells group (see Figure 8.25).
   - ▲ Right-click any cell in the selected column and choose Insert from the context menu (see Figure 8.27).

   The new column appears (**Figure 8.29**, bottom). Other columns affected by the insertion shift to the right.

✔ Tips

- You can also select a single cell in the column where you want to insert the new column. However, you must then choose Insert Sheet Columns from the Insert icon's menu or select Entire column in the Insert dialog box (see Figure 8.26).

- You can insert *multiple* columns by selecting the columns (or a cell in each column) where you want to add the new columns in Step 1 (**Figure 8.30**).

To delete a row:

1. Select the row that you want to delete.

2. *Do one of the following:*
   - ▲ On the Home tab, click the Delete icon in the Cells group.
   - ▲ Right-click any cell in the selected row and choose Delete (see Figure 8.27).

   The row is deleted. Other rows that are affected by the deletion shift up to close the space.

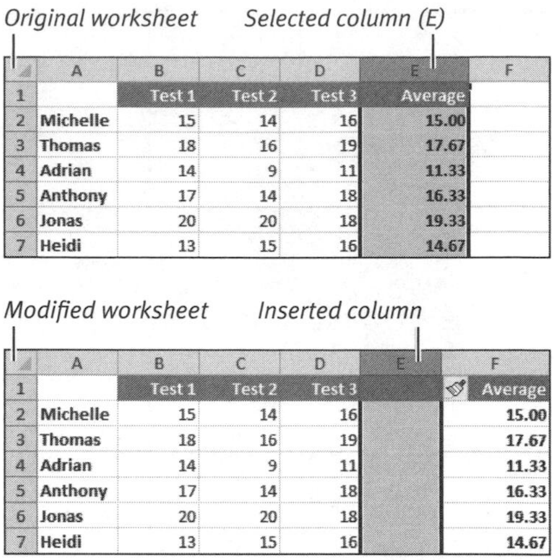

Original worksheet   *Selected column (E)*

Modified worksheet   *Inserted column*

Figure 8.29 Suppose that you need to record a fourth test. When you select column E and issue the Insert command, the original column E shifts to the right to become column F.

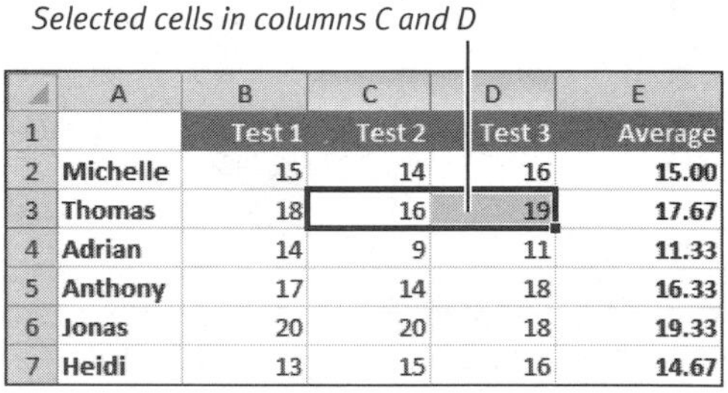

Selected cells in columns C and D

Figure 8.30 You can also begin a column or row insertion by selecting single cells or a range. In this example, to insert new columns in C and D, it's sufficient to select any pair of cells that spans both columns.

Insertion and Deletion Considerations

When inserting or deleting cells, rows, or columns, you must consider the impact on your worksheet. Insertions and deletions often cause other data to move:

◆ When you insert a cell, the current cell must either move to the right or down. Other cells to the right or below the inserted cell will also shift to the right or down.

◆ When you delete a cell, all cells directly below or to the right of the deleted cell must shift up or left to fill the hole created by the deletion.

◆ When you insert a new row, the current row automatically moves down to make room for the new row. Rows below the current row also move down one row.

◆ When you insert a column, the current column and all columns to its right shift one column to the right.

The impact of an insertion or deletion on data *elsewhere* in the worksheet must be considered. For instance, if a worksheet contains a single data array or table, such as an address book, inserting or deleting a row or column will have little impact. And if you discover that you entered the same data in two cells in a row (causing the row to have an extra entry), deleting a duplicate and choosing Shift cells left quickly fixes the problem.

But when a worksheet is complex and has multiple data arrays, an insertion or deletion is liable to create problems elsewhere in the sheet. If this is the case, the safest approach may be to manually rearrange the data rather than make insertions or deletions.

✔ Tips

■ You can also select a cell in the row you want to delete. However, you must then choose Delete Sheet Rows from the Delete icon or select Entire row in the Delete dialog box (see Figure 8.28).

■ To delete *multiple* rows, select the rows (or a cell in each row) that you want to delete in Step 1.

To delete a column:

1. Select the column that you want to delete.

2. *Do one of the following:*
   ▲ On the Home tab, click the Delete icon in the Cells group.
   ▲ Right-click any cell in the selected column and choose Delete from the context menu (see Figure 8.27).

   The column is deleted, and all columns to its right shift to the left.

✔ Tips

■ You can also select a single cell in the column you want to delete. However, you must then choose Delete Sheet Columns from the Delete icon or select Entire column in the Delete dialog box (see Figure 8.28).

■ To delete *multiple* columns, select the columns (or a cell in each column) that you want to delete in Step 1.

■ Deleting cells, rows, or columns isn't the same as clearing their contents. To clear selected cells, switch to the Home tab and choose a command from the Clear icon's menu in the Editing group.

■ Deleting cells, rows, and columns are destructive processes. Because every row and column extends to the end or bottom of the worksheet, be sure not to accidentally delete data that isn't in view.

REORGANIZING A WORKSHEET

Filling Cells

Two situations occur in worksheet creation that can be simplified using the Fill feature:

◆ You have a text constant, numeric constant, or formula that you want to repeat many times in the current row or column.

◆ You have or are creating a series of cell entries in the current row or column that you want to extend.

To fill adjacent cells with a constant:

◆ *Do either of the following:*

▲ Select the cell that contains the text or numeric constant. Move the cursor over the lower-right corner of the cell, click the *fill handle* (**Figure 8.31**), and drag in the direction that you want to fill (**Figure 8.32**).

▲ Select the cell with the text or numeric constant and the cells you want to fill. On the Home tab, choose the fill direction from the Fill icon's menu in the Editing group (**Figure 8.33**).

The cells fill with the constant.

✔ Tips

■ To *duplicate* a cell regardless of the type of data it contains (text, number, date, or time), select the cell immediately to the right or below it and press ⌃R or ⌃D, respectively.

■ You can perform a drag fill in any direction: right, left, down, or up.

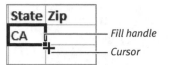

Figure 8.31 You can fill cells by dragging.

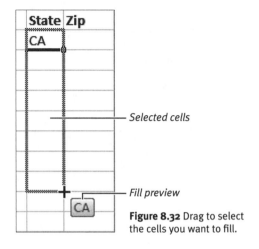

Figure 8.32 Drag to select the cells you want to fill.

Figure 8.33 You can also perform a fill by choosing a direction from the Fill menu.

Formula in E2

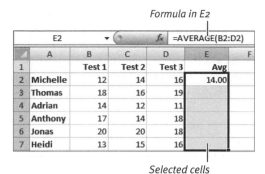

Selected cells

Figure 8.34 Select the cell that contains the formula (E2), as well as the cells you want to fill (E3:E7).

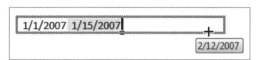

Figure 8.35 This series expands in 14-day increments.

Auto Fill Options icon

Figure 8.36 The Auto Fill Options menu.

- When continuing a series, select enough data to enable Excel to discern the nature of the series. In some cases, such as a day name, month name, or numbered text (Quarter 1, Score 1, or Team 1, for example), *one* item may be sufficient.

- For more complex series (especially numerical ones), you can choose Series from the Fill icon's menu (Figure 8.33) and set options in the Series dialog box. In general, however, you'll be happier if one of the previously described methods works. The Series dialog box can be seriously confusing.

To fill adjacent cells with a formula:

◆ *Do either of the following:*

   ▲ Select the cell with the formula. Click the fill handle and drag in the direction that you want to fill (see Figures 8.31–8.32).

   ▲ Select the cell with the formula, as well as the cells you want to fill (**Figure 8.34**). On the Home tab, click the Fill icon in the Editing group and choose a fill direction: Down, Right, Up, or Left (see Figure 8.33).

   The cells fill with the formula. Note that *relative cell references* (see Chapter 10) in the formula are automatically adjusted in the filled cells.

To continue a series into adjacent cells:

1. If the series doesn't already exist, begin it by typing at least two adjacent entries in a row or column.

   For example, for invoice numbers starting with 1050, you would enter 1050 and 1051. For company divisions, you could type Div1 and Div2, Div. 1 and Div. 2, or Division 1 and Division 2. For days of the week, you could enter Sunday and Monday or Sun and Mon.

2. Select two or more adjacent cells containing members of the series. Drag the fill handle of the rightmost or lowest cell in the direction you want to fill (**Figure 8.35**). As you drag, Excel shows the data each cell will contain.

   Series data fills the cells.

✔ Tips

- When expanding certain series such as dates, an Auto Fill Options icon appears (**Figure 8.36**). Click it to set a fill specification for the series. If you drag-extend the series using the *right* mouse button, similar options appear in a context menu.

FILLING CELLS

Importing Data

You don't have to manually enter the data in every worksheet. If the data exists elsewhere, such as in a table on the Web, in another program, or in a properly formatted text file, you can *import* the data into a new or existing worksheet. Following are examples of common data-importing scenarios.

To import data from a Web table:

1. On the Data tab, click the From Web icon in the Get External Data group.

   A New Web Query dialog box appears.

2. In the Address box (**Figure 8.37**), type or paste the URL for the Web page that contains the data and click Go. (If you recently viewed the page, you may be able to select its URL from the Address box's drop-down menu.)

   The Web page is fetched from the Internet and displayed in the dialog box.

3. Each table on the page is marked with an arrow enclosed in a yellow box. Click the box for each table that you want to import (**Figure 8.38**) and click Import.

   The Import Data dialog box appears (**Figure 8.39**), asking where you want to import the data. By default, the active cell on the current worksheet is proposed.

4. *Select one of the following:*

   ▲ **Existing worksheet.** Specify the starting cell to receive the imported data by typing its address in the box or by clicking the cell on the worksheet.

   ▲ **New worksheet.** Excel will create a new worksheet in the current workbook and import the data into a range beginning with cell A1.

5. Click OK.

   Each table you selected in Step 3 is imported (**Figure 8.40**).

Page address   Select a recently viewed page

Figure 8.37 Enter a page address in the Address box at the top of the New Web Query dialog box.

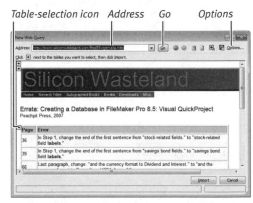

Table-selection icon   Address   Go   Options

Figure 8.38 Click the icon beside each table that you want to import.

Figure 8.39 Specify a destination for the imported data and click OK.

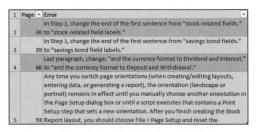

Figure 8.40 Here's the imported data (after applying text wrap to column B and formatting the data set as a table).

IMPORTING DATA

Figure 8.41 To retain formatting, select a Formatting option in the Web Query Options dialog box.

✔ Tips

- After entering a URL in the Address box (see Figures 8.37–8.38), you can interact with the fetched page. You can follow links by clicking them; enter your user name and password (for sites that require a login); and click buttons at the top of the dialog box to go backward or forward, refresh the page, or stop.

- To import data with its original formatting intact, click the Options button at the top of the New Web Query dialog box (see Figure 8.38). In the Formatting section of the Web Query Options dialog box (**Figure 8.41**), select Rich text formatting only or Full HTML formatting, and then click OK.

- Another way to retain a Web table's formatting is to open the page in a Web browser, drag to select the table, and copy (Ctrl C) the data. Select a destination cell in the worksheet and then paste (Ctrl V). See **Figure 8.42** for an example.

- Additional options for a Web import can be viewed by clicking the Properties button in the Import Data dialog box (see Figure 8.39).

IMPORTING DATA

	A	B
1	Page	Error
2	36	In Step 1, change the end of the first sentence from "stock-related fields." to "stock-related field **labels**."
3	39	In Step 1, change the end of the first sentence from "savings bond fields." to "savings bond field **labels**."
4	66	Last paragraph, change: "and the currency format to Dividend and Interest." to "and the currency format to **Deposit** and **Withdrawal**."
5	93	Any time you switch page orientations (when creating/editing layouts, entering data, or generating a report), the orientation (landscape or portrait) remains in effect until you manually choose another orientation in the Page Setup dialog box or until a script executes that contains a Print Setup step that sets a new orientation. After you finish creating the Stock Report layout, you should choose File > Page Setup and reset the orientation to portrait.

Figure 8.42 When moved into a worksheet via copy-and-paste, a Web table retains its fonts, styles, colors, and cell shadings. This can also be achieved by selecting Full HTML formatting in the Web Query Options dialog box.

To export data from another program in Excel format:

1. Open the document in its creating application, such as a database, a spreadsheet, or an address book utility.

2. *Optional:* Select the records (or portion of the document) that you want to use in Excel. If possible, rearrange the data fields to match the order in which you want them to appear in the worksheet.

3. Use the program's Export, Save As, or equivalent command to save a copy of the data as an *Excel (.xls or .xlsx) worksheet file* (**Figure 8.43**).

   Note, however, that not all programs offer this capability.

4. In Excel, click the File tab to go to the Backstage, click Open, and open the exported data file (**Figure 8.44**).

   Alternatively, you may be able to open the file by simply clicking or double-clicking it.

✔ Tips

- The exported data may require cleanup in Excel. For instance, you may need to add or edit column heads, rearrange the columns and change their widths, and add appropriate number and date formatting.

- Most Export and Save As procedures do not export formulas. In general, the *results* of such calculations are exported. If you intend to work with and extend the data in Excel, you'll probably want to recreate the formulas. On the other hand, if the reason you exported the data was so you could use Excel to analyze or chart it, working with the export as is may suffice.

Export filename

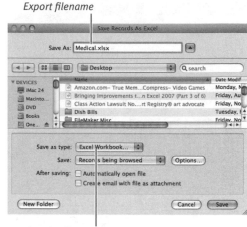

Excel as the file type

Figure 8.43 In FileMaker Pro (Mac version shown), any database can be exported as an Excel file.

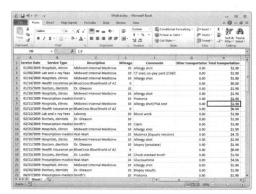

Figure 8.44 Here's the exported database opened in Excel 2010.

IMPORTING DATA

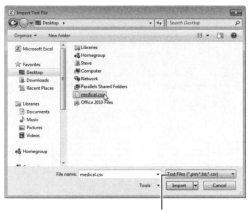

Display these file types

Figure 8.45 Select the exported data file from the files listed in the Import Text File dialog box (Windows 7 shown).

Field-arrangement description

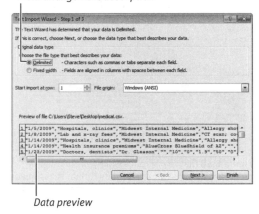

Data preview

Figure 8.46 Examine the data in the preview area and ensure that the correct field-export description is selected.

To export data from another program as a text file:

1. Open the document in its creating application, such as a database, spreadsheet, or address book utility.

2. *Optional:* Select the records (or portion of the document) that you want to use in Excel. If possible, rearrange the data fields to match the order in which you want them to appear in the worksheet.

3. Use the program's Export, Save As, or equivalent command to save a copy of the data as a *tab-delimited* or a *comma-delimited text file.*

   The program may refer to these file types as *tab-separated* and *comma-separated*.

4. In Excel, switch to the Data tab and click the From Text icon in the Get External Data group.

   The Import Text File dialog box appears (**Figure 8.45**).

5. Navigate to the drive/folder that contains the exported data file.

6. *Do one of the following:*
   ▲ If the exported data file appears in the file list, select it and click Import (or Open).
   ▲ If the export file is *not* present in the file list, select All Files from the file-type list (Figure 8.45). Select the export file in the file list and click Import (or Open).

7. In Step 1 of the Text Import Wizard (**Figure 8.46**), ensure that Delimited is selected. Examine the data preview in the bottom of the window, verifying that it is the correct file and displays properly. Click Next to continue.

continues on next page

IMPORTING DATA

8. In Step 2 of the wizard (**Figure 8.47**), ensure that the correct data delimiter is checked. (Data in the Data preview section will be correctly divided into fields when the right delimiter is selected.) Click Next to continue.

9. *Optional:* In Step 3 of the wizard (**Figure 8.48**), you can specify a format for the data in each field. Select the field in the Data preview and click the appropriate Column data format radio button.

   Note that General format is appropriate for most types of data, including dates.

10. *Optional:* If you decide not to import certain fields, select each field in the Data preview and click the Do not import column (skip) radio button.

11. Click Finish.

   The Import Data dialog box appears (see Figure 8.39).

12. *Do one of the following:*

    ▲ To open the file in the current worksheet, select Existing worksheet and specify the starting cell in which to receive the data.

    ▲ To open the file in a new sheet in the workbook, select New worksheet.

13. Click OK to import the data into Excel.

✔ Tips

■ Excel can also import data from files with *fixed-width fields* (see Figure 8.46). Some programs, especially very old database applications, store data in fixed-width fields. When originally creating the file, you had to specify the maximum number of characters for each field. When you entered data but failed to use the allotted characters for a field, the program simply padded the field with spaces.

Select the delimiter character

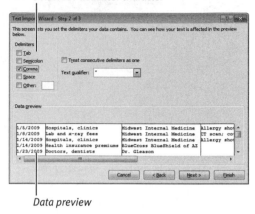

Data preview

Figure 8.47 Select the delimiter character that was used to separate fields in the export file.

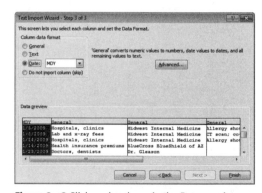

Figure 8.48 Click each column in the Data preview area to ensure that an appropriate format is assigned.

■ Excel can also open comma-separated value (*CSV*) files *directly*, bypassing the Text Import Wizard. Instead of clicking the From Text icon in Step 4, click the File tab, click Open, set the file type to Text Files, and open the .csv file.

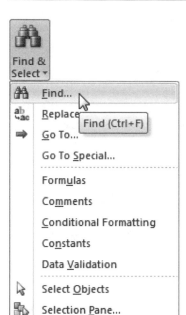

Figure 8.49 Find, Replace, Go To, and Select commands can be chosen from the Find & Select menu.

Show/hide options

Figure 8.50 The Find and Replace dialog box (with options displayed).

Finding/Replacing Data

Although you can scroll through a worksheet to find a particular string (such as a label, data, a cell reference, or a formula element), you may be able to use the Find feature to quickly locate the item. You can optionally replace any found string with another string.

To perform a Find:

1. To restrict the search to a range, select the range. Otherwise, click the cell in which you'd like to begin the search.

2. On the Home tab, choose Find from the Find & Select icon's drop-down menu in the Editing group (**Figure 8.49**) or press Ctrl F.

   The Find and Replace dialog box appears (**Figure 8.50**).

3. Enter a search string in the Find what box.

4. *Optional:* If the additional search options aren't visible, click the Options button to display them. You can set any combination of the following options:

   ▲ **Within.** Indicate whether you want to search within the current worksheet or all sheets in the workbook.

   ▲ **Search.** Specify whether the search will proceed across rows and down (By Rows) or down columns and across (By Columns).

   ▲ **Look in.** Specify the cells to be searched. Choose *Formulas* to consider all cells, *Values* to search all cells except those containing a formula, or *Comments* to search only within comments (ignoring cell contents).

   ▲ **Match case.** When this option is enabled, capitalization within a cell must match that of the search string.

continues on next page

▲ **Match entire cell contents.** Cell contents must exactly match the search string. For example, searching for `Microsoft` will find cells that contain `Microsoft` but ignore `Microsoft Corporation`.

Unless you check this option, a match can be found *anywhere* within a cell. For instance, searching for 3 would match 3, 7.23, 1:37, 5/3/2005, A32, and =B7-G23.

▲ **Format.** To include formatting in the Find criteria, click the Format button and choose one of these options from the drop-down menu (**Figure 8.51**):

Format. Specify format settings in the Find Format dialog box.

Choose Format From Cell. Using the eyedropper cursor, click a cell whose formatting will serve as the criterion.

Clear Find Format. Choose this option to remove previously chosen formatting as a criterion.

5. *Do one of the following:*

▲ Click Find Next to go to the first match (if any are present). Continue clicking Find Next to step through the matches.

▲ Click Find All to display a list of all matches in the bottom of the dialog box (**Figure 8.52**). Click any match to go to that cell.

6. When you're finished, click Close.

✔ Tips

■ To perform a simple search, hide the options in the Find and Replace dialog box by clicking the Options button, and then click Close. Issue the Find command again, enter a search string in the Find and Replace dialog box, and click Find Next or Find All. The search is performed by rows, identifies partial matches, and searches in every cell.

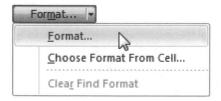

Figure 8.51 To add or remove formatting as a match criterion, click the Format button and choose a command.

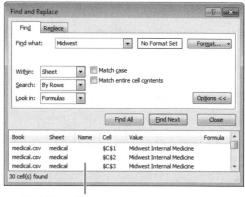

Find All results

Figure 8.52 When you click Find All, matching cells are displayed in a scrolling list.

■ Another way to limit the scope of a Find is to first choose a selection command from the Find & Select icon's drop-down menu (see Figure 8.49).

■ The Find and Replace procedures support the use of *wildcards* as criteria. Use the ? wildcard to replace a single character and * to replace multiple (or 0) characters. For example, you could enter ba?k to find back, balk, bank, bark, and bask. Enter John* to find John, Johns, Johnson, and Johnston.

Show/hide other options

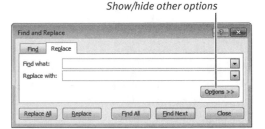

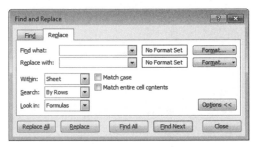

Figure 8.53 The Find and Replace dialog box with options hidden (top) and displayed (bottom).

✔ Tips

- When the Find and Replace dialog box is open, you can switch freely between its modes by clicking the Find or the Replace tab. In fact, a Replace is frequently preceded by a Find, allowing you to first determine if there is anything to replace.

- When making a replacement without checking Match entire cell contents, you will only replace the matching portion of a cell's contents. For example, if you search for `corp` with the intent of replacing it with `corporation`, `scorpio` will be replaced by `scorporationio`.

- You can also use the Find and Replace dialog box to replace formatting without changing cell contents. Leave the Find what and Replace with boxes empty, and set Format options for both.

To perform a Find/Replace:

1. To restrict the Find/Replace to a range, select the range. Otherwise, click the cell in which you'd like to start the search.

2. Open the Find and Replace dialog box by doing one of the following:
   - ▲ On the Home tab, choose Replace from the Find & Select icon's menu in the Editing group (see Figure 8.49) or press Ctrl H.
   - ▲ On the Home tab, choose Find from the Find & Select icon's drop-down menu in the Editing group (see Figure 8.49) or press Ctrl F. In the Find and Replace dialog box, click the Replace tab.

   The Find and Replace dialog box is ready to receive search criteria (**Figure 8.53**).

3. Enter criteria by performing Steps 3–4 of the previous procedure. Enter a replacement string in the Replace with box.

   Note that Format can be set separately for the Find and Replace strings.

4. *Do one of the following:*
   - ▲ To make the replacement decision individually for each match, click Find Next. Excel moves to the first match, if one is found.

     To replace the matching contents with the Replace with string, click Replace. Or to ignore the current match, click Find Next. Excel selects the next matching cell. Repeat for each additional match.
   - ▲ To simultaneously perform all replacements, click Find All. Review the matches in the bottom of the dialog box and click Replace All. Click OK to close the dialog box and view the results of the Replace All.

5. Click Close.

Sorting Data

To maintain data in a particular order (arranging entries in an address list by last name, phone number, or ZIP code, for example), you can *sort* the data. You can sort any column in ascending or descending order, based on the contents of that column. If surrounding data is related to the data in the selected column (created as records), data in the adjacent columns can also be reorganized to match that of the sorted column.

To sort a column or data array:

1. Select the column you want to sort or by which you want to sort all surrounding data (**Figure 8.54**).

2. On the Home tab, click the Sort & Filter icon and choose a sort order, such as Sort A to Z, Sort Smallest to Largest, or Sort Oldest to Newest (**Figure 8.55**).

   The options presented vary with the type of data in the selected column. If there are no adjacent columns on either side of the selected column, the column is sorted as specified.

3. Otherwise, if columns *are* adjacent to the selected column, the Sort Warning dialog box appears (**Figure 8.56**). *Select one of these options:*

   ▲ **Expand the selection.** Treat all contiguous columns (on both sides of the selected column) as a data array.

   ▲ **Continue with the current selection.** Sort only the selected column, leaving any surrounding columns unchanged.

4. Click Sort to sort the data as specified.

Selected column

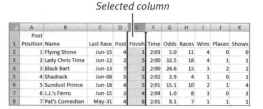

Figure 8.54 Start by selecting the column to sort.

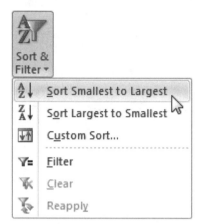

Figure 8.55 Choose a sort command from the Sort & Filter menu.

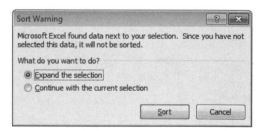

Figure 8.56 To clarify your selection, indicate whether you want to sort the entire array or only the selected column.

SORTING DATA

Figure 8.57 Choose Custom Sort to sort on multiple fields. In this example, a medical expenses data array is sorted on Service Type and then—within Service Type—by Description.

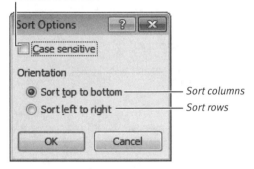

Figure 8.58 Set additional options in the Sort Options dialog box.

■ Another way to analyze a data array is to *filter* it by hiding selected rows (records) or showing only those that satisfy a criterion, such as after 5/1/10:

▲ To add filter capabilities to a single column (whether or not it's part of an array), select the column, switch to the Home tab, click the Sort & Filter icon in the Editing group, and choose Filter from the drop-down menu.

▲ To add filter capabilities to all columns in a data array, select the entire array or any individual cell in the array, and choose Filter from the Sort & Filter icon's drop-down menu.

See Chapter 11 for more information about applying and using filters.

✔ Tips

■ To perform a more complex sort, choose Custom Sort from the Sort & Filter drop-down menu, and then set options in the Sort dialog box (**Figure 8.57**). Options include sorting on multiple columns (last name *and* first name, for example) and performing sorts based on cell or font color.

To sort by rows (rather than by columns) or to use letter case in a sort, click the Options button in the Sort dialog box. Set options in the Sort Options dialog box (**Figure 8.58**) and then click OK to return to the Sort dialog box.

■ To really simplify the process of sorting a data array, consider defining the array as a *table* (see Chapter 11).

■ A sort can also be initiated using other cell and range selections:

▲ If you select only a cell in the column you want to sort or by which you want to sort all surrounding data, the sort is performed immediately. If there are no adjacent columns, the column is sorted as specified. If there *are* adjacent columns, they are treated as an array. The entire array is sorted based on the data in the sort column.

▲ If you select a range that contains multiple columns prior to choosing a Sort command, the selected range will be sorted. The first column is automatically treated as the sort-by column. Other adjacent columns and cells outside the selected range are not changed.

Naming Cells and Ranges

In addition to referencing cells and ranges by their addresses (such as G17 and A1:D8), you can assign names to them. There are two reasons to name certain cells and ranges:

◆ It's easier to find important data in the Go To dialog box (see Figure 8.11) using a name because you don't have to memorize cell or range addresses.

◆ A name can be used in formulas (see Chapter 10) as a replacement for a cell address or range, making the formula easier to create and understand, such as =Total*Tax_Pct.

A name can contain 255 characters: letters, numbers, periods, and underscores (_). The first character must be a letter, underscore, or backslash (\\). Although names cannot contain spaces, you can represent a space with a period or underscore, such as Div_1 or Div.1. Names aren't case-sensitive, so Budget, BUDGET, and budget are considered to be the same name.

To name a cell or range:

1. Select the cell or range that you want to name (**Figure 8.59**).

2. *Do either of the following:*

   ▲ Enter the name in the name box (**Figure 8.60**) and press Enter.

   ▲ On the Formulas tab, click the Define Name icon in the Defined Names group or choose Define Name from the Define Name menu. Complete the information in the New Name dialog box (**Figure 8.61**) and click OK.

Figure 8.59 Select the cell or range to be named. (In this example, column G is selected.)

Figure 8.60 Enter a name for the selected cell or range in the name box.

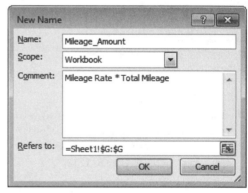

Figure 8.61 Creating a name in the New Name dialog box allows you to set a scope for the name (worksheet or workbook), add an optional comment, and edit the cell or range reference.

Filter the Name list

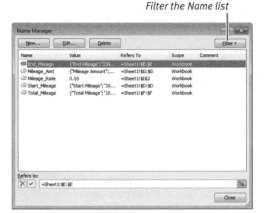

Figure 8.62 You can create, rename, edit, and delete names in the Name Manager dialog box.

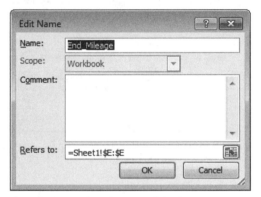

Figure 8.63 Use the Edit Name dialog box to rename a name, add a comment, or change the address or range to which the name refers.

✔ Tip

- To limit the names listed in the Name Manager dialog box to defined names, table names, names scoped to the worksheet or the workbook, or ones with or without errors, click the Filter button and choose an option from the drop-down menu (Figure 8.62).

✔ Tips

- In previous versions of Excel and in other spreadsheets, a name was often referred to as a *range name* or *named range*.

- If Excel can associate a row or column label with the selected range, it will propose the label as the name in the New Name dialog box.

- Every created name has a *scope*; it can be a specific worksheet or all worksheets in the current workbook. When a name is created in the name box, its scope is automatically set to the workbook. If you create the name in the New Name dialog box (see Figure 8.61), you can set either as the scope.

- Tables can also be named. In fact, when you create a table, a default name is assigned to it, based on the number of tables already in the worksheet (Table1, Table2, and so on).

To rename, delete, or modify a name:

1. On the Formulas tab, click the Name Manager icon in the Defined Names group. The Name Manager dialog box appears (**Figure 8.62**).

2. Select a name from the Name list, and click one of these buttons:
   - ▲ **Delete.** Delete the name. To confirm the deletion, click OK in the dialog box that appears.
   - ▲ **Edit.** Change the name, add a comment (or edit the current comment), or change the cell or range to which the name refers (**Figure 8.63**). Click OK to close the dialog box, saving your changes.

3. Click Close to dismiss the Name Manager dialog box.

Password-Protecting Workbooks

Excel provides a variety of tools for protecting data. One that you are likely to use is that of adding *password protection* to a workbook (requiring a password to open and/or modify its contents).

To password-protect a workbook:

1. Click the File tab to go to the Backstage.

2. In the Info section of the Backstage, click the Protect Workbook icon and choose Encrypt with Password (**Figure 8.64**).

    The Encrypt Document dialog box appears (**Figure 8.65**).

3. Type a password and click OK.

    The Confirm Password dialog box opens.

4. Reenter the password and click OK.

    Note that letter case counts; that is, Newt7, newt7, and NEWT7 are all different.

✔ Tip

- You can also set a password while saving a workbook with the Save As command. Open the Tools menu at the bottom of the Save As dialog box and choose General Options. In the General Options dialog box (**Figure 8.66**), *do one of the following:*

    ▲ **Open protection.** To prevent unauthorized users from opening the workbook, enter a password in the Password to open box. Excel encrypts the workbook when saving it.

    ▲ **Modify protection.** To prevent unauthorized users from modifying the workbook but still let them view it, enter a password in the Password to modify box. No encryption is added. Users who cannot supply the password will only be allowed to view the workbook.

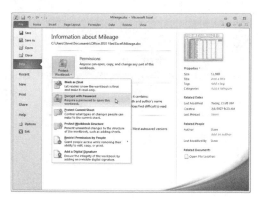

Figure 8.64 You can encrypt and password-protect the current workbook in the Backstage.

Figure 8.65 Type a password in the Encrypt Document dialog box and click OK.

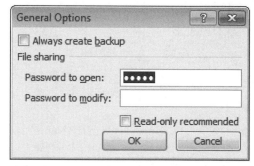

Figure 8.66 Enter a password in the appropriate text box and click OK.

Figure 8.67 This dialog box appears when a password to open has been set for a workbook.

Figure 8.68 This dialog box appears when a password to modify has been set for a workbook.

To open a protected workbook:

1. Open the workbook file.

2. Depending on the type(s) of password protection associated with the file (see previous Tip), one of the following occurs:

   ▲ **Open protection.** A Password dialog box appears (**Figure 8.67**). Enter the password and click OK. If the password is incorrect or Cancel is clicked, the workbook does not open.

   ▲ **Modify protection.** A Password dialog box appears (**Figure 8.68**). Enter the password for permission to modify the workbook or click Read Only for permission to only view the workbook.

To remove or change a password:

1. Open the workbook by supplying the password. The following occurs:

   ▲ **Open protection.** A Password dialog box appears (Figure 8.67). Enter the password and click OK. If the password is incorrect or Cancel is clicked, the workbook does not open.

   ▲ **Modify protection.** A Password dialog box appears (Figure 8.68). Enter the password for permission to modify the workbook.

2. Click the File tab to go to the Backstage, and then click Save As.

3. Open the Tools drop-down menu at the bottom of the Save As dialog box and choose General Options.

4. In the General Options dialog box (see Figure 8.66), *do any of the following:*

   ▲ To eliminate a password, delete it from the appropriate Password text box.

   ▲ To change a password, delete the old password, type a new one, and then confirm the change.

continues on next page

5. Click OK to close the General Options dialog box.

6. *Optional:* In the Save As dialog box, you can change the file's name and/or its location on disk.

7. Click Save.

Any edits made to passwords, as well as password deletions, are recorded in the saved file. The edits and deletions will be in effect the next time you open the file.

✔ Tips

■ Save an unprotected, archival copy of the workbook to CD or another type of removable media—just in case you forget the password(s).

■ Use the Password to modify option when one or more users need to view a workbook but not change it. Restrict access to that password to those few users (or only yourself) who have permission to change the data.

■ If you assign both types of password to a workbook, be sure to use two *different* passwords.

FORMATTING WORKSHEETS AND DATA

Although you're free to accept the default formatting for any worksheet by using the preset column widths, row heights, font, and font size, you're unlikely to do so very often. Simply put, properly formatted worksheets are easier to read and understand than those that use the default settings.

And if you apply Excel's *attractive* formatting features (such as shading and border styles for cells, and fonts, styles, colors, and alignment for data), you can transform a run-of-the-mill worksheet into something worthy of being published in a corporate report.

✔ Tip

- For information on formatting tables, see Chapter 11.

Setting Column Width and Row Height

Unless you've set a specific width for a column or height for a row, each row and column automatically adjusts to fit the data it contains, as follows:

◆ **Row height** adjusts to the largest font size in any cell within the row.

◆ **Column width** adjusts to the longest number in any cell within the column.

A lengthy text string in a cell (**Figure 9.1**), on the other hand, does *not* result in a column-width adjustment. If adjacent cells are empty, the extra text spills into them. If adjacent cells contain data, only the text that fits within the current cell width is displayed.

To set a column width:

1. To select the column(s), *do one or a combination of the following:*

   ▲ **Single column.** Click its letter or select a single cell within the column.

   ▲ **Multiple contiguous columns.** Drag-select the column letters.

   ▲ **Multiple noncontiguous columns.** ⌈Ctrl⌉-click each column letter.

2. On the Home tab, click the Format icon in the Cells group. *Do one of the following:*

   ▲ To set a single width for all selected columns, choose Column Width from the drop-down menu (**Figure 9.2**). In the Column Width dialog box (**Figure 9.3**), enter a number (representing the approximate number of characters), and click OK.

   ▲ Choose AutoFit Column Width. Excel will continually adjust the column width to the longest number or text string that appears anywhere in each of the selected columns.

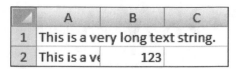

Figure 9.1 Cells A1 and A2 contain the same text string. Because cells B1 and C1 are empty, A1's text spills into them. But because B2 contains data, the text string in cell A2 is truncated.

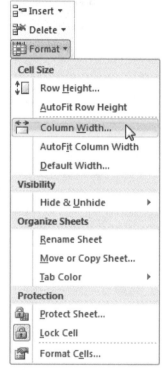

Figure 9.2 Choose a column width or row height command.

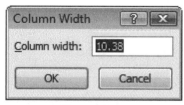

Figure 9.3 Enter a new column width (in characters) and click OK.

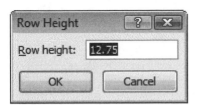

Figure 9.4 Enter a new row height (in points) and click OK.

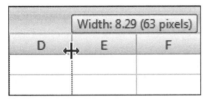

Figure 9.5 Click and drag between column letters to resize the column on the left (in this case, column D).

To set a row height:

1. To select the row(s), *do one or a combination of the following:*

   ▲ **Single row.** Click its number or select a single cell within the row.

   ▲ **Multiple contiguous rows.** Drag-select the row numbers.

   ▲ **Multiple noncontiguous rows.** Ctrl -click each row number.

2. On the Home tab, click the Format icon in the Cells group. *Do one of the following:*

   ▲ To set a single height for all selected rows, choose Row Height from the drop-down menu (see Figure 9.2). In the Row Height dialog box (**Figure 9.4**), enter a height in *points* (72 points per inch) and click OK.

   ▲ Choose AutoFit Row Height. Excel will continually adjust the row height to accommodate the largest font or text wrap in each of the selected rows.

✔ Tips

■ You can *manually* adjust column widths and row heights:

   ▲ **Column width.** Click the right border of the column's letter and drag to the left or right (**Figure 9.5**).

   ▲ **Row height.** Click the bottom border of the row's number and drag up or down.

■ You can simultaneously set a width or height for *multiple* columns or rows. Select the columns or rows, and then manually adjust the width or height of any one of them.

■ To instantly make a column wide enough to accommodate the longest number or text string in the column, double-click the column letter's right border. To adjust a row height in the same manner, double-click the row number's bottom border.

SETTING COLUMN WIDTH AND ROW HEIGHT

189

About Data and Cell Formatting

If you start a new worksheet by simply entering data, it will all have the same formatting. Every text and number entry will use the same font, size, style, and color. Numbers will be displayed using the General format (as typed, unless the column isn't wide enough to show the entire number). Cells will have no background color and no borders.

However, Excel offers many data- and cell-formatting options. To make any worksheet more attractive and easier to interpret, you can do the following:

◆ Apply different fonts, styles, sizes, and/or colors to data within selected cells.

◆ Set paragraph alignment for individual cells (left-, center-, or right-aligned).

◆ Wrap text within cells or shrink it to fit, rather than let it the spill into adjacent cells.

◆ Apply a variety of Number formats to cells that contain numeric data, such as setting the number of decimal places and formatting as currency or percentages.

◆ Use *conditional formatting* to make certain numbers stand out, such as values below the average or values that correspond to a rule of your own creation.

◆ Fill cells with color.

◆ Add *borders* (lines) around cell edges.

✔ Tips

■ If you don't care for the default font used to format worksheets, you can change it. Click the File tab to go to the Backstage, and then click Options. In the General section of the Excel Options dialog box (**Figure 9.6**), choose a new font and/or size, and click OK.

Figure 9.6 You can change the default font and/or font size for all new worksheets.

■ Displaying the gridlines on any worksheet is traditional—*but optional*. To hide the gridlines, click the View tab and remove the check mark from Gridlines in the Show group.

Figure 9.7 Character-formatting commands can be selected from the Font group.

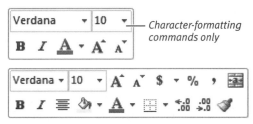

Character-formatting commands only

Figure 9.8 The Mini toolbar displays different formatting commands when text within a cell (top) or the cell itself (bottom) is selected.

Figure 9.9 Choose a style from the Cell Styles gallery to format headings, titles, totals, and good/bad data.

Figure 9.10 Choose paragraph-formatting commands from the Alignment group.

Character and Paragraph Formatting

By choosing commands from the Home tab or the Mini toolbar, you can specify a font for selected text within a cell or the entire cell, as well as change the paragraph alignment.

To set character or paragraph formatting:

1. *Do one of the following:*
   - ▲ To format all text within a cell, select the cell.
   - ▲ To format only certain text within a cell, select the text you want to format.

2. To apply character formatting, *do any of the following:*
   - ▲ On the Home tab, choose character-formatting commands from the Font group (**Figure 9.7**).
   - ▲ Right-click the cell or selected text, and choose formatting commands from the Mini toolbar (**Figure 9.8**).
   - ▲ Click the Cell Styles icon in the Styles group and choose a style from the gallery (**Figure 9.9**). Note that cell styles can only be applied to an entire cell—not to selected text within a cell.

3. To apply paragraph formatting, choose commands from the Alignment group on the Home tab (**Figure 9.10**).

✔ Tip

- ■ Character and paragraph formatting can also be applied to multiple selected cells simultaneously. Use any of the selection techniques described on pages 160–161 prior to choosing formatting commands.

Fitting Text Within a Cell

Occasionally, a cell can contain more text than will fit. To fully display the text, you can allow the additional characters to overflow into adjacent cells, widen the column in which the cell is located, or use one of the methods described below.

To enable text wrap:

1. Select the cell or cells in which you want text to wrap.

2. On the Home tab, click the Wrap Text icon in the Alignment group (see Figure 9.10).

   Text within the selected cells wraps. The row height increases as needed in order to accommodate present and future text in the row (**Figure 9.11**).

To shrink text to fit a cell:

1. Select the cell or cells containing text you want to shrink to fit the cell width.

2. On the Home tab, click the Format icon in the Cells group and choose Format Cells.

   The Format Cells dialog box appears.

3. On the Alignment tab (**Figure 9.12**), click Shrink to fit and then OK.

   Text in the cells is reduced as necessary in order to fit the cell widths.

✔ Tips

■ To eliminate text wrap from selected cells, click the Wrap Text icon again.

■ If you've enabled text wrap, you may also want to set a vertical alignment for the entire row or selected cells within the row (**Figure 9.13**).

■ If you set a specific height for a row, its height will no longer increase to accommodate text wrap.

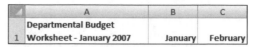

Figure 9.11 Long text, such as the string in cell A1, can be wrapped within its cell.

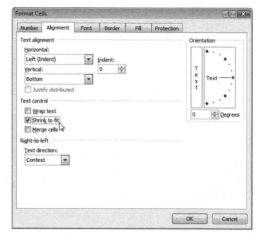

Figure 9.12 Click Shrink to fit and then click OK.

Format Cells dialog box launcher

Top, Middle, and Bottom Align icons

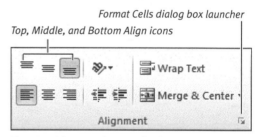

Figure 9.13 Bottom Align was set for the column heads in cells B1 and C1 in Figure 9.11 (above).

■ Wrap Text and Shrink to Fit are mutually exclusive. To enable Shrink to Fit in the Format Cells dialog box, you must first remove the check mark from Wrap Text (if present).

■ You can also open the Format Cells dialog box by clicking the Format Cells dialog box launcher in the Font, Alignment, or Number group (Figure 9.13).

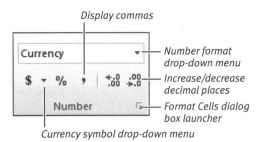

Figure 9.14 Choose common number-formatting options from the Number group.

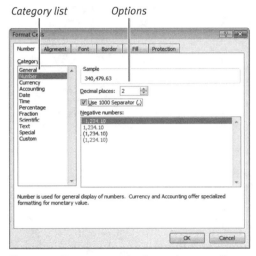

Figure 9.15 For more complex formatting, as well as date and time formats, use the Format Cells dialog box.

Number Formatting

Like any modern spreadsheet application, Excel 2010 offers many formats that you can apply to numeric, date, and time data. You can format numbers as currency, percentages, fractions, or scientific notation, for example. You can optionally display numbers with commas and a fixed number of decimal places.

Note that the display options set for a given cell do *not* affect the way its number is stored or used in calculations. For instance, if you apply a currency format to a cell containing 28.1225, $28.12 will display. The remaining .0025 isn't gone; it simply isn't shown.

To apply a Number format:

1. Select the cell or cells to which you want to apply a Number format.

2. *Do one of the following:*

   ▲ On the Home tab, choose formatting options from the Number group (**Figure 9.14**).

   ▲ Right-click any selected cell and choose format options from the Mini toolbar (see Figure 9.8).

   ▲ Click the Format Cells dialog box launcher (see Figure 9.13). Choose formatting options from those on the Number tab (**Figure 9.15**). Click OK to apply the options to the selected cells.

✔ Tip

■ Be sure to thoroughly explore the Number tab of the Format Cells dialog box. It also includes date and time formatting options. And if you choose the Special category, you'll find formats for ZIP codes, phone numbers, and Social Security numbers.

NUMBER FORMATTING

Conditional Formatting

By specifying *conditional formatting* (formatting that's applied only when specified criteria are met), you can make important data stand out from other elements in a data set. You can do any of the following:

◆ Overlay every member of the data set with a data bar, color, or icon that shows its position in the distribution.

◆ Apply a color highlight to a specific number of items that are highest, lowest, above average, or below average.

◆ Apply a color highlight to items identified by a *rule*, such as bowling averages greater than 200.

Unlike manually applied formatting, conditional formatting updates itself as required. That is, if the data that has been conditionally formatted changes, the items formatted in this manner (highlighted in green, for instance) will automatically change, too.

To apply data bars, color scales, or icon sets to data:

1. Select the cell range to which you want to apply conditional formatting.

2. On the Home tab, click the Conditional Formatting icon in the Styles group.

   A drop-down menu appears (**Figure 9.16**).

3. Choose an option from the Data Bars, Color Scales, or Icon Sets submenu (**Figure 9.17**).

   A live preview is provided for each conditional formatting option.

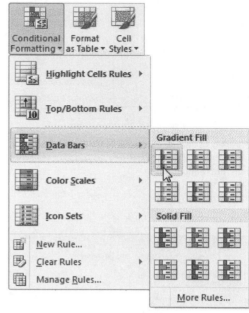

Figure 9.16 Choose conditional formatting from this drop-down menu in the Styles group of the Home tab.

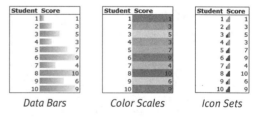

Figure 9.17 You can show the relative size of every item in a data distribution by formatting with data bars, a color scale, or an icon set.

Figure 9.18 Choose an option from the Top/Bottom Rules submenu to select the highest/lowest items or those above/below the average for the data set.

Number or percentage   *Formatting options*

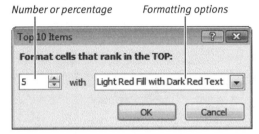

Figure 9.19 Set options for the rule and click OK.

Figure 9.20 Highlight Cells Rules submenu.

To apply a Top/Bottom Rule to data:

1. Select the cell range to which you want to apply a Top/Bottom Rule.

2. On the Home tab, click the Conditional Formatting icon in the Styles group.

3. From the drop-down menu that appears, choose an option from the Top/Bottom Rules submenu (**Figure 9.18**).

4. Set options in the dialog box that appears (**Figure 9.19**). A live preview is shown.
   - ▲ For Average rules, the dialog box allows you to select fill and text colors.
   - ▲ For Top and Bottom rules, you can also set the cutoff point (as a number or percentage), highlighting only the lowest five scores, for example.

5. Click OK to apply the rule to the selected cell range.

To apply a Highlight Cells Rule to data:

1. Select the cell range to which you want to apply a Highlight Cells Rule.

2. On the Home tab, click the Conditional Formatting icon in the Styles group.

3. From the drop-down menu, choose an option from the Highlight Cells Rules submenu (**Figure 9.20**).

4. In the dialog box that appears, set options and click OK to apply the rule.

✔ Tips

- You can apply multiple types of conditional formatting to the same range.

- To remove conditional formatting, select the range, open the Conditional Formatting drop-down menu, and choose Clear Rules > Clear Rules from Selected Cells.

CONDITIONAL FORMATTING

Adding Cell Backgrounds and Borders

In addition to formatting cell content, you can apply formatting to cell borders and backgrounds. For example, you can create a double-line border beneath a row to visually separate data from a totals row. Or you could make critical cells stand out by applying a colored fill to them.

To fill cells with color:

1. Select the cells to which you want to apply a background color.

2. On the Home tab, open the Format Cells dialog box by *doing one of the following:*

   ▲ Click the Format icon in the Cells group and choose Format Cells from the drop-down menu.

   ▲ Click the Format Cells dialog box launcher in the Font, Alignment, or Number group (see Figure 9.13).

   ▲ Right-click one of the selected cells and choose Format Cells from the context menu that appears.

3. In the Format Cells dialog box, click the Fill tab (**Figure 9.21**).

4. *Do one of the following:*

   ▲ **Fill cells with a solid color.** Click a color icon in the Background Color section. (To choose a color that isn't displayed, click More Colors.)

   ▲ **Fill cells with a pattern.** Choose a pattern color and style from the drop-down menus.

   ▲ **Fill cells with a gradient.** Click the Fill Effects button. Set options in the dialog box that appears (**Figure 9.22**) and click OK.

5. Click OK to close the Format Cells dialog box.

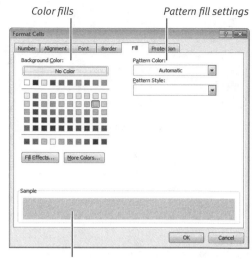

Color fills   *Pattern fill settings*

Preview of color, pattern, or gradient fill

Figure 9.21 Select fill options on the Fill tab of the Format Cells dialog box.

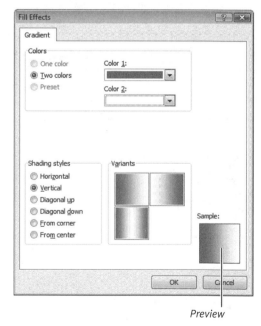

Preview

Figure 9.22 You can apply a custom gradient to cells. Doing so often results in a 3D-like effect.

Line styles   Presets

Line color   Border icons

Figure 9.23 You can add, remove, or modify borders for the currently selected cells.

Custom Conditional Formatting

While you can quickly apply conditional formatting to a range by merely choosing an option from one of the Conditional Formatting submenus (see Figures 9.16, 9.18, and 9.20), you can *customize* the settings for any conditional formatting rule to show only particular values in a specified manner.

Choose More Rules from the bottom of the appropriate Conditional Formatting submenu. Depending on the conditional formatting type, you can specify a minimum and/or maximum plotted value, indicate how negative values will be displayed, or change the number of plotted values for a top/bottom rule, for example.

To add cell borders:

1. Select the cells to which you want to add one or more border lines.

2. On the Home tab, open the Format Cells dialog box by *doing one of the following:*
   ▲ Click the Format icon in the Cells group and choose Format Cells from the drop-down menu.
   ▲ Click the Format Cells dialog box launcher in the Font, Alignment, or Number group (see Figure 9.13).
   ▲ Right-click one of the selected cells and choose Format Cells from the context menu that appears.

3. In the Format Cells dialog box, click the Border tab (**Figure 9.23**).

4. *Do any of the following:*
   ▲ **Add border lines.** Select a line style and color from the left side of the dialog box. To use one of the presets (such as Outline), click its icon. To add a single border line of the selected style and color, click its border icon or the spot in the sample where you want to add the line.
   ▲ **Remove border lines.** To simultaneously remove *all* border lines from the selected cells, click the None preset. To remove a single border, click its border icon or the spot in the sample from which you want to remove the line.
   ▲ **Change border line properties.** To change the style or color of borders, select a new style and/or color, and click the preset or border icon that you want to reformat.

5. Click OK to close the dialog box.

✔ Tip

■ Border styles can also chosen from the drop-down menu in the Font group.

Removing, Replacing, and Reusing Formats

Whether you've applied character, paragraph, number, or conditional formatting, the applied formatting can be removed or replaced. And to simplify the process of applying existing formatting to additional cells or ranges, you can also *reuse* formatting.

To remove formatting:

1. Select the cell range from which you want to remove formatting, and switch to the Home tab.

2. *Do any of the following:*

   ▲ To remove all character, paragraph, and number formatting, click the Clear icon in the Editing group and choose Clear Formats from the drop-down menu (**Figure 9.24**).

   ▲ To selectively remove character style formatting (bold, italic, underline, or double underline) from selected cells or selected characters within a cell, reapply the style formatting option.

   ▲ To remove conditional formatting from the selected cells, open the Conditional Formatting drop-down menu and choose Clear Rules > Clear Rules from Selected Cells.

   ▲ To remove all conditional formatting from the current worksheet, click the Conditional Formatting icon and choose Clear Rules > Clear Rules from Entire Sheet.

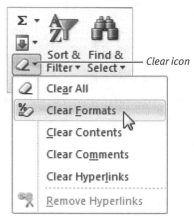

Figure 9.24 Choose Clear Formats to remove all formatting from the selected cells.

✔ Tips

■ Applying Clear Formats also causes cell data to revert to the default font and size.

■ The Clear Formats command can also be used to remove conditional formatting.

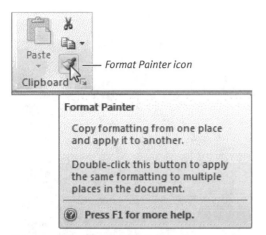

Figure 9.25 Use the Format Painter tool to copy cell formatting to another cell or range.

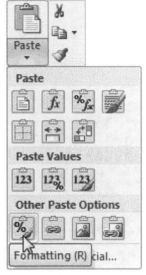

Figure 9.26 To perform a normal paste, click the Paste icon. To paste anything other than copied data (such as formatting), click an icon in the Paste drop-down menu.

To replace formatting:

1. Select the cell range for which you want to replace or modify the current formatting. Switch to the Home tab.

2. *Do any of the following:*
   ▲ To alter paragraph formatting, choose options from the Alignment group (see Figure 9.10).
   ▲ To set a new font or size, select options from the Font group (see Figure 9.7) or the Mini toolbar (see Figure 9.8).
   ▲ To replace or modify Number formatting, select options from the Number group (see Figure 9.14) or the Number tab in the Format Cells dialog box (see Figure 9.15).

To reuse existing formatting:

1. Select a cell that contains the formatting you want to duplicate.

2. On the Home tab, click the Format Painter icon in the Clipboard group (**Figure 9.25**).

3. *Do either of the following:*
   ▲ Click the cell to which you want to apply the formatting.
   ▲ Drag-select the cell range to which you want to apply the formatting.

✔ Tip

■ You can also reapply existing formatting using copy-and-paste. First, copy (Ctrl C) the cell whose formatting you want to reuse. Next, select the target cells, click the Paste icon in the Clipboard group of the Home tab and click the Formatting icon (**Figure 9.26**). You can also specify copied properties that you want to paste by choosing Paste Special from the Paste icon's drop-down menu.

Worksheet Formatting

In addition to specifying a new default font and size, as well as turning off the display of gridlines, you may occasionally want to try some of these sheet-formatting options:

◆ **Background.** You can use any image from your hard disk as a background for the current sheet (**Figure 9.27**). On the Page Layout tab, click the Background icon in the Page Setup group, select an image from the Sheet Background dialog box, and click Open.

◆ **Themes.** If you don't feel like manually selecting fonts, colors, and effects, you can choose a predesigned theme. Select the Page Layout tab and view the Themes gallery in the Themes group. Each theme contains a complementary set of fonts, colors, and effects. When you insert a new chart or SmartArt graphic, for example, theme formatting is automatically used. Similarly, when you select a color for text or an object, the color set will display only variations of the theme colors.

◆ **Tab Color.** You may find it helpful to color-code the sheet tabs in a workbook to make them easier to identify. To do so, right-click a sheet tab and choose a color from the Tab Color pop-out (**Figure 9.28**).

Remove background

Figure 9.27 As long as you apply contrasting font colors, a photo or graphic can serve as an interesting sheet background.

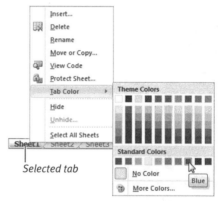

Selected tab

Figure 9.28 Choose a color for the current tab. Choose No Color to remove a previously applied color.

FORMULAS AND FUNCTIONS

After familiarizing yourself with Excel's list management features (using it to record mailing lists and membership rosters, for example), you'll want to explore its extensive calculation capabilities. By combining the contents of specific cells with each other or constants, you can create *formulas*. For example, you can add two cells' contents, divide the contents of one cell by that of another, or multiply a cell's contents by a constant, such as a sales tax percentage or a commission rate.

You can also use Excel *functions* in your formulas. For instance, rather than laboriously adding the contents of several dozen cells, you can use the SUM function to generate a total for the range. In support of your calculation needs, Excel provides more than 300 built-in functions.

In this chapter, you'll learn the basics of combining cell references, constants, and functions into useful formulas. Techniques for troubleshooting formulas are also presented.

About Cell References

Although a formula can be composed solely of constants, such as =12+5, you'll seldom use Excel to perform such calculations. Almost all formulas include *cell references*, such as =A2+5. This formula is interpreted by Excel as: "Take the current contents of cell A2 and add 5 to it."

A1 reference style

By default, Excel worksheets use *A1 reference style* in which columns are lettered and rows are numbered. Each *cell address* is named for the intersection of the column and row in which the cell is located. For example, G7 is the cell found at the intersection of column G and row 7. A *range* is represented as a pair of addresses separated by a colon (:). For example, B3:B6 means all cells between cells B3 and B6 inclusive—that is, B3, B4, B5, and B6. Refer to **Table 10.1** for some additional examples.

3-D reference style

Excel also provides a *3-D reference style* that allows you to include cells and ranges from other sheets in your formulas, as well as perform calculations across workbook sheets:

◆ To include a cell or range from another sheet in a formula, you precede the cell or range address with the sheet's name followed by an exclamation point:

=Sheet2!a7-8

In this example, 8 is subtracted from the contents of cell A7 on Sheet2.

◆ To consolidate data across multiple sheets, precede the cell or range address with the sheet range:

=SUM(Sales1:Sales12!G50)

Table 10.1

A1 Reference Style Examples	
EXAMPLE	EXPLANATION
R5	Cell in column R, row 5
B3:E3	Cells B, C, D, and E in row 3
3:3	Row 3
F:F	Column F
5:8	Rows 5, 6, 7, and 8
A:C	Columns A, B, and C
A1:B3	All cells between cells A1 and B3 inclusive (A1, B1, A2, B2, A3, and B3)

=SUM(Table1[@[Test 1]:[Test 3]])

Figure 10.1 In Table 1 (top), Total (column E) is a calculated column. When the formula is expressed in structured reference style (bottom), it is identical in every cell in the column.

	1	2	3
1	Date	Business Purpose	Destination
2	01/03/2006	Mail	Post Office
3	01/10/2006	Mail	Post Office

Figure 10.2 In R1C1 reference style, both rows and columns are numbered.

Table 10.2

3-D Reference Style Functions

FUNCTION	DESCRIPTION
AVERAGE	Calculates the average (arithmetic mean)
COUNT	Counts the cells that contain numbers
MAX	Returns the largest value in referenced cells
MIN	Returns the smallest value in referenced cells
PRODUCT	Multiplies numbers in referenced cells
STDEV	Calculates the standard deviation, based on a sample
STDEVP	Calculates the population standard deviation
SUM	Adds numbers in referenced cells
VAR	Calculates the variance, based on a sample
VARP	Calculates the population variance

In this example, monthly sales are recorded in the first 12 sheets, each of which is named Sales, followed by the month number. Consolidating data this way assumes you have laid out the data in the sheets (Sales1–Sales12) in identical fashion; that is, the cell (G50, in this case) contains the appropriate number in each sheet, such as total monthly sales or Janice's monthly commissions.

Structured reference style

Excel 2007 introduced *structured reference style*, a simplified means of addressing table data. When you create a formula in a table (a calculated column, for example), table-based structured references are automatically used rather than specific cell addresses (**Figure 10.1**).

✔ Tips

- When referring to a table cell in a formula, you can use structured or A1 reference style. If you point to the cell to add it to the formula, structured reference style is used.

- If you prefer, you can use *R1C1 reference style,* in which both rows and columns are numbered (**Figure 10.2**). R1C1 reference style is generally used in Excel scripts (called *macros*). To enable R1C1, click the File tab to display the Backstage and then click Options. In the Excel Options dialog box, select the Formulas category, click the R1C1 reference style check box in the Working with formulas section, and then click OK.

- In 3-D reference style, only certain functions can be used to consolidate data across sheets. For a list of these functions, see **Table 10.2**. Supported variants of these functions that can be applied to text and logical values include AVERAGEA, COUNTA, MAXA, MINA, STDEVA, STDEVPA, VARA, and VARPA.

ABOUT CELL REFERENCES

Formula Essentials

This section presents the background information you'll need to create formulas.

Anatomy of a formula

A basic formula (**Figure 10.3**) consists of a combination of cell references, constants, and operators. (A *constant* is any data entered in a cell, such as text or a number, date, or time.) To distinguish a formula from data, every formula begins with an equal (=) symbol.

Operators

Operators are used to specify the type of calculation to perform, such as addition or multiplication. Operators can be divided into four categories: arithmetic, comparison, text concatenation, and reference.

◆ **Arithmetic operators.** Used to perform mathematical calculations, producing a numerical result.

◆ **Comparison operators.** Used to perform logical comparisons between two values, resulting in either True or False.

◆ **Text concatenation operator.** Used to combine two text values, producing a single text string.

◆ **Reference operators.** Used to specify cell ranges.

See **Tables 10.3–10.6** for lists of supported operators.

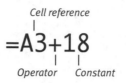

Cell reference

$$=A3+18$$

Operator   Constant

Figure 10.3 In this simple formula, 18 is added to the data in cell A3. As is the case with all formulas, the result is displayed in the cell containing the formula.

Table 10.3

Arithmetic Operators

OPERATOR	DESCRIPTION	EXAMPLE
+	Addition	A3+5
–	Subtraction	18-B7
–	Negation	-17
*	Multiplication	A6*B6
/	Division	G4/3
%	Percent	35%
^	Exponentiation (raise to a power)	A4^2

Table 10.4

Comparison Operators

OPERATOR	DESCRIPTION	EXAMPLE
=	Equal	A3=B5
>	Greater than	D2>12
<	Less than	E3<E4
>=	Greater than or equal to	A6>=15
<=	Less than or equal to	G4<=3
<>	Not equal to	B7<>5

Table 10.5

Text Concatenation Operator

OPERATOR	DESCRIPTION	EXAMPLE
&	Concatenation	"Phone: "&B5

Table 10.6

Reference Operators

OPERATOR	DESCRIPTION	EXAMPLE
:	Range	A3:A8 (all cells from A3 to A8)
,	Union	D2,F2:F5 (cells D2 and F2:F5)
[space]	Intersection	C4:D7 D6:D8 (cells D6 and D7)

Table 10.7

Operator Precedence	
OPERATOR	DESCRIPTION
:	Colon (range)
,	Comma (union)
[space]	Space (intersection)
−	Negation
%	Percent
^	Exponentiation
*, /	Multiplication and division
+, −	Addition and subtraction
&	Concatenation
=, <>, <=, >=	Comparison operators

Precedence

When calculating the result of a formula, Excel evaluates the elements from left to right. However, this holds true only when all operators are of the same importance (called *precedence*). Every operator has a precedence, as shown in **Table 10.7**. The higher in the table an operator appears, the higher its precedence. Thus, when a formula contains operators of differing precedence, the calculations are performed from highest to lowest precedence. Here are some examples:

4+2+3 [=9]

Explanation: All operators have the same precedence, so the formula is evaluated from left to right.

4*2+3 [=11]

Explanation: Multiplication has a higher precedence than addition. But because the multiplication occurs first in the formula, the left-to-right order is still followed (8+3).

4+2*3 [=10]

Explanation: Multiplication has a higher precedence, so 2*3 is evaluated first (4+6).

Note that you can change the order of evaluation by enclosing terms in parentheses. Such items are always evaluated first. When multiple sets of parentheses are used, items in the innermost ones are evaluated first.

4*(2+3) [=20]

Explanation: Because parentheses surround the last two terms, they are evaluated first (resulting in 5). Without the parentheses, the formula would have been evaluated in left-to-right order: 4*2 (or 8), plus 3, for a result of 11.

FORMULA ESSENTIALS

Relative, absolute, and mixed

Cell references in formulas can be relative, absolute, or mixed. When you enter a reference by typing an address (such as entering =(B2+C2+D2)/3 in cell E2), the references to cells B2, C2, and D2 are *relative* to the location of the formula cell (E2). If the formula is moved or copied to another cell, Excel adjusts the cell references to point to the correct cells. For example, copying the formula to cells E3:E7 results in the correct formula in each new cell (**Figure 10.4**).

You use an *absolute reference* (preceding both the column and row with dollar signs) for a cell address that must not change when copied or moved. For example, in a business mileage worksheet (**Figure 10.5**), you could create a formula to calculate Mileage Amount: the trip's total mileage multiplied by a fixed mileage rate (found in cell I2). The initial formula in row 2 would be =F2*$I$2 and then repeated in every cell in column G (for example, =F3*$I$2). Unlike relative references, absolute references never change, no matter where on the worksheet the formula is copied or moved.

Finally, Excel also supports *mixed references* in which the column or the row is absolute and the other is relative, such as $A1 (column A is absolute, row 1 is relative) and A$1 (column A is relative, row 1 is absolute).

✔ Tip

- When a formula is copied or moved (**Figure 10.6**), the cell references change as shown in **Table 10.8**:
  - ▲ Relative references change to match the formula's new location, relative to the original location. This also applies to the relative part of a mixed reference.
  - ▲ Absolute references do not change. The absolute portion of a mixed reference also remains unchanged.

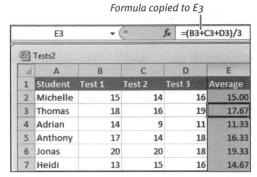

Formula copied to E3

Figure 10.4 When the formula =(B2+C2+D2)/3 in E2 is copied to cells E3:E7, the relative cell references in the formula automatically adjust to refer to the correct cells.

F	G	H	I
Total Mileage	**Mileage Amount**		*Mileage Rate*
10	4.45		0.445
10	4.45		
10	4.45		

Figure 10.5 The formula in column G uses an absolute reference to the fixed mileage rate in cell I2.

	A	B	C	D	E
1	1	4	1		
2	2	5			
3	3	6			
4				D3	
5					

Figure 10.6 If a formula in C1 is copied or moved to cell D3, it changes as described in Table 10.8.

Table 10.8

Result of Copying or Moving a Formula		
FORMULA (C1)	COPIED/MOVED (D3)	REFERENCE TYPE
=A1	=B3	Relative
=$A$1	=$A$1	Absolute
=$A1	=$A3	Mixed (absolute column)
=A$1	=B$1	Mixed (absolute row)

Figure 10.7 The Function Library group organizes Excel functions by category.

Search for a function   *Function categories*

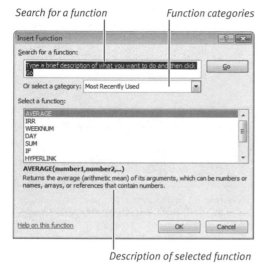

Description of selected function

Figure 10.8 Select a function, and then click OK.

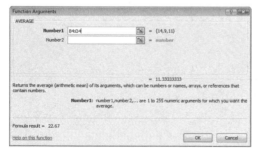

Figure 10.9 You can enter arguments by typing, clicking a cell, or drag-selecting a range.

✔ Tip

■ You can also open the Insert Function dialog box by clicking the ƒx icon in the formula bar or by pressing ⌈Shift⌉⌈F3⌉.

Functions

Functions are formula helpers—built-in computational routines that you can include in formulas to simplify the creation of complex and special-purpose calculations. For instance, rather than laboriously totaling a string of cells with the formula =A1+A2+A3+A4+A5, you can use the SUM function to add the entire range: =SUM(A1:A5).

All but a few functions require *arguments,* the data on which the function operates. Arguments are enclosed in parentheses and— if there are multiple arguments—separated by commas. The argument to the SUM function above is the range A1:A5. In addition to operating on a single range, SUM can be used to total individual cells and constants, as seen in this formula:

=SUM(A1:A5,B7,23)

In this example, the total of cells A1, A2, A3, A4, A5, B7, and 23 is calculated.

When the text insertion mark is at the desired spot in a formula you're creating, you can insert a function in these ways:

◆ Functions for which you know the spelling and syntax can be typed directly into the formula.

◆ On the Formulas tab, you can choose a function by clicking an icon in the Function Library group (**Figure 10.7**).

◆ For guidance in selecting a function, click Insert Function in the Function Library group. In the Insert Function dialog box (**Figure 10.8**), select a function and then click OK.

In the latter two function-insertion methods, the Function Arguments dialog box appears (**Figure 10.9**). Using the guidance provided, enter the argument(s) and click OK to insert the function into your formula.

FORMULA ESSENTIALS

Creating Formulas

Formulas can be created from any combination of cell contents, constants, and functions. Many common formulas, such as sums or averages of a column or row, can quickly be created using the AutoSum tool.

To create a formula without functions:

1. Select the cell that will contain the formula and type an equal sign (=).

2. Construct the formula by typing constants, cell references, and operators (**Figure 10.10**). Press [Enter] or click the ✔ in the formula bar to complete the formula.

   The formula is replaced in the cell by the calculated result (**Figure 10.11**).

To create a formula with functions:

1. Select the cell that will contain the formula and type an equal sign (=).

2. Insert constants and cell references as needed. To insert a function at the text insertion mark, *do one of the following:*

   ▲ Type the function name, a left parenthesis, the argument(s), and a right parenthesis.

   ▲ Choose a function from the Function Library group (see Figure 10.7). In the Function Arguments dialog box (see Figure 10.9), enter the argument(s) and click OK.

   ▲ Click the Insert Function icon in the Function Library group or on the formula bar. In the Insert Function dialog box (see Figure 10.8), select a function and click OK. In the Function Arguments dialog box (see Figure 10.9), enter the argument(s) and click OK.

3. Press [Enter] or click the ✔ in the formula bar to complete the formula.

   The formula is replaced in the cell by the calculated result.

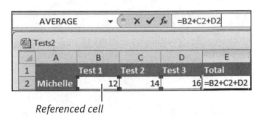

Referenced cell

Figure 10.10 The formula in E2 totals Michelle's three test scores. As you select cells or type their addresses, Excel displays handles around each referenced cell.

Formula   *Result*

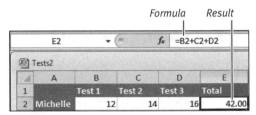

Figure 10.11 When you complete a formula, the result is displayed in the cell. Note that the formula is shown in the formula bar.

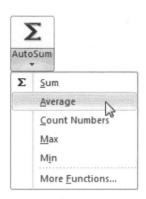

Figure 10.12 Choose a function from the drop-down menu.

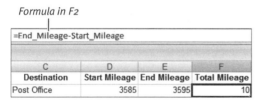

Figure 10.13 To specify a range for this SUM function, type =SUM(and drag-select the range to be totaled. Type the closing parenthesis to complete the formula.

Formula in F2

=End_Mileage-Start_Mileage

C	D	E	F
Destination	Start Mileage	End Mileage	Total Mileage
Post Office	3585	3595	10

Figure 10.14 Columns D and E have been named Start_Mileage and End_Mileage. To calculate total mileage for any cell in column F, the names can be substituted for the two cell references.

	A	B	C	D	E	F
1		Test 1	Test 2	Test 3		
2	Michelle	12	14	16		
3	Thomas	18	16	19		
4	Adrian	14	12	11		
5	Anthony	17	14	18		
6	Jonas	20	20	18		
7	Heidi	13	15	16		
8	=av					
9	AVEDEV					
10	AVERAGE	Returns the average (arithmetic mean)				
11	AVERAGEA					
12	AVERAGEIF					
13	AVERAGEIFS					

Formula cell

Formula AutoComplete drop-down list

Figure 10.15 Double-click a function name to insert it into the formula.

To create an AutoSum formula:

1. Select the cell at the bottom of a column or end of a row that will contain the formula.

   The cells that will serve as the argument to the AutoSum function must be a contiguous string within a single column or row, such as B2:B23 or H7:R7.

2. On the Formulas tab, click the AutoSum icon in the Function Library group (**Figure 10.12**). Choose a function from the drop-down menu or choose More Functions to pick from all Excel functions.

3. Excel highlights the range it thinks you want to use as the argument to the function. Adjust the range, if necessary.

4. Press (Enter) to complete the formula.

✔ Tips

■ When you create a formula, a cell reference can be typed or added by clicking the cell you want to reference. You can type or drag-select a range (**Figure 10.13**) as an argument to a function.

■ Typed cell references can be entered in uppercase or lowercase.

■ As explained in Chapter 8, if you've named cells or ranges, you can substitute the names for the addresses and ranges in formulas (**Figure 10.14**).

■ If required, a formula can contain multiple functions, as well as functions within functions (called *nested functions*).

■ If you can type the first few letters of a function's name when creating a formula, you can use Formula AutoComplete to insert the function (**Figure 10.15**). Double-click the function name in the drop-down list.

■ Functions do *not* ignore empty cells within the argument range(s).

CREATING FORMULAS

Editing Formulas

You can edit existing formulas to correct errors and to change cell or range references. Many of the techniques described below are also applicable to editing data.

To edit a formula:

1. Select the cell that contains the formula you want to edit.

2. You can edit in the cell or the formula bar, whichever is most convenient. *Do one of the following:*

   ▲ Double-click the cell.

   ▲ Click in the formula bar to set the text insertion mark.

3. *Do any of the following:*

   ▲ Use normal text-editing techniques to add, delete, or change the cell contents.

   ▲ To clear the cell, drag-select its contents and press (Backspace), or select the cell and press (Del) or (Delete).

   ▲ To change a cell reference from relative, absolute, or mixed to another reference type, select the address within the formula and repeatedly press (F4).

   ▲ To replace a function, select its name in the formula and begin typing the new function's name. Select the desired function from the Formula AutoComplete list by double-clicking its name (see Figure 10.15). You can also replace a selected function name by choosing a new function from the Function Library group (**Figure 10.16**).

4. Press (Enter) to complete the formula.

✔ Tip

■ To make an entry in a cell in multiple worksheets, (Ctrl)-select the sheet names in the Sheet tab bar, select the cell, and then enter the data or formula.

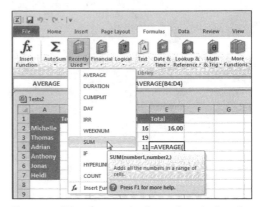

Figure 10.16 Functions can be chosen from the Function Library group's icons. If you regularly use a function, you can often choose it from the Recently Used icon's drop-down menu.

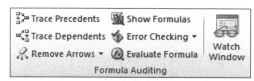

Figure 10.17 Troubleshooting tools are available in the Formula Auditing group of the Formulas tab.

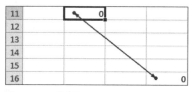

Figure 10.18 This arrow connects two cells that reference each other. The formula in B11 is =D16; the formula in D16 is =B11+8.

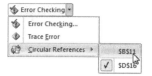

Figure 10.19 You can go directly to a circular reference cell.

Figure 10.20 Click the Evaluate button to replace the underlined formula element with its data. Click Close when you're finished.

	A	B	C	D	E	F	G
2	Jonas	20	20	18	19.33		
3	Thomas	18	16	19	17.67		
4	Anthony	17	14		7.00		
5	Michelle	15	14				
6	Heidi	13	15				
7	Adrian	14	9				
8							
9							
10							
11							
12							

Inconsistent Formula
Copy Formula from Above
Help on this error
Ignore Error
Edit in Formula Bar
Error Checking Options...

Figure 10.21 Click the icon and choose an option.

Troubleshooting Tips

Following are some techniques for finding and correcting errors in formulas. Start by switching to the Formulas tab to make the icons in the Formula Auditing group (**Figure 10.17**) accessible:

◆ **Formulas replaced by data.** To find cells in which you've accidentally replaced a formula with data, click Show Formulas. Any cell containing a formula will now display the formula, rather than the result. Click Show Formulas again to restore the worksheet to its normal state.

◆ **Circular references.** If the formulas in two cells rely on each other, Excel cannot correctly perform the calculations. This is known as a *circular reference* and is denoted on the worksheet by an arrow connecting the two cells (**Figure 10.18**). You can also find circular references by clicking the Error Checking icon and choosing any cell listed in the Circular References submenu, as shown in **Figure 10.19**. In a circular reference, only one of the two formulas can refer to the other cell.

◆ **Incorrect result.** If a formula displays an unexpected result, select the cell and click Evaluate Formula. By repeatedly clicking the Evaluate button in the Evaluate Formula dialog box (**Figure 10.20**), you can step through the elements in the formula, displaying the result for each step. Evaluating a formula often makes it easy to find incorrect cell references and identify flaws in a formula's logic.

◆ **Is it an error?** Excel notifies you immediately if it detects a possible formula error—often by displaying a tiny triangle in the cell's upper-left corner. Select the cell (**Figure 10.21**) and choose a handling option from the drop-down menu.

TROUBLESHOOTING TIPS

WORKING WITH TABLES

	A	B	C	D	E	F	G	H	I	J	K
1	Post Position	Name	Last Race	Post	Finish	Time	Odds	Races	Wins	Places	Shows
2	1	Flying Stone	Jun-15	4	1	2:03	5.0	11	4	0	0
3	2	Lady Chris Time	Jun-12	2	5	2:00	32.5	18	4	1	1
4	3	Black Bart	Jun-13	7	2	2:00	24.6	13	3	2	2
5	4	Shadrack	Jun-08	5	5	2:02	3.9	4	1	0	1
6	5	Sundust Prince	Jun-18	4	5	2:01	15.1	10	2	1	4
7	6	J.J.'s Ferro	Jun-15	3	4	2:04	1.0	8	3	0	3
8	7	Pat's Comedian	May-31	4	8	2:01	8.1	7	1	1	1

Figure 11.1 Worksheets often contain lists of related data. In this harness-racing worksheet, each row is the record for a single horse. Each column is a field, such as post position or horse's name.

Although number-crunching is the purpose of the typical worksheet, many worksheets are used only to record lists of related data, such as addresses, club memberships, or a course roster. New users quickly discover that a worksheet's row-and-column grid is better for handling lengthy lists than a word processing document. Such worksheets are essentially simple databases in which each row is a *record* and each column is a *field* (**Figure 11.1**).

Because so many people use worksheets to manage lists, Microsoft added list-related features to Excel 2003. In Excel 2007, lists were renamed *tables*. Any area of a worksheet can be designated a table, and a worksheet can contain as many tables as you need. Here are some advantages of formatting data as a table rather than using normal Excel formatting and tools to manage your list:

◆ Quickly sort the table by the contents of any field

◆ Filter the data to show only certain records or those that match a criterion

◆ Display a summary statistic for selected columns in an optional *total row*

◆ Simplify the process of performing a calculation on row data using *calculated columns*

Creating a Table

You can create a table in any blank range or convert existing data to a table.

To create a table:

1. *Do one of the following:*
   - ▲ Select a blank range where you want to insert the table.
   - ▲ Select a range with data that you want to convert to a table.

2. *Do one of the following:*
   - ▲ On the Insert tab, click the Table icon in the Tables group or press Ctrl T.
   - ▲ On the Home tab, click the Format as Table icon in the Styles group and choose a table format from the gallery (**Figure 11.2**).

   The Create Table or Format As Table dialog box appears (**Figure 11.3**).

3. If the proposed table range contains a header row, check My table has headers.

4. Click OK to create the table (**Figure 11.4**).

✔ Tips

- ■ The menu icons in each cell of the header row can obscure the header labels. You may want to widen the columns, change the alignment, or apply text wrap to any lengthy headers.

- ■ To quickly select a table, click in any table cell and then move the cursor over one of the table's top corners. Click when the cursor changes to a plus (+) with arrows.

- ■ To delete a table, select the entire table and press Del or Delete.

- ■ To change a table back to a normal range, select any table cell. On the Design tab, click the Convert to Range icon in the Tools group. Click Yes in the confirmation dialog box that appears.

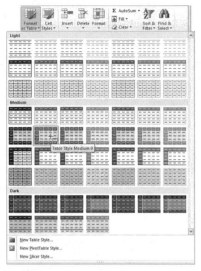

Figure 11.2 One way to create a table is to simply format a cell range as a table.

Figure 11.3 Edit the range (if necessary), indicate whether the range already contains a header row, and then click OK.

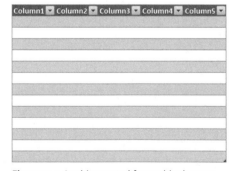

Figure 11.4 A table created from a blank range.

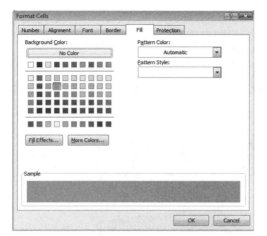

Figure 11.5 A color fill or gradient can be applied to selected table rows, columns, or cells. To display this dialog box, switch to the Home tab, click the Format icon in the Cells group, and choose Format Cells.

Figure 11.6 Click check boxes in the Table Style Options group to hide, show, and format table components.

Formatting a Table

A table is just another worksheet range. As such, if you aren't thrilled with the default formatting, you can format individual cells, rows, columns, or the entire table any way you like.

To format a table:

◆ **Format the entire table.** Select any cell in the table. On the Design tab, select a new style from the Table Styles gallery.

◆ **Format a row, column, or range.** Select the row, column, or range within the table. On the Home tab, select a cell format from the Cell Styles drop-down menu in the Styles group. Alternatively, you can apply a fill color, gradient, or pattern to selected cells by selecting options on the Fill tab of the Format Cells dialog box (**Figure 11.5**).

◆ **Format the first or last column.** The first column often contains record identifiers and the last column is frequently used to summarize each record's data. To apply distinctive formatting to these columns (boldface and, in some cases, a background color), switch to the Design tab and click the First Column and/or Last Column check boxes in the Table Style Options group (**Figure 11.6**).

◆ **Create alternating rows or columns.** On the Design tab, click Banded Rows or Banded Columns in the Table Style Options group (Figure 11.6).

✔ Tip

■ The effect of selecting First Column and Last Column in the Table Style Options group depends on the table's current formatting. For instance, if the entire table is formatted with a single color, only boldface will be applied to the column.

Creating Calculated Columns

Formulas in a table work differently from ones found elsewhere in the worksheet. If you insert a formula, it's automatically copied to all cells in the same column. And if you later add rows to the table, the formula is copied to the new cells in the column, too. Any table column that contains a formula is referred to as a *calculated column*.

To create a calculated column:

1. If necessary, insert a new column into the table in which to place the formula.

   To be treated as a calculated column, the column must be empty when you create the formula. If the column contains *any* data, the formula will be applied only to the current cell.

2. Select a cell in the empty column, and type or paste the formula into the cell.

   Many table formulas are automatically converted by Excel to equivalent *structured references* (**Figure 11.7**).

3. Complete the formula by pressing Enter or clicking ✔ (Enter) in the formula bar (Figure 11.7).

   The formula is automatically copied to all other cells in the column (**Figure 11.8**).

✔ Tips

- If you replace the formula with data in any cell in a calculated column, Excel marks the cell as an *exception*. You can correct an exception by clicking the indicator beside the cell (**Figure 11.9**).

- As long as a calculated column contains no exceptions, you can replace the formula with a new one. Like the original formula, it will automatically copy itself to every cell in the column.

Enter

Figure 11.7 Formulas within tables are often converted into structured references.

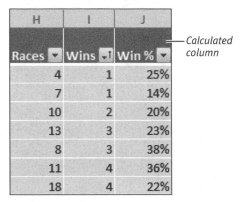

Calculated column

Figure 11.8 The Win % calculated column is based on the formula =Wins/Races.

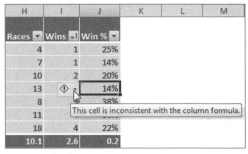

Figure 11.9 An exception cell in a calculated column is denoted by a tiny triangle in the cell's upper-left corner. When you move the cursor over the indicator beside the cell, an explanatory message appears.

CREATING CALCULATED COLUMNS

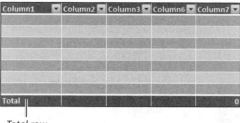

Total row

Figure 11.10 When enabled, a total row appears at the bottom of the table.

8	Sprint	09/24/09	$ 19.00
9	Total	09/18/09	$ 217.71
10			None
11			Average
12			Count
13			Count Numbers
14			Max
15			Min
16			Sum
			StdDev
			Var
			More Functions...

Figure 11.11 Each cell in the total row has a drop-down menu from which you can choose a statistical function.

Adding a Total Row

A table can optionally have a single *total row* at its bottom, enabling you to calculate a summary statistic across all records in the table. Each column can display a different statistic or none at all. For instance, in a donations table, you could compute the total of all donations, the average of the most recent donation (across all donors), or a count of the number of donor records.

To add a total row to a table:

1. Select a cell in the table to make the table active.

2. On the Design tab, click the Total Row check box in the Table Style Options group (see Figure 11.6).

   The total row appears at the bottom of the table (**Figure 11.10**).

3. *Optional:* Edit or delete the *Total* label in the leftmost cell of the total row.

4. To display a summary statistic for a column, click the total row cell beneath the column. Click the icon that appears beside the cell and choose a statistic from the drop-down menu (**Figure 11.11**).

5. Repeat Step 4 for each additional column that you want to summarize.

6. Format the total row cells as desired.

✔ Tips

- If the function you need isn't listed in the drop-down menu, choose More Functions.

- To eliminate the summary statistic for a column, choose None from the drop-down menu (Figure 11.11).

- You can disable and enable the total row as needed. When you re-enable the total row, any statistic previously specified for a column reappears.

ADDING A TOTAL ROW

Sorting and Filtering

Excel provides two tools that simplify viewing and analyzing table data:

◆ **Sorting.** Sort an entire table based on the contents of one or more fields (columns).

◆ **Filtering.** Restrict visible records (rows) to those that match a criterion. If desired, criteria can be chosen from multiple columns. For instance, you might filter a business table to show June absences of employees earning less than $10 per hour.

To sort a table:

1. *Do one of the following:*

   ▲ In the header row, click the icon in the column by which you want to sort (**Figure 11.12**).

   ▲ Right-click in any cell of the column by which you want to sort and open the Sort submenu (**Figure 11.13**).

   ▲ Select any cell in the column by which you want to sort. On the Home tab, click the Sort & Filter icon in the Editing group.

2. Choose a sort order (ascending or descending) from the menu.

   The table is sorted as specified.

✔ Tip

■ You can perform a multi-field sort by choosing Custom Sort. In the Sort dialog box that appears, click the Add Level icon to add additional sort fields, such as sorting by Payee and then by Amount.

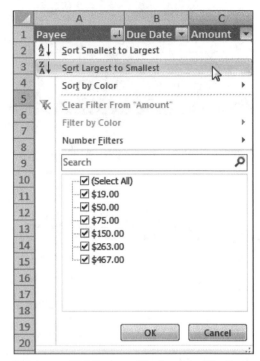

Figure 11.12 Click the icon of the header cell for the column by which you want to sort the table …

Figure 11.13 … or right-click any cell in the column by which you want to sort and choose an option from the Sort submenu.

SORTING AND FILTERING

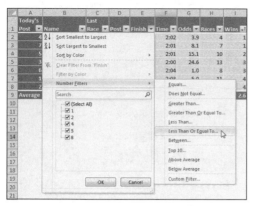

Figure 11.14 There are two ways to set a filter criterion. First, you can clear check boxes to filter out matching data. Second, you can specify a formula-based criterion by choosing a command from the pop-out menu.

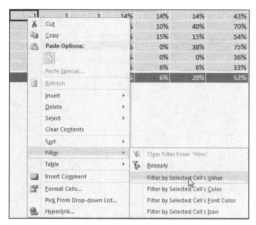

Figure 11.15 You can also filter the data based on the selected cell, but your options are limited.

Figure 11.16 Sort & Filter icon.

To filter a table:

1. *Do either of the following:*
   - ▲ In the header row, click the icon in the column by which you want to filter the table (**Figure 11.14**).
   - ▲ To filter based on a cell's contents or properties, right-click the cell in the column by which you want to filter the table and open the Filter submenu (**Figure 11.15**).

2. Choose or specify a filter criterion.

   Records that do not match the filter criterion are hidden. If present, statistics in the total row are recalculated to reflect only the visible records.

✔ Tips

- ■ To remove all filtering effects from a table (restoring the full record set), switch to the Home tab, click the Sort & Filter icon in the Editing group, and choose Clear from the drop-down menu (**Figure 11.16**).

- ■ To selectively remove one table filter when one or more filters have been applied, click the icon in the column header whose filtering you want to remove and choose Clear Filter From "*field name*."

- ■ If you've added records to a table, you can reapply the current sort instructions and filter criteria to accommodate the new records. On the Home tab, click the Sort & Filter icon in the Editing group and choose Reapply from the drop-down menu (Figure 11.16).

Changing a Table's Size

Table contents can change over time. In addition to editing the data, you may want to add or delete fields (columns), as well as add or delete records (rows).

To change a table's size:

◆ **Insert records (rows) within a table.** Select a cell in the row beneath where you want to insert a new row. (To insert multiple rows in the same spot, begin by selecting that number of cells in adjacent rows.) On the Home tab, click the Insert icon in the Cells group and choose Insert Table Rows Above (**Figure 11.17**).

◆ **Insert fields (columns) within a table.** Select a cell in the column to the right of where you want to insert a new column. (To insert multiple columns in one spot, begin by selecting that number of cells in adjacent columns.) On the Home tab, click the Insert icon in the Cells group and choose Insert Table Columns to the Left (Figure 11.17).

◆ **Increase a table's size by dragging.** Move the cursor over the lower-right corner of the table. When the cursor changes as shown in **Figure 11.18**, drag to the right to add columns or drag down to add rows.

◆ **Delete records (rows).** Select one or more cells in the row or rows you want to delete. On the Home tab, click the Delete icon in the Cells group and choose Delete Table Rows (**Figure 11.19**).

◆ **Delete fields (columns).** Select one or more cells in the column or columns you want to delete. On the Home tab, click the Delete icon in the Cells group and choose Delete Table Columns (Figure 11.19).

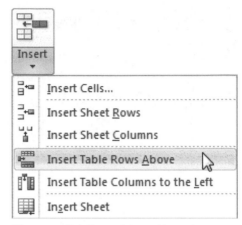

Figure 11.17 To insert or delete table rows or columns, choose a command from the Insert or Delete icon's drop-down menu.

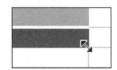

Figure 11.18 You can append rows or columns to a table by dragging the lower-right corner.

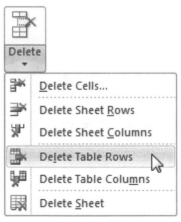

Figure 11.19 You can delete table rows or columns by choosing a command from the Delete icon's menu.

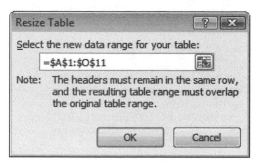

Figure 11.20 Rather than dragging to append new rows or columns to a table, you can type a new range.

✔ **Tips**

■ You can also use the Delete Sheet Rows and Delete Sheet Columns commands in the Delete icon's drop-down menu to modify a table. However, unlike the equivalent Delete Table commands, the Delete Sheet commands also affect data *outside* of the table.

■ You can also resize a table by entering a new range. Select a cell in the table, switch to the Design tab, and click the Resize Table icon in the Properties group. Type a new range in the Resize Table dialog box (**Figure 11.20**) or manually select the range on the worksheet, and then click OK. Unlike resizing by dragging (see Figure 11.18), you can use the Resize Table dialog box to add new rows and columns at the same time.

■ You can move a table to a new location using cut-and-paste or drag-and-drop. Select the table, and then do one of the following:

▲ **Cut-and-paste.** Press Ctrl X or click the Cut icon in the Home tab's Clipboard group. In the destination location, click the cell that will serve as the table's new upper-left corner, and press Enter to perform the paste.

▲ **Drag-and-drop.** Move the cursor over any corner or edge of the table. When the cursor changes to a plus symbol with four arrowheads, click and drag the table to the new location.

Selecting Table Rows or Columns

To select a table column rather than an entire worksheet column, move the cursor over the top edge of the column header. When the cursor changes to a black down-pointing arrow, click to select the table column.

Similarly, to select a table row, move the cursor over the left edge of the row. When the cursor changes to a black right-pointing arrow, click to select the table row.

CHANGING A TABLE'S SIZE

Printing Tables

You can print a table as part of the current worksheet. On the other hand, there may be instances when you prefer to print *only* the table—without printing any of the surrounding worksheet cells.

To print a table:

1. Select the table or a cell within the table that you want to print.

2. Click the File tab to display the Backstage.

3. Click Print.

   The Print settings screen appears.

4. In the Settings area, choose Print Selected Table from the top drop-down menu (**Figure 11.21**).

5. Change other print settings as desired, such as the orientation and printer.

   As you select and change settings, the print preview (**Figure 11.22**) changes to reflect the new settings.

6. Click the Print button.

   The table is sent to the designated printer, the Backstage closes, and the worksheet reappears.

✔ Tip

- You can also print a table by preselecting the entire table on the worksheet and then choosing Print Selection from the same drop-down menu.

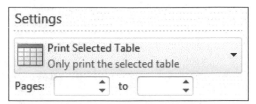

Figure 11.21 To print only a selected table, choose Print Selected Table from the drop-down menu.

Print button *Print preview*

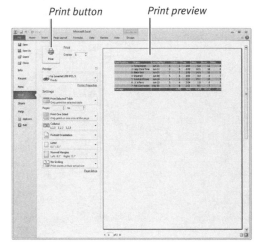

Figure 11.22 A print preview reflects the current print settings (in this case, printing only a selected table).

PRINTING TABLES

12

CREATING CHARTS

In Excel, you can create charts and graphs to display your data visually. Although many kinds of charts can be made from tiny data sets, charts are especially useful for presenting and summarizing large quantities of data.

A normal Excel chart is a *floating object*. As such, you can move a chart to any convenient location on the worksheet or change its size by dragging a corner. You can customize almost any part of a chart, such as its title, axis labels, legend, chart wall, or chart floor. You can also choose which optional elements to display and which ones to hide, such as data labels, gridlines, or the data itself. Finally, if you aren't satisfied with the current chart style, you can replace it with a variation or a completely different kind of chart.

Office 2010 introduces a new chart type called *sparklines*. Rather than float as normal charts do, the tiny sparklines charts are displayed in cells just as data normally is.

Excel's charting tools are also used to create charts in PowerPoint, Word, and Outlook. Charts in these non-Excel documents can be *embedded* (static objects that are unlinked from the worksheet data) or *linked* (objects that are linked with the data and automatically reflect changes to it).

Objects and Charts

You can embellish your worksheets and charts by inserting objects, such as shapes, pictures, SmartArt, clip art, and screen shots. For instructions on inserting, resizing, moving, and rotating objects, see Chapter 3.

Chart Elements

Designing a chart is similar to creating art. You can freely add or remove elements, move them to new positions, and change their size, shape, and formatting. (Of course, you are free to accept the default elements and formatting used in a newly created chart, but you're unlikely to do so very often.)

Because you'll spend so much time working with chart elements, it's important that you be able to *identify* each element. Note that many of the ones shown below (**Figure 12.1**) are optional.

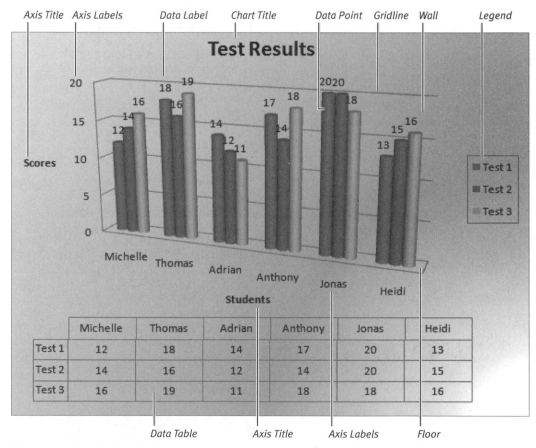

Figure 12.1 A chart and its elements.

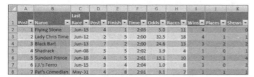

Figure 12.2 In this example, column B (labels) and columns I, J, and K (data) have been selected.

Figure 12.3 Specify the chart type by clicking an icon in the Charts group and choosing a chart style from the drop-down menu that appears.

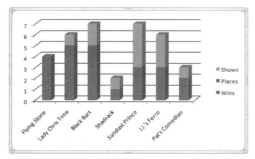

Figure 12.4 Excel adds the chart as a floating object on the worksheet.

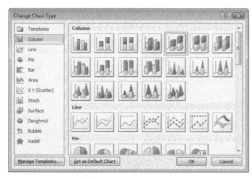

Figure 12.5 You can change an existing chart's type and/or style by clicking an icon in the Change Chart Type dialog box.

Creating a Chart

In many instances, creating a chart is as simple as selecting the labels and data on the worksheet and then picking a chart type. Your chart data can be arranged in columns or rows. However, the columns or rows must be in a specific order for some types of charts.

To create a chart:

1. If necessary, rearrange the data so it conforms to the chart's requirements.

   For example, to create one type of *stock chart*, the data must be in High, Low, Close order. For other chart requirements, see "Create a chart from start to finish" in Excel Help.

2. *Optional:* Sort the data to ensure that it will be in the desired order when charted.

3. On the worksheet, select the labels and data from which the chart will be created.

   Labels and data don't need to be contiguous. For example, in **Figure 12.2**, column B contains the labels and columns I, J, and K contain the data.

4. On the Insert tab, choose a chart type from a Charts group icon's drop-down menu (**Figure 12.3**).

   The new chart appears (**Figure 12.4**).

✔ Tips

- If you select a chart's plot area, the labels and data used to create the chart are highlighted in the worksheet. You can also select the data by switching to the Design tab and clicking the Select Data icon in the Data group.

- To change the chart type or style, select the chart, click the Design tab, and click Change Chart Type in the Type group (**Figure 12.5**).

- To delete a chart, select it and press Del.

225

Changing the Background

If you aren't satisfied with the background formatting on a generated chart, you can change it. You can apply formatting to the entire chart, the plot area, or the legend, as well as to objects you've placed on the chart, such as a title.

To change the background for the chart or a component:

1. Select the chart or component you want to format, such as the plot area, wall, floor, or legend.

2. *Do one of the following:*

   ▲ On the Format tab, choose formatting options from the Shape Styles group (**Figure 12.6**).

   ▲ On the Format or Layout tab, click the Format Selection icon in the Current Selection group.

   ▲ Right-click the selected area and choose Format *item* from the context menu. In the Format *item* dialog box (**Figure 12.7**), set formatting options and click Close.

✔ Tips

■ To easily select a particular chart element, switch to the Format or Layout tab and choose the element from the drop-down menu at the top of the Current Selection group. Then click the Format Selection icon in the same group.

■ You can also modify chart formatting by choosing options from the Background group (**Figure 12.8**) on the Layout tab.

Figure 12.6 You can add an outline, fill, and effects to a selected chart component by selecting options from the Shape Styles group.

Figure 12.7 To simultaneously modify several formatting options, select settings in a Format dialog box.

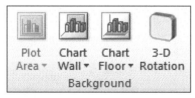

Figure 12.8 To change the wall, floor, or rotation of the plot area, choose options from the Background group.

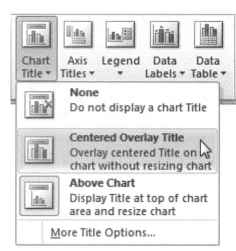

Figure 12.9 Add a title and set its initial position by choosing an option from the Chart Title drop-down menu.

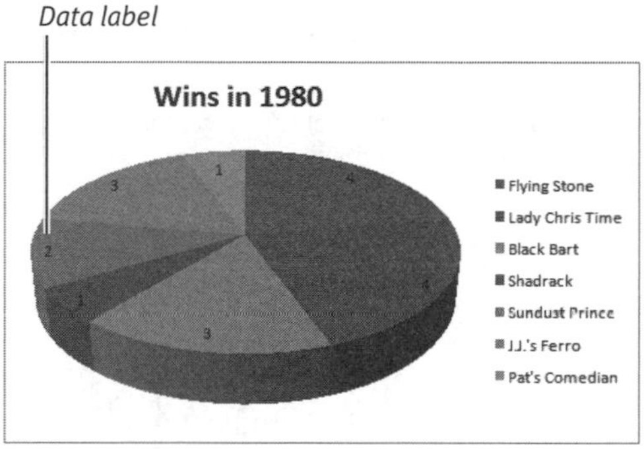

Data label

Wins in 1980

- Flying Stone
- Lady Chris Time
- Black Bart
- Shadrack
- Sundust Prince
- J.J.'s Ferro
- Pat's Comedian

Figure 12.10 Depending on the chart type, it can be useful to display the data on chart elements.

Adding and Formatting Text

Although primarily visual, charts can also include a prodigious amount of text. You can add a title, legend, grid division labels, axis labels, data labels, and text boxes.

To add a text item to a chart:

1. Select the chart.

2. On the Chart Tools contextual tab, select the Layout tab.

3. *Do any of the following:*

   ▲ **Add a chart title.** Click Chart Title in the Labels group and choose an option from the drop-down menu (**Figure 12.9**).

   ▲ **Add an axis title.** Click Axis Titles in the Labels group and choose an option from a Horizontal Axis Title or Vertical Axis Title submenu.

   ▲ **Label the data.** Click Data Labels in the Labels group and choose an option from the drop-down menu. Labeling options vary by chart type (**Figure 12.10**).

   ▲ **Show chart data.** Click Data Table in the Labels group and choose a Show option from the drop-down menu. Doing so displays the chart data in a grid beneath the plot area.

   ▲ **Add other text.** Click Text Box in the Insert group. Click and drag to create a text box on the chart, and then type or paste the text into the box.

ADDING AND FORMATTING TEXT

To format chart text:

1. *Do either of the following:*

   ▲ Select the text object. (Select an object when you want to apply the same formatting to all text within the object.)

   ▲ Within a text object, select the specific text to be formatted. (Only certain chart objects allow this, such as a title, axis label, or text box.)

2. *Do any of the following:*

   ▲ On the Home tab, choose formatting options from the Alignment group or the Font group (**Figure 12.11**).

   ▲ Right-click the selected object or text string, choose Font from the context menu (**Figure 12.12**), select formatting options from the Font dialog box (**Figure 12.13**), and click OK.

   ▲ With text selected, move the cursor up and choose formatting options from the Mini toolbar (Figure 12.12).

   ▲ On the Format tab, choose options from the WordArt Styles group.

✔ Tips

■ Another way to format a text object is to choose More *text object* Options from the element's drop-down menu in the Labels group (see Figure 12.9). A Format dialog box appears in which you can apply a background fill, specify a border style and color, add a shadow, and so on.

■ To remove most text objects, select the object and press Del. You can also remove a specific label type by switching to the Layout tab, clicking the proper icon in the Labels group, and choosing None. For example, you can remove a chart title by choosing None from the Chart Title icon (see Figure 12.9).

Figure 12.11 You can apply text formatting by choosing commands from the Font group.

Selected object   Mini toolbar

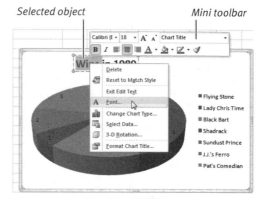

Figure 12.12 You can right-click objects that contain text and choose Font from the context menu.

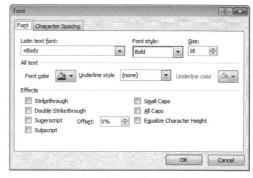

Figure 12.13 For complex text-formatting needs, you may prefer to use the Font dialog box.

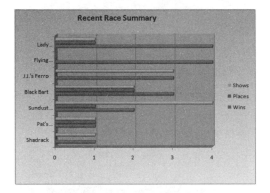

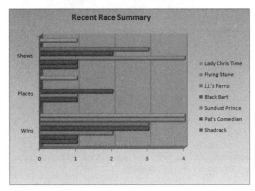

Figure 12.14 By switching rows and columns, you can view the wins, places, and shows for each horse (top) or see how the seven horses compare on number of wins, places, and shows (bottom).

Rows or Columns

Regardless of how your data is organized on the worksheet, you can plot it by rows or by columns. With many types of charts, plotting it *both* ways can give you a new perspective on the data.

To switch rows and columns:

1. Select the chart.

2. In the Data group within the Design tab, click the Switch Row/Column icon.

   The chart updates to reflect the change (**Figure 12.14**).

Changing Layout and Style

One of the simplest ways to modify a chart is to specify a new layout or style. *Layout* refers to the elements appearing on the chart and their positions. *Style* refers to the coloring of chart elements, including the data objects, plot walls, and surrounding background.

To specify a new layout:

1. Select the chart.

2. On the Design tab, click an icon in the Chart Layouts group (**Figure 12.15**).

   The chart is modified to match the selected layout (**Figure 12.16**).

3. If previously undefined text elements appear in the chart (such as a title or axis titles), you can delete them or change their text.

To change the chart style:

1. Select the chart.

2. On the Design tab, choose a different style from the Chart Styles group (**Figure 12.17**).

   The chart is modified to match the chosen chart style.

✔ Tips

- Choosing a new chart style is a destructive process. Elements you've manually formatted, such as gridlines or the background, are replaced with the features specified in the new style.

- When choosing a new chart layout or style, you can scroll through one line of options at a time by clicking the up and down scroll arrows. To view all options simultaneously as a gallery, click the bottom arrow (Figure 12.15).

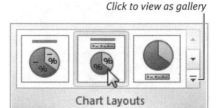

Click to view as gallery

Figure 12.15 Choose a new chart layout from the Chart Layouts group.

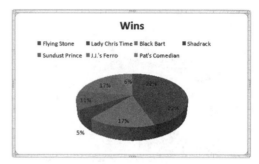

Figure 12.16 The pie chart is automatically modified to match the chosen layout.

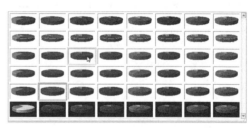

Figure 12.17 To change the style for a selected chart, choose a new style from the Chart Styles gallery.

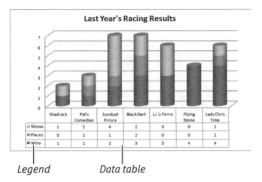

Legend   Data table

Figure 12.18 The data and legend can be combined (shown here) or displayed as separate chart items.

Displaying the Data Set

If a chart is based on a small data set, it can be informative to show the data table on the chart.

To display the data on the chart:

1. Select the chart.

2. *Do one of the following:*

   ▲ On the Layout tab, choose a data display option from the Data Table drop-down menu in the Labels group.

   ▲ On the Design tab, choose a layout from the Chart Layouts group that includes the data table.

   The data table is added to the chart (**Figure 12.18**).

3. If necessary, resize the chart.

✔ Tips

■ To remove the data table, choose None from the Data Table drop-down menu or choose a layout from the Chart Layouts group that doesn't includes the data table.

■ Another way to show data is to place it directly on chart items, such as bars and pie slices. On the Layout tab, choose an option from the Data Labels drop-down menu in the Labels group.

Working with Gridlines

To make it easier to estimate the size of data points, you can display horizontal and/or vertical lines called *gridlines (***Figure 12.19***)* on many kinds of charts. You can modify gridlines by removing them; displaying major, minor, or both types of gridlines for an axis; and setting a new line color or style.

To add, remove, or modify gridlines:

1. Select the chart.

2. On the Layout tab, click the Gridlines icon in the Axes group and choose one of the following options from the Primary Horizontal Gridlines, Primary Vertical Gridlines, or Depth Gridlines submenu (**Figure 12.20**):

▲ **None.** Remove all gridlines of the chosen type.

▲ **Major Gridlines.** Display major data divisions on the chosen axis, such as 1–5 or integers divisible by 5, 10, or 25 (depending on the size and spread of the data).

▲ **Minor Gridlines.** Display subdivisions between major gridlines (whether or not major gridlines are visible).

▲ **Major & Minor Gridlines.** Display both major and minor gridlines for the chosen axis.

▲ **More Primary Gridlines Options.** Open a Format dialog box to set color, style, shadow, glow, or soft edges for horizontal or vertical primary gridlines. Select new settings and click Close.

The chosen option is applied to the chart.

✔ Tips

■ The Depth Gridlines submenu appears only when a true 3-D chart is selected (**Figure 12.21**).

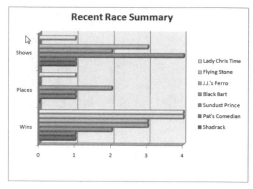

Figure 12.19 Gridlines behind the data can make it easier to see or estimate the size of data points.

Figure 12.20 A Gridlines submenu.

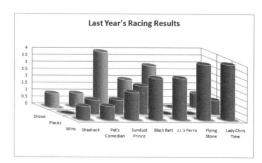

Figure 12.21 A true 3-D chart has depth.

■ You can also remove gridlines by right-clicking them on the chart and choosing Delete from the context menu.

Legend

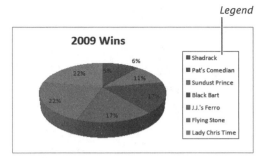

2009 Wins

■ Shadrack
■ Pat's Comedian
■ Sundust Prince
■ Black Bart
■ J.J.'s Ferro
■ Flying Stone
■ Lady Chris Time

Figure 12.22 The legend serves as a key to the chart. Each element in the legend represents a data series.

Legend icon

None
Turn off Legend

Show Legend at Right
Show Legend and align right

Show Legend at Top
Show Legend and top align

Show Legend at Left
Show Legend and align left

Show Legend at Bottom
Show Legend and align bottom

Overlay Legend at Right
Show Legend at right of the chart without resizing

Overlay Legend at Left
Show Legend at left of the chart without resizing

More Legend Options...

Figure 12.23 Add, remove, or change the placement of the legend by choosing an option from this menu.

Figure 12.24 You can specify a new location or custom formatting in the Format Legend dialog box.

- You can also open the Format Legend dialog box by double-clicking the legend.

Working with the Legend

If you select row or column labels when creating a chart, a *legend* (key to the data series) is generally added to the chart (**Figure 12.22**). You can add or remove the legend, specify its placement in relation to the chart, change its properties (such as fill color and border style), and edit its labels.

To add, remove, or modify the legend:

1. Select the chart.

2. *Do any of the following:*

▲ To add, remove, or change the position of the legend, click the Layout tab and choose an option from Legend menu in the Labels group (**Figure 12.23**).

▲ To manually change the size or position of the legend, drag an edge or the center, respectively.

▲ To format the legend, right-click it, choose Format Legend from the context menu, and make the desired changes in the Format Legend Entry dialog box (**Figure 12.24**).

▲ To change the properties of a single data series, select that element in the legend, right-click it, choose Format Data Series or Format Legend Entry, and make any desired changes in the Format Data Series or Format Legend Entry dialog box.

▲ To modify the text used for legend entries, make the edits in the worksheet cells you used as labels.

✔ Tips

■ You don't have to close a Format dialog box immediately. To format a *different* chart element, select that element on the chart. The Format dialog box changes to one appropriate for the selected element.

WORKING WITH THE LEGEND

Adding Trendlines

If data is gathered over time, you can add lines called *trendlines* to the chart that summarize the data and predict future values. Depending on the data set, different trendline types may provide a better *fit* to the data.

To add a trendline:

1. Select the chart.

2. On the Layout tab, click the Trendline icon in the Analysis group and choose an option from the drop-down menu.

   If the chart includes multiple data series, an Add Trendline dialog box appears. Select the data series to which the trendline will be applied and click OK.

   The trendline appears on the chart.

3. *Optional:* To modify a trendline's properties or type, select the trendline. Open the Format Trendline dialog box (**Figure 12.25**) by doing one of the following:

   ▲ Right-click the trendline and choose Format Trendline.

   ▲ Choose More Trendline Options from the Trendline drop-down menu.

4. Make the desired changes and click Close. The new settings are reflected on the chart (**Figure 12.26**).

✔ Tips

■ Adding trendlines is cumulative. That is, you can plot multiple types of trendlines on the same chart.

■ To remove all trendlines from a chart, choose None from the Trendline drop-down menu. To remove one trendline (when multiple trendlines are displayed), select the trendline on the chart and press ⌦ Del ⌫.

Figure 12.25 The Format Trendline dialog box offers additional options, such as other trendline types and displaying predicted values, based on the trendline.

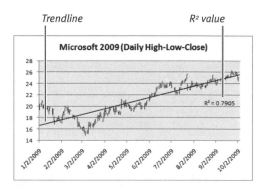

Figure 12.26 A trendline on a stock chart.

■ You may also want to explore these other options in the Analysis group:

   ▲ **Lines.** Show high-low marks (especially useful for stock charts) and/or drop lines that extend up from the X axis to each data point.

   ▲ **Error Bars.** Surround each data point with bars showing a confidence interval based on a percentage, standard deviation, or standard error.

ADDING TRENDLINES

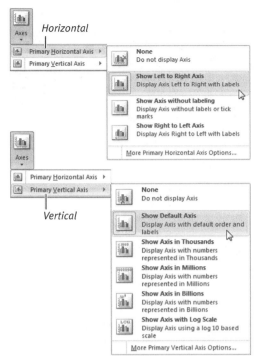

Figure 12.27 Because the horizontal and vertical axes serve different purposes, each has different options.

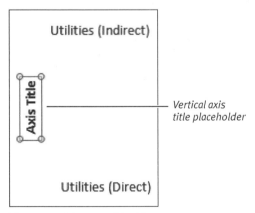

Figure 12.28 You can add a title to either or both axes.

Modifying the Axes

Most charts have a horizontal (X) and a vertical (Y) axis. You can modify either axis by changing its labels or formatting.

To modify an axis:

1. Select the chart.

2. *Do any of the following:*

   ▲ To remove an axis, set the position of the Y axis, or specify numeric units to use for the X axis, click the Layout tab and choose an option from the Axes drop-down menu in the Axes group (**Figure 12.27**).

   ▲ To change the formatting for an axis, right-click the axis labels on the chart and choose Format Axis, or choose More *axis name* Axis Options from the Axes menu (Figure 12.27). Make changes in the Format Axis dialog box and click Close.

   ▲ To change an individual axis label, edit the label's text in its worksheet cell. You can also modify axis labels in the Select Data Source dialog box. Click the Design tab, and click the Select Data icon in the Data group.

   ▲ To add a title to the horizontal or vertical axis, choose a display option from the appropriate Axis Titles submenu on the Layout tab. A title containing placeholder text appears on the chart (**Figure 12.28**). Edit the placeholder text and then change the formatting, if you wish.

MODIFYING THE AXES

Creating Sparklines

New in Office 2010, *sparklines* (**Figure 12.29**) are tiny charts that display and summarize data. Unlike normal charts that are floating, resizable objects, sparklines are presented in individual cells, visually linking them with their data.

To add sparklines:

1. Select the data range or the range into which you want to insert the sparklines.

2. Click the Insert tab. In the Sparklines group (**Figure 12.30**), click a sparkline format icon.

   The Create Sparklines dialog box appears (**Figure 12.31**).

3. Fill in the two range text boxes by typing or drag-selecting on the worksheet.

   If you preselected a range in Step 1, it will already be specified in the dialog box. Edit it, if necessary.

4. Click OK.

   The sparklines appear in the designated Location Range.

✔ Tips

- As with other Excel charts, if you edit the data on which sparklines are based, the sparklines automatically update.

- To change their style or formatting, select the sparklines and set new options on the Design tab (within the Sparkline Tools contextual tab).

- You can change the formatting of an individual sparkline by selecting only its cell, rather than all sparkline cells.

- Sparkline cells can also contain data.

- To remove all or selected sparklines, choose a Clear command from the Group group on the Design tab.

Sparklines

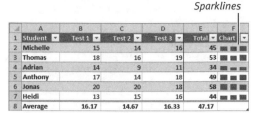

Figure 12.29 In this example, column sparklines show each student's three test scores.

Figure 12.30 Select a sparkline format by clicking an icon.

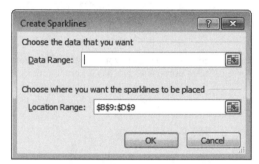

Figure 12.31 Specify the data range and location range for the sparklines.

CREATING SPARKLINES

Original chart data

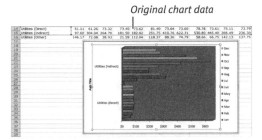

Figure 12.32 With the chart selected, drag a corner handle of the data selection rectangle to select the original and new data.

Specify a new range

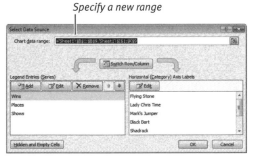

Figure 12.33 To change the data on which a chart is based, edit the ranges in the Select Data Source dialog box or select new ranges on the worksheet.

Changing the Chart Data

Even if you've created a chart and carefully formatted it exactly the way you wanted, a problem sometimes occurs. The data on which the chart is based changes! A column or row in the data source may need to be deleted, data in one or more cells may need to be edited, or you may want to include additional rows or columns.

To modify chart data:

1. Select the chart.

2. *Do any of the following:*

   ▲ **Edit existing data.** If you edit data in the cells on which the chart is based, the chart automatically updates to reflect the edited data.

   ▲ **Delete rows or columns.** If you delete rows or columns within the range(s) used to create the chart, the data is automatically removed from the chart.

   ▲ **Add new rows or columns.** Adding new rows or columns within the range of the original chart data triggers an update of the chart.

   To add new rows that are immediately adjacent to the existing rows, select the chart. This causes the original chart data to be selected on the worksheet. Drag a corner of the data selection rectangle to encompass the new rows or columns (**Figure 12.32**).

✔ Tip

■ You can also add new data to a chart by switching to the Design tab and clicking the Select Data icon in the Data group. The Select Data Source dialog box appears (**Figure 12.33**). Edit the ranges in the dialog box or select new ranges on the worksheet. Click OK.

Part IV: Microsoft PowerPoint

GETTING STARTED WITH POWERPOINT 2010

You can use PowerPoint to create presentations for almost any occasion, such as a business meeting, government forum, school project or lecture, church function, or club fund-raiser. A presentation is designed as a slide show and can be based on one of the included themes, use a company-provided theme, or be created from scratch.

Presentations can feature within-slide animations (such as flying text) and between-slide transitions (such as dissolves). Slides can include embedded movies and audio clips, as well as recorded narration. You can add notes on each slide to use when giving the presentation and to distribute as handouts.

The resulting slide show can be run on your computer, printed, output to transparencies for viewing on an overhead projector, converted to a high-quality video, or saved as HTML for viewing using a browser on the Web, an intranet, or a recipient's computer.

✔ Tip

- When distributing a presentation, your audience doesn't need PowerPoint. They can download PowerPoint Viewer 2010 from Microsoft's site. (When you use the Package Presentation for CD feature, a link from which PowerPoint Viewer can be downloaded is included on the CD.)

The PowerPoint Interface

Figure 13.1 (below) shows the interface elements you'll use when creating presentations. Many of them, such as the Ribbon and Quick Access Toolbar, can also be found in Word, Excel, and Outlook.

File tab. Click this tab to perform file-related actions in the Backstage (**Figure 13.2**), such as creating, opening, saving, and printing. Click Options to set PowerPoint preferences. To open a presentation on which you've recently worked, click its name in the Recent list. The Exit command can also be found here.

File tab

Recent files list

Set preferences
Quit PowerPoint

Figure 13.2 Office Backstage.

File tab *Quick Access Toolbar* *Tab (Animations)* *Placeholder* *Group (Drawing)* *Close*

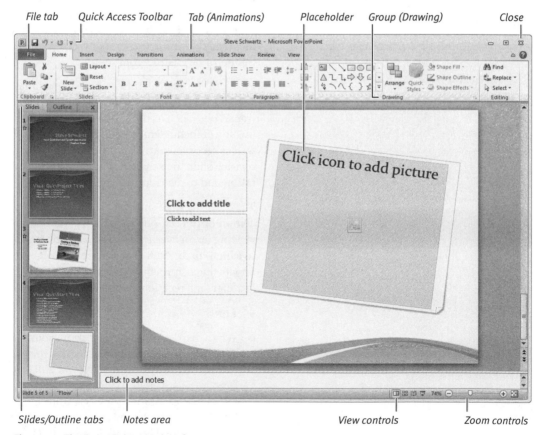

Slides/Outline tabs *Notes area* *View controls* *Zoom controls*

Figure 13.1 The PowerPoint 2010 interface.

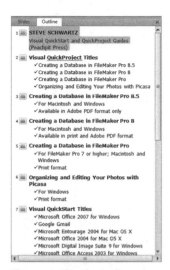

Figure 13.3 Use the Outline tab to rearrange slides and edit content.

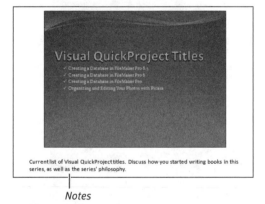

Notes

Figure 13.4 When printed, you can use the note pages to assist you in the presentation or give them out as handouts. Here's a typical slide in Notes Page view.

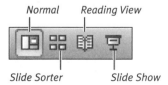

Normal   Reading View

Slide Sorter   Slide Show

Figure 13.5 You can switch views by clicking an icon at the bottom of the window.

Quick Access Toolbar. Icons for performing common commands, such as Save, Undo, and Redo, can be found here.

Ribbon. As in Office 2007, you choose commands from the Ribbon rather than from menus. Similar commands and procedures are listed together on a *tab*, such as Insert or View. Within each tab, procedures are further divided into *groups*, based on similarity of function. To perform a command, you switch to the appropriate tab by clicking its name and then click the command's icon or control.

Slides/Outline tabs. In Normal view, when the Slides tab is selected, thumbnails of your slides (in their current order) are displayed (see Figure 13.1). Click a thumbnail to work with that slide. Click the Outline tab to view and work with the presentation in outline mode (**Figure 13.3**).

Placeholders. Every PowerPoint theme contains a predefined set of layouts. In each slide layout, placeholders are provided in which you can add your own formatted text, pictures, and so on.

Notes. To assist with a presentation, you can type notes in this area and print them out, along with a miniature version of the slide to which the notes refer (**Figure 13.4**).

View controls. Click an icon to switch views (**Figure 13.5**). You can also change views by selecting the View tab and clicking an icon in the Presentation Views group.

Zoom controls. Change the current magnification by dragging the slider or by clicking + (Zoom In), – (Zoom Out), the zoom percentage, or the Fit slide to current window icon.

Close. Click the close box to close an open presentation or to quit PowerPoint. (When the current presentation is the only one open, clicking the close box quits PowerPoint.) You can also close a presentation by clicking Close in the Backstage (see Figure 13.2).

THE POWERPOINT INTERFACE

Working in Different Views

Depending on what you want to do at the moment, you'll work in one of PowerPoint's many *views*. To switch views, you can click an icon in the View controls (see Figures 13.1 and 13.4) or in the Presentation Views group on the View tab (**Figure 13.6**). Because creating a presentation is an interactive process, you'll switch views frequently.

The PowerPoint views are as follows:

◆ **Normal.** Create, edit, and delete slides (see Figure 13.1).

◆ **Slide Sorter.** Rearrange, delete, and hide slides (**Figure 13.7**).

◆ **Notes Page.** Add and edit notes for each slide in a convenient full-screen format (see Figure 13.4).

◆ **Slide Show.** View the presentation as a full-screen slide show as it will appear to your audience.

◆ **Reading View.** New in PowerPoint 2010, you can use Reading View to step through a presentation and its animations within the document window. Reading View is also useful when delivering a presentation to someone on their computer. To exit Reading View, press ⎋ Esc or click a view icon at the bottom of the document window (see Figure 13.5).

◆ **Slide, Handout, and Notes Masters.** Switch to a Master view to create or modify the underlying theme for slides, note pages, and handouts. For instance, changes made to a master slide (such as setting a different font, size, or color for heading text on a title slide) instantly affect all current and new title slides (**Figure 13.8**).

Figure 13.6 Change views by clicking an icon in the Presentation Views group.

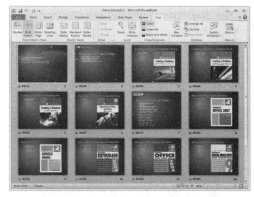

Figure 13.7 In Slide Sorter view, a thumbnail of each slide in the presentation is displayed. Rearrange the slides by dragging them to new positions.

Figure 13.8 If you don't care for a particular font, you can change it on its master slide.

Figure 13.9 When creating a new presentation, you can make one from scratch or start with a template.

Figure 13.10 Select a theme from the Themes group.

Creating a Presentation

If you've never made a PowerPoint presentation, the following are the basic steps in the process. Note that many of the steps, such as creating notes and handouts, are optional. In addition, because presentation design is seldom a linear process, you can change the step order as your creative flow dictates.

To create a presentation:

1. **Make an outline.** This step can help you decide what to present and the approximate order in which you intend to cover the material.

    You can use Word's Outline mode (see Chapter 6) for this task.

2. **Create a new PowerPoint presentation.** *Do one of the following:*

    ▲ If you just launched PowerPoint, a new presentation is started for you.

    ▲ If a presentation is currently open, click the File tab and then click New in the Backstage. Select Blank Presentation from the Available Templates and Themes list (**Figure 13.9**). (If you prefer, you can base the presentation on a template by selecting a category from those stored on disk or at Office.com.)

3. **Select a theme.** If a theme wasn't set in Step 2, choose a theme from the Themes group on the Design tab (**Figure 13.10**).

    A theme gives a consistent look to all slides in the presentation.

4. **Create the slides.** From the New Slide gallery in the Slides group on the Home tab, select a slide style (such as Section Header or Picture with Caption) to add to the presentation. Replace placeholders with appropriate text and pictures.

    continues on next page

New Presentation Tips

◆ To quickly create a Blank Presentation without switching to the Backstage, press Ctrl N.

◆ Regardless of the format intended for a presentation (such as HTML for display on the Web), you should save the working version in a native PowerPoint format: PowerPoint Presentation or PowerPoint 97-2003 Presentation.

5. **Add notes.** If you like, you can add comments to the slides to assist you when delivering the presentation. Notes can be entered in Normal or Notes Page view (see Figures 13.1 and 13.4).

6. **Organize the slides.** In Slide Sorter view (see Figure 13.7), arrange the slides in the order in which you want to present them. Delete or hide unwanted slides.

7. **Add within-slide animations.** You can add motion (fly-in or spin, for example) to slide elements, such as text objects and pictures. With the object selected, select effects from the Animation group on the Animations tab (**Figure 13.11**).

8. **Add between-slide transitions.** You can also specify visual and/or auditory transition effects that play when you move from one slide to the next. Common transitions include fades, dissolves, and wipes, for instance. By choosing effects from the Transition to This Slide group on the Transitions tab (**Figure 13.12**), you can set a different transition for each slide or apply one transition to all slides.

9. **Play and rehearse the presentation.** To play the presentation, switch to Slide Show view or click an icon in the Start Slide Show group on the Slide Show tab. As the show plays, rehearse what you'll say while each slide is onscreen. On the Transitions tab, you can specify that each slide will advance in response to a mouse click or be based on timing established during a rehearsal.

10. **Print notes and handouts, if any.**

11. **Output the show in its final format.** In addition to playing the slide show on a computer, you can convert it to a movie, save it as a PDF, package it for distribution on CD, or output the show in HTML for viewing in a browser.

Show gallery

Figure 13.11 Use the scroll arrows to find an effect or click the bottom arrow to reveal the entire gallery.

Figure 13.12 You can select a between-slide transition effect for the current slide from the Transition to This Slide gallery.

✔ Tips

■ You can also use Reading View to preview and fine tune presentations.

■ PowerPoint 2010 allows you to divide lengthy presentations into *sections*. Like points in a Word outline, you can collapse selected sections to make it easier to concentrate on one part of a presentation at a time.

CREATING A PRESENTATION

CREATING A PRESENTATION

In this chapter, you'll learn the mechanics of creating a presentation and the tools used in the process:

◆ Starting a new presentation and choosing a theme

◆ Adding and deleting slides

◆ Replacing slide placeholders with text, images, charts, tables, and objects

◆ Adding other types of items to slides, such as shapes, text boxes, date/time stamps, and slide numbers

◆ Creating a photo album slide show

◆ Previewing a presentation onscreen as a slide show

For information on working with and formatting slide text and objects (such as pictures, clip art, tables, charts, and text boxes), see Chapter 3.

Beginning a Presentation

As explained in Chapter 13, there are several ways to begin a presentation.

To create a new blank presentation (no theme):

◆ *Do one of the following:*

▲ Launch PowerPoint 2010. By default, a blank presentation is created.

▲ With PowerPoint open, press Ctrl N.

▲ Click the File tab. In the Backstage, click New to display the Available Templates and Themes (**Figure 14.1**). Select the Blank Presentation icon and click the Create button.

To create a new presentation based on a template or theme:

1. Click the File tab to go to the Backstage.

2. Click New to display the Available Templates and Themes (Figure 14.1).

3. Select one of the following categories from the Templates list:

▲ To base the presentation on a template that's on your hard disk, select Sample templates or My templates. Select a template from the ones that appear and click the Create button.

▲ To base the presentation on the default Blank Presentation but with a theme applied, select Themes. Select a theme icon from the ones that appear and click Create.

▲ To base the presentation on an online template, select a category from the Office.com Templates section. Select one of the listed templates and click Download (**Figure 14.2**). The template downloads from Office.com and is added to the My templates category.

Figure 14.1 To create the same blank presentation that appears at startup, select the Blank Presentation.

Office.com template   *Preview*

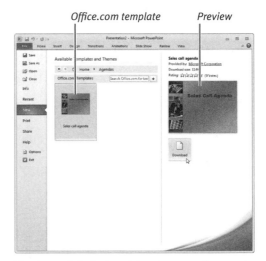

Figure 14.2 Select a template category, review templates available for download, and select a template that's appropriate for your project.

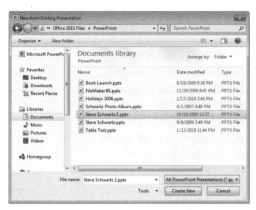

Figure 14.3 Select one of your previous presentations from this dialog box.

— *Save icon*

Figure 14.4 Click Save to save the presentation.

Current folder

Filename   *File type*

Figure 14.5 Save the new presentation in the Save As dialog box (Windows 7 shown).

Back   *Main page*   *Current folder*

Figure 14.6 The navigation bar.

▲ To base the presentation on one of your previous presentations, select New from existing. The New from Existing Presentation dialog box appears (**Figure 14.3**). Navigate to the folder that contains your presentation, select it, and click Create New.

The presentation opens in a new window.

4. Any time after generating the new presentation, you can save it to disk by doing one of the following:

   ▲ Click the Save icon in the Quick Access Toolbar (**Figure 14.4**).

   ▲ Press ⌃Ctrl S.

   ▲ Click the File tab to go to the Backstage. Select Save or Save As.

   A Save As dialog box appears (**Figure 14.5**).

5. Navigate to the folder in which you want to save the presentation, name the file, select a file type from the Save as type drop-down list, and click Save.

✔ Tips

■ Note that the Available Templates and Themes section contains navigation icons (**Figure 14.6**).

■ Periodically, you should save the changes made to your presentation. Click the Save icon in the Quick Access Toolbar, click the File tab and select Save, or press ⌃Ctrl S.

■ If you decide you don't want to use or keep the presentation, close it without saving.

■ Regardless of the presentation-creation method you choose, you can change the *theme* applied to the slides. See the next section for instructions on setting a theme.

BEGINNING A PRESENTATION

Setting the Theme

A *theme* provides a consistent background and fonts for a presentation. Unless your new presentation already has a theme (as it will if the presentation is based on a template or an existing presentation), the first step is to select a theme (**Figure 14.7**, below).

To apply a theme to a presentation:

1. Switch to the Design tab.

2. *Do any of the following:*

▲ Choose a theme from the gallery in the Themes group.

▲ Choose a new color scheme for the current theme from the Colors drop-down list (**Figure 14.8**).

▲ Choose a different combination of fonts from the Fonts drop-down list.

▲ Choose a different color or gradient from the Background Styles gallery.

These theme elements all provide a *live preview* on the current slide when you hover the cursor over one of them. Click an option to apply it to the presentation.

✔ Tips

■ You can change the *current* theme and elements, too. However, the sooner in the design process that you finalize your theme choices, the fewer modifications you'll have to make to existing slides.

■ For more extensive background options, choose Format Background from the Background Styles drop-down menu.

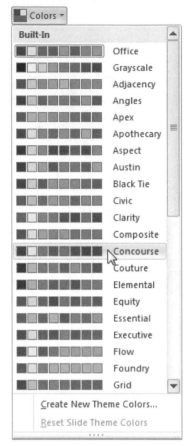

Figure 14.8 You can pick a new color scheme from the Colors list.

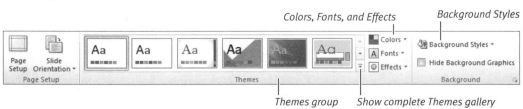

Colors, Fonts, and Effects

Background Styles

Themes group

Show complete Themes gallery

Figure 14.7 Apply theme and theme element changes by choosing options from the Design tab.

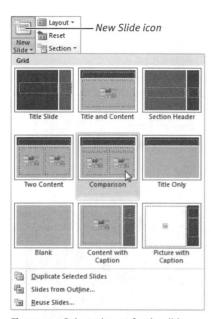

Figure 14.9 Select a layout for the slide you're adding to the presentation.

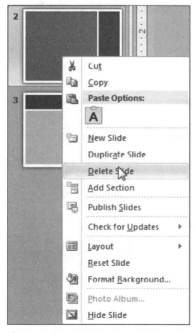

Figure 14.10 You can also delete a slide by right-clicking its thumbnail.

Adding and Deleting Slides

You can add new slides and delete ones that you decide not to use in the presentation.

To add a slide to a presentation:

1. Switch to Normal, Slide Sorter, or Notes Page view by clicking an icon in the Presentation Views group of the View tab.

2. Click the Home tab.

3. Select the slide after which you want the new slide to be added.

4. Click the New Slide icon in the Slides group and select the slide type to insert from the drop-down gallery (**Figure 14.9**). The new slide appears after the current slide.

To delete a slide:

1. Switch to Normal or Slide Sorter view by clicking an icon in the Presentation Views group of the View tab.

2. Click the Home tab.

3. *Do either of the following:*

   ▲ Select the slide's thumbnail and press [Del].

   ▲ Right-click the slide's thumbnail and choose Delete Slide from the context menu (**Figure 14.10**).

   The slide is deleted from the presentation.

✔ Tip

■ To modify a slide's layout (changing it from one slide style to another), switch to the Home tab in Normal or Slide Sorter view and choose a layout from the Layout icon's gallery in the Slides group.

ADDING AND DELETING SLIDES

251

Replacing Placeholders

Most slide layouts contain *placeholders* for text or graphics (**Figure 14.11**). To use the placeholders, you replace them with your own material. Replacing placeholders and other design work is done in Normal view.

To replace a text placeholder:

1. Click a "Click to add title," "Click to add text," or similarly worded placeholder (**Figure 14.12**).

   The placeholder text vanishes.

2. Type your text (**Figure 14.13**). If additional paragraphs are required, press Enter to begin each new paragraph.

To replace a picture or movie-clip placeholder:

1. Click the picture or movie-clip placeholder icon (Figure 14.11).

   An Insert Picture or Insert Video dialog box appears, respectively.

2. Navigate to the folder that contains the picture or movie clip, select its file icon, and click Open or Insert, respectively.

   The picture or movie appears in the placeholder frame.

To replace a clip art placeholder:

1. Click the clip art placeholder icon (Figure 14.11).

   The Clip Art pane appears on the right side of the PowerPoint window.

2. Follow the procedure in "Adding Clip Art" (Chapter 3) to find, select, and insert a clip art image.

   After the clip art appears on the slide, close the Clip Art pane by clicking its close box (X).

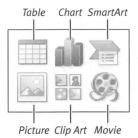

Table   Chart   SmartArt

Picture   Clip Art   Movie

Figure 14.11 Object placeholder icons.

Subtitle text placeholder

Title text placeholder

Figure 14.12 This title slide has two text placeholders.

Figure 14.13 The replacement text adapts the character and paragraph formatting of the placeholder.

REPLACING PLACEHOLDERS

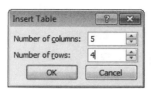

Figure 14.14 Set the number of columns and rows.

Figure 14.15 A table with the specified number of columns and rows appears in the placeholder area.

Chart categories   *Chart styles*

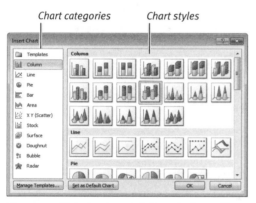

Figure 14.16 Select a chart style from the Insert Chart dialog box. Click OK.

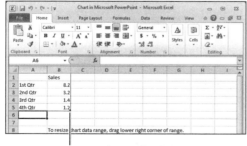

Drag to change the chart range

Figure 14.17 Replace the sample data with your data.

To replace a table placeholder:

1. Click the table placeholder icon (see Figure 14.11).

   The Insert Table dialog box appears (**Figure 14.14**).

2. Enter the number of columns and rows for the table, and then click OK.

   The new table appears (**Figure 14.15**).

3. Complete the table by entering labels and data.

To replace a chart placeholder:

1. Click the chart placeholder icon (see Figure 14.11).

   The Insert Chart dialog box appears (**Figure 14.16**).

2. Select a chart category.

3. Click the icon that represents the style of chart you want to create, and click OK.

   Excel launches and opens a worksheet containing sample data (**Figure 14.17**).

4. Replace the chart labels and data with your information. To change the chart range (by adding or removing columns and/or rows), drag the lower-right corner of the range. Click the worksheet's close box (X) when you're done entering data.

   The chart appears on the slide.

5. *Optional:* With the chart selected on the slide, Chart Tools contextual tabs (Design, Layout, and Format) appear. Choose commands from these tabs to change the chart type, layout, or formatting.

REPLACING PLACEHOLDERS

To replace a SmartArt placeholder:

1. Click the SmartArt placeholder icon (see Figure 14.11).

   The Choose a SmartArt Graphic dialog box appears (**Figure 14.18**).

2. Select a graphic category from the list on the left and then select a graphic from the center of the dialog box. Click OK.

   The SmartArt graphic appears in the image placeholder.

3. Replace the text placeholders in the SmartArt graphic with your own text.

4. *Optional:* Choose options on the Design (**Figure 14.19**) and Format tabs to change the colors and style of the SmartArt graphic (**Figure 14.20**).

✔ Tips

■ To remove an unneeded placeholder from a slide, select it and press [Del].

■ To alter the format, appearance, rotation, size, or position of placeholders and other elements (such as background graphics) throughout the presentation, make the changes on the master slides. Changes made to a master Title Slide, for example, will automatically be applied to all current and new Title Slides.

Categories   *SmartArt graphics*   *Preview*

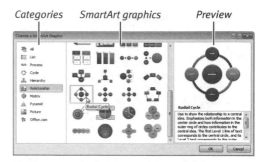

Figure 14.18 Select a SmartArt graphic from the center of the dialog box.

Change Colors gallery

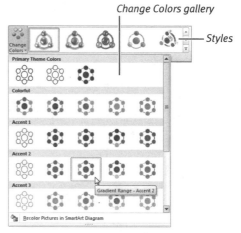

Styles

Figure 14.19 You can alter the SmartArt by choosing a new style and colors.

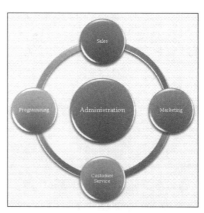

Figure 14.20 A SmartArt graphic example.

REPLACING PLACEHOLDERS

Shapes icon

Figure 14.22 Choose a shape from the Shapes drop-down gallery.

Shape Styles group   WordArt Styles group

Figure 14.23 To change the formatting for a shape, choose options from the Shape Styles group. To alter text (stand-alone or inside an object), you can choose options from the WordArt Styles group.

Figure 14.24 A formatted shape containing WordArt decorative text.

Inserting Other Items

In addition to replacing placeholders with objects or text, you can place items *anywhere* on a given slide by choosing options from the Insert tab (**Figure 14.21**, below). Position the inserted item by clicking a location on the slide or by dragging the item into position.

To insert a table, picture, clip art, SmartArt, chart, movie, or audio clip, see the instructions in "Replacing Placeholders" on the previous pages. For instructions on inserting screenshots, see Chapter 3.

To insert a shape:

1. Switch to the Insert tab. In the Illustrations group, choose a shape from the Shapes gallery (**Figure 14.22**).

2. Click and drag to draw the shape on the slide. (To maintain the shape's original proportions, press Shift as you drag.)

3. *Optional:* To change the shape's color and formatting, choose settings from groups on the Format tab (**Figure 14.23**).

4. *Optional:* To add text inside the shape, *do either of the following:*
   ▲ Right-click the shape and choose Edit Text from the context menu.
   ▲ On the Insert tab, click the Text Box icon in the Text group and click inside the shape to set the text insertion mark.

   Type and format the text (**Figure 14.24**).

INSERTING OTHER ITEMS

Figure 14.21 You can add text and objects anywhere on a slide by choosing commands from the Insert tab.

To insert a text box:

1. Switch to the Insert tab. Click the Text Box icon in the Text group (see Figure 14.21). A text box insertion cursor appears.

2. Click where you want to add the text or drag to set the box's approximate width (**Figure 14.25**).

3. Type the text (**Figure 14.26**). Press ⌈Enter⌋ to begin each additional paragraph.

4. *Optional:* Change the text formatting by performing any of these actions:
   ▲ **Character/Paragraph Format.** Set new character and paragraph formatting by choosing commands from the Font and Paragraph groups on the Home tab (**Figure 14.27**) or from the Mini toolbar.
   ▲ **Rotate.** Click the rotation handle (Figure 14.26) and drag to the left or right to change the text rotation angle.
   ▲ **Stylize.** Choose options from the WordArt Styles group on the Format tab (see Figure 14.23).
   ▲ **Wrap.** Reduce or increase the width of the text box by dragging the center handle on either side. The text within the box will automatically rewrap as required.

5. *Optional:* Reposition the text by moving the cursor over any edge. When a plus cursor with arrowheads appears, you can drag the text box to a new location.

Figure 14.25 This new text box is ready to receive typed or pasted text.

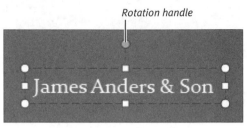

Figure 14.26 The text box automatically expands as you type or paste the text.

Figure 14.27 Common character and paragraph formatting commands are prominently displayed on the Home tab.

Duplicating Slides

After you've created several slides, one of the fastest ways to move the creation process along is to duplicate slides and then edit the duplicates, rather than design every new slide from scratch.

To duplicate a slide, select its thumbnail in the current view, such as Normal or Slide Sorter. Switch to the Home tab, click the New Slide icon in the Slides group, and choose Duplicate Selected Slides from the drop-down menu.

INSERTING OTHER ITEMS

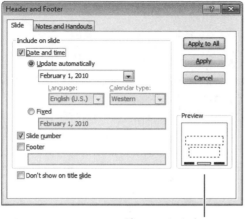

Placement preview

Figure 14.28 Set date/time and numbering options, and then click Apply or Apply to All.

Inserted date

Figure 14.29 Date/time appears on the left edge of the footer, numbering appears on the right, and footer text is centered between the two.

To add a slide number or date/time:

1. Switch to the Insert tab. Click the Header & Footer, Date & Time, or Slide Number icon in the Text group (see Figure 14.21).

   The Header and Footer dialog box appears (**Figure 14.28**). If it isn't selected, click the Slide tab.

2. To number the slides consecutively, click the Slide number check box.

3. To display the date, time, or both, click the Date and time check box, and *do one of the following:*

   ▲ To always display the current date and/or time, click Update automatically and select a date/time format from the drop-down list.

   ▲ To stamp the slide(s) with the present date/time, click Fixed and enter the text to display, such as *8/23/2010*.

4. *Optional:* To prevent the slide number and date information from being shown on title slides, click the Don't show on title slide check box.

5. *Do one of the following:*

   ▲ To add the number and date information to all slides in the presentation (**Figure 14.29**), click Apply to All.

   ▲ To add the number and date information only to the current slide, click Apply.

✔ Tips

■ You can enter *any* text you want in the Fixed text box. You aren't restricted to date/time information.

■ To add text that will be centered in the footer (between the date/time and slide number), click the Footer check box and type the text in the box.

Tips for Working with Objects

Here's some additional information that you may find helpful when working with objects on slides:

◆ Inserted objects can be laid over one another. For example, you can draw a shape around a text box to frame the text or combine shapes to create an illustration. After combining objects, you can *group* them to prevent individual items from accidentally being moved. Select the objects you want to group. On the Home tab, choose Group from the Arrange drop-down menu in the Drawing group. Or on the Format tab, choose Group from the Group icon in the Arrange group.

◆ To change the layering of objects, select an object and choose a command (such as Send to Back) from the Arrange group on the Format tab (**Figure 14.30**). Layering commands are also available on the Home tab from the Arrange drop-down menu in the Drawing group (**Figure 14.31**).

◆ For help in selecting objects, open the Selection and Visibility task pane by doing one of the following:

　▲ On the Format tab, click the Selection Pane icon (Figure 14.30) in the Arrange Group.

　▲ On the Home tab, choose Selection Pane from the Arrange icon's menu in the Drawing group (Figure 14.31).

　▲ On the Home tab, choose Selection Pane from the Select icon's menu in the Editing group.

Click any item in the pane to select it on the slide, regardless of the item's layer and whether it's visible or buried under other items.

Figure 14.30 You can change the layering of a selected object by choosing a command from the Arrange group icons.

Figure 14.31 You can also choose a layering command from the Arrange menu.

◆ Sometimes after carefully formatting and adding text to a shape, the shape just doesn't "work." Rather than create another shape and add the same text and formatting, you can *replace* the original shape with a new one. On the Format tab, click the Edit Shape icon in the Insert Shapes group, choose Change Shape from the drop-down menu, and choose a replacement from the gallery.

Select files   Pictures in album   Preview area

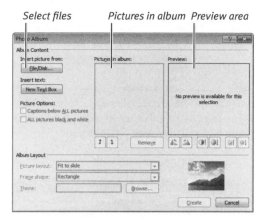

Figure 14.32 The Photo Album dialog box.

Selected photo   Preview of photo

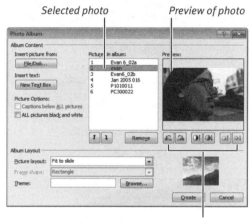

Rotation, contrast, and brightness controls

Figure 14.33 Photos are added to Pictures in album in the order in which they're inserted. (In a mass insertion, they're added alphabetically by filename.)

Creating a Photo Album

A *photo album* is a special presentation you can create to present a slide show of personal or business photos.

To create a photo album:

1. On the Insert tab, click Photo Album in the Illustrations group and choose New Photo Album from the drop-down menu. The Photo Album dialog box appears (**Figure 14.32**).

2. To add photos, click the File/Disk button. The Insert New Pictures dialog box opens.

3. Navigate to the folder that contains the photos. *Do one of the following:*
   ▲ To add a single photo, click its icon.
   ▲ To simultaneously add multiple photos from the folder, Ctrl-click each file.
   ▲ To simultaneously add *all* image files from the folder, select any photo and then press Ctrl A to select them all.

4. If the Insert New Pictures dialog box is still present, click Insert (or Open). The selected photo(s) are added to the Pictures in album list (**Figure 14.33**).

5. As necessary, repeat Steps 2–4 to add more photos. To remove a photo, select its name in the Pictures in album list and click Remove (Figure 14.33).

6. *Optional:* The order of photos in the Pictures in album list will match the slide order. To change a photo's position in the list, select it, and click the up or down arrow button beneath the list.

7. *Optional:* You can alter the rotation, contrast, and/or brightness of a selected photo by clicking icons below its Preview.

continues on next page

CREATING A PHOTO ALBUM

8. In the Album Layout area of the dialog box (**Figure 14.34**), select a layout from the Picture layout drop-down list.

If you select a "with title" layout, every slide will contain a text placeholder.

9. If you chose any layout other than Fit to slide in Step 8, you can select a frame from the Frame shape drop-down list.

A preview of the selected Picture layout and Frame shape settings is shown to the right (see Figure 14.33).

10. *Optional:* To apply a theme to the slides, click the Browse button. Select a Power-Point theme in the Choose Theme dialog box (**Figure 14.35**) and click Select/Open.

11. *Optional:* In the Picture Options area of the dialog box (**Figure 14.36**), click check boxes to add a caption and/or display the photos in black and white.

By default, each photo's filename is used as its caption. You can edit the captions after the slides have been generated.

12. Click the Create button.

PowerPoint creates a presentation from the selected photos.

13. *Optional:* Edit the album title on slide 1.

14. To save the presentation, click the Save icon on the Quick Access Toolbar, press Ctrl S, or click the File tab and select Save or Save As in the Backstage.

✔ Tips

■ You can treat the photo album as a finished presentation or enliven it by adding PowerPoint features such as animations, transitions, and audio.

■ After generating the presentation, you can change its settings or add new photos by clicking the Photo Album icon and choosing Edit Photo Album. Make the changes and click Update.

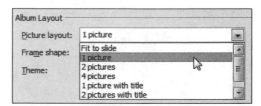

Figure 14.34 Select a slide layout in the Album Layout section of the Photo Album dialog box.

Figure 14.35 You can optionally apply a theme to the slides in your photo album presentation.

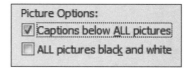

Figure 14.36 Picture Options.

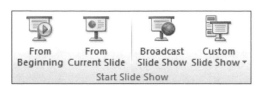

Figure 14.37 If you can't remember the keyboard shortcuts, you can start the show by clicking one of these icons.

Figure 14.38 The slide show runs in full-screen mode.

Previewing the Slide Show

Every slide show is a work in progress. As such, you'll want to periodically preview it onscreen to check the effect of changes, the application of special effects, the addition of new slides, and so on.

To preview a slide show:

1. *Optional:* To begin the slide show with a particular slide (other than the first), select or switch to that slide.

   You can select a slide in Normal, Slide Sorter, or Notes Page view.

2. *Do one of the following:*
   ▲ To run the show starting with the first slide, press F5.
   ▲ To run the show starting with the current slide, press Shift F5.
   ▲ On the Slide Show tab, click the From Beginning or From Current Slide icon in the Start Slide Show group (**Figure 14.37**).

   The show begins (**Figure 14.38**).

3. *Do any of the following:*
   ▲ To step forward through the slides and within-slide animations (if any), click the mouse or press n, Enter, Page Down, Spacebar, →, or ↓.
   ▲ To move backward through the slides and within-slide animations (if any), press p, Page Up, Backspace, ←, or ↑.
   ▲ To end the show, press Esc.

✔ Tips

■ You can also navigate by clicking the faint onscreen controls at the bottom-left corner of the screen.

■ You can press Esc to halt a slide show at *any* time—after the final slide has been displayed or in the middle of the show.

■ Another way to preview a slide show—but restrict its size to the PowerPoint window rather than use the entire screen—is to switch to the new Reading View.

Wrapping Up a Presentation

In this chapter, you'll learn about putting the finishing touches on a presentation:

◆ Add within-slide animations, incoming slide transitions, and action buttons

◆ Make minor edits to movies you've placed on slides

◆ Rearrange slides to match their final order, as well as delete and hide slides

◆ Rehearse the presentation while recording the time spent on each slide and on the total presentation

◆ Print notes, handouts, and other material you'll need for the presentation

◆ Save the presentation in other formats (such as PDF) and package its contents on a CD or DVD

◆ Present the slide show in person or broadcast it over the Internet

✔ Tip

■ To run a finished presentation, follow the steps in "Previewing the Slide Show" in Chapter 14.

Animating Objects and Text

To add motion to a presentation, you can animate any object on a slide, such as a text block, picture, chart, or SmartArt object. You can choose animation effects from the Animation or Add Animation gallery. You can fine-tune an effect by choosing commands from the Animations tab or by opening the Animation Pane. Any slide can contain multiple animated objects. You can even assign multiple animations to the same object.

To assign an animation to an object:

1. In Normal view, select the object on the current slide that you want to animate. Switch to the Animations tab.

2. Choose an effect from the Animation gallery (**Figure 15.1**, below).

   As you hover the cursor over an effect, an animation preview appears on the slide. After you pick an effect, a number appears beside the object that shows the order in which the effect will play (**Figure 15.2**).

3. *Optional:* To add another effect to the object, choose it from the Add Animation gallery in the Advanced Animation group.

Number

Figure 15.2 Each animation is numbered to show the sequence in which it will play.

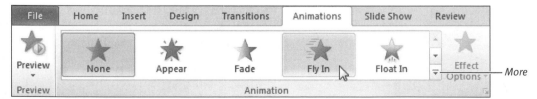

Figure 15.1 View different animation effects by clicking the scroll arrows or click More to see the entire animation gallery.

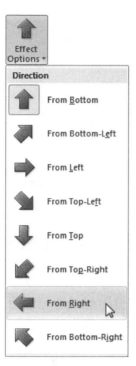

Figure 15.3 When available, effect options differ for each effect.

Figure 15.4 You set options for a selected effect in an effect-specific dialog box. This is where you can associate a sound with an effect, for example.

To set options for an effect:

1. In Normal view, switch to the Animations tab. On the slide, select the number of the animation effect that you want to modify.

2. *Do any of the following:*
   - ▲ Choose an option from the Effect Options menu (**Figure 15.3**).
   - ▲ Click the dialog box launcher icon at the bottom of the Animation group and set options in the dialog box that appears (**Figure 15.4**).
   - ▲ Click the Animation Pane icon in the Advanced Animation group. In the pane, select the animation that you want to modify. Then choose an option from the Effect Options menu, click the Effect Options dialog box launcher, or choose Effect Options from the drop-down menu to the right of the object name.

✔ Tips

- ■ Even information in the footer, such as the slide number, can be animated.

- ■ To view additional effects, choose a More… command from the Animation gallery or Add Animation drop-down menu.

- ■ To set an effect for multiple objects that will all play simultaneously, select all of the objects and then choose the effect.

- ■ To apply one object's animations to another object, select the object with the animation you want to copy, click the Animation Painter icon in the Advanced Animation group, and then click the target object.

continues on next page

ANIMATING OBJECTS AND TEXT

- When animating a *complex object* composed of multiple elements, such as a SmartArt graphic or chart, you can animate it as though it were a single object, one element or item type at a time, and so on.

- To replace one animation with another, select the effect step for the object in the Animation Pane and choose a replacement effect from the Animation gallery.

- You can view a slide's animations by clicking the Preview icon in the Preview group or by clicking Play in the Animation Pane.

- To change the order in which animations will play, open the Animation Pane, select the effect that you want to move, and then *do any of the following:*

  ▲ Drag the effect up or down to a new position in the list.

  ▲ Click a Re-Order icon at the bottom of the Animation Pane (**Figure 15.5**).

  ▲ Click a Reorder Animation icon (Move Earlier or Move Later) in the Timing group (**Figure 15.6**).

- To remove an animation from a selected object, *do one of the following:*

  ▲ Select None in the Animation gallery.

  ▲ Choose Remove from the effect's drop-down menu in the Animation Pane (**Figure 15.7**).

  ▲ Select the effect in the Animation Pane or select the effect's number on the slide and press ⌈Delete⌋.

- Don't overuse animations. A few can draw attention to key elements on important slides; too many can turn a presentation into a carnival sideshow.

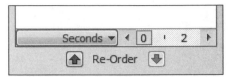

Figure 15.5 You can click a Re-Order icon at the bottom of the Animation Pane to move a selected animation step to a different position.

Figure 15.6 Or you can click the Move Earlier or Move Later icon in the Timing group. Each click moves the effect one step up or down in the animation list.

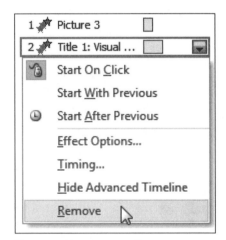

Figure 15.7 To remove an effect, you can select it in the Animation Pane and choose Remove from the effect's drop-down menu.

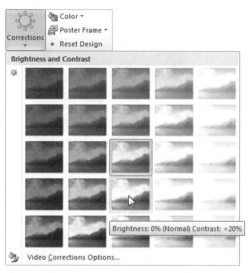

Figure 15.8 You can alter the brightness/contrast and color cast of a movie by choosing thumbnails from the Corrections and Color galleries.

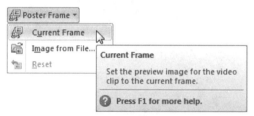

Figure 15.9 You can set a poster frame for a video.

Editing Movies

Office 2010 provides tools for editing videos. When you select a movie on the current slide, the Video Tools contextual tab appears. You can choose new settings from its Format and Playback tabs.

Format tab tools

Using commands on the Format tab of the Video Tools contextual tab, you can perform the following edits on a selected movie clip:

◆ **Correct brightness/contrast.** Choose a brightness/contrast thumbnail from the Corrections gallery in the Adjust group (**Figure 15.8**). For more precise settings, choose Video Corrections Options from the bottom of the gallery menu.

◆ **Recolor movies.** To display the video in *grayscale* (shades of gray) or with an overall color cast, choose a thumbnail from the Color gallery in the Adjust group. Choose More Variations if you want to use a color that isn't shown.

◆ **Set a poster frame.** A *poster frame* is an image used to represent the movie when it's not playing. To select a movie frame, advance the movie to the frame and choose Current Frame from the Poster Frame drop-down menu in the Adjust group (**Figure 15.9**). If you prefer, you can select a picture from your hard disk to serve as the poster frame.

◆ **Add a border.** If you want to surround the movie with a border, choose settings from the Video Border drop-down menu in the Video Styles group. Alternatively, you can click the Format Video dialog box launcher (found at the bottom of the Video Styles group) and select settings from the Border Color and Border Style categories.

◆ **Apply object formatting.** You can add a fancy frame or alter the shape of a video clip by choosing commands from the Video Styles group (**Figure 15.10**).

◆ **Resize movies.** You can resize any movie frame by doing any of the following:

▲ Click a corner and drag.

▲ Type new numbers or click the arrows in the Video Height and Video Width boxes in the Size group (**Figure 15.11**).

▲ Click the dialog box launcher in the Size group (Figure 15.11) to enter specific dimensions or scaling numbers.

◆ **Reset formatting.** To remove all applied formatting changes, click Reset Design in the Adjust group (see Figure 15.8).

✔ Tip

■ Other than selecting a poster frame to ensure that a consistent image appears when the slide is first presented, it's unlikely that you'll use many of the commands on the Format tab to modify the appearance of your movies.

Playback tab tools

Using commands on the Playback tab of the Video Tools contextual tab, you can specify how a selected movie clip will play during the presentation:

◆ **Trim videos.** Click the Trim Video command in the Editing group to remove unwanted frames from the start or end of a video clip. In the Trim Video dialog box (**Figure 15.12**), drag the green start marker and/or the red end marker to new positions, and then click OK.

Figure 15.10 To add a stylized frame or border to a movie, choose options from the Video Styles group.

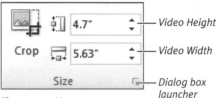

Figure 15.11 You can set a new size for a movie by entering dimensions in the Size group.

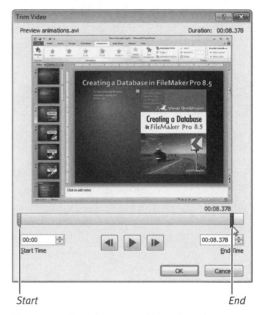

Figure 15.12 Drag the start and/or end markers to new positions to cut out unwanted frames. As you drag, a live preview of the movie is shown.

EDITING MOVIES

Figure 15.13 Create or delete bookmarks by clicking icons in the Bookmarks group.

Figure 15.14 You can apply a fade in or fade out to any movie clip.

Figure 15.15 Apply additional settings from the Video Options group.

Embedded vs. Linked Videos

Normally, inserted movies are *embedded* in the presentation. The video is saved with the PowerPoint file, ensuring that it will always be available whenever and wherever the show is presented. Another option is to *link* the movie to the presentation—using either a movie from a Web site or a file on disk. To play such a movie, you must have access to the Internet or to the file's location, such as a flash drive or DVD.

To link a movie file, select a slide placeholder, click the Insert tab, click the Video icon in the Media group, and choose Video from File or Video from Web Site. When choosing the latter, you will be asked to paste the "embed code" provided by the Web site.

◆ **Add/remove bookmarks.** You can mark key points in a movie by assigning *bookmarks* to them. Bookmarks enable you to jump directly to that frame or can be used to trigger animations.

▲ To add a bookmark, move the movie slider to the desired spot and then click the Add Bookmark icon in the Bookmarks group (**Figure 15.13**).

▲ To delete an unwanted bookmark, select its bookmark icon on the movie slider and click Remove Bookmark.

◆ **Fade in or out.** You can instruct a movie to smoothly fade in or out by entering numbers (in whole and fractional seconds) in the Fade Duration boxes in the Editing group (**Figure 15.14**).

◆ **Other playback options.** The self-explanatory tools in the Video Options group (**Figure 15.15**) are used to set key playback behaviors, such as audio volume, whether the clip will play automatically or wait for a mouse click, and so on.

✔ Tips

■ You can remove inserted videos that you no longer want. Select the video on the slide and press (Delete) or (Del).

■ To reduce the size of all embedded videos in a presentation, switch to the Backstage by clicking the File tab. Select the Info category and choose a quality setting from the Compress Media drop-down menu. View the results by running the show. If you aren't satisfied, you can undo or change the compression by revisiting the Compress Media command.

EDITING MOVIES

Organizing the Slides

In Slide Sorter view (**Figure 15.16**), you can rearrange the slides to match their final order. You can also delete unwanted slides, as well as hide ones you want to keep but won't be using in the current presentation.

To organize the slides:

1. Switch to Slide Sorter view by clicking its icon in the Presentation Views group on the Views tab or at the bottom of the document window.

2. Adjust the magnification controls to clearly display the slide thumbnails.

3. *Do any of the following:*

   ▲ To change a slide's order in the show, drag its thumbnail to a new position.

   ▲ To delete a slide, right-click its thumbnail and choose Delete Slide from the context menu (**Figure 15.17**).

   ▲ To hide a slide, right-click its thumbnail and choose Hide Slide from the context menu. The slide number shows a slide's hidden status (**Figure 15.18**). In Normal view, hidden slides' thumbnails are fuzzy.

✔ Tips

■ If you need to modify a slide, double-click its thumbnail. The slide appears in Normal view, ready for editing.

■ You can play a slide's animations in Slide Sorter view by clicking the animation indicator beneath the lower-left corner of the thumbnail (Figure 15.18).

■ You can also organize slides in Normal view. To change a slide's position, drag its thumbnail to a new location in the list. To delete or hide a slide, right-click the thumbnail and choose Delete Slide or Hide Slide from the context menu.

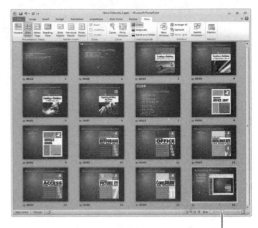

Magnification controls

Figure 15.16 Slide Sorter view.

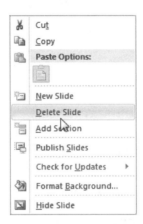

Figure 15.17 Right-click a thumbnail to delete or hide a slide.

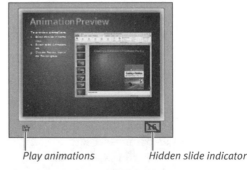

Play animations   *Hidden slide indicator*

Figure 15.18 When a slide is hidden, its number is displayed with a slash.

Effect Options

Figure 15.19 Select a transition effect from the gallery.

Sound and speed settings *Advance Slide options*

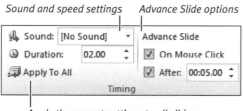

Apply the current settings to all slides

Figure 15.20 You can set additional options in the Timing group.

And What About Sections?

Although we've gotten along without them for 20+ years, PowerPoint 2010 now allows you to group your slides into logical *sections*. Because you can expand or collapse a section in Normal or Slide Sorter view, sections are especially useful for focusing on specific parts of a large presentation.

To insert a section, switch to the Home tab, select the slide that will be the first one in the new section, and choose Add Section from the Section icon in the Slides group. To name the section, click its bar and choose Rename Section from the Section icon.

You can collapse or expand a section by clicking the triangle that precedes the section name. To simultaneously collapse or expand *all* sections, choose the appropriate command from the Section icon's drop-down menu.

Adding Transitions

A *transition* is an effect that appears when switching to a new slide during a slide show. You can use the same transition for every slide change, different transitions for different slides, or no transitions at all (when presenting real slides or using an overhead projector, for example). When setting transitions, note that they are applied to the current slide's *entrance*—not its exit.

To specify a transition:

1. In Normal or Slide Sorter view, select the slide thumbnail to which you want to add a transition.

2. Click the Transitions tab.

3. Choose an effect from the Transition to This Slide gallery (**Figure 15.19**).

   A live preview is presented for any transition over which you hover the cursor.

4. *Optional:* To change the direction of the effect, choose an option from the Effect Options menu (Figure 15.19).

   Effect options are different for different effects.

5. *Optional:* To add a sound effect to the transition, choose one from the Sound menu in the Timing group (**Figure 15.20**). To change the length of the transition effect, enter a new Duration (in seconds).

6. Select an Advance Slide option to determine whether the slide will advance manually (under presenter control) or automatically (based on time).

7. *Optional:* To apply the transition to every slide in the presentation, click Apply To All.

ADDING TRANSITIONS

✔ Tips

- To view transitions in Normal or Slide Sorter view, click the Preview button in the Preview group.

- Transitions can be skipped if you won't be presenting on a computer.

- To change a transition effect and options for a slide, select the slide and select new settings from the Transitions tab (see Figures 15.19 and 15.20).

- To remove a transition from a selected slide, select the None transition (see Figure 15.19). To remove transitions from *all* slides, set any slide's transition to None and then click Apply to All.

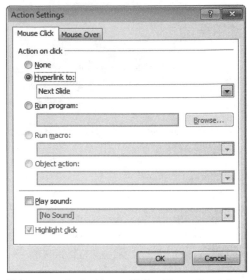

Figure 15.21 On the Mouse Click or Mouse Over tab, specify a button action and click OK.

Adding Action Buttons

An *action button* is a shape you can place on a slide that performs a function when clicked, such as returning to the first slide, playing a sound effect, or launching an application.

To add an action button to a slide, switch to Normal view, click the Insert or Home tab, and choose a button from the Action Buttons section of the Shapes gallery. Click and drag to draw the button on the slide. (To keep the button proportional to its original dimensions, press [Shift] as you drag.) Like other objects, you can move, resize, or format an action button.

In the Action Settings dialog box (**Figure 15.21**, above), specify the action you want the button to perform in response to a mouse click or *mouse over* (moving the mouse over the button). Close the Action Settings dialog box by clicking OK.

Figure 15.22 Click Rehearse Timings to record the time you spend on each slide.

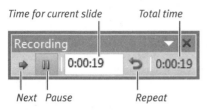

Time for current slide   *Total time*

Next   Pause   *Repeat*

Figure 15.23 Use the Recording toolbar to view slide timings, pause the show, or perform the next action.

Figure 15.24 If the rehearsal went well, you can save the slide timings for use during the presentation.

Rehearsing a Presentation

You'll want to rehearse your presentation before giving it to an audience. In addition to helping prepare what you'll say for each slide, a rehearsal can record the time spent per slide and on the total presentation. This serves two purposes. First, by reviewing slide timings, you can determine if you're spending too much or too little time on some slides or the presentation. Second, if the presentation will run in kiosk mode, timings can be used to automatically advance slides.

To rehearse slide timings:

1. On the Slide Show tab, click Rehearse Timings in the Set Up group (**Figure 15.22**). The slide show begins.

2. Present the show as you intend to give it to your audience, advancing through the slides by clicking the mouse, pressing a keyboard shortcut (see "Previewing the Slide Show" in Chapter 14), or clicking the Next button on the Recording toolbar (**Figure 15.23**).

   As you switch slides, PowerPoint notes the amount of time spent on each one.

3. During the rehearsal, you can also use the Rehearsal toolbar as follows:

   ▲ Click the Pause button if you need to take a break. Click Pause again when you're ready to continue.

   ▲ To restart the timing for the current slide, click the Repeat button.

4. When the show ends, a dialog box displays the total time and asks if you'd like to save the slide timings (**Figure 15.24**). Click Yes to save or No if you prefer not to save the timings.

✔ Tip

■ To replay a presentation using the saved timings, switch to the Slide Show tab, click the Use Timings check box (Figure 15.22), and click From Beginning in the Start Slide Show group. The slide show will play and automatically advance through the animations and slides using the saved timings.

REHEARSING A PRESENTATION

Printing Notes and Handouts

In preparation for the presentation, you can print your notes and audience handouts.

To print notes:

1. Click the File tab to go to the Backstage. Select the Print category.

   A print preview (**Figure 15.25**) allows you to see the output prior to routing it to your printer.

2. Choose a printer from the Printer drop-down menu.

   If your printer isn't shown, choose Add Printer.

3. Using the following drop-down menus in the Settings section, enter these settings:

   ▲ **Menu 1.** Specify the slides you want to include in the printout, such as Print All Slides.

   ▲ **Menu 2.** Choose Notes Pages.

   ▲ **Menu 5.** Choose an orientation (portrait or landscape) for the printout.

   ▲ **Menu 6.** Indicate whether the notes should be printed in shades of gray (*grayscale*), black-and-white, or color.

4. To review the slides and notes as they'll print, click the page controls beneath the preview (Figure 15.25).

5. *Optional:* To edit the header or footer, click Edit Header & Footer. Make any desired changes on the Notes and Handouts tab of the Header and Footer dialog box that appears (**Figure 15.26**).

6. In the Print section, specify the number of copies to print.

7. Click the Print button.

   When you print, the notes print one slide per page.

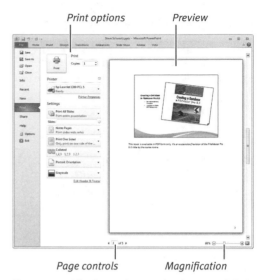

Print options   Preview

Page controls   Magnification

Figure 15.25 All print settings can be chosen and their effects previewed in the Backstage.

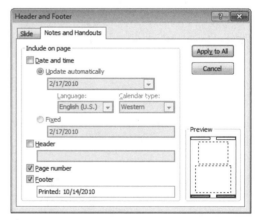

Figure 15.26 By default, only the slide number is included as footer data on a notes page. However, you can customize the header and footer, if you wish.

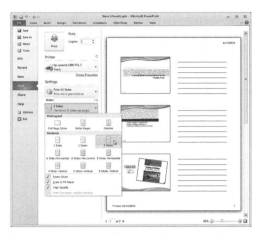

Figure 15.27 Choose a Handouts layout from this drop-down menu.

To print audience handouts:

◆ Perform the "To print notes" task list. In Step 3, however, choose a Handouts layout (**Figure 15.27**) from the second drop-down menu rather than choosing Notes page.

✔ Tips

■ Choose Full Page Slides from the second drop-down menu to print an enlarged version of each slide (one slide per page).

■ In a printed handout, the 3 Slides option provides lines on which the audience can write notes (Figure 15.27).

■ It can be helpful to choose Outline from the second drop-down menu. The printout (**Figure 15.28**) provides a slide-by-slide listing of the text contained on each slide.

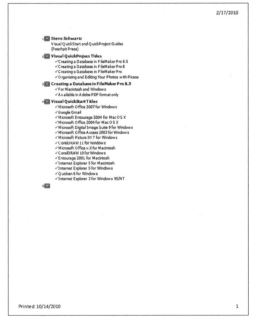

Figure 15.28 Choose Outline to print slide text in outline form.

Saving a Presentation In Other Formats

If the slide show will be presented or needs to be delivered to recipients in a form other than as a PowerPoint 2010 presentation, you can generate an additional copy of it in the necessary format. In PowerPoint 2010, all of the essential commands can be found in the Share section of the Backstage. From this area, you can save or convert the current presentation to a variety of popular formats. In this section, you'll learn to save presentations in alternative PowerPoint formats, convert a presentation to a PDF file, package a presentation for distribution on CD, and generate a PowerPoint video from a presentation.

To save a presentation in an alternative PowerPoint format:

1. In the Share section of the Backstage, select Change File Type.

   A file type list appears (**Figure 15.29**).

2. Select an output file type from the Change File Type list.

   A Save As dialog box appears (**Figure 15.30**). The correct file type is preselected in the Save as type list.

3. Navigate to the drive and folder in which you will save the file, rename the file (optional), and click Save.

✔ Tips

- You can also save in an alternate format by selecting Save As in the Backstage. When the Save As dialog box appears, simply select the desired file type from the Save as type list (Figure 15.30).

- If an intended recipient has an older version of PowerPoint, choose *PowerPoint 97-2000 Presentation* as the output file type.

Figure 15.29 Select an output file type from this list.

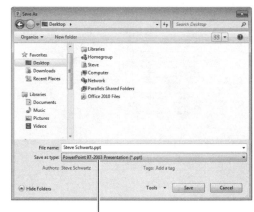

Save As type list

Figure 15.30 Select a location in which to save the new file and then click Save.

Figure 15.31 Use this modified file output dialog box (Windows 7) to specify a name, disk location, and quality for the PDF file.

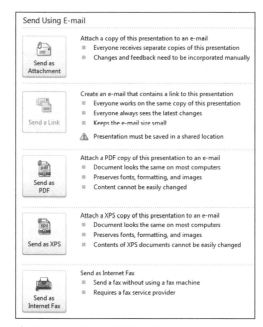

Figure 15.32 Two popular Send Using E-mail options are Send as PDF and Send as Attachment.

To save a presentation as an Adobe Reader (PDF) file:

1. In the Share section of the Backstage, select Create PDF/XPS document.

2. Click the Create a PDF/XPS button.

   The Publish as PDF or XPS dialog box appears (**Figure 15.31**).

3. *Optional:* If you want to specify a subset of slides to include or publish handouts, notes, or an outline view of the presentation, click the Options button and change the settings in the Options dialog box that appears.

4. At the bottom of the Publish as PDF or XPS dialog box, specify whether to generate a Standard or Minimum size (compressed, lower resolution) file by clicking the appropriate radio button.

5. Navigate to the drive and folder in which you will save the file, rename the file (optional), and click Publish to create the PDF file.

   The resulting PDF file can be viewed in Adobe Reader, Apple's Preview, and similar utilities.

✔ Tip

- If you intend to email the PDF file, you can streamline the process by selecting Send Using E-mail in the Share section of the Backstage and clicking the Send as PDF button (**Figure 15.32**). Similarly, if you want to share the *actual* presentation via email (enabling it to be edited and viewed by the recipient in a current version of PowerPoint), click Send as Attachment.

To package a presentation for distribution on CD or DVD:

1. In the Share section of the Backstage, select Package Presentation for CD and click the Package for CD button.

   The Package for CD dialog box appears (**Figure 15.33**).

2. Type a short name for the CD/DVD in the Name the CD text box.

3. If you want to add other presentations to the same CD/DVD, click Add. Select the additional presentation filename(s) from the Add Files dialog box and click Add.

   The presentation names are added to the list in the Package for CD dialog box. You can change their order by selecting a filename and clicking the up- or down-arrow button.

4. *Optional:* If you want to password-protect a presentation to prevent it from being opened or modified by unauthorized users, click the Options button and make the necessary changes in the Options dialog box (**Figure 15.34**).

5. Click the appropriate Copy button as described below. Note that if you intend to create a DVD rather than a CD, you *must* use Copy to Folder and then create the DVD using separate DVD burning software.

   ▲ **Copy to CD.** Insert a blank CD into your CD or DVD burner. In the dialog box that appears, click Yes or No to include linked files on the CD. Office burns the selected presentation(s) onto the CD.

   A recipient can view the presentations with PowerPoint or PowerPoint Viewer (2007 or higher). Instructions for down-loading and installing PowerPoint Viewer are provided on the CD.

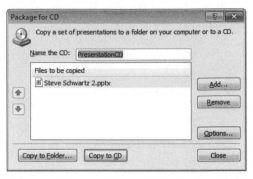

Figure 15.33 The current presentation is automatically included in the Files to be copied list. Add other presentations (if desired), set options, and copy the files to a CD or a folder.

Figure 15.34 In the Options dialog box, you can add password-protection to the copied presentations.

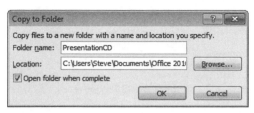

Figure 15.35 Specify a disk location and new folder name, and then click OK.

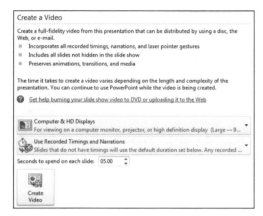

Figure 15.36 Set options for the video and click OK.

▲ **Copy to Folder.** Click this button to copy the presentations and supporting files to disk for later burning to CD or DVD. If desired, you can set the same options as described previously by clicking the Options button. In the Copy to Folder dialog box (**Figure 15.35**), select an output location by clicking Browse, name the presentation folder, and click OK.

✔ Tips

■ A presentation CD contains normal copies of your PowerPoint files. If you don't want to allow these files to be opened or edited in PowerPoint, set password(s) in the Options dialog box (see Figure 15.34).

■ If you want to avoid the requirement that recipients have PowerPoint or PowerPoint Viewer on their computer, you may prefer to create a Windows Media Video (WMV) of the presentation as described below.

To create a video from a presentation:

1. *Optional:* Record the slide timings (Rehearse Timings on the Slide Show tab) or timings and narrations (Record Slide Show on the Slide Show tab). These elements can be incorporated into the video.

2. In the Share section of the Backstage, select Create a Video.

   Create a Video options appear on the right side of the page (**Figure 15.36**).

3. From the first drop-down menu, choose an output size/quality setting.

4. From the second drop-down menu, you can elect to use recorded timings and narrations or a default duration per slide.

continues on next page

SAVING A PRESENTATION IN OTHER FORMATS

5. In the Seconds to spend on each slide box, enter a default duration to use for displaying each slide.

If you chose Don't Use Recorded Timings and Narrations in Step 4, this timing will be applied to all slides in the presentation. If you chose Use Recorded Timings and Narrations in Step 4, this timing will be applied to every slide for which a timing hasn't been recorded.

6. Click the Create Video button.

A Save As dialog box appears (**Figure 15.37**).

7. Name the output file, select a disk and folder in which to save it, and click Save.

A progress bar appears in PowerPoint's status area, enabling you to track the video-creation process (**Figure 15.38**). At its conclusion, the WMV file is saved to disk. The video can be played on a PC using Windows Media Player and similar programs, as well as on other devices that can play WMV videos.

✔ Tip

■ Before running, saving, or exporting a presentation, it's a good idea to review the settings in the Set Up Show dialog box. Options enable you to create a self-running presentation (*kiosk mode*) and specify whether recorded timings will automatically advance slides. To open the dialog box, click the Set Up Slide Show icon in the Set Up group of the Slide Show tab.

Figure 15.37 Name the file, select a location in which to save it, and click Save.

Figure 15.38 A progress bar appears in the status area. If necessary, you can click Cancel to halt the video-creation process.

Figure 15.39 Before presenting the show, make sure these settings are correct.

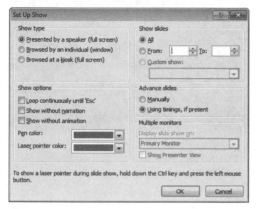

Figure 15.40 The most important pre-show settings can be managed in the Set Up Show dialog box.

Delivering the Presentation

Of course, delivering the presentation is the ultimate goal of your work in PowerPoint. In this final section, you'll learn how to present a show in person or broadcast it over the Web.

Delivering an in-person show

The following steps show how the majority of slide shows are presented to an audience.

To deliver an in-person presentation:

1. *Optional:* To begin the show with a slide other than the first, select or switch to that slide in Normal, Slide Sorter, or Notes Page view.

2. On the Slide Show tab, set options in the Set Up (**Figure 15.39**) and Monitors groups as follows:

   ▲ **Hide Slide.** Select each slide that you want to skip and click Hide Slide.

   ▲ **Use Presenter View.** If you'll be using multiple monitors to present the show, enable this option in the Monitors group.

   ▲ **Set Up Slide Show.** Click this icon to open the Set Up Show dialog box (**Figure 15.40**). You can set these primary show options here or click check boxes in the Set Up and Monitors groups.

3. *Do one of the following:*

   ▲ To run the show starting with the first slide, press F5.

   ▲ To run the show starting with the current slide, press Shift F5.

   ▲ On the Slide Show tab, click the From Beginning or From Current Slide icon in the Start Slide Show group.

   The presentation begins.

continues on next page

DELIVERING THE PRESENTATION

4. *Do any of the following:*

▲ If Use Timings is checked in the Set Up group (see Figure 15.39), the show will play automatically from start to finish.

▲ To manually step forward through the slides and within-slide animations (if any), click the mouse or press ⒩, ⎡Enter⎤, ⎡Page Down⎤, ⎡Spacebar⎤, →, or ↓.

▲ To move backward through the slides and within-slide animations (if any), press ⒫, ⎡Page Up⎤, ⎡Backspace⎤, ←, or ↑.

▲ To end the show, press ⎡Esc⎤.

Broadcasting a slide show

In PowerPoint 2010, you can broadcast a presentation over the Internet that invited audience members can view with a browser (**Figure 15.41**). PowerPoint provides two methods for broadcasting a presentation:

◆ To broadcast over a network, the company must use SharePoint Services 4.

◆ To broadcast over the Internet using the PowerPoint Broadcast Service, you must have a Windows Live or Hotmail account.

Note the following limitations of a broadcast:

◆ The PowerPoint presentation file must be 20 MB or smaller.

◆ Audience members must use Internet Explorer, Firefox, or Safari to view the presentation.

◆ Although most animations will play correctly, all assigned transitions will be shown as a Fade.

◆ Audio (sound effects or narration) will not be transmitted.

In this section, you'll learn how to perform a Web broadcast. For information on broadcasting via SharePoint, contact your network administrator.

View full screen

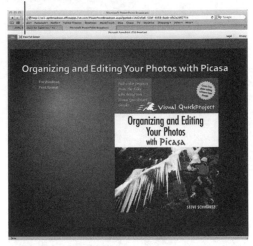

Figure 15.41 The audience can view the broadcast in their browser. New slides and animations appear based on individual slide timings or the presenter's mouse clicks.

Figure 15.42 The Broadcast Slide Show dialog box.

Figure 15.43 Enter your Windows Live or Hotmail sign-in information and click OK.

Figure 15.44 Communicate the show's URL to your audience.

To broadcast a slide show using the PowerPoint Broadcast Service:

1. Open the PowerPoint presentation that you intend to broadcast.

2. On the Slide Show tab, set options for the show as instructed in Step 2 of the previous step list.

3. Click Broadcast Slide Show in the Start Slide Show group.

   The Broadcast Slide Show dialog box appears (**Figure 15.42**).

4. Click the Start Broadcast button.

5. If a Windows Security dialog box appears (**Figure 15.43**), enter your Windows Live or Hotmail address and password. Click OK to continue.

6. Office connects to the PowerPoint Broadcast Service and prepares the show for broadcast. A link to the Web presentation appears (**Figure 15.44**). *Do any of the following:*

   ▲ **Copy Link.** Click Copy Link or press Ctrl C to copy the selected URL to the Clipboard for pasting into an email or an instant message. Instruct the recipient to paste the URL into their browser's address box. (If it is received as link text, they can just click it.)

   ▲ **Send in Email.** Click Send in Email to generate an email message containing the link. Address the message, edit the message text as desired, and click Send.

7. When audience members have the presentation URL opened in their browser, click Start Slide Show (Figure 15.44).

   The slide show begins (see Figure 15.41).

   continues on next page

DELIVERING THE PRESENTATION

8. When the presentation is finished, click the mouse button or press Esc to return to the PowerPoint window. Click the End Broadcast button beneath the Ribbon (**Figure 15.45**, below) and then confirm.

✔ Tip

■ When contacting the audience prior to beginning a broadcast, you may want to ask them to confirm they're ready by clicking Reply in response to your email announcement.

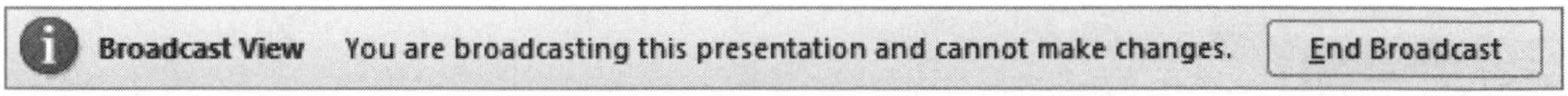

ⓘ **Broadcast View** You are broadcasting this presentation and cannot make changes. [**End Broadcast**]

Figure 15.45 When the show is finished, click End Broadcast (found immediately beneath the Ribbon).

Part V:
Microsoft Outlook

GETTING STARTED WITH OUTLOOK 2010

16

Even if you're new to the Internet, you've heard the term *email* bandied about. Short for *electronic mail*, email is a text message sent from one person's Internet account to another's. With most email accounts, you must have a computer program known as an *email client* to compose and send messages, as well as to receive and read messages from others. In addition to serving as your email client, Outlook can manage your appointments, handle to-do lists, and receive Really Simple Syndication (RSS) Web site feeds.

In this chapter, you'll set up your email accounts in Outlook, learn how to subscribe to RSS feeds, and explore the following essential Outlook topics:

◆ Understanding the Outlook interface

◆ Creating and using profiles

◆ Creating groups to schedule automatic send/receive operations

◆ Using the new Outlook Social Connector

◆ Working online and offline

◆ Setting options to customize the way Outlook works

◆ Getting help while running Outlook 2010

Types of Email Accounts

Outlook supports three types of Internet mail account: Post Office Protocol (*POP3*), Internet Message Access Protocol (*IMAP*), and Microsoft Exchange. Outlook can send and retrieve email from all such accounts. If you aren't certain what account type(s) you have, your Internet Service Provider (*ISP*), company, or school can tell you.

POP3 accounts

The majority of ISP email accounts are POP3. When Outlook connects with the ISP to check for new mail, the mail is downloaded to your PC from a POP3 server. After you've received the new mail, it's automatically deleted from the server. Thus, POP3 mail servers act only as temporary repositories for outgoing and incoming mail.

IMAP accounts

Unlike a POP3 account, an IMAP account is *not* a temporary repository for email. The email never actually leaves the IMAP server. Instead, the server acts like a node on a network to which you can connect. Rather than downloading your new mail to your PC, you're simply *viewing* it on the IMAP server. IMAP is rapidly catching up with POP3 as the most common email account type.

Exchange Server accounts

Exchange Server accounts are primarily used by individuals in large companies, educational institutions, and the like. With many Exchange-compatible clients, you must have an active connection to the server in order to read your current messages. However, you can enable Outlook's *Cached Exchange Mode* to store copies of messages on your PC, enabling you to view them even when you're offline.

Windows Live Hotmail accounts

Windows Live and Hotmail accounts are Web-based. Normally, you interact with such services using a browser rather than an email client. However, after installing the Microsoft Outlook Connector for Windows Live Hotmail, you can use Outlook 2010 to send and receive email via Microsoft's POP3 servers.

✔ Tips

■ A few ISPs require you to use their proprietary software to send/receive email. You cannot use Outlook for such accounts.

■ Web-based accounts other than Hotmail may be supported by Outlook via POP3 or IMAP. For this to occur, the Web-based email service must provide auxiliary mail servers to which email clients can connect. For example, Google's Gmail is handled this way. Yahoo! Mail provides similar support, but only for paying Yahoo! Mail Plus customers.

■ Some email accounts can be accessed in multiple ways. For instance, many ISPs now offer both POP3 and IMAP support. You can configure Outlook to use either account type.

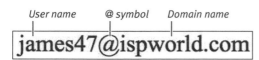

User name   @ symbol   Domain name

Figure 16.1 Every email address consists of these three components.

Figure 16.2 In addition to a name and email address, an Outlook contact record can store mailing and telephone information, a Web site, and a picture.

Email from Anywhere

You don't have to restrict email activities to your home or work computer. In fact, odds are excellent that you can interact with your ISP's mail servers from anywhere you can get Internet access.

Simply create a new account in the current computer's email client using the same settings you used when adding the account in Outlook 2010. Delete the account when you're done using the computer.

Note: Many ISP email accounts can also be accessed with a browser. Contact your ISP or its Web site for details.

About Email Addresses

Regardless of the type of email account you have, each is identified by a unique address, such as jpt417@msn.com or bobp@linetop.net. The address consists of three parts: a user name, the @ (at) symbol, and a domain name (**Figure 16.1**). When you create the account, you normally get to choose your user name. The domain name is the name of the company or organization that is providing email access. In many cases, the same entity also provides your Internet access.

When people want to send you a message, they address it to your email address. And when you want to send someone else a message, you send it to that person's email address. Because you may know dozens or even hundreds of people, there's little point in attempting to memorize email addresses. Programs such as Outlook generally provide an Address Book (**Figure 16.2**) in which you can record important email addresses. When you want to create a new message, you can select addresses from the Address Book rather than type them from memory. See Chapter 17 for instructions on using the Address Book.

✔ Tips

- A proper email address cannot include blank spaces. The underscore (_) character and period (.) are commonly used to represent spaces.

- Letter case is ignored in an email address. Thus, the convention is to type email addresses using all lowercase letters.

- Domains in countries other than the United States often end in a country abbreviation, such as .ca (Canada), .uk (United Kingdom), or .jp (Japan).

The Outlook 2010 Interface

Whether you'll be using the Mail, Contacts, Calendar, Tasks, or Notes component of Outlook 2010, it's important that you familiarize yourself with the parts of the new interface (**Figure 16.3**) and what they do.

As you may know, Outlook 2007 was spared the Ribbon interface that was added to the other core applications. Outlook 2010, however, is now on par with those applications. As a result, if you've used earlier versions of Outlook, your first challenge for Outlook 2010 will be to learn where the former menu commands can be found in this new interface.

Figure 16.3 The Outlook 2010 main window with important interface elements marked with numbers.

THE OUTLOOK 2010 INTERFACE

File tab *Choose commands*

Categories

Figure 16.4 Select a category tab for the operation you want to perform and then choose a command. To exit the Backstage, click the File tab or press Esc.

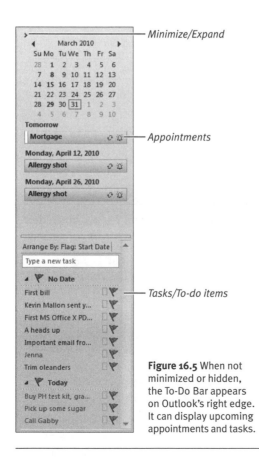

Minimize/Expand

Appointments

Tasks/To-do items

Figure 16.5 When not minimized or hidden, the To-Do Bar appears on Outlook's right edge. It can display upcoming appointments and tasks.

❶ Ribbon. Click the Ribbon tabs to reveal important command groups. To learn more, see "Using the Ribbon" in Chapter 2.

❷ File tab/Backstage. Click the File tab to open the Backstage (**Figure 16.4**), where you can print, manage your accounts and RSS feeds, and set preferences.

❸ Quick Access Toolbar. The Send/Receive All Folders and Undo commands can always be found here, regardless of the Ribbon tab that's currently selected.

❹ Navigation Pane. When the Mail button is selected, all email accounts, RSS feeds, and their folders are shown. Messages from the folder selected in this pane are displayed in the message list (**❺**). Click a button in the Navigation Pane to work with a different Outlook component, such as your Contacts or Calendar.

❺ Message list. Displays message headers from the folder that's selected in the Navigation Pane. The name of the selected folder is shown in the window's title bar.

❻ Instant Search box. Type here to search the current folder (or all folders) for matching text in a message or item.

❼ Reading Pane. The text of the selected email message or RSS feed is shown here.

❽ To-Do Bar. Displays to-do items and upcoming appointments (**Figure 16.5**).

❾ Help icon. Click the question mark (?) icon to open Outlook Help.

❿ Status bar. This bar at the bottom of the window shows messages about Outlook's state (Offline, for example) and current activity, such as performing a send/receive.

Detailed instructions for using these Outlook interface components will be presented in later chapters.

THE OUTLOOK 2010 INTERFACE

Adding Email Accounts

If a previous version of Outlook is on your PC, Outlook 2010 will automatically use the old version's data: all email accounts, messages, contacts, appointments, and so on. However, if no previous version of Outlook is found, you must add the email accounts that you want Outlook to manage.

New accounts can be added *automatically* with Outlook attempting to discern settings from your email address or *manually* by hand-entering the required information.

To automatically add an account:

1. Click the File tab. Select the Info category in the Backstage.

2. Click the Add Account text link, or click the account listed at the top of the Account Information pane and choose Add Account from the drop-down menu.

   The Add New Account dialog box appears (**Figure 16.6**).

3. Enter the requested information. Click Next.

   Outlook contacts the domain's mail server, attempts to configure the account, and then sends a test message.

4. *Do one of the following:*
   - ▲ If the test is successful, the final screen appears. Click Finish to add the new account.
   - ▲ If Outlook can't contact the server, the user name and password aren't recognized, or the server can't handle encrypted messages, instructions for correcting the problem appear. Follow them to retry or click Cancel.

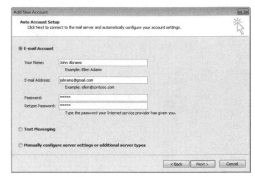

Figure 16.6 Enter your name as you want it to be shown in outgoing messages, the account's email address, and the account password.

Why Configure Manually?

There are two important reasons you might want to configure a new account manually:

- ◆ First, although automatic configuration works better than it did in Outlook 2007, it can still fail.

- ◆ Second, some accounts can be configured as multiple types, such as POP3 and IMAP. Automatic configuration will automatically select a type for you. To switch account types, you must delete the original account and then configure a new one manually.

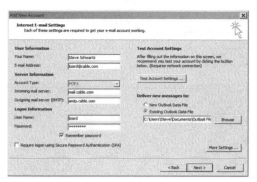

Figure 16.7 Enter your name, email address, account password, and incoming and outgoing mail servers. Select an account type from the drop-down list.

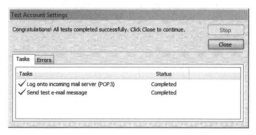

Figure 16.8 In a successful test, Outlook logs onto the account and sends a test message.

Add a new email account

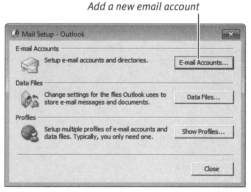

Figure 16.9 Exchange accounts must be set up using the Mail Control Panel. Outlook cannot be running.

To manually add a POP3 or IMAP account:

1. Perform Steps 1 and 2 from the previous task list.

2. In the Add New Account dialog box (see Figure 16.6), select Manually configure server settings or additional server types. Click Next.

   The Choose Service screen appears.

3. Select Internet E-mail. Click Next.

   The Internet E-mail Settings screen appears (**Figure 16.7**).

4. Enter the requested account information.

   You'll need the names of the incoming and outgoing mail servers. You can obtain them from your ISP or from most Web-based accounts' online help.

5. *Optional:* If available, click the Test Account Settings button to send a test message using the provided settings.

   A successful test (**Figure 16.8**) ensures that the basic settings are correct and that you'll be able to send and receive mail.

6. Click Next and then click Finish.

To manually add an Exchange account:

1. Quit Outlook if it is currently running, and open the Mail Control Panel.

   The Mail Setup - Outlook dialog box appears (**Figure 16.9**).

2. Click the E-mail Accounts button.

   Outlook 2010's Account Settings dialog box appears.

3. Click the New icon.

   The Choose Service dialog box appears.

continues on next page

ADDING EMAIL ACCOUNTS

4. Select Microsoft Exchange, POP3, or IMAP. Click Next.

5. In the Auto Account Setup screen, select Manually configure server settings or additional server types. Click Next.

The Choose Service screen appears.

6. Select Microsoft Exchange. Click Next.

The Microsoft Exchange Settings screen appears (**Figure 16.10**).

7. Enter the information provided to you by your Exchange Server administrator. Click Next to move to subsequent screens.

8. When you're done creating the account, click Close in both the Account Settings and the Mail Setup - Outlook dialog boxes.

✔ Tips

■ You can also begin an automatic or manual setup by choosing Account Settings > Account Settings in the Backstage. In the Account Settings dialog box, select the E-mail tab and click New. In the dialog box that appears, select Microsoft Exchange, POP3, or IMAP. Click Next. Continue with Step 3.

■ Try the automatic approach first. If it doesn't work at all, you can use the manual method. If it works but not perfectly, you can modify the settings by selecting the account in the Account Settings dialog box and clicking Edit.

■ Hotmail and Gmail (Google) accounts are readily handled by Outlook's automatic configuration. As a bonus, Gmail accounts are now configured as IMAP rather than POP3 accounts.

■ Unless you are told by ISP or network personnel that your account uses Secure Password Authentication, assume that it is neither required nor supported.

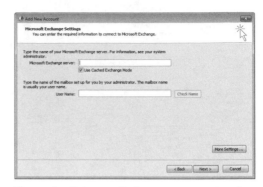

Figure 16.10 Enter your Exchange server name and user name.

■ Messages in an Exchange Server account are normally readable only when you're online. To automatically download copies of all messages so they can also be read when you're offline, click the Use Cached Exchange Mode check box (Figure 16.10).

Selected account

Figure 16.11 In the Account Settings dialog box, select an account to modify.

Name the account

Figure 16.12 On the General tab, you can enter a new display name for the account that will be used to identify it in the Navigation Pane.

Changing Account Settings

After adding an email account automatically or working with the account for a while, you may want to modify the account's settings to make it behave in a different manner.

You can also specify a *default account* from which all outgoing mail will be sent unless another account is specified, change an account's position in the Account Settings list, test an account, or delete an account.

To edit an account's settings:

1. In the Backstage, select the Info category and choose Account Settings > Account Settings.

   The Account Settings dialog box appears (**Figure 16.11**).

2. *Do either of the following:*

   ▲ Select the account and click Change.

   ▲ Double-click the account's name.

   A Change Account dialog box appears, similar to the one shown in Figure 16.7.

3. Make any desired changes to the settings, such as the name used to identify your outgoing messages or mail server names.

4. *Optional:* To view other account-specific settings, click More Settings. The Internet E-mail Settings dialog box appears (**Figure 16.12**). Settings you might want to change include the following:

   ▲ **General tab, Mail Account:** Enter a descriptive name for the account, such as Home or the ISP's name.

   ▲ **General tab, Reply E-mail:** When someone replies to a message from you, the reply is addressed to the account from which you sent the message. To direct replies to a *different* account (a work account, for example), enter that email address here.

continues on next page

CHANGING ACCOUNT SETTINGS

▲ **Advanced tab (POP3 accounts only), Leave a copy of messages on the server:** Normally, when you retrieve a message from a POP3 server, the message is simultaneously deleted from the server. If you're retrieving the account's mail from *multiple* computers (work and home, for example), enable this option on the secondary computers (**Figure 16.13**). Doing so ensures that all messages retrieved on a secondary computer will also be downloaded to your main computer before being deleted from the server.

Click OK to save all changes made in the Internet E-mail Settings dialog box or click Cancel to ignore the changes.

5. To save the changes to the account, click Next and then Finish. Or click Cancel if you don't want to save the changes.

6. Click Close to close the Account Settings dialog box.

To change the default email account:

◆ In the Account Settings dialog box (see Figure 16.11), select an account and click Set as Default.

To change an account's position in the Account Settings list:

◆ In the Account Settings dialog box (see Figure 16.11), select the account and click the up- or down-arrow button.

To check a malfunctioning account:

◆ In the Account Settings dialog box (see Figure 16.11), select the account and click Repair.

To delete an account:

◆ In the Account Settings dialog box (see Figure 16.11), select the account, click Remove, and confirm the deletion.

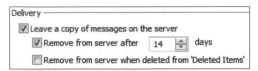

Figure 16.13 For POP3 accounts, you can specify the circumstances under which delivered messages are deleted from the mail server.

✔ Tip

■ Different account types have different More Settings options. Hotmail accounts, for example, have very few options that can be set or changed.

Current profiles

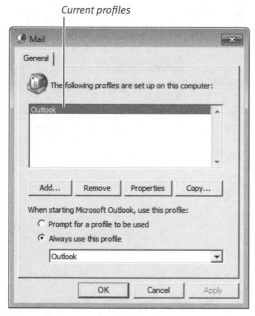

Figure 16.14 You create, delete, or set startup options for profiles in the Mail dialog box.

Figure 16.15 Name the profile and click OK.

Working with Profiles

Outlook uses *profiles* to determine which mail accounts should be displayed in an Outlook session. When you install Outlook, a single profile is created for all your accounts. However, if several people use the PC, each will need his or her own profile. Similarly, if you want to keep your work and home accounts separate, you can create another profile.

Note that on most single-user PCs, one profile will suffice. Even if you have multiple Exchange accounts, Outlook 2010 allows you to store them in a single profile.

To create a new profile:

1. Quit Outlook if it is currently running, and open the Mail Control Panel.

   The Mail Setup - Outlook dialog box appears (see Figure 16.9).

2. Click the Show Profiles button.

   The Mail dialog box appears (**Figure 16.14**).

3. Click Add.

   The New Profile dialog box appears (**Figure 16.15**).

4. Name the new profile and click OK.

   The Add New Account dialog box appears (see Figure 16.6).

5. *Do either of the following:*
   - ▲ Add the first email account for the new profile (described in "Adding Email Accounts," earlier in this chapter).
   - ▲ Click Cancel to create the profile without specifying the first email account.

✔ Tip

- Additional email accounts can be added to a profile at any time within Outlook or in the Mail Control Panel.

To set a startup profile:

1. Quit Outlook if it is currently running, and open the Mail Control Panel.

   The Mail Setup - Outlook dialog box appears (see Figure 16.9).

2. Click the Show Profiles button.

   The Mail dialog box appears (see Figure 16.14).

3. *Do either of the following:*

   ▲ To automatically use a certain profile, click Always use this profile and select a profile from the drop-down list.

   ▲ To be prompted to select a profile at the start of every Outlook session (as shown in **Figure 16.16**), select Prompt for a profile to be used.

4. Click OK.

✔ Tips

- You cannot switch profiles from within Outlook 2010. If the wrong profile is active, quit Outlook, and *do one of the following:*

   ▲ If Outlook is set to Prompt for a profile to be used, relaunch Outlook and select the correct profile.

   ▲ If Outlook is set to Always use this profile, open the Mail Control Panel, click Show Profiles, select the desired profile from the drop-down list, and click OK.

- Outlook profiles aren't password protected. While profiles are convenient for keeping your mail, appointments, and contacts separate from those of other Outlook users, there's nothing to prevent one user from viewing another's material. If security and privacy are concerns, a better approach is to create a separate password-protected Windows user account for each person.

Figure 16.16 You can configure Outlook to prompt for a profile to use each time it's run. Select a profile from the drop-down list and click OK.

The Case for Web Accounts

Why bother with Web-based accounts if you already have an ISP or a company-provided email account? Here are three excellent reasons:

◆ If you travel, you can access a Web-based account from anywhere in the world using a Web browser on any PC or Mac.

◆ Because Web accounts are often free, you can use them to handle email that you'd rather not have cluttering up your ISP email account. When registering at Web sites, for example, you are usually asked for an email address. To avoid volumes of unwanted advertising mail (called *spam*) flooding your primary account, you can direct it all to your Web account.

◆ Some Web-based services, such as Hotmail and Gmail, also provide POP3 or IMAP support that enables you to use them in Outlook and other email clients.

Create new group

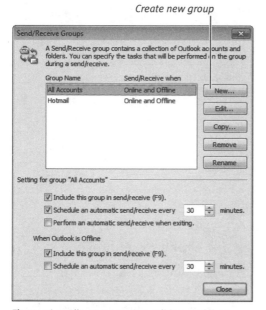

Figure 16.17 All group creation, editing, or deletion begins in the Send/Receive Groups dialog box.

Include the selected account in this group

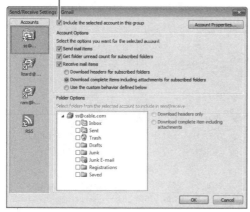

Figure 16.18 Change group membership and individual account settings in this dialog box.

Working with Send/Receive Groups

Outlook automatically sends and receives email every so many minutes. By creating *send/receive groups* (each containing one or more email accounts), you can specify a different send/receive schedule for each group. (When you initially set up Outlook, it creates a default All Accounts group that consists of all defined email accounts and RSS feeds.)

To create a group:

1. On the Send/Receive tab in the Send & Receive group, click the Send/Receive Groups icon. Choose Define Send/Receive Groups from the icon's menu.

   The Send/Receive Groups dialog box appears (**Figure 16.17**).

2. Click the New button.

3. In the Send/Receive Group Name dialog box, type a name for the new group and click OK.

   The Send/Receive Settings dialog box for the new group appears (**Figure 16.18**).

4. In the Accounts list on the left, group member icons contain blue "refresh" arrows and non-member icons have a red *X*. To change an account's membership in the group, select its icon and click the Include the selected account in this group check box.

5. For each included account, select its icon in the Accounts list, and set options by clicking check boxes and radio buttons. Click OK when you're done examining the settings of all included accounts.

   The Send/Receive Groups dialog box reappears.

6. Set send/receive options for the new group and click Close.

To modify a group's settings:

1. On the Send/Receive tab in the Send & Receive group, click the Send/Receive Groups icon. Choose Define Send/Receive Groups from the icon's menu.

    The Send/Receive Groups dialog box appears (see Figure 16.17).

2. Select the group name whose settings you want to modify.

3. Change any of the top three settings (**Figure 16.19**):

    ▲ **Include this group in send/receive:** When this option is enabled, all accounts and RSS feeds in the group will perform a send/receive when you press F9 or click the Send/Receive All Folders icon on the Send/Receive tab or the Quick Access Toolbar.

    ▲ **Schedule an automatic send/receive every X minutes:** When this option is enabled, all accounts and RSS feeds in the group will automatically perform a send/receive at the designated interval. To change the interval, type in the text box or click the up or down arrow.

    ▲ **Perform an automatic send/receive when exiting:** When this option is enabled, a final send/receive will be performed for the accounts in the group each time you quit Outlook.

4. Click Close.

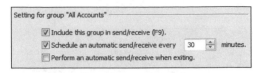

Figure 16.19 The top three settings govern online send/receive behavior for the selected group.

Group-Creation Tips

The easiest way to decide how many groups you need is to base the decision on send/receive schedules. Schedules often differ by account type:

◆ POP3 accounts offered by your ISP can usually support a send/receive every 1–2 minutes, allowing you to instantly receive most incoming messages.

◆ IMAP and Exchange accounts normally don't need to be included in *any* group because they are automatically checked and synched about once per minute.

◆ Web-based accounts (such as Hotmail and Gmail) and RSS feeds may have restrictions on how often you can perform scheduled send/receives, such as once every 5 or 15 minutes (although you can usually perform manual send/receives as often as you like). See the site's Help for details.

In addition, you may have some seldom-used accounts that you don't want to include in any group. For such accounts, it may suffice to do a manual send/receive every now and then.

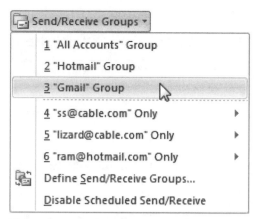

Figure 16.20 To perform a manual send/receive, choose the group or account name from this menu.

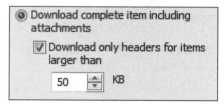

Figure 16.21 You can set this option for a POP3 account that regularly receives mail with large, unwanted attachments.

✔ Tips

■ A group can contain only one account, if you like.

■ All RSS feeds—regardless of whether they have one or many sources—are treated as a single account. You may want to lump them together into a single group.

■ Remove any account from the All Accounts group that needs to be checked on a different schedule. For instance, I have only POP3 accounts in this group, set to be checked once per minute. It would be overkill to check Web-based accounts or RSS feeds on this schedule.

■ To change a group's membership or edit an account's options within a group, select the group in the Send/Receive Groups dialog box (see Figure 16.17) and click Edit.

■ To change the name of a selected group, click Rename. To delete an unneeded group, select it in Send/Receive Groups dialog box and click the Remove button.

■ For a dial-up connection, you may want to set the group that includes your ISP account to perform a send/receive every few minutes. Doing so ensures regular line activity that can prevent disconnects.

■ To perform a manual send/receive for a group, choose its name from the Send/Receive Groups menu (**Figure 16.20**). To check a single account for new messages, choose *account name* Only > Inbox from the Send/Receive Groups menu.

■ If people routinely send huge, unwanted attachments to your POP3 account, you can enable the Send/Receive Settings dialog box option to Download only headers for items larger than *X* (**Figure 16.21**). Set the size to 100 KB or less.

Subscribing to RSS Feeds

Many Web sites now offer to deliver their latest information to you via Really Simple Syndication (*RSS*) feeds. Subscribed-to feeds can be received by and viewed in Outlook 2010.

To subscribe to a feed:

1. Click the File tab to go to the Backstage. With the Info category selected, choose Account Settings > Account Settings.

   The Account Settings dialog box appears (see Figure 16.11).

2. Click the RSS Feeds tab, and then click New.

   The New RSS Feed dialog box appears (**Figure 16.22**).

3. Enter or paste the address of the feed (obtained from the site's instructions) and click Add.

   The new feed is added to the list in the Account Settings dialog box.

4. Click Close to dismiss the Account Settings dialog box.

✔ Tips

■ Many Web sites simplify the process of subscribing to feeds by providing links for you to click. For an example, visit `http://dealmac.com/rss.html`.

■ If you want to receive feeds on a schedule, make sure that the RSS account is in a send/receive group. You can also use the Send/Receive Settings dialog box to selectively include and exclude certain feeds (see Figure 16.18). To *delete* a feed, select it on the RSS Feeds tab of the Account Settings dialog box and click Remove.

■ Feed publishers may set an *update limit* (a minimum time between updates). To view this limit, double-click the feed's name in the Account Settings dialog box to view the RSS Feed Options (**Figure 16.23**).

Figure 16.22 Type or paste the feed's URL into this box.

Use provider limit   *Provider limit*

Figure 16.23 You can view the feed provider's update recommendation in the RSS Feed Options dialog box.

Filter icons   Pane divider   Collapse/expand

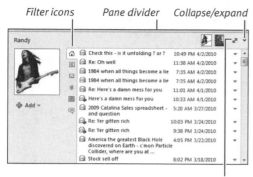

Toggle views

Figure 16.24 The People Pane shows exchanged mail.

Figure 16.25 To filter the item list to show only certain material, click an icon.

✔ Tip

■ To install or configure social networking add-ins, choose Account Settings from the People Pane icon's menu. In the Social Network Accounts dialog box that appears, you can do the following:

▲ To download and install social networking site add-ins, click the "View social network providers available online" text link.

▲ Click Settings to view or edit social networking options, such as how updates will occur.

▲ For each installed social networking add-in listed, click its pencil-and-paper icon to set options for the site.

Outlook Social Connector

Outlook 2010 has a new area called the People Pane (**Figure 16.24**) that may appear under the Reading Pane when you select a message header or contact record. The People Pane has several purposes. First, it shows material related to the participants or the record, such as message headers. Second, if you belong to the same social networking site (such as MySpace) and have installed the site's Outlook Social Connector add-in, you can view their updates. Finally, if you're on the same SharePoint Server, updates such as changes to contact info also appear in the People Pane.

You can do the following with the People Pane:

◆ **Enable/disable the pane.** On the View tab, choose Normal or Minimized from the People Pane icon in the People Pane group. To disable the pane, choose Off.

◆ **Change the pane's height.** When the pane is displayed, drag the double line that separates it from the Reading Pane.

◆ **Collapse/expand the pane.** Click the arrow icon at the pane's top-right edge.

◆ **Display items.** Click any item in the pane to open it in its own window.

◆ **Display an item class.** Click an icon to filter the list (**Figure 16.25**).

◆ **Display material for multiple people.** Some selected items, such as meetings or email messages, may be related to several people. To view items relevant to a particular person, click her or his icon at the top of the pane. Each person's icon has a ToolTip to identify him or her. If you prefer, you can click the Toggle views icon to see larger icons.

Working Online and Offline

In addition to working with Outlook interactively by reading and replying to email messages while online, you can work while you are *offline* (not connected to the Internet).

Why would you want to work offline? Here are a few common reasons:

◆ If you have a dial-up account and use your phone line for both voice calls and Internet access, you can work offline to free up the phone line.

◆ When traveling with a portable computer, you can read previously received email messages and compose new messages that will be sent the next time you connect to the Internet.

◆ If the Internet account you're currently using (such as one at an Internet cafe) doesn't provide unlimited access, you can save on time-based connect charges by doing much of your work offline.

To go offline, click the Work Offline icon in the Preferences group on the Send/Receive tab. When you're working offline, the icon is colored gold (**Figure 16.26**) and the status bar shows *Working Offline*.

While offline, you can read previously downloaded email and RSS feeds. You can also compose new messages. When you click the Send button, Outlook stores them in your Outbox until the next time you're online.

To resume working online, click the Work Offline icon again. If you've also disconnected from the Internet, you'll need to reconnect.

Note: If you have dial-up Internet, quitting Outlook or going offline does *not* disconnect you from the Internet. To do so and free up your phone line, you'll also have to disconnect.

— *Working offline*

Figure 16.26 When enabled, the Work Offline icon is gold.

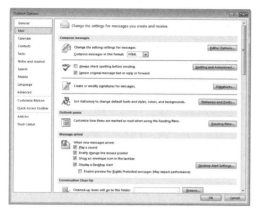

Figure 16.27 Many important Outlook preferences can be viewed or set in the Outlook Options dialog box.

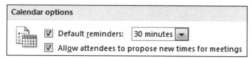

Figure 16.28 Set spell-checking options for outgoing messages in the Compose messages section of the Mail options.

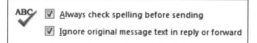

Figure 16.29 When you set a reminder for a new appointment, Outlook proposes the default period specified in this preference setting.

Figure 16.30 Calendar appointments always reflect your time zone. When working out of town or to accommodate Daylight Saving Time, ensure that these preferences are correct. Changes here are used to automatically update all appointment times.

Setting Preferences

You can customize the way Outlook works by setting preferences in the Outlook Options dialog box (**Figure 16.27**). To open the dialog box, click the File tab and select the Options category in the Backstage. Make any desired changes and click OK.

The default Options settings are initially fine for most users. However, after using Outlook for a bit, it's worth exploring the options. Here are some of the more useful ones:

◆ **Mail, Replies and forwards:** Specify whether original text is quoted in replies and forwards and how it is formatted.

◆ **Mail, Message arrival:** Specify how you're notified when new mail arrives.

◆ **Mail, Compose messages (Spelling):** Determine whether an automatic spell check occurs before you send each message and whether quoted text is also checked (**Figure 16.28**).

◆ **Mail, Compose messages (Signatures):** Create *signatures* to append to outgoing messages. A signature can be your full name, a Web address, additional contact information, or a witty saying, for example.

◆ **Calendar, Work time:** Specify your work hours and the days of the work week.

◆ **Calendar, Calendar options:** Set the default reminder period and add holidays to the Calendar (**Figure 16.29**).

◆ **Calendar, Display options:** Change the Calendar's color.

◆ **Calendar, Time zones:** Specify or change your time zone (**Figure 16.30**).

◆ **Tasks, Task options:** Select display colors for overdue and completed tasks.

continues on next page

SETTING PREFERENCES

◆ **Notes and Journal, Notes options:** Set a default color, size, and font for notes.

◆ **Search, Results:** Indicate how Instant Search will work and present its results (**Figure 16.31**).

◆ **Advanced, Outlook Panes:** Specify the buttons displayed in the Navigation Pane, when messages are marked as read, and the contents of the To-Do Bar.

◆ **Advanced, Outlook start and exit:** Set Outlook's startup folder and indicate whether the Deleted Items folders will automatically be emptied at the end of each session.

◆ **Advanced, AutoArchive:** Set options for archiving or deleting old mail.

◆ **Advanced, Reminders:** Change the sound that plays when a reminder occurs.

◆ **Advanced, Other:** Indicate whether you want to be prompted to confirm deletions.

✔ Tip

■ As you'll see in subsequent chapters, not all preferences are set in the Outlook Options dialog box. For example, junk email preferences are found on the Home tab (**Figure 16.32**) and IMAP folder purging options are set on the Folder tab.

Figure 16.31 Use Search preferences to set a default scope for searches and indicate whether matching text within found items will be highlighted.

Figure 16.32 Not all preference settings can be found in the Outlook Options dialog box. Be sure to check Ribbon icon menus.

Close box

Figure 16.33 The Outlook Help window.

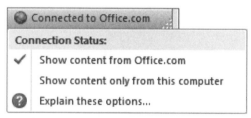

Figure 16.35 Select a help source.

Getting Help

Help with commands and procedures is only a button click away. Help is presented in the Outlook Help window (**Figure 16.33**).

To view help information:

◆ To open Outlook Help, click the Help (?) icon in the upper-right corner of the Outlook window or press F1 . To dismiss Outlook Help, click its close box.

◆ To view help text for the current dialog box, click the ? button in the upper-right corner of the dialog box.

To use the Outlook Help window:

◆ To view Outlook Help's start page, click the Home icon (**Figure 16.34**, below).

◆ To view a help topic, select it in the table of contents or click the blue text that's presented as a search result.

◆ To go back or forward to previously viewed help pages, click the arrow icons.

◆ To search for help on a subject, enter search text and click the Search button.

◆ To print the current help page or selected text on the page, click the Print icon.

◆ You can view help from the file stored on your hard disk or from Office.com (requires an active Internet connection). Choose a help source by clicking the text in the bottom-right corner of the Outlook Help window (**Figure 16.35**).

Search text   View table of contents   Perform search

Back   Forward   Home Print Font   Keep on top

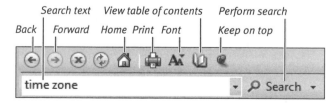

Figure 16.34 The Outlook Help toolbar.

GETTING HELP

WORKING WITH CONTACTS

Contacts is the repository of your contact information for people, companies, institutions, organizations, and Internet mailing lists. After you create records for your contacts, you can address email to them simply by typing part of the recipient's name.

In addition to standard address information (such as name, home and work addresses, phone numbers, and email addresses), a contact record can store other information, such as a Web page address, a photo, and notes.

You can do any of the following in the Contacts window:

◆ Record multiple email addresses, mailing addresses, and phone numbers for each contact

◆ Browse through and search for contacts

◆ Import contact information from older versions of Outlook, as well as other email, database, and address applications

◆ Create an Electronic Business Card, enabling you to easily share your contact information with others

◆ Create contact groups to simplify mass mailings

The Contacts Window

To view or work with your contacts, click the Contacts button in the Navigation Pane or press Ctrl 3. In the Contacts window (**Figure 17.1**), you can change views; view and edit contacts; and find specific contacts by scrolling, clicking alphabetical icons, or searching.

✔ Tip

- To quickly find an email address without switching to the Contacts window, click Address Book in the Find group on the Home tab (Ctrl Shift B). You can address a new message to a selected contact by pressing Ctrl N.

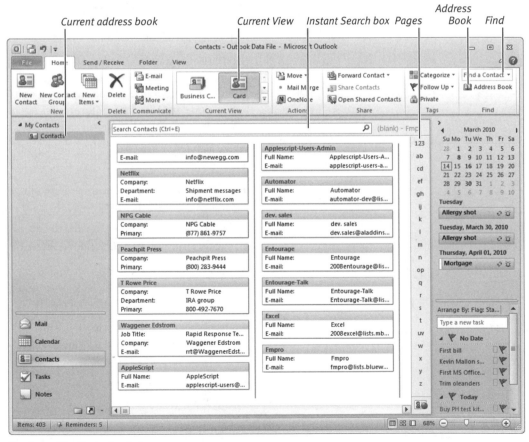

Figure 17.1 The Contacts window.

General *Details*   *Close box*

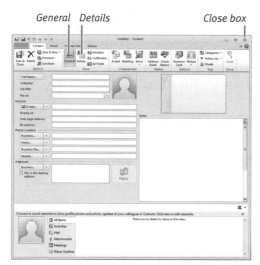

Figure 17.2 In addition to a name and email address, an Outlook contact record can store a wealth of data.

Figure 17.3 If you want to create several contact records for the same company, choose this command to avoid some repetitive typing.

✔ Tips

- Although many contacts will contain information only on their General page, you can click Details in the Show group on the Contact tab (Figure 17.2) to enter secondary information, such as data about the person's family.

- As you can with other Outlook elements, you can categorize contact records. See "Categorizing Messages" in Chapter 20 for help with assigning categories.

Creating Contact Records

There are several ways to create new contact records. You can do any of the following:

- ◆ Manually create records from scratch

- ◆ Create a contact record from a received email message

- ◆ Import contact records from another copy of Outlook 2010, an earlier version of Outlook, or another email program or database

To manually create a new contact:

1. *Do either of the following:*
   - ▲ In any Outlook component, select the Home tab, click the New Items icon in the New group, and choose Contact ($\boxed{\text{Shift}}\boxed{\text{Ctrl}}\boxed{\text{C}}$).
   - ▲ In Contacts, switch to the Home tab and click the New Contact icon in the New group ($\boxed{\text{Ctrl}}\boxed{\text{N}}$).

   An Untitled - Contact window appears (**Figure 17.2**).

2. Fill in as much information as desired.

3. *Do one of the following:*
   - ▲ To save the record and close its window, click the Save & Close icon in the Actions group.
   - ▲ To save the record and immediately create another, click the Save & New icon in the Actions group.
   - ▲ To save the record and immediately create another using the same company information, click the down arrow beside the Save & New icon and choose Contact from the Same Company (**Figure 17.3**).
   - ▲ If you decide not to save the record, click its close box (X) or the Delete icon and then confirm this action.

To create a new contact record from a received email message:

1. While viewing the message in the Reading Pane or its own window, move the cursor over the sender's name/address. In the window that appears (**Figure 17.4**), choose Add to Outlook Contacts.

   A new, partially completed contact record for the person or organization appears.

2. *Optional:* Enter additional information for the new contact.

3. Click the Save & Close icon in the Actions group to save the record and close its window.

   If this is a new, unique record, the record is saved and its window closes.

4. If a record for this person or organization already exists, a Duplicate Contact Detected dialog box appears (**Figure 17.5**). *Do one of the following:*

   ▲ To avoid creating a duplicate record (discarding the new record), click Cancel.

   ▲ To modify the existing record for this person or organization using the new data, ensure that Update information of selected Contact is selected and click Update.

   ▲ To save the new record (creating a duplicate), click the Add new contact radio button and then click Add.

✔ Tip

■ You can also create a new record by right-clicking the sender's name/address and choosing Add to Outlook Contacts from the context menu.

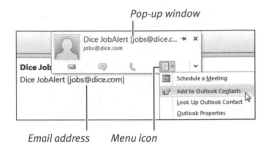

Pop-up window

Email address   Menu icon

Figure 17.4 Choose Add to Outlook Contacts from the drop-down menu.

Handling options

Figure 17.5 This dialog box appears when your new record is believed to already exist.

Hotmail/Windows Live Contacts

Although the typical home user will have only one Contacts database, Outlook 2010 supports multiple databases. For example, if you add a Hotmail or Windows Live account to Outlook, its associated address book will automatically be added as a new Outlook folder. To view or work with those contact records, select its folder (such as `Contacts - steve01@Hotmail.com`) in the Navigation Pane.

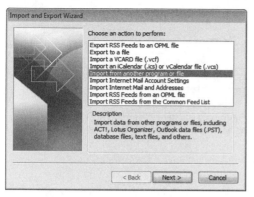

Figure 17.6 In the Import and Export Wizard, begin by selecting the type of data you want to import.

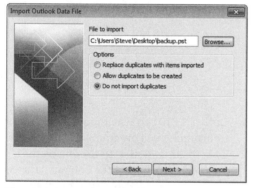

Figure 17.7 Locate the export file you created and indicate how duplicate records should be handled.

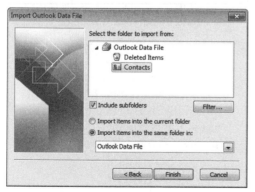

Figure 17.8 Select the Contacts folder and direct the data into the appropriate Outlook folder.

To import contact data from another copy of Outlook 2010 or a prior version:

1. To export from Outlook 2010, click the File tab, select Open, and click the Import icon. To export from an earlier version of Outlook, choose File > Import or Export.

2. *Do the following (in order):*
   - ▲ Select Export to a file.
   - ▲ In Outlook 2010, select Outlook Data File (.pst) as the output format. In Outlook 2007 or earlier, select Personal Folder File (.pst).
   - ▲ Select Contacts as the folder from which to export the data.
   - ▲ Set a location for the export file by clicking the Browse button. Select Do not export duplicate items.
   - ▲ Click Finish to create the export file.

   The file is created. Move it over the network or via removable media, such as a flash drive, to the target computer.

3. To import the data into Outlook 2010, click the File tab, select Open, and click the Import icon.

   The Import and Export Wizard appears (**Figure 17.6**).

4. Select Import from another program or file. Click Next.

5. On the new screen, select Outlook Data File (.pst). Click Next.

6. On the new screen (**Figure 17.7**), click Browse to locate the export file created in Steps 1–2. Specify how duplicates are to be handled and click Next.

7. On the final screen (**Figure 17.8**), select Contacts as the import folder, select the folder that will receive the imported data, and click Finish.

   The records are imported into the specified Contacts database.

✔ Tips

- To edit a contact record, double-click it in the Contacts window, make the necessary changes, and click Save & Close in the Actions group.

- When creating or editing contact data, you should note that each record can have multiple email addresses and phone numbers. To add other email addresses, click the E-mail down arrow and choose E-mail 2 or E-mail 3. When adding phone numbers, select a phone type from the drop-down list beside each phone field.

- To display a photo for a contact, click the picture placeholder, or click Picture in the Options group and choose Add Picture. To modify a picture, choose Change Picture or Remove Picture from the Picture menu in the Options group.

- The File as field (**Figure 17.9**) on the General tab is critical because the records are sorted by it in most views. It is important to use a consistent naming convention to enable you to easily browse through your contacts. For corporate contacts, I ensure that File as displays as *company (person)*, for example.

- To delete a contact record, select it in the Contacts window and click the Delete icon in the Delete group on the Home tab, press Ctrl D, or press Del. If the record is open, click the Delete icon in the Actions group on the Contact tab.

- To restore an accidentally deleted record, select the record in Mail's Deleted Items folder and drag it onto the Contacts button in the Navigation Pane.

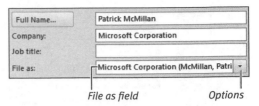

File as field   *Options*

Figure 17.9 To change the contents of a record's File as field, click the down arrow to the right of the field.

- Outlook 2010 can also import contact data from other email programs and databases. The process is similar to the one on the previous page. Export the contact data to an Outlook-compatible file format, such as Outlook Data File, tab-delimited, or Excel. Then import the data into Outlook. (You may have to instruct Outlook on the manner in which fields from the export file should map to Outlook fields.)

- If the contact records you're importing are from Outlook Express or Eudora, you can import your email at the same time by selecting Import Internet Mail and Addresses in the Import and Export Wizard. This is extremely useful if you're replacing either program with Outlook.

Figure 17.10 When the Home tab is selected, the quickest way to change views is to click an icon.

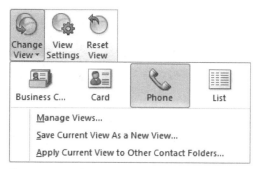

Figure 17.11 To change the view, you can also choose an icon from this menu.

Figure 17.12 After opening a record, you can edit it or select and copy text (such as an email or Web address) for pasting elsewhere.

Viewing Contact Records

Rather than searching for a specific record using the Instant Search box (described later in this chapter), you'll often find yourself just flipping through contacts to find the one you want. There are four built-in display *views* you can use when browsing for contacts; each can be easily customized.

To browse through contact records:

1. Select a view by doing one of the following:
   ▲ Click an icon in the Current View group on the Home tab (**Figure 17.10**).
   ▲ On the View tab, choose a view from the Change View menu in the Current View group (**Figure 17.11**).

2. In the contact list, *do any of the following:*
   ▲ Click the scroll arrows, click in the scroll bar, or drag the scroll box to a new position. Depending on the current view, the scroll bar will be on the right or bottom of the screen.
   ▲ In Business Cards and Card view, click a letter (see Figure 17.1) to view contacts beginning with that letter.

3. *Optional:* To view a complete contact, double-click the record, or select the record and press (Ctrl)(O).
   The record opens in a new window (**Figure 17.12**).

To customize a view:

1. On the View tab, select the view you want to customize from the Change View icon's menu (see Figure 17.11).

2. Click the View Settings icon in the Current View group.

   The Advanced View Settings: *view name* dialog box appears (**Figure 17.13**).

3. Click a button and change its properties.

4. Click OK to close the Advanced View Settings dialog box.

   The view changes to reflect the new settings.

5. *Optional:* Choose Save Current View As a New View from the Change View icon's menu (see Figure 17.11), name the view in the Copy View dialog box, and click OK.

   The new view is added to the Change View and Current View lists, enabling you to switch to the view whenever you like.

✔ Tips

- Different views have different properties you can change. Here are some to consider:

  ▲ **Columns.** Change the fields shown and their display order (**Figure 17.14**).

  ▲ **Group By.** Set record grouping fields, such as Company (**Figure 17.15**).

  ▲ **Sort.** Set a default sort order for the view. If you specify multiple sort fields, records will be sorted by the first field and—within that sort order—sorted by subsequent fields. For example, you could specify Company as the primary sort field, followed by Last Name and then by First Name.

  ▲ **Filter.** Apply a filter to generate a list of only records that meet certain criteria. For example, by specifying that the Company field must contain Microsoft, you can create a Microsoft-only view.

Properties   *View name*

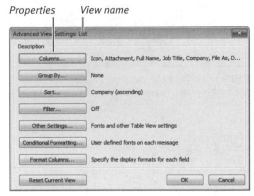

Figure 17.13 To change properties of the current view, click the appropriate button(s).

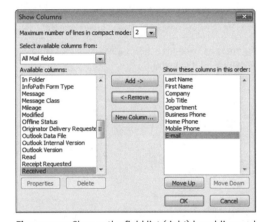

Figure 17.14 Change the field list (right) by adding and removing fields. To change their display order, drag the fields or click the Move Up/Move Down buttons.

Collapse/expand group

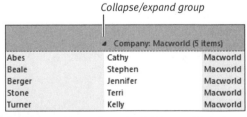

Figure 17.15 When a Group By field is specified, the records are organized in the view according to their group membership.

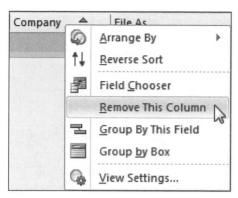

Figure 17.16 For simple changes to a list view, right-click a column heading and choose options from this context menu.

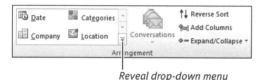

Reveal drop-down menu

Figure 17.17 The Arrangement group on the View tab.

■ You can change views at any time. Outlook remembers the most recent view selected—even between computing sessions.

■ When working in a columnar list view (such as Phone or List), you can change the sort order by clicking a column heading. Click the heading a second time to reverse the sort order.

■ When working in a columnar list view, you can right-click a column heading to quickly change the sort field(s), apply a grouping, change the field list, or remove the column (**Figure 17.16**).

■ If you've specified a Group By field for a view, you can collapse or expand the group by clicking the tiny icon that precedes the group's name (see Figure 17.15).

■ The Arrangement group on the View tab (**Figure 17.17**) has useful commands for modifying the current view. However, with the exception of Reverse Sort, they apply only to a columnar list view.

▲ **Reverse Sort.** Resort the records in reverse of their current order.

▲ **Add Columns.** Add or remove columns from the view.

▲ **Group By fields.** To group records by a field, select its field name (such as Company) and choose Show in Groups from the drop-down menu.

■ To restore the current view to its original state (field list, field order, and so on), switch to the View tab and click Reset View in the Current View group (see Figure 17.11).

Searching for a Contact

If you want to quickly find a contact without browsing through records, Outlook provides several tools you can use.

To search from the Find group box:

◆ On the Home tab in any Outlook component, enter a search string in the box in the Find group (**Figure 17.18**) and press [Enter].

One of the following occurs:

▲ If only one match is found, its contact record opens.

▲ If no match is found, an alert dialog box appears. Click OK to dismiss it.

▲ If multiple matches are identified, the Choose Contact window appears (**Figure 17.19**). Select a contact and click OK to open it, or click Cancel if the desired record isn't shown.

To perform an Instant Search:

1. Click in the Instant Search box at the top of the Contacts window (see Figure 17.1).

   The Search Tools contextual tab appears (**Figure 17.20**)

2. Type the search string.

   Potential matches are displayed as you type (**Figure 17.21**).

3. *Do any of the following:*

   ▲ Double-click a found record to open it.

   ▲ To repeat a previous search, click the Recent Searches icon in the Options group and choose a search to repeat.

   ▲ To perform a more complex or specific search, set criteria using the icons in the Refine group.

   ▲ To resume viewing all contact records, click the X beside the Instant Search box or the Close Search icon.

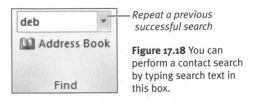

Repeat a previous successful search

Figure 17.18 You can perform a contact search by typing search text in this box.

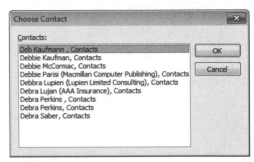

Figure 17.19 If the desired contact is shown, select it and click OK; otherwise, click Cancel.

Close Search

Figure 17.20 When you perform an Instant Search, the Search Tools contextual tab appears. Use its tools to refine the current search by adding criteria or to repeat a search.

Search results   *Instant Search box*   *Close*

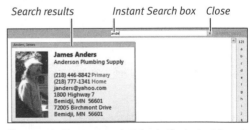

Figure 17.21 Enter a search string in the Instant Search box. Matching records appear as you type.

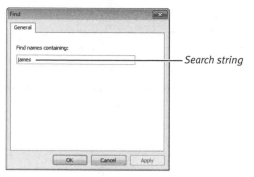

Figure 17.22 Enter part of the name for which you're searching. Click OK.

Search string

To perform a search in Address Book:

1. On the Home tab of any Outlook component, click the Address Book icon in the Find group.

   The Address Book window appears.

2. Choose Tools > Find, click Advanced Find, or press Shift Ctrl F.

   The Find window appears (**Figure 17.22**).

3. Enter search text and click OK.

   All matching records are displayed.

4. Double-click an entry to open its Outlook contact record in a new window.

✔ Tips

- To find a contact you've previously found using the Find group search box, click the arrow beside the box (see Figure 17.18) and select a record from the ones listed.

- After finding and opening a contact, you can create a new email message to the person or company by clicking the E-mail icon in the Communicate group.

- In an Instant Search (**Figure 17.23**), criteria chosen from the Refine group build the query text in the Instant Search box. Choices made from the Categorized, Has Phone Number, or Has Address icons are added directly to the query text. Fields chosen from the More icon (such as City and Company) display new text boxes in which you can type criteria.

Added field   Remove field   Added field   Remove field   Expanded query   End the search

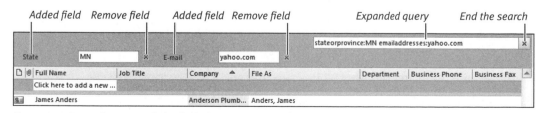

Figure 17.23 To conduct a search that looks in only particular fields, add them to the query.

Using Business Cards

If people often ask for your contact information, Outlook provides a way for you to email your contact record as an *Electronic Business Card* (EBC) or *vCard*. If the recipient is an Outlook user, he or she can quickly create a contact record for you, too.

To create or edit a business card:

1. Open your personal contact record. (Create the record if it doesn't exist.)

2. If you want to display additional elements on the card, complete those fields now.

3. Click the Business Card icon in the Options group of the Contact tab.

   The Edit Business Card window appears (**Figure 17.24**).

4. *Do any of the following:*

   ▲ To change the placement of a photo, company logo, or background image, choose an option from the Layout drop-down menu.

   ▲ To use a different image, click the Image: Change button. To change the image's alignment on the card, choose an option from the Image Align menu.

   ▲ To remove a selected field, click Remove. To add a field, click Add and choose the field to add.

   ▲ To change a field's vertical placement, select the field in the Fields list and click the up arrow or down arrow.

   ▲ To change a field's formatting, select the field in the Fields list and pick formatting options from the Edit toolbar.

5. Click OK to save the business card.

   The finished business card appears above the record's Notes area (**Figure 17.25**).

6. Click the Save & Close icon in the Actions group.

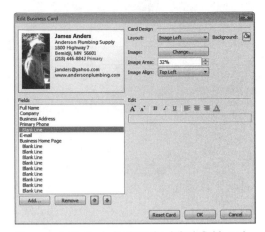

Figure 17.24 Outlook displays the default fields and layout for a new business card. (If the card already exists, the current version is shown.)

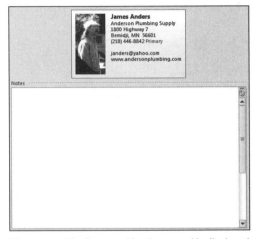

Figure 17.25 The formatted business card is displayed in the contact record.

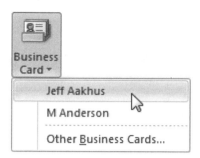

Figure 17.26 Choose a business card to attach to the current email message.

View the email message

View the business card

Figure 17.27 When you receive email with an attached business card, you can view the message or the card by clicking these tabs.

- To quickly save an open record as a .vcf file, click the File tab and then click Save As. In the Save As dialog box that appears, the Save as type is automatically set to vCard Files (*.vcf).

To email a business card:

1. Create a new email message.

2. On the Insert tab, click the Business Card icon in the Include group (**Figure 17.26**), and *do one of the following:*.

   ▲ Choose the card from the menu.

   ▲ If the card isn't listed, choose Other Business Cards and select the desired contact record.

   The card is inserted into the message as a graphic and attached as a .vcf file.

To save a received business card as an Outlook contact record:

1. Display the received email message in the Reading Pane or open it in its own window. If you like, you can view the card fields by clicking the .vcf attachment tab above the message body (**Figure 17.27**).

2. Right-click the business card image and choose Add to Outlook Contacts.

   A contact record for the business card appears.

3. *Do either of the following:*

   ▲ To save the record, click the Save & Close icon in the Actions group. (If desired, you can edit the information.)

   ▲ If you decide not to save the contact or believe it is a duplicate, click the close box (X) or click the Delete icon in the Actions group.

✔ Tips

- You can forward a contact record as a business card by selecting it in a Contacts list, selecting the Home tab, clicking the Forward Contact icon in the Share group, and choosing As a Business Card. Prior to doing so, you may wish to modify the card's field list as explained on the previous page.

USING BUSINESS CARDS

Creating Contact Groups

Do you ever find yourself repeatedly address-ing email to the same group of people? A project manager, for example, might want a weekly update delivered to all group members. When you need to regularly send messages to a clearly defined group, you can create a con-tact group (called a *distribution list* in prior versions of Outlook).

To create a contact group:

1. *Do one of the following:*

   ▲ On the Home tab of the Contacts window, click the New Contact Group icon in the New group.

   ▲ On the Home tab of any other Outlook component, click the New Items icon in the New group and choose More Items > Contact Group.

   ▲ Press Shift Ctrl L.

   An Untitled - Contact Group window appears.

2. Enter a name for the contact group in the Name box.

   Choose a descriptive name. It's how the group will be identified in your Contacts list.

3. To add members with contact records to the group, click the Add Members icon in the Members group and choose From Outlook Contacts or From Address Book (**Figure 17.28**).

   The Address Book window opens. To add someone to the group, select his or her name and click the Members button (**Figure 17.29**). Repeat for each additional member and then click OK. The new members are added to the contact group (**Figure 17.30**).

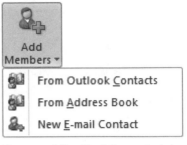

Figure 17.28 To add existing contacts to a group, start by choosing their source.

Figure 17.29 Chosen members are added to this box at the bottom of the Address Book window.

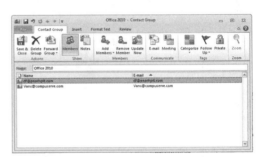

Figure 17.30 After you close the Address Book window, the chosen members appear in the contact group.

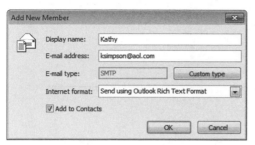

Figure 17.31 You can also add members who aren't in your Address Book. Click Add to Contacts if you'd like to create a contact record for the person.

4. To add a member to the contact group who does not have contact record, click the Add Members icon and choose New E-mail Contact.

The Add New Member dialog box appears (**Figure 17.31**). Enter the person's name and email address, and then click OK.

5. To save the contact group record, click the Save & Close icon in the Actions group.

To modify a contact group:

1. *Do any of the following:*

▲ To remove a member, open the contact group record, select the member to be removed, and click the Remove Member icon in the Members group.

▲ To add new members, perform Step 3 or 4 from the previous task list.

▲ If any list member's data has changed (a new email address, company name, or display name, for example), click Update Now in the Members group to update his or her contact data with the current information.

2. To save your changes, click the Save & Close icon in the Actions group.

✔ Tips

■ A group's contact record is denoted by two faces or the word *Group*, depending on the current view.

■ To address a message to a contact group, enter the group's name in the email message's To, Cc, or Bcc box.

■ To delete a contact group, select its record and click the Delete icon in the Delete group on the Home tab; right-click it and choose Delete; or press (Ctrl)(D), (Delete), or (Del). If the group's contact record is open, click the Delete Group icon in the Actions group.

COMPOSING AND SENDING MAIL

18

While much of a new user's email experience will consist of receiving and reading messages from supervisors, mailing list subscriptions, unwanted advertisements, and jokes from friends, most of you will eventually participate in the other part of the process: sending mail to others. You can create new messages, reply to incoming messages, and forward received messages to others.

Whether you are composing a new message, writing a reply, or forwarding email to a co-worker, the process of composing and sending a message consists of these steps:

1. Open a window for the new message, reply, or message to be forwarded.

2. Specify recipients and enter a Subject.

3. Select a message format: Plain Text, HTML, or Rich Text.

4. Compose the message.

5. Add optional attachments, such as a photo, text document, or worksheet.

6. Send the message.

In this chapter, you'll learn how to create new messages, reply to and forward received mail, and use Outlook tools to ensure that your messages are correct and attractive.

The Message Window

You can create three types of email messages in Outlook 2010:

◆ **New messages.** Messages you compose from scratch.

◆ **Replies.** Responses to received messages.

◆ **Forwarded messages.** Received messages you are sending to someone else.

All messages are composed in a message window (**Figure 18.1**). The main window sections include the Ribbon, the message header or address pane (the To, Cc, Bcc, and Subject boxes), the attachment list, and the message body (the text of the message).

The window title differs for each message type, showing *Untitled* for a blank original message, the Subject for a message you're composing, *RE:* for a reply, *FW:* for a forwarded message, and the original Subject for a message you're resending.

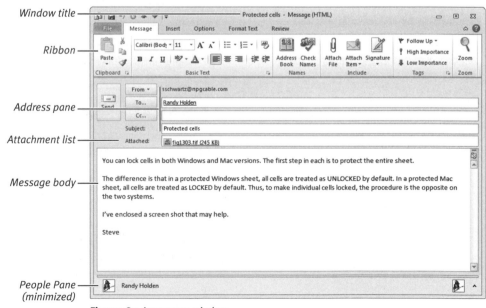

Figure 18.1 A message window.

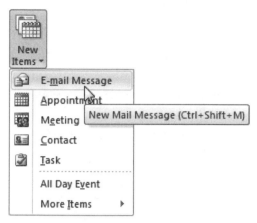

Figure 18.2 You can create a new message by choosing E-mail Message from the New Items icon.

Proposed account

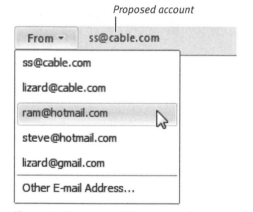

Figure 18.3 You can send the message from the proposed account or from another account selected in the From list.

Figure 18.4 You can type a few letters of a contact's first name or email address and then select from a list of potential matches.

Creating Messages

To let a relative know what's new, send a Web link or photo to a friend, or inform your supervisor how a project is progressing, you start by creating a new message. You can also create email by replying to or forwarding a received message. And you can resend any previously sent message—either to the same person or to someone else.

To create a new message:

1. *Do one of the following:*

   ▲ When working in Mail, switch to the Home tab and click the New E-mail icon in the New group ($\boxed{\text{Ctrl}}\boxed{\text{N}}$).

   ▲ When working in *any* component (Mail, Calendar, Contacts, Tasks, or Notes), switch to the Home tab and choose E-mail Message from the New Items icon in the New group (**Figure 18.2**) ($\boxed{\text{Ctrl}}\boxed{\text{Shift}}\boxed{\text{M}}$).

   A message window opens (see Figure 18.1). The cursor is positioned in the To box, ready for you to enter the recipients. The message will be sent from the active account in the Navigation Pane or, when another Outlook component is active, from your default account (see Chapter 16). If you like, you can select a different account from the From list (**Figure 18.3**).

2. Enter primary recipients in the To box. Specify the first To email address by doing one of the following:

   ▲ Start typing the person's name or email address. As you type, a list of matching recipients drawn from addresses you previously typed in the address pane appears (**Figure 18.4**). Select a recipient or continue typing.

   continues on next page

▲ Click the To button, click the Address Book icon in the Names group on the Message tab (**Figure 18.5**), or press Ctrl Shift B. To add a person from the Address Book, select them and click the To button or double-click their name. Click OK.

3. *Optional:* To enter more To addresses, click in the space following the last address and repeat Step 2. Note that each address pair must be separated by a semicolon (;).

4. *Optional:* Persons in the Cc (*carbon copy*) box represent secondary recipients. To add Cc recipients, click in the Cc box and follow Steps 2–3.

5. *Optional:* A message can also have Bcc (*blind carbon copy*) recipients. Addresses in the Bcc box are hidden from all recipients. If the Bcc box isn't visible, click the Options tab and then click the Bcc icon in the Show Fields group (**Figure 18.6**). To add Bcc recipients, click in the Bcc box and follow Steps 2–3.

6. Click in or Tab into the Subject box. Enter a subject to identify the message.

7. Click in or Tab into the message area and type the message text.

8. Click Send to send the message.

✔ Tips

■ You can also paste a copied email address into the To, Cc, or Bcc box. Click the Paste icon in the Clipboard group on the Message tab or press Ctrl V.

■ You can drag addresses between the To, Cc, and Bcc boxes.

■ The AutoComplete drop-down list (see Figure 18.4) does not suggest contacts from the Address Book. However, if you type a contact's full name, Outlook will email the message to the correct address.

Figure 18.5 When entering message recipients, it can be helpful to consult your Address Book.

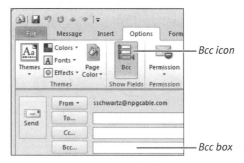

Figure 18.6 Click the Bcc icon to reveal the normally hidden Bcc box.

Exchange Email Gets Smarter

Outlook 2010 has a new Exchange-only feature called *MailTips*. Whenever you send a message from an Exchange account, Outlook performs a number of checks to ensure that the message can be delivered, is within size limits, and isn't improperly addressed to someone who doesn't have an account on the server, for example.

If problems are detected for a message, informative MailTips are shown beneath the Ribbon, identifying and enabling you to correct the problem(s).

CREATING MESSAGES

Figure 18.7 Select the desired contact and click OK. If you can't find the individual, click Cancel.

Reply text

Quoted text from original message

Figure 18.9 When replying to email, enter your reply above the author's quoted text and click Send.

- If you enter only a partial name in an address box and click Send, the Check Names dialog box appears (**Figure 18.7**). Select the correct person and click OK.

- Outlook remembers and uses the most recent Bcc setting in subsequent sessions.

- You can create a pre-addressed message by clicking an email address in the body of a received message or an email link on a Web page (**Figure 18.8**, below).

To create a reply:

1. In the message list, select the header of the message to which you are replying or open the message in its own window.

2. Click the Reply icon in the Respond group or press Ctrl R.

   A copy of the message appears in a new window, addressed to the original author. The author's text is *quoted* (repeated) at the bottom of the message (**Figure 18.9**). The Subject is changed to RE: *original Subject* and the text insertion mark is positioned above the quoted text.

3. *Optional:* You can add additional recipients in the address pane boxes.

4. Type your reply to the message.

5. Edit the quoted text, if desired (removing extraneous material, for example).

6. Click the Send icon.

   Replies are sent from the account to which the original message was addressed.

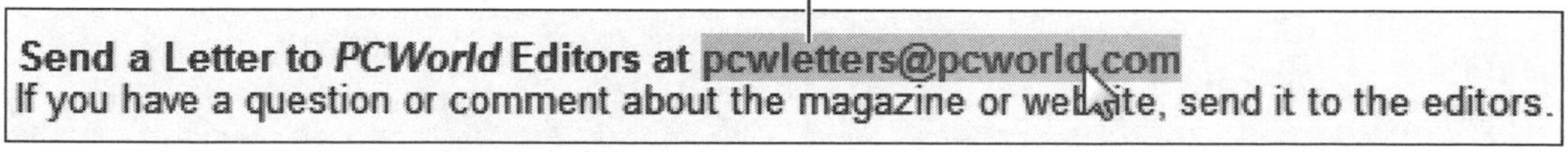

Mailto: link example

Send a Letter to *PCWorld* Editors at pcwletters@pcworld.com
If you have a question or comment about the magazine or website, send it to the editors.

Figure 18.8 Some Web pages contain *mailto:* links. Click the link to create a new pre-addressed message in Outlook.

✔ Tips

- When writing a reply, you shouldn't edit the automatically generated Subject. The RE: *original Subject* shows the recipient the message to which you're responding.

- Reply and forwarding options are set in the Replies and forwards section of the Outlook Options dialog box (**Figure 18.10**). Click the File tab to go to the Backstage, click Options to open the Outlook Options dialog box, and select the Mail Category.

- To reply to everyone in the To and Cc lines of a received message, click Reply All in the Respond group ([Ctrl] [Shift] [R]).

To forward a received message:

1. Select the header of the message you want to forward or open the message in its own window.

2. Click the Forward icon in the Respond group or press [Ctrl] [F].

   The author's text is repeated *(quoted)* at the bottom of the message. The Subject is automatically changed to FW: *original Subject* (**Figure 18.11**).

3. In the address pane, specify recipients for the forwarded message.

4. *Optional:* You can edit the original text, as well as insert your own comments.

5. Click the Send icon.

   Forwarded messages are sent from the account to which the original message was addressed.

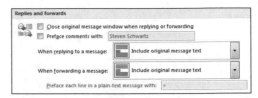

Figure 18.10 You can specify the formatting of quoted text in replies and forwarded messages.

New text   Forwarded text

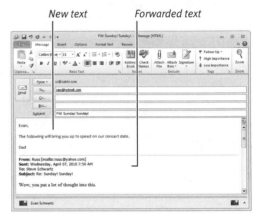

Figure 18.11 When forwarding email, you can add your own comments, as well as edit the forwarded text.

Sending Messages from Different Accounts

If you just click the Send icon to send a new message, it is sent from the currently selected account or, if you're working in a non-Mail part of Outlook, from your default account. When you click the Send icon to send a reply or forwarded message, it is sent from your account that received the original message.

To send any message from a *different* Outlook account, click the From button and select the account you'd like to use.

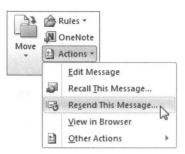

Figure 18.12 Choose Resend This Message from the drop-down menu.

Figure 18.13 If one of your sent messages has yet to be read by an Exchange Server recipient, you can delete the message or replace it with another.

Recalling a Sent Message

If a message recipient has an Exchange Server account, you can optionally *recall* a message you've mistakenly sent to them or one that contains errors.

1. Open the previously sent message.

2. Choose Recall This Message from the Actions icon in the Move group (Figure 18.12).

3. Select an option in the Recall This Message dialog box (**Figure 18.13**, above) and then click OK.

✔ Tips

■ In addition to forwarding a message as quoted text, you can forward it as an attachment. With the header selected or the message open in its own window, click the More icon in the Respond group and choose Forward as Attachment.

■ When forwarding jokes, news items, and the like, don't forward multiple layers of attachments; that is, a message within a message within a message. Open all layers of the received message until you locate the original and then forward *that* message. Also, you may want to remove the email addresses of the last sender and previous recipients to ensure their privacy.

To resend a previously sent message:

1. In a Sent or Sent Items folder, locate the previously sent message and open it in its own window.

2. On the Message tab in the Move group, click the Actions icon and choose Resend This Message (**Figure 18.12**).

   A copy of the original message appears.

3. *Optional:* Change the intended message recipient(s).

4. Click the Send icon.

✔ Tip

■ You can use the Resend This Message command to send the same message to multiple people, one at a time. Just change the recipient each time.

About Message Formats

Every message you create must be in one of three formats: Plain Text, HTML, or Rich Text.

◆ **Plain Text** is a universally readable, single-font format. It provides no support for character formatting (such as boldface, italic, or color) or paragraph formatting.

◆ **HTML** is meant for messages that must contain formatting. You can format text with specific fonts and colors, create bulleted and numbered lists, embed pictures in the message body, insert links, and use stationery backgrounds.

◆ **Rich Text** is a format readable only by Microsoft email clients. Rich Text messages sent over the Internet are automatically converted to HTML format. They are sent unaltered only to other Exchange Server accounts within your network.

You can set a default format to be used for new messages, as well as change the format of the message you're currently writing.

To specify a default message format:

1. Click the File tab. In the Backstage, click Options.

   The Outlook Options dialog box appears.

2. Select the Mail category and choose a default format in the Compose messages section (**Figure 18.14**).

3. Click OK to save your changes and close the Outlook Options dialog box.

To set a format for the current message:

◆ On the Format Text tab of the message you're composing, click an icon in the Format group (**Figure 18.15**).

   You can set or change the format at any time during the message-creation process.

Choose a message format

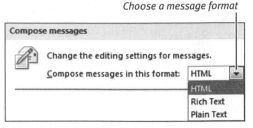

Figure 18.14 By default, all new messages will use the chosen format.

Figure 18.15 Select a format for the message. The current format is highlighted.

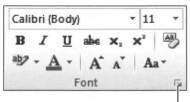

Font dialog box launcher

Figure 18.16 The Font group on the Format Text tab provides the most complete array of character-formatting commands.

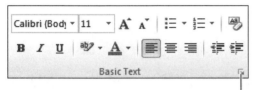

Font dialog box launcher

Figure 18.17 The left side of the Basic Text group presents a subset of the most common character-formatting commands.

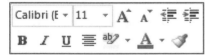

Figure 18.18 The pop-up Mini toolbar has frequently used character- and paragraph-formatting commands.

Table 18.1

Character-Formatting Keyboard Shortcuts	
KEYPRESS	**DEFINITION**
Ctrl B	Boldface
Ctrl I	Italic
Ctrl U	Underline (single)
Ctrl Shift K	Small capital letters (small caps)
Ctrl =	Subscript
Ctrl Shift +	Superscript
Ctrl Shift <	Decrease font size
Ctrl Shift >	Increase font size

Formatting Message Text

When creating an HTML or Rich Text format message, you can selectively apply character and paragraph formatting. Like Word, Outlook 2010 provides the Format Painter tool for quickly duplicating character formatting.

To apply character formatting:

1. *Do either of the following:*
   - ▲ Select the text you want to format. (You can make multiple noncontiguous selections by holding down Ctrl as you make each selection.)
   - ▲ Position the text insertion mark where you want the new character formatting to begin.

2. *Do any of the following:*
   - ▲ On the Format Text tab, select character-formatting options from the Font group (**Figure 18.16**).
   - ▲ On the Message tab, select character-formatting options from the Basic Text group (**Figure 18.17**).
   - ▲ Select the text to be formatted and move the cursor up. The Mini toolbar appears (**Figure 18.18**), presenting common formatting commands.
   - ▲ Click the Font dialog box launcher at the bottom of the Font or Basic Text group. In the Font dialog box, select character-formatting options and click OK to apply the formatting. (For more information on working with the Font dialog box, see Chapter 5.)
   - ▲ Enter a formatting command's keyboard shortcut, such as Ctrl B for Bold. To view the keyboard shortcut for a command, rest the cursor on its icon in the Basic Text or Font group. **Table 18.1** lists many of the character-formatting keyboard shortcuts.

To apply paragraph formatting:

1. Position the text insertion mark in the paragraph you want to format.

   You can also preselect multiple paragraphs or select some text within a paragraph.

2. *Do any of the following:*

   ▲ On the Format Text tab, select paragraph-formatting commands from the Paragraph group (**Figure 18.19**).

   ▲ On the Message tab, select paragraph-formatting commands from the Basic Text group (see Figure 18.17).

   ▲ If you've selected text in one or more paragraphs, move the cursor up to display the Mini toolbar (see Figure 18.18). Several paragraph-formatting commands are available.

   ▲ Click the Paragraph dialog box launcher, choose settings from the Paragraph dialog box, and click OK.

   ▲ Enter a paragraph-formatting command's keyboard shortcut, such as Ctrl J for Justify. (To see the keyboard shortcut for a command, rest the cursor on its icon in the Paragraph or Basic Text group.)

To apply a Quick Style to text:

1. Select the text to be formatted or position the text insertion mark in the paragraph to be formatted.

2. Select the Format Text tab. Open the Quick Styles gallery in the Styles group (**Figure 18.20**).

3. As you move the cursor over a style in the gallery, a preview of that style is applied to the selected text or paragraph. Click a style to apply it.

   If you decide not to apply any of the styles, click outside the gallery.

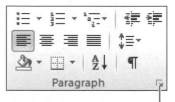

Paragraph dialog box launcher

Figure 18.19 The Paragraph group contains the general paragraph-formatting commands.

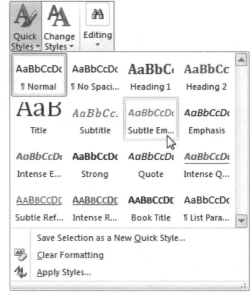

Figure 18.20 To easily apply complex, attractive formatting to selected text or paragraphs, choose a style from the Quick Styles gallery.

More Quick Styles

If you don't like the look of the default Quick Styles, there are other style sets from which you can choose. You can also change the colors and fonts used. Click the Change Styles icon to explore the options. See "Working with Styles" in Chapter 5 for more information on using Quick Styles.

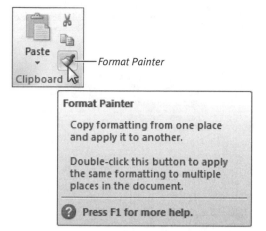

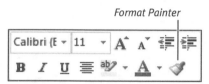

Figure 18.21 Select formatted text that you want to apply elsewhere and click the Format Painter in the Clipboard group (top) or on the Mini toolbar (bottom).

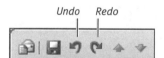

Figure 18.22 To undo your most recent action, click the Undo icon on the Quick Access Toolbar.

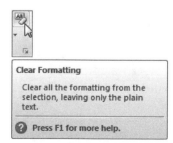

Figure 18.23 Click Clear Formatting to remove all applied character formatting from the selected text.

To apply character formatting:

1. Select specific text or a paragraph that contains the formatting you want to copy.

2. Click the Format Painter in the Clipboard group of the Message tab or on the Mini toolbar (**Figure 18.21**).

3. Drag to select the text you want to format. When you stop dragging, the copied formatting is applied to the selected text.

To remove character formatting:

1. Select the text from which you want to remove previously applied formatting.

2. *Do one of the following:*

   ▲ If your most recent action was to apply the character formatting, press Ctrl Z or click the Undo icon in the Quick Access Toolbar (**Figure 18.22**).

   ▲ Select the same formatting command on the Ribbon or Mini toolbar.

   ▲ Click the Clear Formatting icon in the Font group (**Figure 18.23**) to remove *all* previously applied formatting from the selected text.

✔ Tips

■ When using the Format Painter, you can apply the copied format to a word by double-clicking the word.

■ You can't reverse the Text Highlight Color or Font Color of selected text by clicking the same icon again. Select the original color or click Clear Formatting.

■ Most paragraph formatting can't be reversed by clicking the icon again. To restore the original formatting, click the appropriate icon in the Paragraph group. (However, you *can* eliminate Bullets and Numbering formatted paragraphs by clicking their icons again.)

FORMATTING MESSAGE TEXT

Adding Attachments

One popular use of email is to transmit documents and photos with your messages. These files are known as *attachments*.

To add an attachment to a message:

1. On the Message or Insert tab, click the Attach File icon in the Include group.

   The Insert File dialog box appears (**Figure 18.24**).

2. Navigate to the correct drive and folder, select a file, and click Insert. (You can select multiple files within a folder by Ctrl-clicking them.)

   The file is added to the Attached list (**Figure 18.25**). You can add other attachments by repeating these steps.

✔ Tips

■ You can also add attachments by dragging their file icons from the desktop or any open folder onto the open message.

■ To remove an attachment, select it in the Attached list and then press Backspace or Del. You can also right-click an attachment and choose Remove from the context menu (**Figure 18.26**).

■ Check the total size of the attachments before sending a message. First, ISPs have a maximum message size, and attachments tend to get larger when encoded for transmission. Second, not everyone has broadband Internet access. If you email a huge video or audio clip to a friend with a dial-up account, you'll tie them up for a very long time.

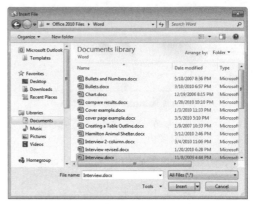

Figure 18.24 Select one or more files and click the Insert button (Windows 7 shown).

Figure 18.25 The Attached box shows the names and sizes of all attached files.

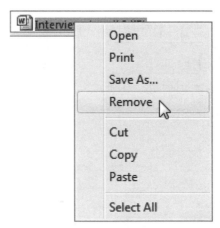

Figure 18.26 The context menu contains a Remove command.

Picture Tools contextual tab

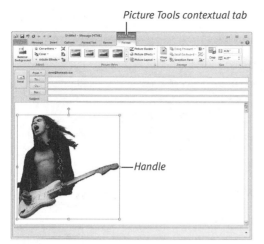

Figure 18.27 When an inserted image is selected, image editing and enhancement commands appear.

Figure 18.28 Select a business card to insert.

vCard file attachment

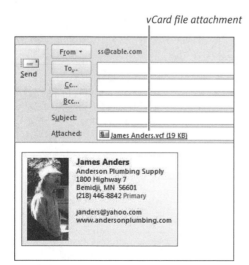

Figure 18.29 The business card is added to the message as an image and as an attachment.

Inserting Items

The Insert tab contains tools for inserting items directly into the body of HTML and Rich Text messages, such as tables, charts, horizontal lines, and clip art. In this section, you'll learn how to insert three common items: photos, business cards, and hyperlinks.

To insert a photo or other image:

1. Position the text insertion mark at the spot in the message body where you want to insert the image.

2. On the Insert tab, click the Picture icon in the Illustration group.

   The Insert Picture dialog box appears.

3. Navigate to the drive/folder that contains the image, select the file, and click Insert.

   The image appears in the message body (**Figure 18.27**).

4. *Optional:* With the image selected, you can resize it by dragging any corner handle. To rotate the image, drag the green circle. You can also perform advanced image enhancement, editing, and formatting by selecting commands from the Picture Tools contextual tab.

To insert a business card image:

1. Position the text insertion mark at the spot in the message body where you want to insert the business card image.

2. On the Insert tab, click the Business Card icon in the Include group. Choose a card from the ones listed in the drop-down menu (**Figure 18.28**).To send contact info for someone whose name isn't listed, choose Other Business Cards.

   A graphic version of the business card is inserted into the message body. The business card (vCard) file is also included as an attachment (**Figure 18.29**).

To insert a clickable Web page link:

1. Position the text insertion mark at the spot in the message body where you want to insert the Web link.

2. On the Insert tab, click the Hyperlink icon in the Links group or press Ctrl K.

   The Insert Hyperlink dialog box appears.

3. Select Existing File or Web Page in the Link to list and Browsed Pages in the inner list (**Figure 18.30**).

4. Select a recently viewed page from the list in the scroll box or from the Address drop-down list. You can also type or paste a Web address (URL) into the Address box.

5. *Optional:* Edit the text in the Text to display box. This text will represent the link.

6. Click OK.

   The link text is inserted into the message (**Figure 18.31**). When the recipient clicks the link, the specified page will load in the person's default Web browser.

To insert a clickable email link:

1. Position the text insertion mark at the spot in the message body where you want to insert the email (*mailto:*) link.

2. On the Insert tab, click the Hyperlink icon in the Links group or press Ctrl K.

   The Insert Hyperlink dialog box appears (Figure 18.30).

3. Select E-mail Address in the Link to list.

4. Type or paste the destination address into the E-mail address box.

   A *mailto:* prefix is automatically added to the address.

5. *Optional:* Edit the Text to display.

6. *Optional:* Enter a Subject for the message (**Figure 18.32**).

Link text to display in message

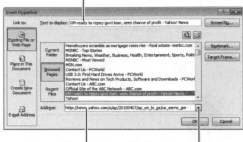

Page address   Recently viewed pages

Figure 18.30 You can create a Web page hyperlink by specifying the page's address and the wording for the link text.

Link

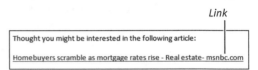

Figure 18.31 When inserted into a message, a Web link looks and acts like one on a Web page.

Figure 18.32 You can also insert an email (*mailto:*) link that generates a new message to the specified address when clicked by the recipient.

INSERTING ITEMS

Selected hyperlink

Figure 18.34 To convert a hyperlink to normal text, select the link text, right-click it, and choose Remove Hyperlink.

7. Click OK.

The link text is inserted into the message (**Figure 18.33**, below). When the recipient clicks the link, a new email message addressed to the specified recipient appears.

✔ Tips

■ You can also create a hyperlink by typing or pasting ([Ctrl][V]) a complete address into the message body. Outlook automatically converts the text to a hyperlink if the text is recognized as a proper link (www.hotmail.com, for example).

■ You can also convert existing message text to a hyperlink. Select the text and then skip to Step 2. The selected text is automatically treated as the Text to display.

■ Hyperlinks work best in HTML/Rich Text messages. Although hyperlinks can also be used in Plain Text messages, these restrictions are present:

▲ The Hyperlink command is unavailable, so you must enter links manually.

▲ Long URLs may be broken up, rendering them inoperable when clicked.

■ To convert a hyperlink back to normal text, select the text, right-click it, and choose Remove Hyperlink from the context menu (**Figure 18.34**).

Embedded email link

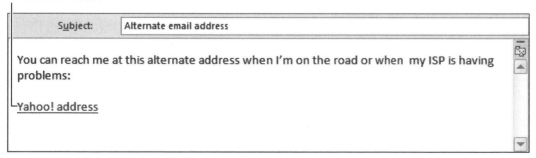

Figure 18.33 When the recipient clicks the embedded *mailto:* link, a new pre-addressed message is generated.

INSERTING ITEMS

Correcting Spelling Errors

Unless you're both an exceptional speller and typist (or you trust that your recipients will simply *know* what you're trying to say, regardless of what you type), it's a good idea to run each outgoing message through Outlook's spelling checker. Outlook provides two spell-checking options:

◆ Outlook can check for and flag potential errors as you type.

◆ You can perform a full spelling check on request or automatically before each message is sent.

To check spelling as you type:

1. This option is enabled by default. If you've disabled it, click the File tab and then click Options in the Backstage.

2. In the Outlook Options dialog box, select the Mail category. In the Compose messages section, click the Spelling and Autocorrect button.

3. In the Editor Options dialog box, click Check spelling as you type (**Figure 18.35**) and then click OK.

4. As you type a message, Outlook checks each word. Suspect words are marked with a squiggly red underline. For each flagged word, you can do the following:

   ▲ Ignore the error (because you believe the word is spelled correctly).

   ▲ Edit the word to correct the error.

   ▲ Right-click the word and select a correction option (**Figure 18.36**).

   You can select the correct spelling or choose Ignore to accept this instance, Ignore All to accept all instances of this spelling in the message, or Add to Dictionary to accept the spelling and add it to your spelling dictionary (so it will be recognized in other messages).

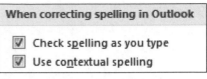

Figure 18.35 The top check box determines whether spelling errors are automatically flagged as you compose each message.

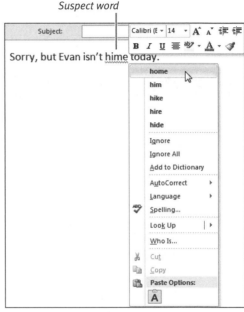

Figure 18.36 To quickly correct an actual error, you may be able to select the correct spelling from the suggestions.

CORRECTING SPELLING ERRORS

Suspect word   *Options*

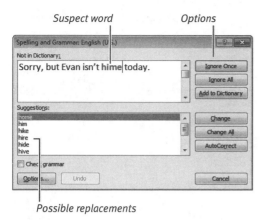

Possible replacements

Figure 18.37 When you perform a manual spelling check, Outlook displays each suspect word in this dialog box.

Automatically check spelling before sending

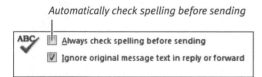

Figure 18.38 Enable this Compose messages option to automatically request a spelling check of every outgoing message.

To perform a manual spelling check:

1. Click the Spelling & Grammar icon on the Review tab or press [F7].

   If any errors are found, the Spelling and Grammar dialog box appears (**Figure 18.37**). Otherwise, you are notified that the spelling check is complete.

2. Each suspect word is displayed in red boldface. *Do one of the following:*

   ▲ Select a replacement word from the Suggestions list and click Change to correct the error. (If you think you've made the same mistake elsewhere in the message, click Change All.)

   ▲ Edit the word in the Not in Dictionary box and then click Change.

   ▲ Click Ignore Once to ignore this instance of the spelling, leaving the current word unchanged.

   ▲ Click Ignore All to ignore all instances of this spelling, leaving all instances of the word in this message unchanged.

   ▲ If the word is spelled correctly and you want it recognized in future spelling checks, click Add to Dictionary.

3. Repeat Step 2 for additional suspect words. The spelling check ends when all suspect words have been examined or you click Cancel.

✔ Tips

■ If you'd rather defer spelling checks until you're done writing each message, check Always check spelling before sending in the Mail category of the Outlook Options dialog box (**Figure 18.38**). Whenever you click Send for an outgoing message, a spell check will be performed.

■ Enable the Use contextual spelling option (see Figure 18.35). It instructs Outlook to consider context when determining whether a word is spelled correctly.

Using Signatures

Optionally, an outgoing message can end with a *signature*: text or an image that provides your name and mailing address, Web address, electronic business card, or a snappy quote. A signature can automatically be added to every outgoing message or manually added to only certain messages. You can create as many signatures as you like.

To create a signature:

1. Create a new mail message. On the Message tab, click the Signature icon in the Include group and choose Signatures.

   The Signatures and Stationery dialog box appears (**Figure 18.39**).

2. Click New to create a new signature.

   The New Signature dialog box appears.

3. Name the new signature (**Figure 18.40**) and click OK.

   The name is added to the list of defined signatures.

4. Enter one or multiple lines of signature text, formatted as you want them to appear when appended to a message. You can also:

   ▲ Format selected text by applying fonts, sizes, and other formatting options from the toolbar.

   ▲ Insert your electronic business card as an image, a photo, or a hyperlink (such as your Web site address) by clicking toolbar icons.

5. When you're done writing and formatting the signature (**Figure 18.41**), click Save.

6. You can continue creating, editing, and deleting signatures or click OK to close the Signatures and Stationery window.

Defined signatures   *Formatting toolbar*

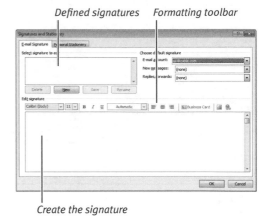

Create the signature

Figure 18.39 You create, edit, and delete signatures in the Signatures and Stationery window.

Figure 18.40 Enter a name to identify this signature and click OK.

Signature name

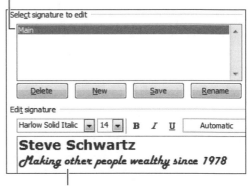

Signature text

Figure 18.41 This simple signature includes my name and a memorable quote.

USING SIGNATURES

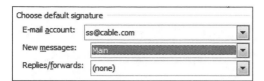

Figure 18.42 You can specify a default signature to automatically be added to certain types of messages from a given account. Choose None if you prefer no signature or would rather add one manually.

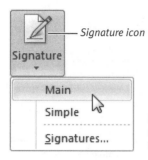

Figure 18.43 Select a signature to include in the current message.

To set a default signature for an email account:

1. In the Signatures and Stationery window, select the mail account to which a default signature will be applied (**Figure 18.42**).

2. *Do any of the following:*
   ▲ To specify a default signature that will be added to all new messages from the account, select a signature name from the New messages drop-down list.
   ▲ To specify a default signature to be added to all replies and forwarded messages from the account, select a name from the Replies/forwards list.

3. Click OK to save your changes.

To manually add a signature to a message:

1. Click to set the text insertion point in your message. Normally, this will be beneath the final message line.

2. On the Message or Insert tab, select a signature from the Signature icon's drop-down list (**Figure 18.43**).

✔ Tips

■ To edit a signature, select it in the Select signature to edit list (see Figure 18.41) and make the desired changes. To delete or rename a signature, select it in the same list and click the appropriate button.

■ To replace a message's signature with a different one, select the other signature from the Signature icon's drop-down list.

■ You can also use a signature to store a *complete message*, such as one notifying people that you're out of the office.

■ If you create a formatted signature and append it to a Plain Text message, an unformatted version of the signature is automatically used.

USING SIGNATURES

Other Message Options

While not essential to most users (or most messages), this section briefly explores some other Outlook message-creation options.

Requesting a receipt

If a message is very important, you can request a delivery or read receipt. A *delivery receipt* is an email notification that the message has been delivered to the recipient. A *read receipt* indicates that the recipient has actually opened and read the message.

To request a delivery or read receipt:

◆ Prior to sending the message, click the appropriate check box(es) in the Tracking group on the Options tab (**Figure 18.44**).

If a delivery receipt was requested, email notification will be sent to you when the message is delivered. If a read receipt was requested and the recipient's email client supports this feature, they will be asked to confirm that the message has been read (**Figure 18.45**).

Setting a message priority

You can set a *priority* for an outgoing message to indicate its level of importance. Setting a priority, however, has no impact on the manner in which it is delivered. Note that not all email programs recognize and display priorities.

To set a priority for a message:

◆ Prior to sending a message, click the High Importance or Low Importance icon in the Tags group on the Message tab.

By default, all outgoing messages are sent Normal priority. Unless you want to set a *different* priority, you don't need to click an Importance icon.

Properties dialog box launcher

Figure 18.44 Click check boxes in the Tracking group to request receipts.

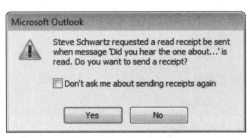

Figure 18.45 In Outlook, this dialog box asks the recipient to verify that the message has been read. Note that the recipient isn't required to respond.

Drafts: Works in Progress

You aren't required to immediately send each message. If you're still working on a message, you can save it as a *draft*. To save a message in progress, click the Save icon in the Quick Access Toolbar, click Save in the Backstage, press Ctrl S, or close the message and elect to save it when prompted. Saved messages are stored in an account's Drafts folder, where you can continue working on them at your convenience.

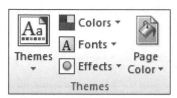

Figure 18.46 You can apply colorful themes, fonts, and backgrounds to a message by choosing options from the Themes group.

Themes and stationery   *Preview*

Options

Figure 18.47 Select a theme from the Choose a Theme list. Set options for the selected theme by checking or clearing check boxes.

Applying page colors, themes, and stationery

In addition to allowing formatted text, HTML messages can have a *theme* (a coordinated set of fonts, bullets, colors, and effects) or be written on *stationery* (a colorful background). These elements can be applied on a message-by-message basis or to all new messages.

To apply a background color or theme to a single message:

1. Create a new message. On the Format Text tab, click the HTML icon in the Format group to set the message type to HTML.

2. *Optional:* Select a background color from the Page Color palette in the Themes group of the Options tab (**Figure 18.46**).

3. *Optional:* To apply a theme to the message, choose options from the other menus and palettes in the Themes group.

To use stationery for a single message:

1. In the New group on the Home tab, click the New Items icon and choose E-mail Message Using > More Stationery.

   The Theme or Stationery dialog box appears (**Figure 18.47**).

2. Select a stationery option from the Choose a Theme list. Click OK.

   A blank HTML message window appears, formatted to match the selected stationery.

3. Address and compose the message, and then click Send.

OTHER MESSAGE OPTIONS

To set a default theme or stationery:

1. Click the File tab. In the Backstage, click Options to open the Outlook Options dialog box.

2. In the Mail category, click the Stationery and Fonts button in the Compose Messages section.

   The Signatures and Stationery dialog box appears, open to the Personal Stationery tab (**Figure 18.48**).

3. Click the Theme button.

   The Theme or Stationery dialog box appears (see Figure 18.47).

4. Select a theme or stationery format.

5. Dismiss all open dialog boxes by clicking OK in each one.

   The theme or stationery will automatically be applied to every new HTML message you create.

✔ Tips

■ To remove a default theme, select (No Theme) from the Choose a Theme list in the Theme or Stationery dialog box.

■ Even if you don't want to designate a default theme, you can use the Signatures and Stationery dialog box to specify a default font to be used to compose new messages, reply to messages, or forward messages (Figure 18.48).

■ You also may want to enable the option to Pick a new color when replying or forwarding (Figure 18.48). This ensures that any text you add to a reply or forwarded message will be in a different color from the original author's text.

■ You can set other message options by clicking the dialog box launcher in the Tracking group (see Figure 18.44).

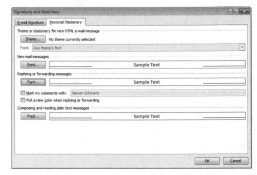

Figure 18.48 If you want certain types of messages to use the same theme or stationery, you can set defaults.

OTHER MESSAGE OPTIONS

19

RECEIVING MAIL

In this chapter, you'll learn how to check for new email (manually and automatically); select and read messages; change your *view* and display *message conversations;* search for messages in a folder or in all mail folders; preview, open, and save attachments; and print messages or a list of message headers.

For information on replying to and forwarding received messages, see Chapter 18. To learn about managing your email (including deleting, copying, and moving messages, and managing conversations), see Chapter 20.

✔ Tips

■ Much of the information in this chapter applies not only to incoming mail but to *sent* messages, too.

■ If you have a Microsoft Exchange account, Office 2010's support for *Unified Messaging* (UM) will enable you to receive voice mail and faxes in your Outlook Inbox. Contact your network administrator for assistance with Exchange support issues.

Checking for New Mail

Outlook 2010 provides two ways to check for incoming mail:

- **Automatically.** While Outlook is running and you are online, all accounts in a given *send/receive group* (see Chapter 16) are automatically checked for new incoming messages every so many minutes, based on the group's schedule.

- **Manually.** To immediately check for new messages in a given account or an entire send/receive group, you can perform a manual send/receive as described below.

To perform a Send/Receive All Folders:

- *Do one of the following:*
  - ▲ Click the Send/Receive All Folders icon in the Quick Access Toolbar (**Figure 19.1**).
  - ▲ On the Send/Receive tab, click the Send/Receive All Folders icon in the Send & Receive group.
  - ▲ Press F9.

To perform a send/receive for a group:

- On the Send/Receive tab, click the Send/Receive Groups icon in the Send & Receive group and choose a group from the drop-down menu (**Figure 19.2**).

To perform a send/receive for a single account folder:

1. In the Navigation Pane, select the account folder you want to check.

2. On the Send/Receive tab, click Update Folder in the Send & Receive group (Shift F9).

   Note that this procedure is available only for certain folders. If a selected folder is ineligible, Update Folder will be grayed out.

CHECKING FOR NEW MAIL

Send/Receive All Folders icon

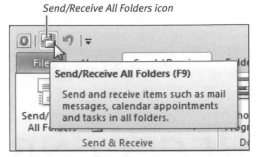

Figure 19.1 You can perform a manual Send/Receive All Folders by clicking this Quick Access Toolbar icon.

Figure 19.2 To initiate a manual send/receive for an Outlook group, choose the group from this drop-down menu.

✔ Tips

- Even if a given group is set for automatic send/receives, you can still perform manual send/receives whenever you like.

- Exchange and IMAP accounts are continuously synched with the server, so they don't need a schedule.

- By default, the All send/receive group contains every account group you've defined in Outlook. To change a group's inclusion in this group, see "Working with Send/Receive Groups" in Chapter 16.

- The notification methods used to signal new mail are determined by the settings in Outlook Options > Mail > Message Arrival.

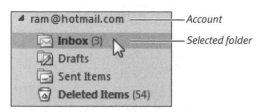

Figure 19.3 Select a message folder in the Navigation Pane.

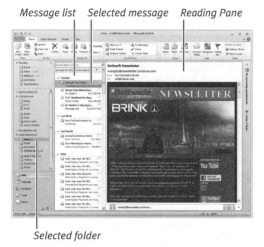

Figure 19.4 It's more convenient to read most messages in the Reading Pane than it is to open them in a separate window.

Reading Messages

You can read any message that's displayed in Outlook, whether it's received mail, sent mail, or an RSS feed message. You can even read mail in the Deleted Items folder until the folder is emptied. And unless you have an uncached Microsoft Exchange account (see the sidebar on this page), you don't need an active connection with the mail server in order to read messages.

To read messages:

1. In the Navigation Pane, select the account folder (**Figure 19.3**) that contains the messages you want to read (such as the Inbox). If you can't see the account's folders, click the triangle that precedes the account name.

   Message headers for the selected folder are displayed in the message list. The name of the currently selected folder is shown in Outlook's title bar.

2. *Do either of the following:*

   ▲ In the message list, select the header of the message you want to read. The message is displayed in the Reading Pane (**Figure 19.4**).

   ▲ To read a message in its own window, double-click its header in the message list. (You can also open a selected message by pressing [Enter] or [Ctrl][O].)

   After you view a message, it is automatically marked as *read*; that is, the boldface is removed from the message header.

3. If you're reading a message in its own window, close the window by clicking its close box.

Enabling Cached Exchange Mode

To determine whether your Exchange messages are *cached* (copies are stored on your computer), *do the following:*

1. Click the File tab and choose Account Settings > Account Settings.

2. On the E-mail tab of the Account Settings dialog box, select the Exchange account and click Change.

3. Ensure that Use Cached Exchange Mode is enabled.

✔ Tips

- If a folder in the Navigation Pane contains at least one unread message, the folder name is displayed in boldface and is followed by the number of unread messages in parentheses, such as **Inbox (8)**.

- Whether a message is in the Reading Pane or open in its own window, you can navigate within the message by using the vertical scroll bar. Drag the scroll box, click in a blank area of the scroll bar, or click the scroll arrow at either end.

- You can press [Spacebar] and [Shift][Spacebar] to move forward and backward, respectively, through any lengthy message.

- With a message open in its own window, you can also use normal navigation keys to move through the message, such as [Page Down], [Page Up], [↓], and [↑]. You can use these keys in the Reading Pane, too, if you first click in the message body.

- If you open a message in its own window, you can read additional messages in the same window. Just click the Next Item or Previous Item icon in the Quick Access Toolbar (**Figure 19.5**) to read the next or previous message in the message list. (Note that if you go past either end of the message list, the message window will automatically close.)

- Read/unread message status is automatically determined by certain rules. To change the current behavior, click the Reading Pane icon in the Layout group of the Home tab and choose Options.

- You can manually change a message from unread to read (or vice versa) by right-clicking the message header and choosing the appropriate command (**Figure 19.6**), as well as by clicking the Unread/Read icon in the Tags group of the Home tab.

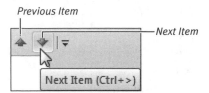

Previous Item

Next Item

Figure 19.5 Click these icons to read consecutive messages in an open message window.

Figure 19.6 To change a message's read status, choose Mark as Read or Mark as Unread.

Missing Pictures?

By default, Outlook doesn't download linked graphics in messages, representing each by a boxed red X. Such graphics are sometimes used by spammers to verify email addresses. If a message is from a trusted source, click the "Click here to download..." text beneath the Subject and choose Download Pictures from the drop-down menu that appears.

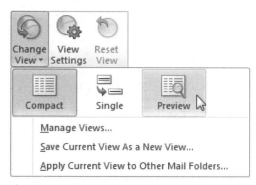

Figure 19.7 You can choose a new view or save a custom view by clicking the Change View icon.

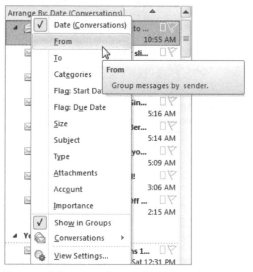

Figure 19.8 Choose an Arrange By option to reorganize the message list for the current folder.

Zoom Controls

To make it easier to view messages in the Reading Pane, you can change the magnification using the zoom controls at the bottom of the window. They work as they do in other Office 2010 documents. Note that the zoom setting affects *all* messages in the current folder. When you change folders, the zoom level is reset to 100%.

Changing the View

To make it easier to read your mail, you can set or change the *view* whenever you wish. Here are some ways you can modify the view.

To change the current view:

◆ *Do any of the following:*

▲ To change the size of the panes, click and drag any dividing line that separates a pair of panes.

▲ Choose a new view from the Change View gallery (**Figure 19.7**) in the Current View group on the View tab.

▲ The Reading Pane can be displayed on the right or bottom, or it can be hidden by choosing a command from the Reading Pane icon in the Layout group on the View tab. Note that if you choose Off, you'll only be able to read messages by opening them in their own window.

▲ To reorganize a message list, select an icon in the Arrangement gallery on the View tab. Or you can click the Arrange By text at the top of the message list and choose an option from the drop-down menu that appears.

For example, you could sort your Inbox by From (**Figure 19.8**) to alphabetize received messages by sender.

✔ Tips

■ To limit the display to only the message list and the current message, click the Reading icon at the bottom of the window.

■ When choosing an Arrange By option, it's often useful to check Show in Groups. Doing so creates separate display groups for each sort unit. For example, if From is the Arrange By field, a group will be created for each unique sender. You can expand/collapse a group by clicking the triangle icon that precedes its name.

CHANGING THE VIEW

Viewing Conversations

In Office 2010, the default Arrange By setting is Date (Conversations). Thus, related messages are automatically formed into a *conversation* (**Figure 19.9**), similar to the *message threads* you'll find in Web forums and newsgroups.

A conversation consists of two or more messages that share the same Subject. With Date (Conversations) as a folder's Arrange By setting, such messages can now be found and read in a single convenient location. You'll no longer need to flip between the Inbox and Sent Item folders or scan for messages that may be scattered throughout the Inbox to follow a multi-message mail exchange.

See "Managing Conversations" in Chapter 20 to learn more about conversations.

To enable conversations for a folder:

1. Select the folder in the Navigation Pane.

2. Click the View tab. In the Arrangement group, click the Conversations icon and ensure that Show Messages in Conversations is checked (**Figure 19.10**).

3. *Do either of the following:*
   ▲ Click Date (Conversations) in the Arrangement gallery.
   ▲ Click the Arrange By text at the top of the message list and choose Date (Conversations) from the menu.

4. To set display options for conversations in the current folder, enable them in the Conversations menu (**Figure 19.10**).

   When you select a message header that represents a conversation and Always Expand Conversations is enabled (Figure 19.10), the related messages are shown. Otherwise, click the triangle icon to the left of the message header to view the conversation.

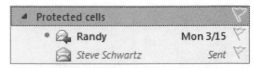

Figure 19.9 This simple conversation contains two messages, both with a subject of Protected cells.

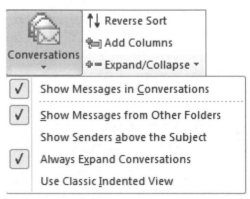

Figure 19.10 When conversations are enabled for a folder, you can view or change the display options via the Conversations menu in the Arrangement group.

VIEWING CONVERSATIONS

Highlighted match

Figure 19.11 As you type the search text, Outlook scans the selected folder and displays matching messages.

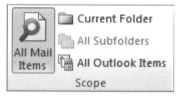

Figure 19.12 Click an icon to change the search's scope. For example, All Outlook Items will consider items other than email in the search.

■ To find a message from someone whose name you've forgotten but whose company or ISP you *do* remember, search for the domain or ISP. For example, enter microsoft.com to see all messages from Microsoft employees or earthlink.net to find messages from Earthlink users.

Searching for Messages

In many cases, the simplest way to find a particular message in a folder is to sort the message list by choosing a command from the Arrange By drop-down menu (as explained in "Changing the View"). For example, to find all messages you received from a particular person, you could sort your Inbox by From.

But if you can't find a message by sorting or manually hunting, Outlook also provides an Instant Search box that you can use to quickly find messages that contain a given text string.

To perform an Instant Search:

1. In Mail, select the account folder in the Navigation Pane that you want to search. The message list for the folder is shown.

2. Type a search string in the Instant Search box (found above the message list).

   As you type, Outlook filters the message list to show only matches (**Figure 19.11**). Matches can be anywhere within a message: addresses, Subject, message body, or attachments. The matching text is highlighted in each message.

3. To restore the message list, click the Close Search box (X) on the Instant Search box or in the Close group.

✔ Tips

■ To narrow a search's focus and show fewer (but more exact) matches, continue typing. For instance, type microsoft rather than micro.

■ To change the search's *scope*, click an icon in the Scope group of the Search tab, such as All Mail Items (**Figure 19.12**).

■ Refer to Chapters 17 and 21 for help with building search queries.

Working with Attachments

Attachments (images, documents, and other file types) can be sent to you as part of any email message. In the message list, mail with an attachment is marked with a paper clip icon (**Figure 19.13**). When viewed in the Reading Pane or in their own window, such messages show the attached files under the address information (**Figure 19.14**).

Depending on an attachment's file type and the programs installed on your computer, options for handling an attachment can include previewing it in the Reading Pane or message window, opening it in an appropriate program, and saving it to disk so it can later be opened without using Outlook.

Previewing attachments

You can view many attachments in the Reading Pane or message window. Whether or not you can depends on the attachment's file type and whether the necessary *attachment previewer* is installed. (Office 2010 installs and enables several previewers that rely on other Office applications to read, open, and display various types of attachments in Outlook.)

To preview an attachment:

◆ Click the attachment file icon, or right-click it and choose Preview from the context menu. If the file can be opened in Outlook, one of the following will occur:

▲ Common graphic file types will open and be displayed.

▲ Other file types for which you have a previewer installed, such as PDF, WMV, or XPS, will present a Preview file button that you must click to view the attachment (**Figure 19.15**).

Attachment icon

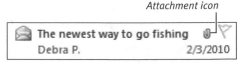

Figure 19.13 In a message list, attachments are denoted by a paper clip to the right of the subject.

View message   Handle attached file

Figure 19.14 Attached files, if any, are shown beneath the addresses. To resume viewing the message after previewing an attachment, click the Message icon.

Figure 19.15 Click the Preview file button to display the attachment in the current window.

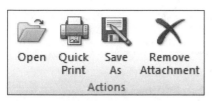

Figure 19.16 Common actions that you can perform on an attachment can be executed by clicking one of these icons.

Figure 19.17 If you have the appropriate program installed (such as Windows Photo Viewer for viewing certain graphic files), you can open the attachment.

Figure 19.18 If Windows can't identify an installed program that can open the attachment, this dialog box appears.

Opening attachments

Rather than previewing an attachment in Outlook, you may prefer to open it in an appropriate program that's installed on your computer. Doing so will enable you to use the program's tools to view, edit, and save the file.

To open an attachment in another application:

1. Double-click the attachment's file icon (see Figure 19.14), right-click the icon and choose Open from the context menu, or select the attachment and click the Open icon in the Actions group on the Attachments tab (**Figure 19.16**).

   The Opening Mail Attachment dialog box appears (**Figure 19.17**).

2. Click the Open button.

   If a compatible program is installed, the attachment opens in that program. Otherwise, a dialog box appears (**Figure 19.18**). You can either search the Web for a program or select one from your currently installed applications.

Saving attachments

To avoid having to scour Outlook for the message that contains a critical attachment whenever you want to view, work with, or print it, you can save the attachment to disk.

To save an attachment:

1. *Do one of the following:*
   ▲ Drag the attachment icon(s) from the message window (see Figure 19.14) onto the Desktop or into a folder.
   ▲ Select an attachment and click Save As in the Actions group (Figure 19.16).
   ▲ Right-click the attachment icon and choose Save As from the context menu.

   A Save Attachment file dialog box appears.

   continues on next page

2. Navigate to the drive and folder in which you want to save the file and click Save (**Figure 19.19**).

The file is saved to disk.

✔ Tips

■ If a message has *several* attachments, you can elect to save them all with a single command. Select one of their file icons and click the Save All Attachments icon in the Actions group. Verify that you want to save them all and then select a destination folder in which to store them.

■ Unless you delete a message, any attachments it contains will continue to take up space on your hard disk. If the text of such a message is important but you don't need the attachment, click the attachment's icon and then click the Remove Attachment icon in the Actions group. Confirm the deletion in the dialog box that appears.

■ To periodically rid yourself of unwanted attachments (or the message/attachment combination), you need a way to find messages with attachments. Select a mail folder in the Navigation Pane, and *do one of the following:*

  ▲ Choose Attachments from the Arrange By menu (see Figure 19.8) and set With on top as the sort order. All messages with attachments will be shown at the top of the message list.

  ▲ Click in the Instant Search box and click the Has Attachments icon in the Refine group (**Figure 19.20**).

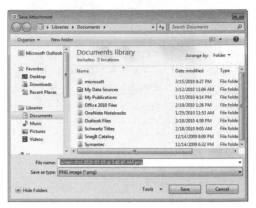

Figure 19.19 Select a location on disk in which to save the attachment.

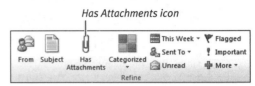

Figure 19.20 One way to identify messages that contain attachments is to search for them by clicking Has Attachments.

Print   Selected printer   Preview

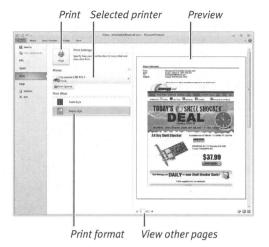

Print format   View other pages

Figure 19.21 In the Print area of the Backstage, you can set options and see their effects in the print preview.

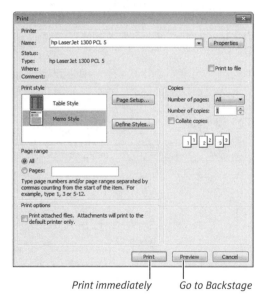

Print immediately   Go to Backstage

Figure 19.22 Set options (such as number of copies and the page range) in the Print dialog box.

Printing Messages

You can print the contents (and the attachments) of selected messages, as well as a list of message headers from the current view.

To print a message:

1. Select the message to print in the message list or open it in its own window.

2. *Do either of the following:*
   ▲ Click the File tab, and then select Print.
   ▲ Press Ctrl P.
   The Print Settings area of the Backstage appears (**Figure 19.21**). A print preview is displayed, based on the current settings.

3. Ensure that the correct printer is selected.

4. Select Memo Style in the Print What area.

5. *Optional:* To set print options, click the Print Options button. In the Print dialog box (**Figure 19.22**), set options as desired. To view or change Page Setup settings, such as the page size, orientation, or margins, click the Page Setup button.
   Click Print to print immediately using the current settings or click Preview to return to the Backstage to examine the effects of the new settings prior to printing.

6. Click the Print button (Figure 19.21) to print the message.

✔ Tips

■ You can also print several messages at once. Select contiguous messages in Step 1 by clicking the first message and then Shift-clicking the last one. To select noncontiguous messages, Ctrl-click each message header.

■ To immediately print a message using the default settings, right-click its header in the message list and choose Quick Print from the context menu.

PRINTING MESSAGES

To print a message list:

1. In the Navigation Pane, select the message folder whose headers you want to print.

2. *Optional:* To print only certain headers from the list, select the ones to be printed.

   To select multiple contiguous headers, click the first header and (Shift)-click the last one. To select noncontiguous headers, (Ctrl)-click each one.

3. *Do either of the following:*

   ▲ Click the File tab to go to the Backstage, and then select Print.

   ▲ Press (Ctrl)(P).

   The Print Settings area of the Backstage appears (see Figure 19.21).

4. Ensure that the correct printer is selected. Select Table Style in the Print What area (**Figure 19.23**).

5. Click the Print Options button.

   The Print dialog box appears.

6. Select an option from the Print range area (**Figure 19.24**):

   ▲ To print all message headers from the selected folder, click All rows.

   ▲ To print only the currently selected headers, click Only selected rows.

7. *Optional:* To set a paper size, fonts, or margins, click Page Setup.

8. Do one of the following:

   ▲ Click Print to print immediately using the current settings.

   ▲ Click Preview to return to the Backstage to preview the effects of the new settings prior to printing.

9. Click the Print button (see Figure 19.21) to print the message header list.

Figure 19.23 Select Table Style to print selected headers or an entire folder of message headers.

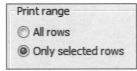

Figure 19.24 Print all visible headers or only selected ones.

✔ Tip

■ Prior to printing a list of headers, you may want to perform an Instant Search to restrict the list's contents and/or choose a sort order from the Arrange By drop-down menu.

MANAGING THE MAIL

In addition to sending, receiving, and reading messages, you'll want to spend time organizing and managing your mail. As you'll learn in this chapter, you can do the following:

◆ Manually set the status of messages to unread or read

◆ Delete unneeded messages

◆ Clean up or ignore conversations

◆ Move or copy messages to other folders

◆ Create message folders in which to organize your messages by project, account, and so on

◆ Categorize or flag messages for follow-up

◆ Set options to avoid junk email and phishing attempts

◆ Create rules to automate the handling of certain messages

◆ Design and use Quick Steps that you can manually apply to selected messages

◆ Archive and back up your Outlook data

Marking Messages as Read

One of the simplest ways to manage email is to change a message's read status to read or unread. Unread messages (shown in bold in the message list) stand out and demand attention; read messages (shown in normal type) can be ignored or handled at your leisure.

A message's read status can be changed whenever and as often as you like. For example, to ensure that a previously viewed message will receive additional attention, you can reset it to unread. Similarly, messages you want to ignore can immediately be set to read—even though you've never viewed them. You can change a message's read status *automatically* (via a setting in Reading Pane options or in response to a message rule) or *manually* (by choosing a new status).

To set an automatic read option:

1. On the View tab, click the Reading Pane icon in the Layout group and choose Options from the drop-down menu.

   The Reading Pane dialog box appears (**Figure 20.1**).

2. To automatically mark new messages as read, click the first or second check box:

   ▲ **Mark items as read when viewed in the Reading Pane.** Any message header that is selected longer than the specified number of seconds will be treated as read.

   ▲ **Mark item as read when selection changes.** Whenever you select a different message, the currently selected message will be marked as read.

3. Click OK to close the Reading Pane dialog box.

Figure 20.1 Select one of the first two mutually exclusive options to specify when messages will automatically be marked as read.

Figure 20.2 You can manually change the read status by right-clicking a message header.

Mark All as Read

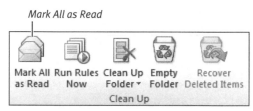

Figure 20.3 To mark all messages in the current folder as read, click the Mark All as Read icon.

To manually change a message's read status:

◆ *Do either of the following:*

▲ Right-click the message header in the message list. In the context menu that appears (**Figure 20.2**), choose Mark as Read or Mark as Unread. (Only the opposite read status is displayed.)

▲ Select a header in the message list. On the Home tab, click the Unread/Read icon in the Tags group to toggle the message's status.

▲ Select a message header in the message list. Press Ctrl U to mark it as unread or Ctrl Q to mark it as read.

✔ Tips

■ You can simultaneously change the status of *multiple* selected messages. Note that you can set only one read status for all selected messages, even if they are a mixture of read and unread.

■ You can mark all messages in a folder as having been read. This is especially useful for quickly catching up on seldom-read RSS feeds or mailing lists. Start by selecting the folder in the Navigation Pane. Click the Mark All as Read icon in the Clean Up group on the Folder tab (**Figure 20.3**).

■ To automatically set certain incoming messages as read, include the `mark it as read` action in a message rule. I use such rules to mark incoming mailing list messages as read. To learn how to create message rules, see "Creating Rules," later in this chapter.

■ You can also mark a message as important by *flagging* it for follow-up. For instructions, see "Flagging Messages," later in this chapter.

MARKING MESSAGES AS READ

Deleting Messages

To reduce message list clutter and the size of your email account databases, you can delete unwanted messages.

To delete email or RSS messages:

1. Select one or more message headers in the message list.

2. *Do one of the following:*

    ▲ On the Home tab, click the Delete icon in the Delete group.

    ▲ Press Del, Delete, or Ctrl D.

    ▲ Right-click one of the selected messages and choose Delete from the context menu (see Figure 20.2).

    The message(s) are deleted or marked for deletion, depending on the account type, settings, and current view.

To restore deleted email or RSS messages:

◆ *Do any of the following:*

    ▲ Drag the item from the account's Deleted Items or Trash folder into the original message folder, such as the Inbox or Sent Items.

    ▲ Right-click the item in the Deleted Items or Trash folder and choose a destination folder from the Move submenu.

    If the folder isn't listed, choose Move > Other Folder. In the Move Items dialog box (**Figure 20.4**), select the destination folder and click OK.

    ▲ *IMAP accounts only:* When view is set as IMAP Messages (displaying messages marked for deletion using strikethrough), you can right-click any message marked for deletion and choose Undelete from the context menu (**Figure 20.5**).

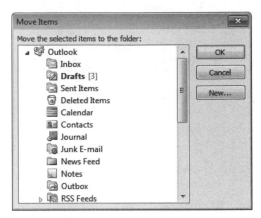

Figure 20.4 To move selected messages from the Trash or Deleted Items folder, select a destination folder in the Move Items dialog box and click OK.

Figure 20.5 Use the Undelete command to restore deleted IMAP messages.

Figure 20.6 IMAP messages marked for deletion are displayed in strikethrough text. To delete the messages from the server, choose an appropriate Purge command.

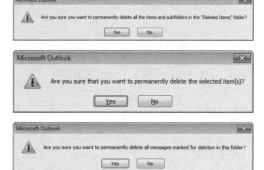

Figure 20.7 When you empty a folder (top), select items for removal (middle), or purge a folder (bottom), you'll be asked to confirm the action.

Archiving vs. Deleting

If there's a chance you might eventually need an older message, you can *archive* it rather than delete it. The AutoArchive procedure executes at regular intervals, archiving all messages older than a certain age by moving them into Archive Folders in the Navigation Pane.

To set AutoArchive options for the current folder, select the Folder tab and click the AutoArchive Settings icon in the Properties group. To perform a manual archive, go to the Backstage, click the Cleanup Tools icon, and choose Archive.

▲ *Exchange accounts only:* Select the account's Deleted Items folder or the folder in which the message was originally stored, such as the Inbox. On the Folder tab, click the Recover Deleted Items icon in the Clean Up group. In the Recover Deleted Items dialog box, select one or more deleted messages and click Recover Selected Items.

To remove deleted items from a folder:

1. In the Navigation Pane, select the folder that contains the deleted messages.

   Folders that you might want to empty include Deleted Items, Trash, and Junk E-mail, for example.

2. Depending on the account type and its settings, *you can do the following:*

   ▲ On the Folder tab, click the Empty Folder icon in the Clean Up group.

   ▲ Right-click the folder in the Navigation Pane and choose Empty Folder from the context menu.

   ▲ Select the previously deleted items and press [Del], [Delete], or [Ctrl][D]; click the Delete icon in the Delete group on the Home tab; or right-click one of the selected items and choose Delete from the context menu.

   ▲ *IMAP accounts only:* On the Folder tab, choose a command from the Purge icon's menu in the Clean Up group (**Figure 20.6**).

   A confirmation dialog box appears (**Figure 20.7**).

3. Click Yes to confirm or click No to cancel the empty, purge, or item deletion.

✔ Tips

■ To delete a message that's open in its own window, click the Delete icon in the Delete group or press Ctrl D.

■ Deleted messages aren't immediately deleted. In fact, what happens to a deleted message depends on its account type:

▲ Most POP3, Hotmail, and RSS feed messages are moved to the Deleted Items folder where they remain until the folder is emptied or the individual messages are selected and deleted.

▲ An IMAP message can be *marked* for deletion (**Figure 20.8**) or moved to a designated folder (Trash, for example), depending on an account setting. When the folder is *purged* by choosing a command from the Purge menu (see Figure 20.6), the messages are removed from the server.

■ To specify a method of handling deleted IMAP messages, go to the Backstage. Select the Info tab and choose Account Settings > Account Settings. In the Account Settings dialog box, select the IMAP account and click Change. In the Change Account dialog box, click More Settings. In the Internet E-mail Settings dialog box (**Figure 20.9**), set the handling method.

■ Be sure to explore the deleted item settings for any other types of accounts you may have. For example, on the Advanced tab for a POP account, messages that you delete in Outlook can automatically be deleted from the server at the same time.

■ The Deleted Items folders can be emptied automatically at the end of each Outlook session. Click the Advanced tab in the Outlook Options dialog box to see this setting (**Figure 20.10**).

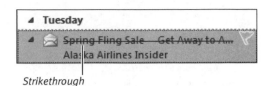

Strikethrough

Figure 20.8 IMAP messages marked for deletion can be displayed with strikethrough text.

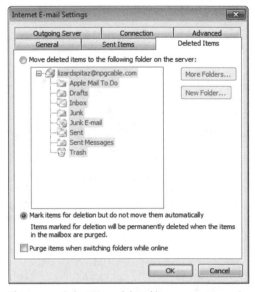

Figure 20.9 Select Move deleted items... to automatically move deleted messages to a particular folder. Or select Mark items... to mark deleted items with strikethrough rather than move them to a folder.

Figure 20.10 You can automate the emptying of all Deleted Items folders.

■ To make an IMAP account *work* like a POP account, select Move deleted items... (Figure 20.9). To make it *look* like a POP account when viewing a message list with Mark Items... selected, set the view to Hide Messages Marked for Deletion.

Figure 20.11 You can instruct Outlook to delete redundant messages in the selected conversation.

Figure 20.12 Specify conversation cleanup criteria in the Mail category of the Outlook Options dialog box.

Figure 20.13 If you no longer want to participate in or read mail for a given conversation, you can ignore it.

✔ Tip

- To rid an entire folder of redundant messages, select the folder and choose Clean Up > Clean Up Folder in the Delete group on the Home tab.

Managing Conversations

In addition to deleting messages, Outlook provides two methods of managing conversations. You can clean up a conversation by removing redundant messages, and you can elect to ignore future email pertaining to a particular conversation.

To clean up a conversation:

1. In the message list, select the header of any message in the conversation.

2. In the Delete group on the Home tab, choose Clean Up > Clean Up Conversation. The Clean Up Conversation dialog box appears (**Figure 20.11**).

3. *Optional:* Click Settings to review the Conversation Clean Up preferences in the Mail category of Outlook Options (**Figure 20.12**). If you make any changes, click OK to save them; otherwise, click Cancel.

4. Click Clean Up (Figure 20.11).

   If no qualifying messages are identified by Outlook, a dialog box informs you. Otherwise, the redundant messages (as you've defined them in the Conversation Clean Up settings) are moved to the account's Deleted Items or Trash folder.

To ignore a conversation:

1. In the message list, select the header of any message in the conversation.

2. In the Delete group on the Home tab, click Ignore or press Ctrl Del.

   The Ignore Conversation dialog box appears (**Figure 20.13**).

3. Click the Ignore Conversation button.

   The conversation and all future messages that would be part of it are moved to the account's Deleted Items or Trash folder.

Copying and Moving Mail

Another way to organize your messages is to move or copy them to other folders. You've already seen how you can move mail out of the Deleted Items folder and back into your Inbox, for example. Similar procedures are used to copy or move messages between almost any pair of folders—including folders in different accounts.

To copy a message to another folder:

◆ *Do either of the following:*

▲ Right-click and drag the message header onto the destination folder in the Navigation Pane. When you release the mouse button, select Copy from the context menu (**Figure 20.14**).

▲ Select a message header. On the Home tab in the Move group, click the Move icon and choose Copy to Folder. In the Copy Items dialog box (**Figure 20.15**), select a destination folder and click OK.

A copy of the selected message is stored in the designated folder.

To move a message to another folder:

◆ *Do one of the following:*

▲ Right-click and drag the message header onto the destination folder in the Navigation Pane. When you release the mouse button, select Move from the context menu (Figure 20.14).

▲ Select a message header. On the Home tab in the Move group, click the Move icon and choose a listed folder.

▲ Select a message header. On the Home tab in the Move group, click the Move icon and choose Other Folder (or press Ctrl Shift V). In the Move Items dialog box, select a destination folder and click OK.

The message is moved to the designated folder and deleted from the source folder.

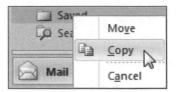

Figure 20.14 You can copy or move the selected message into a folder by choosing a context command.

Figure 20.15 Select a destination folder and click OK.

✔ Tips

■ You can also move or copy *multiple* selected messages using these techniques.

■ In the Copy Items or Move Items dialog box, you can create a new folder to receive the copied or moved message(s) by clicking the New button (Figure 20.15).

Name the folder

Figure 20.16 New folders are created in the Create New Folder dialog box.

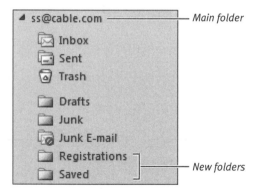

Main folder

New folders

Figure 20.17 This account contains two user-created folders.

Creating Message Folders

Although deleting, copying, and moving messages are essential to managing email, one of the best ways to organize messages is to create additional folders for them. For instance, you can create a folder to store project-related messages, save Web and software registrations, or store permanent copies of critical messages. You can use any such folder as the target of message moves and copies. And as you'll learn later in this chapter, you can create *message rules* to automatically route incoming messages to specific folders.

To create a new message folder:

1. *Do one of the following:*
   ▲ On the Folder tab, click the New Folder icon in the New group.
   ▲ Right-click an account folder in the Navigation Pane and choose New Folder from the context menu.
   ▲ Press Ctrl Shift E.
   The Create New Folder dialog box appears (**Figure 20.16**).

2. Enter a name for the new folder.

3. Choose Mail and Post Items from the Folder contains drop-down menu.

4. Select a *parent* (containing) folder from the list in the dialog box. The new folder will be a subfolder of the selected folder.

5. Click OK to create the new folder.
   The folder is added to the Navigation Pane (**Figure 20.17**).

✔ Tips

■ By default, the folder that's selected or right-clicked when you issue the New Folder command is assumed to be the parent folder. Of course, you're still free to choose *any* other folder as the parent.

CREATING MESSAGE FOLDERS

- Folders can be nested within folders. For example, to handle book-related correspondence, I could create a Peachpit folder within the account folder or Inbox. Within that folder, I can create additional folders—one per book.

- To rename a folder, click its name twice in the Navigation Pane and edit the name (**Figure 20.18**). You can also select the folder and click the Rename Folder icon in the Actions group on the Folder tab.

- Although you can't reorder account folders, you can move one folder inside another by dragging it onto the destination folder in the Navigation Pane. You can also right-click the folder and choose Move Folder from the context menu.

- You can delete any user-created folder that you no longer need. Select the folder in the Navigation Pane and click the Delete Folder icon in the Actions group on the Folder tab. Click Yes in the confirmation dialog box. The folder and its messages are moved into the account's Deleted Items or Trash folder.

  If you change your mind about deleting the folder and haven't emptied the Deleted Items or Trash, you can move the folder back into the folder list.

- For obvious reasons, you can't delete most of the automatically created folders, such as Inbox and Sent Items.

- To make it easy to access an important folder (such as the Inbox), drag it into the Favorites section in the Navigation Pane. Or you can select the folder and click Show in Favorites in the Favorites group on the Folder tab (**Figure 20.19**). To remove a folder from Favorites, select it and click Show in Favorites again.

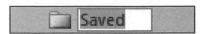

Figure 20.18 This is an example of a folder name selected for editing.

Figure 20.19 The Show in Favorites command works as a toggle to add or remove a folder from the Favorites section of the Navigation Pane.

Category box

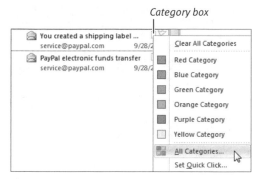

Figure 20.20 To assign a category to a message or open the Color Categories dialog box, you can right-click the Category box in the message header.

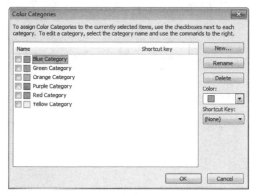

Figure 20.21 You can create, delete, rename, or set options for categories in the Color Categories dialog box.

Categorizing IMAP Messages

At this writing, you cannot apply categories to IMAP messages. If you select an IMAP message in the message list or open one in its own window, you won't see a Categorize icon in the Tags group. Similarly, if you right-click an IMAP header, no Categorize submenu will appear in the context menu. Whether this is a technical difficulty that will eventually be resolved or is a deliberate design decision remains to be seen.

Categorizing Messages

To further help organize your mail, you can assign *categories* (colored labels) to certain messages. Categories can be applied manually or automatically (via message rules). You can use the default categories or create ones of your own, such as Quarterly Report, Work, or Family.

Initially, category names match their color indicators, such as Red Category. For each category, you can specify a name, a color, and a keyboard shortcut. Although you can also create *new* categories, you'll probably start by modifying the default categories.

To modify a category:

1. *Do either of the following:*
   ▲ On the Home tab, click the Categorize icon in the Tags group and choose All Categories.
   ▲ Right-click the Category box in any message header (or the header itself) and choose All Categories from the context menu (**Figure 20.20**).
   The Color Categories dialog box appears (**Figure 20.21**).

2. To rename a selected category, double-click the category name or click the Rename button. Enter a new name.

3. To change the color indicator for the selected category, select a color from the Color drop-down palette.

4. To assign a keyboard shortcut to a selected category, select one from the Shortcut Key drop-down list.

5. Click OK to save the changes.

To create a new category:

1. Open the Color Categories dialog box (see Figure 20.21) using one of the techniques described in the previous task list.

2. Click the New button.

   The Add New Category dialog box appears (**Figure 20.22**).

3. Enter a name for the new category in the Name text box and select a color from the Color drop-down list.

4. *Optional:* To assign a keyboard shortcut to the category, select one from the Shortcut Key drop-down list.

5. Click OK to save the new category.

To set the Quick Click category:

1. *Do one of the following:*
   - ▲ On the Home tab, click the Categorize icon in the Tags group and choose Set Quick Click.
   - ▲ Right-click the Category box in any message header (or the header itself) and choose Set Quick Click (see Figure 20.20).

   The Set Quick Click dialog box appears (**Figure 20.23**).

2. Select a category from the drop-down list and click OK.

   The Quick Click category will be applied whenever you click the Category box of a message or other item.

Figure 20.22 Set options for the new category in the Add New Category dialog box.

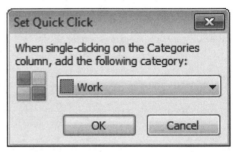

Figure 20.23 Use this dialog box to set your most frequently used category as the Quick Click category.

Figure 20.24 Specify search criteria in the New Search Folder dialog box.

Creating a Category Search Folder

To create a category search folder, follow these steps:

1. In the Navigation Pane, right-click the Search Folders icon within the appropriate email account and choose New Search Folder.

2. In the New Search Folder dialog box, select Categorized mail in the Organizing Mail section (**Figure 20.24**, above).

3. Click the Choose button. In the Color Categories dialog box (see Figure 20.21), select the search category (or categories) by clicking check boxes. Click OK.

4. Click OK to close the New Search Folder dialog box. The search folder appears as a new subfolder beneath the Search Folders icon.

Whenever you click the search folder's icon, it will automatically display all messages assigned the specified category.

To assign a category to an item:

◆ *Do any of the following:*

▲ To assign the Quick Click category to a message, click the Category box in the message header.

▲ Select a message header and choose a category from the Categorize icon's drop-down menu.

▲ Right-click a message header and choose a category from the Categorize submenu.

✔ Tips

■ Categories can also be assigned to tasks, calendar events, and contact records. Any item can have zero, one, or many categories assigned to it.

■ To remove a category from an item, choose the same category again. To remove the Quick Click category from an item, click the item's Category box. To remove *all* categories from a selected item, choose the Clear All Categories command.

■ To sort and group the current message list by categories, click the Categories icon in the Arrangement group on the View tab or choose Categories from the Arrange By drop-down menu above the message list.

■ To delete an unwanted category, open the Color Categories dialog box, select the category, click Delete, confirm the deletion, and click OK.

■ To view all messages assigned a particular category, select the category from the Filter E-mail menu in the Find group on the Home tab.

Flagging Messages

If you need to *do* something about a message (such as respond to it at a later date or schedule a meeting concerning it), you can *flag* the message for follow-up. Flagged messages are denoted by a colored flag in the message header. A flagged message can optionally have a reminder and/or be marked as completed. You can also specify a Quick Click flag that will be applied whenever you click the Follow Up box of a message or other item.

To set the Quick Click flag:

1. Select a message header in the message list, and *do one of the following:*

   ▲ On the Home tab, click the Follow Up box in the Tags group and choose Set Quick Click from the drop-down menu.

   ▲ Right-click the Follow Up box in any message header and choose Set Quick Click from the context menu.

   The Set Quick Click dialog box appears (**Figure 20.25**).

2. Choose a flag from the drop-down menu and click OK.

To set a follow-up flag for an item:

◆ *Do any of the following:*

   ▲ Click the Follow Up box in any message header to assign the Quick Click flag to the message.

   ▲ Select a message header and choose a flag from the Follow Up icon in the Tags group on the Home tab (**Figure 20.26**).

   ▲ Right-click the Follow Up box in any message header (or the header itself) and choose a flag from the context menu that appears.

Figure 20.25 Set the default follow-up flag in this dialog box.

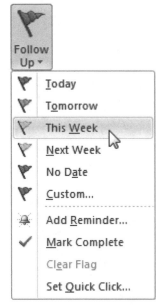

Figure 20.26 Choose a follow-up flag for the selected message.

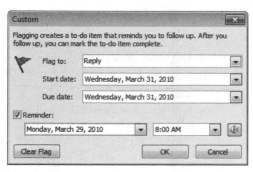

Figure 20.27 Use the Custom dialog box to set a custom follow-up date and/or reminder for an item.

Alarm icon

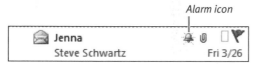

Figure 20.28 A flagged item can also have a reminder.

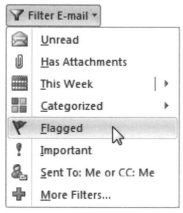

Figure 20.29 You can filter a message list to display only flagged messages.

✔ Tips

■ Flags can also be assigned to tasks, calendar events, and contact records. An item can have only one flag.

■ Flagged items automatically appear in the To-Do Bar and the To-Do List (in Tasks).

■ To create a follow-up item without a due date, choose No Date as the flag setting.

■ To set a follow-up for a date other than those listed, choose Custom. Set options in the Custom dialog box (**Figure 20.27**) and click OK.

■ To set a reminder (alarm) for a flagged item, choose Add Reminder (see Figure 20.26). In the Custom dialog box (Figure 20.27), ensure that the Reminder box is checked, set a date and time for the reminder, and click OK. An alarm icon is added to the item's message header (**Figure 20.28**).

■ To remove a flag from an item, choose Clear Flag. You can simultaneously clear a flag and mark the item complete by choosing Mark Complete.

■ To toggle between the flag setting for an item and marking the item complete, click the item's Follow Up box.

■ Choose Flag: Start Date or Flag: Due Date from the Arrange By menu above a message list to sort and group the current mail by flagged items.

■ To view all flagged messages in the current folder, click the Filter E-mail icon in the Find group on the Home tab and choose Flagged from the drop-down menu (**Figure 20.29**).

FLAGGING MESSAGES

Handling Junk Mail and Phishing Attempts

Everyone eventually receives junk mail or *spam*—generally consisting of unwanted advertisements for mortgages, weight loss products, penis and breast enlargers, and the like. If you use your regular email address to register on Web sites or if you send email to corporations, newsgroups, or mailing lists, your volume of received junk mail is liable to increase dramatically. Using the Junk E-mail Options feature, you can filter out much of this time-wasting, annoying email.

Outlook 2010 also offers protection against *phishing* (attempts via email to con you into providing important personal data, such as bank account numbers, credit card information, and Web site passwords).

To set junk mail and phishing options:

1. Select an account in the Navigation Pane. On the Home tab, click Junk in the Delete group and choose Junk E-mail Options.

   The Junk E-mail Options dialog box appears (**Figure 20.30**).

2. On the Options tab, click a radio button to set the desired protection level.

3. To enable phishing protection, check Disable links and other functionality in phishing messages.

4. *Optional:* To automatically delete potential junk mail, check Permanently delete suspected junk e-mail instead of moving it to the Junk E-mail folder.

5. Click OK to save the new settings.

   When received in this email account, suspected junk mail is automatically moved to the Junk E-mail folder or deleted, depending on the settings on this tab.

6. Repeat for your other email accounts.

Junk mail protection level

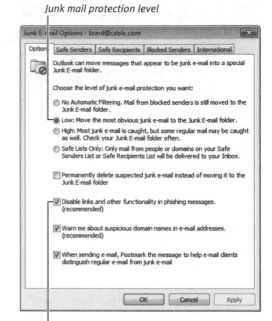

Phishing protection

Figure 20.30 Set junk mail and phishing options on the tabs of the Junk E-mail Options dialog box.

Figure 20.31 You can block future messages from specific users, companies, or domains by adding them to the Blocked Senders list.

Figure 20.32 Certain countries are notorious for generating junk mail. To ignore all email from such a country, add it to the list on the International tab.

- You can specify other actions for junk mail by creating *rules* (discussed in the next section).

- Junk E-mail Options are account-specific. Remember to set them for each email account you're tracking with Outlook.

✔ Tips

- Outlook maintains a Blocked Senders list for each account that you can use to automatically classify new mail from certain addresses as junk. To add someone to the list, click the Blocked Senders tab of the Junk E-mail Options dialog box (**Figure 20.31**), click Add, enter the person or company's email address, and click OK. To add someone to the list based on a received message, select the message, switch to the Home tab, and choose Block Sender from the Junk icon's menu in the Delete group.

- You can also block all email from a *domain*. Doing so is useful when you notice that you're receiving many junk messages from a domain, but each has a different user name. For instance, to block all email from krypton.net, add `krypton.net` or `@krypton.net` to the Blocked Senders list.

- To prevent Outlook from classifying mail from certain senders as junk, create contact records for them and ensure that Also trust e-mail from my Contacts is checked on the Safe Senders tab of the Junk E-mail Options dialog box. Or you can add their email addresses to the list on the Safe Senders tab.

- Using the International tab of the Junk E-mail Options dialog box, you can classify all email from certain *countries* as junk. Click the Blocked Top-Level Domain List button, select countries to block (**Figure 20.32**), and click OK.

- Outlook will occasionally mark a received message as junk that is actually legitimate email. To reclassify a selected or open message, choose Not Junk or Never Block Sender from the Junk icon's menu.

Creating Rules

By defining *rules*, you can instruct Outlook to automatically perform actions on new incoming or outgoing mail. A rule could store all incoming email from Peachpit.com in a Peachpit folder rather than the Inbox, for example. A rule can be based on a template or created from scratch. You can also create a rule based on a particular received message.

To create a rule from a template or from scratch:

1. On the Home tab in the Move group, click the Rules icon and choose Manage Rules and Alerts, or go to the Backstage and click the Manage Rules & Alerts button on the Info tab.

   The Rules and Alerts dialog box opens (**Figure 20.33**).

2. Select the account and folder to which the rule will be applied from the Apply changes to this folder drop-down list.

3. Click the New Rule icon.

   The Rules Wizard appears (**Figure 20.34**).

4. Select a template on which to base the rule. If an appropriate template isn't listed, you can create the rule from scratch by selecting a blank rule. Click Next.

5. Add or remove conditions for the rule by clicking check boxes. Condition placeholders are displayed as blue underlined text in the Step 2 area of the wizard. Click each placeholder and replace it with appropriate data. Click Next to continue.

6. Add or remove actions to be performed by the rule by clicking check boxes. Action placeholders are displayed as blue underlined text in the Step 2 area of the wizard. Click each placeholder and replace it with appropriate data. Click Next to continue.

Apply to this folder   *Defined rules are listed here*

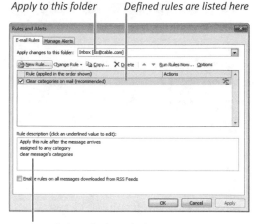

Description of selected rule

Figure 20.33 Rules are created and maintained in the Rules and Alerts dialog box.

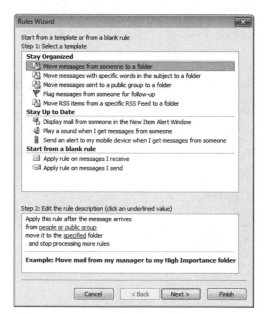

Figure 20.34 Select a template on which to base the rule. On the screens that follow, you can add, remove, and specify rule conditions, actions, and exceptions.

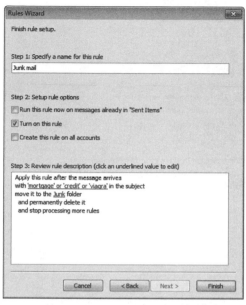

Figure 20.35 To complete a rule definition, name and set initial options for the rule.

Figure 20.36 To test a new or revised rule, you can run it on the messages in a selected folder. (Click Browse to select the folder.)

7. Specify exceptions to the rule by clicking check boxes. Placeholders for exceptions are displayed as blue underlined text in the Step 2 area of the wizard. Click each placeholder and replace it with appropriate data. Click Next to continue.

8. On the final wizard screen (**Figure 20.35**), name the rule and set rule options by clicking check boxes.

9. Click Finish to save the rule. Then click OK to close the Rules and Alerts dialog box.

✔ Tips

- You can temporarily disable a rule by clearing its check mark in the Rules and Alerts dialog box (see Figure 20.33). To permanently eliminate a rule, select it and click the Delete icon.

- To edit a rule, double-click it in the Rules and Alerts dialog box. Or you can select it, click Change Rule, and choose Edit Rule Settings from the drop-down menu.

- To alter only a rule's conditions, actions, or exceptions, it isn't necessary to edit the rule. Just select it in the Rules and Alerts dialog box to display the rule and click the placeholder you want to change.

- Rules are executed in the order in which they're listed in the Rules and Alerts dialog box. To change the order, select a rule and click the Move Up or Move Down icon.

- To test a rule, click Run Rules Now in the Rules and Alerts dialog box. In the Run Rules Now dialog box (**Figure 20.36**), select the rule to test, specify the folder on which to run the rule, and click Run Now.

- Until a message-deletion rule has been successfully tested, do not use the `permanently delete it` action. Instead, use `delete it`, which merely moves items into the Deleted Items folder.

CREATING RULES

To create a rule based on a message:

1. Select the message header of the message on which you want to base the rule.

   For example, you might want to route all messages from the sender directly into the Deleted Items or Trash folder. Or you may want to save them all in a custom folder you've created.

2. On the Home tab in the Move group, click the Rules icon and choose Create Rule.

   The Create Rule dialog box appears (**Figure 20.37**).

3. Set options in the dialog box by clicking check boxes, editing text, and clicking buttons. When you're satisfied, click OK.

✔ Tips

- If the options in the Create Rule dialog box aren't sufficient to completely define the rule, click Advanced Options. The Rules Wizard dialog box appears (see Figure 20.34). Any options you specified in the Create Rule dialog box will also be set in the Rules Wizard.

- Because rules created in this manner are automatically named, you may want to open the rule for editing so you can rename it.

Figure 20.37 In many cases, you can quickly create a rule from a received message without resorting to the Rules Wizard.

Backing Up Outlook Folders

To safeguard your email and contacts, you may want to occasionally back up your data. Using the following procedure, you can export one account folder at a time:

1. In the Backstage, select the Open category and click the Import icon.

2. In the Import and Export Wizard, select Export to a file. Click Next.

3. Select Outlook Data File (.pst) as the file type. Click Next.

4. Select an account folder to export, such as Inbox or Contacts.

5. Specify a location for the exported data file. Click Finish.

6. Repeat for other folders that you want to back up.

Microsoft offers a free Outlook Personal Folders Backup tool for versions 2002–2007 that simplifies the backup process. Check www.microsoft.com/downloads for an updated version that supports Outlook 2010.

CREATING RULES

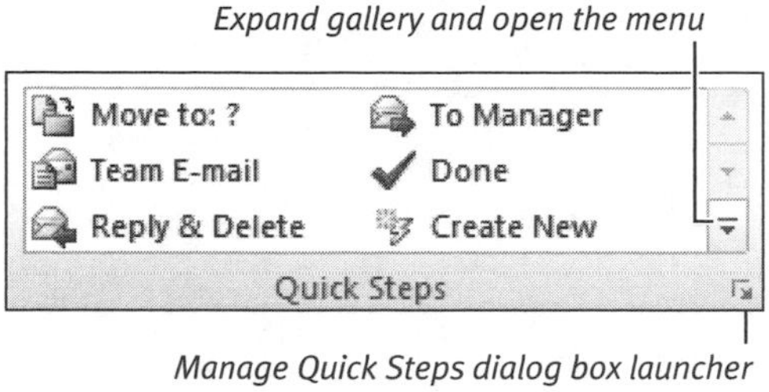

Expand gallery and open the menu

Manage Quick Steps dialog box launcher

Figure 20.38 The Quick Steps gallery on the Home tab.

Figure 20.39 The Manage Quick Steps dialog box.

Figure 20.40 The Edit Quick Step dialog box.

Working with Quick Steps

Quick Steps are single- or multiple-action scripts that you can use to help manage your email. In the Quick Steps group on the Home tab (**Figure 20.38**), Outlook provides default Quick Steps that you can use as is or customize. You can also create Quick Steps from scratch.

To modify an existing Quick Step:

1. *Do one of the following:*
   ▲ Right-click the Quick Step's icon in the Quick Steps group and choose Edit *name* from the context menu.
   ▲ Click the Manage Quick Steps dialog box launcher or choose Manage Quick Steps from the Quick Steps menu. Select the Quick Step in the Manage Quick Steps dialog box (**Figure 20.39**) and click Edit.

   The Edit Quick Step dialog box appears (**Figure 20.40**).

2. If the Quick Step contains an unwanted action, click its X to remove it.

3. To add other actions, click Add Action and select an action from the drop-down menu.

4. *Optional:* Up to nine Quick Steps can have a shortcut key ([Shift][Ctrl], plus a digit between 1–9). To assign one to this Quick Step, choose it from the Shortcut key menu.

5. *Optional:* Edit the ToolTip text.
   The ToolTip will appear whenever you rest the cursor over this Quick Step.

6. Edit the Quick Step name in the Name box.
   The name will be displayed in the Quick Steps gallery.

7. Click Save to replace the original Quick Step with this edited version.

8. Click OK to dismiss the Manage Quick Steps dialog box.

To create a Quick Step from a template:

1. Choose a template from the New Quick Step submenu (**Figure 20.41**).

   A First Time Setup dialog box appears (**Figure 20.42**).

2. *Do either of the following:*

   ▲ Fill in the necessary information and click Finish.

   ▲ If you prefer to work with the full Edit Quick Step dialog box (see Figure 20.40), click Options. Fill in the necessary information and click Save.

   The Quick Step is added to the gallery.

To create a Quick Step from scratch:

1. Click the Create New icon in the gallery or choose New Quick Step > Custom from the gallery's menu (Figure 20.41).

   The Edit Quick Step dialog box appears (see Figure 20.40).

2. Follow Steps 2–6 in "To modify an existing Quick Step." Add actions, name the Quick Step, and so on.

3. When you're done, click Finish.

To apply a Quick Step:

1. Select the message(s) to which you want to apply the Quick Step.

2. Click the Quick Step icon in the gallery.

✔ Tips

■ Every Quick Step that you create is account-specific; that is, it will only be listed and accessible from the account that was active when it was created.

■ When creating or editing a Quick Step, you can select a new icon for it by clicking the icon to the left of the Name text box.

■ To remove a Quick Step, right-click its icon and choose Delete (**Figure 20.43**).

Figure 20.41 Open the gallery menu and choose a category from the New Quick Step submenu.

Figure 20.42 For simple Quick Steps, the First Time Setup dialog box will often suffice.

Figure 20.43 You can right-click a Quick Step in the gallery to choose common commands, such as Edit, Duplicate, and Delete.

TASKS AND APPOINTMENTS

In addition to handling your email and Really Simple Syndication (RSS) feeds, Outlook has exceptional appointment, event, and task management capabilities.

You use the Calendar pane to schedule one-time appointments (such as a project meeting or dinner with a friend), accompanied by a pop-up reminder before the event. You can also schedule recurring events, such as birthdays and weekly staff meetings.

You use the Tasks pane to manage items on your to-do list, such as mowing the lawn, buying a bathrobe, or writing a proposal. Unlike Calendar appointments, a task is not required to have a due date or a reminder, although it can optionally have either or both.

Calendar Basics

To work with the Calendar pane (**Figure 21.1**, below), click the Calendar button in the Navigation Pane and select a viewing option, such as day, week, or month. *Events* (all-day items) are shown at the top of each day, and *appointments* (items with a particular start and end time) are listed by their start times.

To change or view the details for an event or appointment (**Figure 21.2**), double-click the item on the Calendar.

Figure 21.2 Open a Calendar item to change its start or end time, add notes, or set a reminder for it.

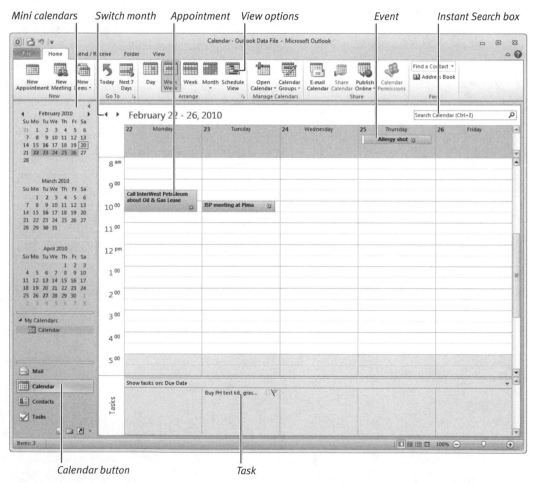

Mini calendars *Switch month* *Appointment* *View options* *Event* *Instant Search box*

Calendar button *Task*

Figure 21.1 The Calendar pane.

CALENDAR BASICS

Save   Subject   Location   Reminder   Event

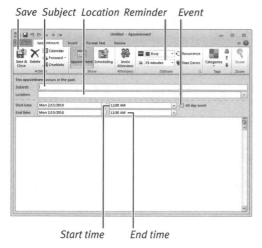

Start time   End time

Figure 21.3 You can create a new appointment or event in a window.

Figure 21.4 Rather than open a window to add an appointment or event, it's often faster to click in a date/time slot and type the item's subject.

- You can quickly create an appointment or event by selecting a time or event slot on the Calendar and then typing the item's subject (**Figure 21.4**).

- To delete a selected appointment or event, click the Delete icon in the Actions group, right-click the item and choose Delete from the context menu, or press Delete.

Recording an Appointment or Event

To track or be reminded of an appointment or event, you must first add it to the Calendar.

To record an appointment or event:

1. *Do one of the following:*
   - ▲ **From any pane.** Click the New Items icon in the New group on the Home tab. Choose Appointment(Ctrl Shift A) from the drop-down menu.
   - ▲ **From the Calendar pane.** Click the New Appointment icon in the New group (Ctrl N) or choose All Day Event from the New Items drop-down menu.

   An Untitled - Appointment or Untitled - Event window opens (**Figure 21.3**).

2. Enter a subject for the appointment or event. You can also specify a location.

3. *Do either of the following:*
   - ▲ To treat this item as an event, click the All day event check box.
   - ▲ To treat this item as an appointment, set start and end dates and times.

4. *Optional:* To set an alarm for this item, choose a time from the Reminder menu in the Options group.

   A reminder will appear the specified number of minutes, hours, or days before the appointment or event's scheduled start.

5. Click the Save & Close icon.

✔ Tips

- You can create an event or appointment in an Event or Appointment window. The All day event check box is all that distinguishes an event from an appointment.

- By clicking icons in the Tags group, you can categorize an item or mark it as High Importance or Low Importance.

Creating Recurring Events

Not all appointments and events are one-time activities; many repeat at regular intervals. For example, you may attend weekly staff meetings or belong to a club that meets at 7 PM every third Tuesday of the month. Birthdays and anniversaries are also examples of recurring events.

To set a recurring schedule for an event or appointment:

1. *Do one of the following:*

   ▲ On the Home tab of the Calendar pane, click the New Items icon in the New group and choose Recurring Event, Appointment, or Meeting from the More Items submenu.

   ▲ Create a new event or appointment by following Steps 1–4 of "To record an appointment or event."

   ▲ Select or open an existing event or appointment that you want to change into a recurring item.

2. If the Appointment Recurrence dialog box isn't open, *do the following:*

   ▲ If the item's window is open, click the Recurrence icon in the Options group of the Appointment or Event tab.

   ▲ If you've selected an appointment or event on the Calendar, click the Recurrence icon in the Options group of the Appointment tab.

3. In the Appointment Recurrence dialog box (**Figure 21.5**), set a recurrence pattern. If the event or appointment has a known end date, specify it in the Range of recurrence area.

4. Click OK to close the dialog box.

5. If the appointment or event window is open, click the Save & Close icon in the Actions group.

Recurrence pattern

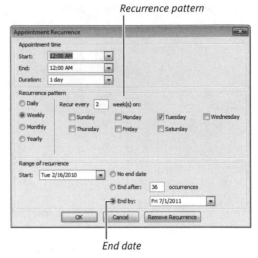

End date

Figure 21.5 You can set or modify a recurring schedule for an event or appointment.

✔ Tips

■ If a recurring appointment or event is scheduled for a specific time, you can enter a Start and End time. If it's an all-day event or one without a scheduled time, ignore Start and End.

■ You can set a reminder for a recurring appointment or event.

■ To change a recurring item to a one-time appointment or event, select it on the Calendar or open it in its own window. Open the Appointment Recurrence dialog box by clicking the Recurrence icon and then click the Remove Recurrence button (Figure 21.5). All recurrences from that date forward are deleted.

CREATING RECURRING EVENTS

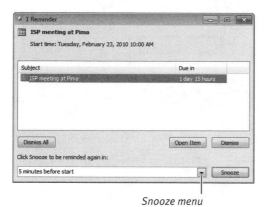

Snooze menu

Figure 21.6 Current and overdue reminders are shown as a scrolling list in the Reminders window.

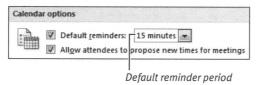

Default reminder period

Figure 21.7 You can change the default reminder period in the Calendar section of the Outlook Options dialog box.

Responding to Reminders

Any event, appointment, or task can have a *reminder* (alarm) associated with it. If Outlook is running when a reminder is triggered, the Reminders window (**Figure 21.6**) appears. The window can also be opened by clicking the Reminders Window icon in the Window group on the View tab.

To respond to a reminder:

1. In the Reminders window, select the reminder to which you want to respond.

2. *Do one of the following:*

   ▲ Click the Dismiss button. This turns off the alarm associated with the item. (To disable the alarm for *every* listed item, click Dismiss All.)

   ▲ To repeat the reminder at a later date or time, choose a snooze period from the drop-down menu and click Snooze.

   ▲ To view or edit the item, click Open Item or double-click the item.

3. When you're done responding to this and other reminders, close the Reminders window by clicking its close box (X).

✔ Tips

■ You can change the default appointment reminder period by going to the Backstage, clicking Options, and selecting the Calendar category in the Outlook Options dialog box (**Figure 21.7**). This period is automatically used for each new appointment. However, you can set a different period or disable the reminder for any new item by choosing None.

■ Although you won't receive additional reminders for a dismissed item, the item is *not* removed from the Calendar. You must delete an item to remove it from the Calendar. See the next section for item deletion methods.

Modifying Events and Appointments

You can change the subject, date, start or end time, reminder schedule, or other elements of an existing event or appointment.

To change an event or appointment:

◆ *Do any of the following:*

▲ To edit only the subject, select the appointment or event on a Calendar page, click a second time to set the text insertion mark in the subject (**Figure 21.8**), and edit as desired.

▲ To delete an appointment or event, select it on a Calendar page. Click the Delete icon in the Actions group or press Del, Delete, or Ctrl D.

▲ To change an item's starting date or time, you can drag the item to a new Calendar location. (To change only the date while keeping the same start and end times, you can drag the item onto a new date on a mini calendar or a date in Month view.)

▲ To change *any* aspect of an event or appointment, double-click the item on any Calendar page or select the item and click Open in the Actions group (Ctrl O). When you're done making changes, click the Save & Close icon.

✔ Tips

■ To find old appointments and events, you can flip through the mini calendars. All dates in bold (**Figure 21.9**) have at least one scheduled appointment or event.

■ When deleting a recurring event or appointment, you can delete only the current occurrence or all occurrences (**Figure 21.10**).

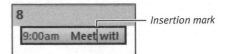

Figure 21.8 Set the text insertion mark and edit the subject as you wish.

Figure 21.9 Dates that contain events or appointments are shown in bold on the mini calendars.

Figure 21.10 When deleting or editing a recurring appointment or event, the deletion or edits can be applied to the selected item or to the entire series.

Custom Calendar Color

If you don't care for the Calendar's color scheme, you can personalize it by choosing a new color from the Color icon in the Color group on the View tab. You can also set the color in the Display options section of the Calendar preferences in the Outlook Options dialog box.

Search Calendar (Ctrl+E)

Figure 21.11 To perform a simple search, type search text in this box above the Calendar.

Searching for an Event or Appointment

Flipping through Calendar pages or mini calendars (see Figure 21.1) isn't always an efficient way to find an appointment or event—especially when you have only a vague idea of when the appointment or event will occur or has already happened. You can use the Instant Search box to quickly find most items.

To search the Calendar:

1. To search all elements of appointments and events (including their attachments), type search text in the Instant Search box (**Figure 21.11**).

   As you type, Outlook displays a results list of matches (**Figure 21.12**). The Search Tools contextual tab appears on the Ribbon.

2. *Optional:* To perform a more specific or complex search, select refinement categories from the Refine group on the Search tab (Figure 21.12).

   Each selection adds a component to your search query, such as subject:(keywords) or hasattachments:yes. Modify the components as necessary by replacing keywords with search text, changing the yes to no, and so on.

continues on next page

Search criteria   Search tab   Close Search   Close search

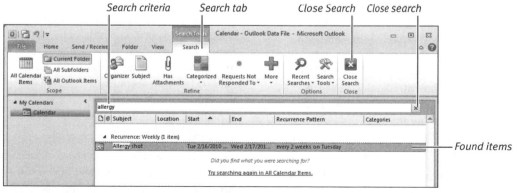

Found items

Figure 21.12 Search results list.

SEARCHING FOR AN EVENT OR APPOINTMENT

3. You can do the following with the search results list:

- ▲ Double-click a found item to open it.
- ▲ To delete a found item from the Calendar, select it in the list and press [Delete] or [Del].
- ▲ To edit a found item (changing its Subject or Start, for example), click in the field in the search results list and make the necessary edits.

4. To return to the Calendar, click the Close Search icon beside the Instant Search box in the search results window or the Close Search icon in the Close group on the Search tab (see Figure 21.12).

✔ Tips

- ■ If you don't feel comfortable editing the query text generated by clicking icons in the Refine group, you can choose fields from the More icon's menu (**Figure 21.13**). Each adds a field to your search query that you can complete by typing text or choosing an option from the field's drop-down menu (**Figure 21.14**).

- ■ Added More fields are automatically displayed when you conduct new searches. You can remove an unwanted search field by clicking its close (X) box.

- ■ By default, searches are AND searches; that is, if you specify multiple criteria, they must *all* be satisfied to constitute a match. However, you can generate an OR search (finding items that match this *or* that criterion) by typing the word OR to separate the criteria, such as Ken OR hasattachments:yes. In this example, found appointments and events will contain the word Ken somewhere within the item or they'll have an attached file.

- ■ To repeat a search, you can select it from Recent Searches list in the Options group.

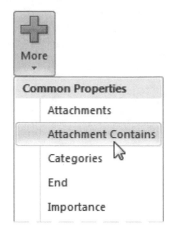

Figure 21.13 Add query fields by choosing them from the More icon's menu.

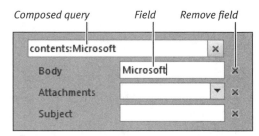

Figure 21.14 Until removed, the chosen query fields are presented for each new search. As you fill the fields, Outlook automatically constructs the query.

Multiple Calendars

Although most users will have only one Calendar, you can create others for different purposes. Switch to the Folder tab and click New Calendar in the New group. Adding Hotmail accounts to Outlook will automatically add their associated calendars, too.

To display any of these other calendars, click their check boxes in the Navigation Pane. You can simultaneously show multiple calendars side-by-side, if you like.

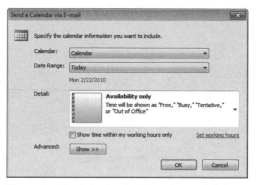

Figure 21.15 Set Calendar-sharing options and click OK.

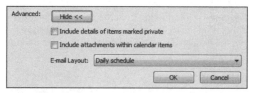

Figure 21.16 You can customize the Calendar data that will be shared.

Displaying a Date

Whether you're searching for an appointment, intend to create one, or just want to check your schedule, you can go to a particular date by doing the following:

◆ Click the scroll arrows in the upper-left corner of the Calendar.

◆ Click the date on a mini calendar or drag-select a range.

◆ On the Home tab, click Today or Next 7 Days in the Go To group.

◆ Specify the date in the Go To Date dialog box. Display the dialog box by clicking the Go To Date dialog box launcher beneath the Go To group or by pressing Ctrl G.

Emailing a Calendar

While most of your work with the Calendar will be solitary, Outlook also provides ways to share your schedule with others. One of the simplest sharing methods is to email a date range of your appointments and events.

To email a calendar:

1. Create a new email message.

2. Set the text insertion mark in the message area, and *do either of the following*:

   ▲ On the Message tab, click the Attach Item icon in the Include group and choose Calendar.

   ▲ On the Insert tab, click the Calendar icon in the Include group.

   The Send a Calendar via E-mail dialog box appears (**Figure 21.15**).

3. Select the dates you wish to include by choosing an option from the Date Range drop-down menu.

   To set a different range or include past dates, choose Specify dates.

4. From the Detail menu, set the amount of appointment information to include:

   ▲ **Availability only.** Shows only whether you're free or busy (in general terms).

   ▲ **Limited details.** Shows free times, plus the Subject for booked times.

   ▲ **Full details.** Shows free times, plus full details for booked times.

5. *Optional:* Click the Show button to set Advanced options (**Figure 21.16**):

   ▲ **Include details of items marked private.** Check to share private items; leave unchecked to omit these items. (This option is available only when you have selected Limited details or Full details.)

continues on next page

- ▲ **Include attachments within calendar items.** If an appointment or event has an attachment (such as a picture or document) and this option is checked, the attachment will also be sent to the recipient. (This option is available only when Full details is selected.)

- ▲ **E-mail Layout.** *Daily schedule* is the standard layout, providing information on both free and booked times. *List of events* shows only booked times.

6. Click OK.

The Calendar information is added to the message body (**Figure 21.17**) and added as an attachment that can be opened and viewed by another Outlook user.

7. Click Send to send the message.

✔ Tips

- ■ When an Outlook 2010 user receives an emailed Calendar, he or she can open the attached file in Outlook and view the two Calendars side-by-side. Doing so makes it simple to see times when you're both free. Appointments from the received file can be dragged onto the recipient's Calendar, if desired.

- ■ Users with a Microsoft Exchange account can share their default Calendar with other users on the server by clicking Share Calendar in the Share group of the Home tab.

- ■ You can also make your Calendar available online to other Outlook users. In the Share group on the Home tab, click Publish Online and choose Publish to Office.com. Complete the Microsoft Office Online Registration wizard. In the Publish Calendar to Office.com dialog box (**Figure 21.18**), choose options and click OK. In the next dialog box, you can generate an email to invite others to subscribe to and view your calendar.

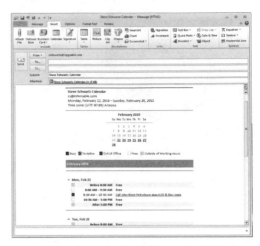

Figure 21.17 Information from the specified Calendar dates is added to the message. This example shows the full details of events scheduled during the period.

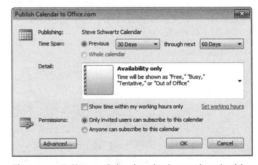

Figure 21.18 Choose Calendar-sharing options in this dialog box and click OK.

- ■ To *stop* sharing a calendar online at Office.com, click the Publish Online icon in the Share group and choose Remove from Server.

Figure 21.20 In addition to disabling/enabling the To-Do Bar, you can specify the components to show.

Task Basics

Click the Tasks button in the Navigation Pane to make the Tasks pane active (**Figure 21.19**, below). Use the Tasks pane to view, create, and manage a to-do list. You can change the view, delete tasks, mark tasks as complete, or edit any aspect of a task.

✔ Tips

■ The distinction between appointments and tasks is up to you. Because a task can occur at a specific time and also have an alarm that appears in the Reminders window, such items can be recorded as tasks *or* appointments.

■ No matter which Outlook component is currently active, your tasks can be viewed in the To-Do Bar (Figure 21.19). To change the To-Do Bar display, switch to the View tab and choose a command from the To-Do Bar menu in the Layout group (**Figure 21.20**). You can minimize or maximize (Normal) the To-Do Bar by clicking the arrow icon above it.

Change View *Create task* *Search the To-Do List*

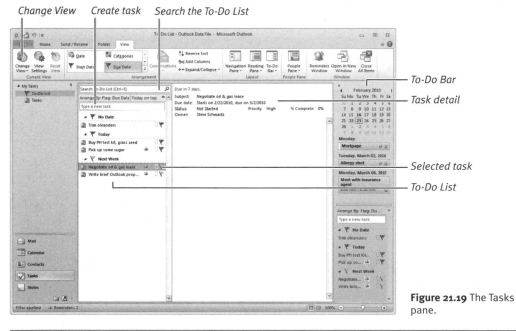

Figure 21.19 The Tasks pane.

TASK BASICS

Creating a Task

You can record as many new tasks as you like.

To create a task:

1. *Do either of the following:*

   ▲ From any pane, click the New Items icon in the New group on the Home tab and choose Task from the drop-down menu ([Ctrl][Shift][K]).

   ▲ From the Tasks pane, click the New Task icon in the New group on the Home tab ([Ctrl][N]).

   An Untitled - Task window opens (**Figure 21.21**).

2. Enter a Subject for the task.

3. *Optional:* For a time-sensitive task, enter a start and/or due date.

   For a task with no specific start and/or due date, leave the dates set to None.

4. *Optional:* To set an alarm for this task, click the Reminder check box and set a reminder date and time.

   At the appropriate time, the reminder will appear in the Reminders window (see Figure 21.6).

5. *Optional:* Choose a progress setting from the Status drop-down menu.

   If you choose In Progress, you can also specify the % Complete.

6. *Optional:* Choose High or Low from the Priority drop-down menu (or click the High Importance or Low Importance icon in the Tags group). Otherwise, the default setting of Normal is assumed.

7. *Optional:* Enter task notes or details in the scrolling text area.

8. Click Save & Close in the Actions group.

   The new task is added to the To-Do List.

Figure 21.21 Like Calendar appointments and events, tasks are typically created in a special window.

Type here to create a new task

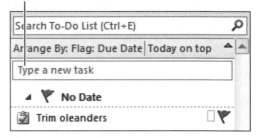

Figure 21.22 To quickly create a new task, type its Subject. If you later need to add details (such as a Due Date), open the task and make the changes.

✔ Tips

■ You can also create a task by typing the Subject directly into the text box above the To-Do List, Tasks list, or the Tasks list area of the To-Do Bar. The text box normally contains "Type a new task" in faint gray text (**Figure 21.22**).

■ Another way to remind yourself that you need to follow up on a task is to select a colored, date-based flag from the Follow Up icon in the Tags group.

■ To generate an email that delegates the task to someone else, click Assign Task in the Manage Task group on the Task tab.

Figure 21.23 Choose a view of the tasks list from the Current View (Home) or Change View (View) gallery.

Figure 21.24 When you open a task in its own window and switch to Detail view, you can enter additional useful information.

Modifying Tasks

When a task is completed or you make progress on it, you can mark it as complete or change the % Complete setting. You can also delete tasks that you no longer want to track.

To modify a task:

1. In the Navigation Pane, select the list that contains the item you want to edit. Normally, this will be To-Do List or Tasks.

2. In the Current View group on the Home or View tab, choose a view that displays the fields you want to change (**Figure 21.23**).

3. *Optional:* You can change the sort order of most lists by clicking a column head. To change the groupings, click an icon in the Arrangement gallery on the View tab.

4. *Optional:* To change the displayed fields, click Add Columns in the Arrangement group.

5. *Do either of the following:*

   ▲ Double-click the task to open it in its own window, make desired changes, and click Save & Close.

   ▲ Make changes by directly editing the task information displayed in the list.

✔ Tips

■ When a task is displayed in its own window, icons in the Show group on the Task tab determine your *view*. When Task is selected, the normal view is presented. In Details view (**Figure 21.24**), you can record other information, such as mileage and hours worked.

■ Views can improved by enabling the Reading Pane. The Reading Pane lets you view the details of any selected task or flagged item. Switch to the View tab and choose Bottom or Right from the Reading Pane menu in the Layout group.

- To mark a task as complete, click the task's check box in the Tasks list (**Figure 21.25**). Or you can select it in any list and click the Mark Complete icon in the Manage Task group on the Home tab. (To reverse the completion status, repeat this process).

- To delete a task you no longer want to track, select it in any list, switch to the Home tab, and then click Delete in the Delete group, click Remove from List in the Manage Task group, or press Ctrl D, Del, or Delete. (Note that most task deletions are carried out immediately—without a warning.)

- Another way to delete a task or change its completion status is to right-click the task in the To-Do Bar or a task list and choose a command from the context menu that appears (**Figure 21.26**).

- Like appointments and events, some tasks can be *recurring* (tasks that repeat at defined intervals). Examples might include paying your mortgage, making semiannual vet visits, or writing a weekly departmental report. To set or remove recurrence for an item, open the item by double-clicking it, click Recurrence in the Recurrence group of the Task tab, and set options in the Task Recurrence dialog box.

- As you can with appointments and events, you can optionally assign categories to tasks. Select the task in any list and choose a category from the Categorize icon in the Tags group on the Home tab. You may find it quicker, however, to right-click the task and choose a category from the context menu. To rename the categories (changing Blue Category to Work, for example), choose All Categories from the Categorize icon's menu.

Completed task

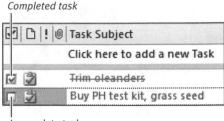

Incomplete task

Figure 21.25 Click the check box to toggle a task's status between incomplete and complete.

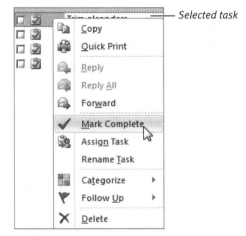
Selected task

Figure 21.26 You can make some changes by right-clicking a task.

Tasks vs. To-Do Items

You're undoubtedly noted and are wondering why the Tasks pane has *two* lists: Tasks and To-Do List. Don't feel bad. Whenever I write an Office book, I have to refresh my memory concerning the distinction between tasks and to-dos.

- **Tasks.** These are items you've created by clicking the New Task icon or issuing the New Task keyboard shortcut.

- **To-do items.** These items include all defined tasks, *plus* any items you've flagged for follow-up.

Part VI:
Office on the Web

OFFICE WEB APPS

In January 2010, Microsoft launched Windows Live SkyDrive, providing 25 GB of free online file storage to anyone with a Windows Live account. Later in 2010, the new Office Web Apps were rolled out. Unlike Office, the Office Web Apps aren't programs installed on your computer. They reside on Microsoft servers. Using them is an example of *cloud computing*.

Using SkyDrive storage and the Office Web Apps individually or together, users can now do the following with a browser and Office 2010:

◆ Use SkyDrive to store backup copies of Office and non-Office documents.

◆ Create and make minor edits to Word, Excel, PowerPoint, or OneNote documents using Internet Explorer, Safari, or FireFox— even without having an installed copy of Office on the current computer.

◆ Save and open files on SkyDrive from within Office (treating SkyDrive as just another hard drive).

◆ Share selected Office files on SkyDrive with others and also allow collaborative, simultaneous editing of those documents.

Microsoft Moving Targets

Although I delayed writing this chapter until the last moment, the Office Web Apps weren't finished when this book went to the printer. Furthermore, because the Office Web Apps will be free and Web-based, it's a safe bet that Microsoft will continue to develop and refine them *after* their official release—making them true *moving targets*.

Thus, unlike Parts I–V of this book, the material in this chapter should be treated as preliminary. It represents the state of the Office Web Apps in May 2010.

Creating an Account

SkyDrive is the repository for the Office files you'll be creating, editing, and sharing with the Office Web Apps. Each time you use SkyDrive, you *must* log in to Windows Live. If you haven't registered for Windows Live, you can gain access by creating a free Hotmail or Windows Live account.

To create a Windows Live or Hotmail account:

1. Go to www.live.com or www.hotmail.com in any browser.

2. Click the Sign up button (**Figure 22.1**).

3. On the Create your Windows Live ID screen, choose live.com or hotmail.com as the account type and enter your desired user name in the Windows Live ID box (**Figure 22.2**).

   If the entered name is already in use (**Figure 22.3**), try a different name, try a variation of the current name, or select one of the Available IDs suggestions.

4. Enter an account password and the information requested for the other fields.

5. Click I accept to complete the registration.

✔ Tips

- A Windows Live or Hotmail account has advantages in addition to SkyDrive access. For instance, you can send and receive email from the account using a browser or an email client such as Outlook (see Chapter 16), use Messenger for instant messaging, and create photo albums.

- Because Hotmail is many years older than Windows Live, most simple words and word combinations are already taken as user names. You may find, however, that an unavailable user name in Hotmail can be yours in Windows Live.

Figure 22.1 Click the Sign up button to begin the account-creation process.

Figure 22.2 Choose a service (live or hotmail) and enter a user name. If you don't immediately receive a response, click the Check availability button.

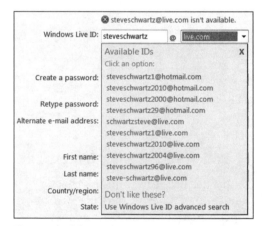

Figure 22.3 If the user name is already taken, similar alternatives are proposed. Select one or try again by entering a different name.

- If the user name you want isn't available, try combining it with some numbers.

Working with SkyDrive

You can use SkyDrive as a external drive for storing backups of important files, or you can view and edit the Office documents you've uploaded to it using Office 2010 or the Office Web Apps. Regardless of how you intend to use SkyDrive, you'll need to familiarize yourself with its folder- and file-management procedures.

To access your SkyDrive:

1. In Internet Explorer, FireFox, or Safari, log into your Windows Live, Hotmail, or MSN account.

2. Click the More drop-down menu at the top of the Web page and choose SkyDrive.

   The SkyDrive screen appears (**Figure 22.4**). By default, each account has four folders: *My Documents* and *Favorites* (private), *Shared Favorites* (accessible to others by invitation only), and *Public* (accessible to anyone). In addition, you can create other folders as your needs dictate.

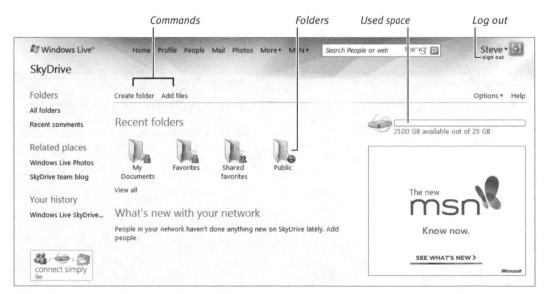

Figure 22.4 If you haven't created additional folders, this is what you'll see when you log into your SkyDrive.

WORKING WITH SKYDRIVE

Folder management

SkyDrive folders can be created and managed to organize your files any way you like.

To create a folder:

1. Click the Create folder link on the main SkyDrive page (see Figure 22.4).

The Create a folder page appears (**Figure 22.5**).

2. Enter a name for the new folder.

3. Choose a Share with option from the drop-down menu. Click Next.

The Add files to *folder name* page appears.

4. *Do one of the following:*

▲ To immediately add one or more files to the new folder, click Browse buttons to select files from your hard drive (**Figure 22.6**). When you are done selecting files, click the Upload button.

▲ To initially leave the new folder empty, click Cancel.

✔ Tip

■ You can also create folders within folders. Open the *parent* (enclosing) folder and click Create folder. Subfolder permissions always match those of the parent folder.

To navigate among the folders:

◆ *Do any of the following:*

▲ To open a folder, go to the SkyDrive main page by clicking the SkyDrive link at the top of the page (**Figure 22.7**). Then click the icon of the folder you want to open. If the destination folder is a subfolder of the current folder, continue clicking folder icons until the desired folder is open.

▲ To go up in the folder hierarchy, click a folder link at the top of the page or click Skydrive to return to the root.

Figure 22.5 Name the folder and choose a sharing option for all files that will reside in the folder.

Selected file

Figure 22.6 Click a different Browse button for each file you want to upload into the folder.

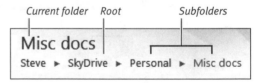

Figure 22.7 The current folder's name is shown at the top of the page. Beneath it is the path to the current folder or the SkyDrive page name.

More ▼

Download as .zip file

Edit permissions

Delete

Rename

Properties

Figure 22.8 This is the More menu for a private, user-created folder. Listed commands differ for other folder types.

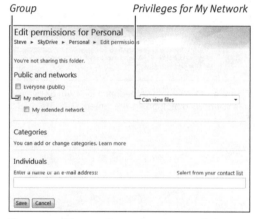

Group   Privileges for My Network

Figure 22.9 When setting or changing permissions for a folder, you can specify who (other than yourself) can access its files and in what manner.

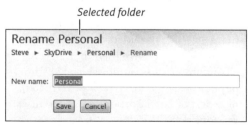

Selected folder

Figure 22.10 To rename the current folder, type the new name and click Save.

To modify a folder:

1. Open the folder that you want to modify.

2. Click the More menu (**Figure 22.8**) and choose one of these commands:

   ▲ **Download as .zip file** (download the folder's files as a Zip archive). Click Save in the dialog box that appears, select a location for the download, and click Save again. See the sidebar on the following page for information about Zip archives.

   ▲ **Edit permissions** (modify access privileges). Available only for root folders, choose this command to change the sharing status and permissions for the current folder and any subfolders (**Figure 22.9**). To switch from shared to private or to remove sharing privileges from certain groups or people, clear their check boxes. To share a currently private folder, click check boxes and specify the permissions for each group or person. Click Save to save the new permissions.

   ▲ **Delete** (delete folder). Confirm the deletion of the folder and its contents.

   ▲ **Rename** (change folder name). The Rename folder name page appears (**Figure 22.10**). Enter a name in the New name box and click Save.

   ▲ **Properties** (modify folder properties). Click links to add a folder description, change permissions, or change the folder type.

✔ Tip

■ Currently, there is no command to *move* a folder. As such, think carefully about where on SkyDrive you create each folder.

WORKING WITH SKYDRIVE

File management

File-management actions you can perform on SkyDrive are similar to those available for your computer's hard drive. In addition to uploading files to SkyDrive, you can click links (**Figure 22.11**) to perform other common actions on a selected file.

To upload files to a folder:

1. Open the SkyDrive folder into which you want to add a file or files.

2. Click the Add files link.

   The Add files to *folder name* page appears (see Figure 22.6).

3. For each file that you want to upload (up to five), click a Browse button, select a file from your hard drive in the Choose File to Upload dialog box, and click Open.

4. When you've finished selecting files, click Upload.

   A progress bar appears at the bottom of the page to show the transfer's status. When the transfer is finished, the folder's file list is shown.

To download a file to your hard drive:

1. Open the folder that contains the file you want to download.

2. Click the icon of the file that you want to download and click the Download link.

   A File Download dialog box appears (**Figure 22.12**).

3. Click one of the following buttons:

   ▲ **Save.** Download and save the file to your hard drive. Specify a location in which to save the file and click Save.
   Open. Download and open the file in an appropriate program.

   The file downloads from SkyDrive to your computer.

Figure 22.11 After double-clicking a file in its SkyDrive folder, a file-handling menu appears.

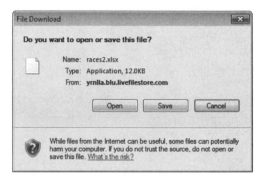

Figure 22.12 When downloading a file from SkyDrive, this Windows dialog box is presented.

About Zip Archives

An *archive* is a file that contains one or more files and/or folders that have been compressed to reduce their total size. A zip archive uses a compression algorithm popularized by WinZip (www.winzip.com), now part of Corel Corporation. Current versions of the Windows and Macintosh operating systems can extract the contents of a Zip archive, restoring them as files and folders.

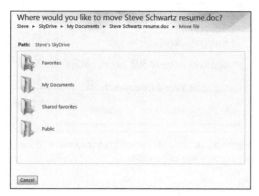

Figure 22.13 Click to open folders until you've opened the destination folder.

Current folder

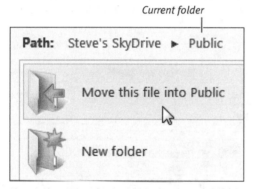

Figure 22.14 When you're within the destination folder, click the Move (or Copy) option to complete the process.

Current name of selected file

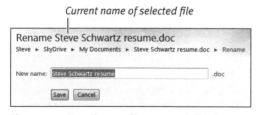

Figure 22.15 Type the new filename and click Save.

To delete a file:

1. Open the folder that contains the file you want to delete. Click the file's icon.

2. Click the Delete link.

3. Click OK in the confirmation dialog box.

To move or copy a file to another folder:

1. Open the folder that contains the file you want to move or copy. Click the file's icon.

2. Click the Move or the Copy link.

   The Where would you like to move (copy) *filename* page appears (**Figure 22.13**). The root folders of your SkyDrive are displayed.

3. Click the folder or parent of the folder in which you want to move or copy the file.

4. Continue opening folders until the destination folder is shown. Click Move (copy) this file into *folder name* (**Figure 22.14**).

To rename a file:

1. Open the folder that contains the file you want to rename. Click the file's icon.

2. Click the Rename link.

3. Enter a new filename in the New name box (**Figure 22.15**) and click Save.

✔ Tips

■ If you previously saved a file to SkyDrive from within Office, it's only necessary to download the file if you want a local backup of the current version. To continue working with the document, open the SkyDrive copy from within Office.

■ If you click the Open button when downloading a file, don't forget to save the file, too—assuming that you want to keep a copy of it on your hard drive.

■ You can also download an entire folder's contents as a Zip archive.

WORKING WITH SKYDRIVE

About the Office Web Apps

Think of the Office Web Apps as *lite* browser-based versions of Word, Excel, PowerPoint, and OneNote. That is, although the Web Apps are *real* applications and are useful for light work, they lack the power, speed, and flexibility of their Office counterparts. Here are some useful facts about the Office Web Apps:

◆ You can access the Office Web Apps using Internet Explorer, Safari, or FireFox.

◆ Your computer is not required to have an installed version of Microsoft Office. On the other hand, if Office *is* installed, you can switch from the Web Apps to Office when editing needs demand it.

◆ The Office Web Apps have no Save command because changes are automatically saved as you work.

Within Windows Live, you can connect to the Web Apps through SkyDrive by opening an existing Office document or creating a new one.

To create a new Office document:

1. Log into SkyDrive and open one of your folders.

2. Click the New link and choose the type of Office document you'd like to create (**Figure 22.16**).

To open an existing Office document:

1. Log into SkyDrive and open the folder that contains the Office document you'd like to view or edit. Click the document icon.

   A new page appears (**Figure 22.17**).

2. Click View or Edit.

   The document opens in an Office Web App for viewing or editing, respectively (**Figure 22.18**).

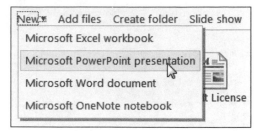

Figure 22.16 The New menu lists the types of Office documents you can create.

Figure 22.17 If the current file is an Office document, you can open it in the Office Web Apps by clicking the View or Edit link.

Figure 22.18 This is an Excel workbook opened for editing in the Office Web Apps.

✔ Tip

■ Although you can't make changes in View mode, you can perform normal viewing activities, such as executing Finds, recalculating worksheets, and printing.

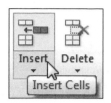

Figure 22.19 Although you'll be familiar with most icons from having used Office 2010, each icon has a ToolTip.

File tab

Figure 22.20 Each application's File tab provides a menu with commands similar to those you'd find in Office 2010's Backstage.

Using the Office Web Apps

You can use the Office Web Apps to view and edit your own documents as well as ones that others have elected to share with you. Regardless of whether you're viewing or editing a document, the Office Web Apps works much like Office:

◆ Each Web App features the tabbed Ribbon interface introduced in Office 2007 (see Figure 22.18). Within each *tab* (such as Home and Insert), commands are organized into functional *groups*.

◆ ToolTips appear for the Ribbon icons (**Figure 22.19**).

◆ Certain commands present dialog boxes.

◆ Click the File tab (**Figure 22.20**) to reveal a menu of file-related commands, such as saving a copy of the document, printing, and opening the document in Office.

◆ There are no contextual menus; that is, right-clicking is not supported.

✔ Tips

■ All edits are saved automatically. While this relieves you of having to remember to save manually, it also means that *every* change is saved. To avoid saving inadvertent changes, there are two options:

▲ Save a backup copy of the document at the start of each editing session. You can choose Save As or Download a Copy from the File tab menu, or you can make a copy of the file using the procedure described on page 403.

▲ Repeatedly click the Undo icon to step back through the changes you want to discard.

■ If you need the full editing power of Office, click the Open in *application* icon in the Office group on the Home tab or choose this command from the File tab.

Office Documents and SkyDrive

After you upload an Office document to SkyDrive, you can view and edit it with the Office Web Apps. And if you have Office 2010 installed on the current PC, you can access Office documents on SkyDrive in these additional ways:

◆ While viewing or editing with the Office Web Apps, you can launch Office to perform more advance editing on the current document.

◆ While working in Office, you can save the current document to SkyDrive.

◆ Documents that have been saved to or uploaded to SkyDrive can be opened from within Office.

To launch Office from a Web App:

1. In Office Web Apps, open the SkyDrive Office document for viewing or editing.

2. *Do either of the following:*

   ▲ Click the Open in *Office application* icon. When editing a document, this icon can be found in the Office group on the Home tab (**Figure 22.21**). When viewing a document, the icon is next to the File tab (**Figure 22.22**).

   ▲ Choose Open in *Office application* from the File tab menu (see Figure 22.20).

To save a document to SkyDrive from Office (first save):

1. Click the File tab to go to the Backstage.

2. Select Share > Save to SkyDrive.

   The Save to SkyDrive pane appears (**Figure 22.23**).

3. If you aren't currently signed in to your Windows Live account, do so now.

Figure 22.21 When editing in a Web App, click this icon to open the current document in Office.

Figure 22.22 When viewing a document in a Web App, click this icon to open the current document in Office.

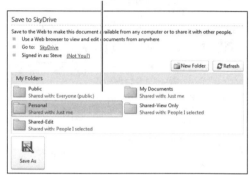

Figure 22.23 If the current Office document has never been saved to SkyDrive, visit the Backstage.

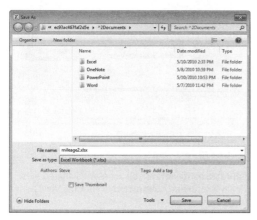

Figure 22.24 Navigate to the desired SkyDrive folder, edit the filename (if desired), and click Save.

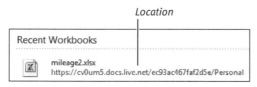

Figure 22.25 A SkyDrive document in the Recent list will show that it's located on the Web (https://).

Figure 22.26 Click Save to overwrite the SkyDrive document with the current edited version.

4. In the My Folders section of the pane, *do one of the following:*

   ▲ Double-click the destination root folder.

   ▲ Select the destination root folder and click the Save As button.

   A Save As dialog box appears (**Figure 22.24**).

5. *Optional:* Navigate to a different SkyDrive folder, such as a subfolder of the selected root folder.

6. *Optional:* Change the filename and/or the file type.

7. Click Save.

To open an Office document stored on SkyDrive:

1. Click the File tab to go to the Backstage.

2. Do one of the following to open the document that you previously saved or uploaded to SkyDrive:

   ▲ If you *uploaded* the document, you may be able to find it by clicking Open and navigating to it in the Open dialog box.

   ▲ If you previously *saved* the document to SkyDrive, you may find it in the Recent documents list (**Figure 22.25**) or the Open dialog box.

To save a document to SkyDrive from Office (subsequent saves):

1. Open the document by loading it from SkyDrive.

2. After editing the document, you can save the changed version to SkyDrive by clicking the Save icon in the Quick Access Toolbar (**Figure 22.26**), pressing Ctrl S, or clicking Save in the Backstage.

✔ Tip

■ You can go directly to SkyDrive by entering www.skydrive.com in the browser's address box.

OFFICE AND SKYDRIVE FILES

Sharing and Co-editing Office Documents

A sharing status is set for every SkyDrive root folder and its subfolders. The specified access privileges apply to every file in the folder(s), as well as to other files that you later save in or upload to the folder(s). An Office document in any shared folder can be accessed individually or simultaneously by any combination of Office and Office Web App users.

✔ Tips

- When you set or change sharing permissions for a SkyDrive folder, an email notification can be sent to the folder sharers (**Figure 22.27**). The message will contain a View folder link they can click to access documents in the shared folder(s). To speed future access to the SkyDrive, they can save the link as a browser favorite or bookmark.

- When a SkyDrive document is opened in Office, it may open in Protected View. To allow editing, click the Enable Editing button (**Figure 22.28**).

View folder

Figure 22.27 To view or edit someone's shared files, the mail recipient is instructed to click the View folder button.

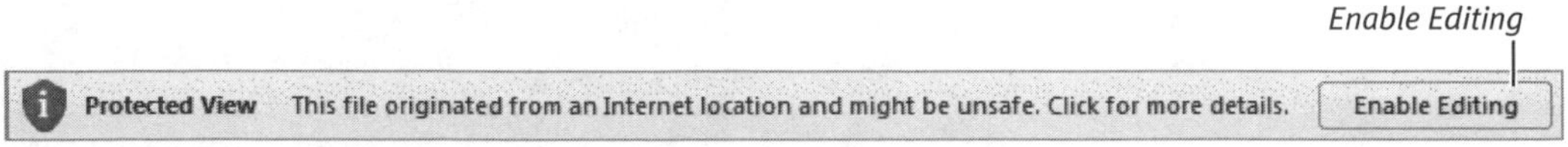

Enable Editing

Figure 22.28 Web-based documents often open in Protected View. If you trust the source and want to be able to modify the document's contents, click the Enable Editing button.

INDEX

Meet Creative Edge.

A new resource of unlimited books, videos and tutorials for creatives from the world's leading experts.

Creative Edge is your one stop for inspiration, answers to technical questions and ways to stay at the top of your game so you can focus on what you do best—being creative.

All for only $24.99 per month for access—any day any time you need it.

creative edge

creativeedge.com